Databrarianship

The Academic Data Librarian in Theory and Practice

Edited by Lynda Kellam
and Kristi Thompson

Association of College and Research Libraries
A division of the American Library Association
Chicago, Illinois 2016

The paper used in this publication meets the minimum requirements of American National Standard for Information Sciences–Permanence of Paper for Printed Library Materials, ANSI Z39.48-1992. ∞

Names: Kellam, Lynda M., editor. | Thompson, Kristi editor.
Title: Databrarianship : the academic data librarian in theory and practice / edited by Lynda Kellam and Kristi Thompson.
Description: Chicago : Association of College and Research Libraries, a division of the American Library Association, 2016.
Identifiers: LCCN 2016010849| ISBN 9780838987995 (pbk.) | ISBN 9780838988015
(epub) | ISBN 9780838988022 (kindle)
Subjects: LCSH: Academic libraries--Effect of technological innovations on. | Academic librarians--Effect of technological innovations on. | Data curation. | Data libraries. | Database management. | Libraries--Special collections--Electronic information resources. | Research--Data processing. | Academic libraries--Relations with faculty and curriculum. | Libraries and colleges. | Communication in learning and scholarship--Technological innovations.
Classification: LCC Z675.U5 D34 2016 | DDC 027.7--dc23 LC record available at https://lccn.loc.gov/2016010849

Printed in the United States of America.

20 19 18 17 16 5 4 3 2 1

Table of Contents

Part II. Data in the Disciplines

Part III. Data Preservation and Access

Part IV. Data: Past, Present, And Future

Acknowledgments

EDITING THIS BOOK was a wonderful opportunity to work with a great many skilled and generous people. First and foremost, thank you goes to the ACRL Publications Advisory Board for recognizing the need for a book-length treatment of academic data librarianship and supporting us in realizing this project. Special thanks to ACRL Content Strategist Kathryn Deiss for her guidance through this process and her patience and grace. Thanks also to our eagle-eyed copy editor Melanie Hawks and our anonymous peer reviewer. Any errors that remain in the book are solely our responsibility; we thank the above-named for the many that do not.

Other individuals assisted us at various points in the process and made what could have been a daunting job much easier. In particular, we would like to acknowledge our colleague Katharin Peter, who provided considerable input during the early development of the book and gave the introduction a close reading. Her wry comments and editor's eye are always welcome. Thanks also to fellow librarians and friends Jenny Dale, Anne Kaay, and Valentina Radoman Ciric, who served as sounding boards and provided feedback on the introduction and overall structure of the book.

Our wonderfully supportive families deserve far more appreciation than we can possibly give them. Kristi would like to specifically thank husband and fellow data professional Daniel Edelstein for encouragement, listening, and insightful feedback, and father Earl Thompson for helping her believe she could do any harebrained thing she set her mind to. Lynda would like to thank her husband Daniel McMillan for his unwavering support. He understands like no other person her compulsion to take on too many projects. At least one is now done! She would also like to thank her parents for listening to her rants and laughing along even when they have no idea what she is talking about.

This book would not exist without the efforts of the many librarians, academics, and other specialists who developed academic data services as a distinct specialty. Without their pioneering endeavors, there would be no databrarianship to write about. We would particularly like to note IASSIST and the many who have been involved with making that organization into such a vital source of support and professional development. Most importantly, we would like to thank the authors who contributed chapters to this book for their hard work, patience, professionalism, and willingness to share their expertise and experiences.

Introduction

Kristi Thompson and Lynda Kellam, editors

WITH THE APPEARANCE of big data, open data, and particularly research data curation on many libraries' radar screens, data services has become a topic of increasing interest in academia, but in academic libraries, this area has long been a central concern. The term "databrarian" dates to a 2013 *Library Journal* article that discussed the results of the 2012 Placements & Salaries survey and noted "several new job titles," including Research Data Librarian, Data Coordinator, and Data Curation Specialist.[1] While practitioners welcomed the increased recognition, data librarianship as a field is hardly new, as it encompasses a diversity of forms, functions, and specializations that are vital to academic research and teaching. Drawing on the expertise of a diverse community of practitioners, the goal of this edited volume is to provide an overview of the major areas within data librarianship. By covering the data lifecycle from collection development to preservation, examining the challenges of working with different forms of data, and exploring service models suited to a variety of library types, this volume provides a toolbox of strategies that will allow librarians and administrators to respond creatively and effectively to the data deluge.

In this collection, we use the term databrarianship to describe a field that is characterized by a diversity of interests but united by our commitment to ensuring access to data, be they primary research data created by our institutions' researchers or secondary data used for analysis. Our contributors have widely diverse primary positions and backgrounds. Some are reference librarians who support data access, which requires a fluency with data concepts and sources not typically taught in the library school reference class. Some are data curators who share more in common with metadata specialists and bring a unique understanding of preservation methods for long-term data access. Some are library instructors who teach data source discovery and use datasets and statistics as part of their library's larger information literacy program. Several are data support specialists without MLIS degrees who work in research grant or IT offices and provide unique insights into the support of researchers. All have a passion for data and for supporting our faculty and students.

Although this specialty area has been around for many years, relatively few texts have been written exclusively about it, and in many cases these publications have remained within the data librarian community. During the summer institute at the Inter-university Consortium for Political and Social Research (ICPSR), a leading data archive, many budding data librarians were introduced to the field by Diane Geraci, Chuck Humphrey and Jim Jacobs and their excellent textbook, *Data Basics: An Introductory Text.*[2] In addition, *IASSIST Quarterly*, the journal of the International Association for Social Science Information Services and Technology (IASSIST), the leading professional organization for data services, has been a key resource for social science data support since 1976. In both cases, these publications have primarily reached audiences already involved in data librarianship and support. Beyond these key texts, little has been written for a wider audience. A few major figures such as Geraci, Jacobs, Judith Rowe, and others wrote articles in the 1980s and 1990s discussing the possibility of bringing data files (at that time on magnetic tape) into library collections and data support into the skill set of reference librarians.[3] While these articles were featured in general librarianship journals, they were few and far between. In the mid-2000s, increased interest in data and access to data through the Internet led to a growth in the number of articles and books about supporting data services. Eleanor Read's 2007 article in *Reference and User Services Quarterly* helped many new data services librarians have a better understanding of support for data and assessment of services.[4] Moreover, the 2011 volume *Numeric Data Services and Sources for the General Reference Librarian* by Lynda Kellam and Katharin Peter aimed to introduce a wider audience to support for data discovery and instruction.[5] In recent years, more volumes have emerged focusing on research data management with Jake Carlson (formerly of Purdue University) taking a lead with the Data Information Literacy Toolkit, a toolkit for having discussions about data with faculty, and the subsequent book *Data Information Literacy: Librarians, Data, and the Education of a New Generation of Researchers* in 2014.[6] While all of these works have filled necessary niches, no one work has tried to span the breadth of the primary concerns of the profession for a general audience. With this collected edition, our authors explore more traditional areas like data reference as well as the emerging area of data management. We hope this text provides an introduction to the scope of databrarianship as well as the variety within the profession.[†]

Data librarian and archivist positions emerged in response to the varied needs of researchers and data producers, and at first these professionals organized and communicated informally through a variety of venues. A major event in the history of databrarianship was the Conference on Data and Program Library Services that was held in conjunction with the World Sociology Congress meeting in Toronto in 1974. This meeting led to the founding of the IASSIST by librarians and archivists from Canada, the U.S., and Europe.[7] The influence of IASSIST can

† Access links, extra appendices, and more on our companion website: https://databrarianship.wordpress.com/.

be seen to this day and is evident in this book in a two major ways. First, Americans, Canadians, and Europeans played key roles in the early development of the profession and its identity, in collaboration and dialogue with each other. Consequently, the editors made an effort to include voices from beyond the American experience. A second factor is the roots of databrarianship as a profession in the quantitative social sciences. The astute reader will note that a number of chapters, particularly in the section on services, focus on quantitative survey data. To ensure that other forms of data were covered, we recruited authors to write about data from other disciplinary focuses.

Despite this effort to include a variety of perspectives, much is still missing. One clear gap is that we were unable to cover the full range of international experiences. Descriptions of data support in countries outside of the U.S., Canada, and Western Europe are missing. This does not mean that data librarians are not active in these countries, and we are aware that excellent work is being done by data librarians in places as diverse as South Africa, Japan, and Croatia, and undoubtedly many others. The work experiences of these data librarians may be quite different from the position of the data librarian in North America, as Rice's chapter discusses.[‡] We hope that other publications will investigate these differences and develop a more global perspective on databrarianship.

Before moving into our chapters, however, this introduction must lay the groundwork for what is to come. Those new to data librarianship will encounter many new terms throughout this book, and our authors do an excellent job of providing concise definitions. One critical term must be discussed first though, and that is the word *data*. The term *data* is used in a variety of ways depending on field and context. A computer scientist might use the term to refer to the flow of zeros and ones that stream through data cables and are used to transmit videos, web pages, and the like, or to the aggregate of all the information available on the Internet. A statistician or survey researcher might think of a numeric dataset structured for use in a statistical package, such as the results in a public opinion poll. In general, we take an intermediate approach. The data we are concerned with here are the product of taking that raw informational input and assembling it into a structured form for analysis. Data are a product of research as well as an input for research. Research data collections (or *datasets*) are generally in electronic form and are accompanied by or incorporate metadata, or documentation that describes the structure and content of the data. In brief, unless specified otherwise, data will be taken to mean electronic files containing information that has been collected systematically, structured, and documented to serve as input for further research. Data are the raw materials for research, produced through any systematic collection of information for the purpose of analysis. Data are the lifeblood

‡ For more information about data support in Great Britain and Europe, see the chapter in this volume by Robin Rice called "View from Across the Pond."

of data librarianship, but as you can see in this book, the term does not belong to one discipline or one research methodology, and we will cover the wide range of interests and concerns in our profession.

We have grouped the chapters into four major sections that give some idea of the division of interests within the field: *Data Support Services for Researchers and Learners*, *Data in the Disciplines*, *Data Preservation and Access*, and *Data: Past, Present, and Future*. The first section, *Data Support Services for Researchers and Learners*, is intended to serve as a toolbox for developing academic library services for data creators and consumers, encompassing data-focused perspectives on familiar librarian activities, such as reference and information literacy, and also branching out to cover topics specific to databrarianship, such as data wrangling and support of researchers working with restricted data. We begin with a pair of chapters that contrast the merits of two different modes of service provision. Samantha Guss describes offering a suite of functions at a tightly focused service point in "A Studio Model for Academic Data Services," while Cynthia Hudson considers how one might instead integrate as a databrarian seamlessly into the campus at point of need with "Embedded Options." Our next pair of chapters offers another study in contrasts, this time comparing top-down and bottom-up techniques for service development. Bobray Bordelon's "Data Reference" offers advice and encouragement for individual subject specialists looking to incorporate reference for microdata into their job descriptions, with or without the assistance of a dedicated data librarian, while Alicia Hofelich Mohr, Lisa Johnston, and Thomas Lindsay take a systemic approach to configuring campus-wide services in the "Data Management Village." Next, Ryan Clement looks at options for libraries working on a much smaller scale, demonstrating that specialized data services incorporating reference, management, and statistical consulting are not out of reach of "The Data Librarian in the Liberal Arts College." The role of librarians in teaching novices is not neglected, as Adam Beauchamp and Christine Murray consider the needs of beginning data users in their information literacy-focused take on "Teaching Foundational Data Skills in the Library," which is followed by a discussion of technical skills with Harrison Decker and Paula Lackie's "technical Data Skills for Reproducible Research." Finally, Jen Darragh takes on the needs of researchers using restricted access data, a type of data that requires protections such as a secure facility or computer. As Darragh demonstrates in "Restricted Data Access and Libraries," the library may be uniquely positioned to help researchers use this type of data.

Data in the Disciplines ventures across the campus to look at a few of the many specialty areas of concern for data support. Our first two chapters tackle geospatial data, a popular and, for some, newer area of support. Nicole Scholtz begins a discussion of "Supporting Geospatial Data" by looking at the wider context of data services and provides suggestions for libraries with an interest in developing their geospatial services. Joy Suh follows with an in-depth case study of geospatial academic support that looks at how a service evolves to meet advanced user needs in "From Traditional to Crowd and Cloud: Geospatial Data Services at GMU." Next, Mandy Swygart-Hobaugh gives qualitative research much-needed attention—and encourages other librarians to do the same—in her survey chapter "Qualitative Research and Data Support: The Jan Brady of Social Sciences Data Services?" Karen Grigg rounds out the section with an overview of the unique needs and challenges of providing support for "Data in the Sciences."

The third section, *Data Preservation and Access*, looks at the place of data in scholarly communication and delves further into the growing field of research data management. Hailey Mooney kicks things off with an exploration of the integral role of data in the production of scientific knowledge in "Scholarly Communication and Data." Joel Herndon and Rob O'Reilly next present the results of a comparative study of the "Data Sharing Policies in Social Sciences Academic Journals," focusing on how the policies of leading social science journals have evolved over time. Collection development policies and procedures are the focus of Christopher Eaker's "Selection and Appraisal of Digital Research Data," and Susan McKee has a collection development case study in "Local Data Success Story: The University of Calgary Library's Ten Years with the City of Calgary." The concluding two chapters in this section consider the different forms that metadata can take and how it can best be used for data preservation and dissemination. Jane Fry and Amber Leahey consider how data professionals can collaborate to produce structured metadata for social science data, specifically the popular standard known as DDI in "Metadata for Social Science Data: Collaborative Best Practices." Finally, Lizzy Rolando, Lisha Li, Ameet Doshi, Alison Valk, and Karen Young take an opposite approach and investigate ways of encouraging individual users to develop unstructured, discipline-specific metadata in "Exploring Disciplinary Metadata and Documentation Practices to Strengthen Data Archiving Services."

We conclude with *Data: Past, Present, and Future*. Two chapters examine the history of how data librarianship developed in two very different sets of circumstances. Robin Rice tells the story of the European context in "View from Across the Pond: A UK Perspective," while Elizabeth Hill and Vincent Gray return us to North America in "The Academic Data Librarian Profession in Canada: History and Future Directions." Danianne Mizzy examines the many career paths librarians and informationists take when developing as data services professionals in "Data Librarianship: A Day in the Life—Science Edition." Concluding the volume, Michael McCaffrey and Walter Giesbrecht look to the future as they describe a course designed to teach the fundamentals of databrarianship to a new crop of library students and lay out a proposal for a full curriculum in "Teaching Data Librarianship to LIS Students."

By now it should be clear that academic data librarianship is not a single specialty but rather a varied collection of overlapping but distinct roles that center on providing access to, documenting, and preserving data, much as traditional librarianship has done for print resources. Most databrarians will share certain base skill sets, having knowledge of file formats, documentation and metadata standards, and disciplinary research practices, but beyond that, their jobs can take a myriad of forms. Underlying many of our chapters is the idea that data librarianship is a collaborative endeavor across our libraries and our universities. The needs of our patrons are diverse as are the skill sets required to assist them. As editors, our motivation with this collection is to demonstrate the wide breadth of data librarianship and all of the component positions. From data discovery to data instruction techniques to data curation and metadata knowledge, databrarianship is a broad field with a world of opportunity for collaboration and innovation. We hope this volume provides some insight into that world.

---

1. Stephanie L. Maatta, "The Emerging Databrarian," *Library Journal* 138, no. 17 (Oct 15, 2013): 26.
2. Diane Geraci, Chuck Humphrey, and Jim Jacobs, *Data Basics: An Introductory Text,* (Ann Arbor, Michigan: ICPSR, 2008).
3. Judith Rowe, "Expanding Social Science Service to Meet the Needs of Patrons More Adequately," *Library Trends* 30, no. 3 (Winter 1982): 327–334; Kathleen M. Heim, "Introduction: Data Libraries for the Social Sciences," *Library Trends* 30, no. 3 (Winter 1982): 321–325; Ray Jones and Colleen Seale, "Expanding Networks: References Services for MRDF," *Reference Services Review* 16, no. 1 (July 8, 1988): 7–12; Deborah Rinderknecht, "Non-Bibliographic Databases: Determining Level of Service," *RQ* 30, no. 4 (July 1991): 528–533; James A. Jacobs, "Providing Data Services for Machine-Readable Information in an Academic Library: Some Levels of Service," *The Public-Access Computer Systems Review*, 2 (1992): 119–132; Diane Geraci and Linda Langschied, "Mainstreaming Data: Challenges to Libraries," *Information Technology and Libraries* 11, no. 1 (March 1992): 10–19; Wendy Treadwell and James A. Cogswell, "The Machine Readable Data Center: A Model Approach to Data Services in Academic Research Libraries," *Library Hi Tech* 12, no. 1 (1994): 87–92.
4. Eleanor J. Read, "Data Services in Academic Libraries: Assessing Needs and Promoting Services, *Reference & User Services Quarterly* 46, no. 3 (2007): 61–75.
5. Lynda M. Kellam and Katharin Peter, *Numeric Data Services and Sources for the General Reference Librarian,* (Oxford: Chandos Publishing, 2011).
6. Jake Carlson and Lisa R. Johnston, *Data Information Literacy: Librarians, Data, and the Education of a New Generation of Researchers,* (West Lafayette, IN: Purdue University Press).
7. For more on the early history of data librarianship, see Margaret O'Neill Adams, "The Origins and Early Years of IASSIST," *IASSSIT Quarterly* 30 (Fall): 5–14, http://www.iassistdata.org/sites/default/files/iq/iqvol303adams.pdf.

PART I

Data Support Services for Researchers and Learners

CHAPTER 1

A Studio Model for Academic Data Services

Samantha Guss

THIS BOOK SERVES as proof that there are plenty of effective ways to provide data services in an academic environment and that there can never be a one-size-fits-all approach. It is still valuable, however, to look closely at others' service models—to learn from successes, to borrow concepts and metaphors from other realms, and to think about one's own services through new lenses. A service model is a framework used to describe and understand the "who, what, where, when, and how" of a service from different stakeholders' perspectives; it can serve as a useful tool for developing and improving data services to best meet the needs of a community.

There are many such service models for developing data support. This chapter adds to that list by developing the idea of a "studio model" for academic data services—a user-centered model that focuses on patrons as creators and consumers of information—and by defining an academic data service as a public good that bridges the research and teaching and learning missions of an institution. This service model also emphasizes why libraries, in collaboration with campus partners, are ideally situated to house and steward data services. After theoretical aspects of the studio model are explored, New York University's Data Services department is described as a case study.

Conceptualizing a Data Service Model

Perhaps the most important conceptual model in the data services community is that of the *data lifecycle*, which describes the cyclical process of planning and conceptualizing a study, collecting data or discovering and accessing existing data, processing and analyzing data, and archiving and preserving data. The data lifecycle has been described and visualized in many ways[1] and is also sometimes called a research lifecycle, but all model the actions taken by scholars as they perform research with data. The data lifecycle is a useful model for designing services because it encourages service providers to think about users' activities, and how those activities can be supported. For example, scholars who need to find existing data to use in their research might be helped by a catalog of datasets, membership in the Inter-university Consortium for Political and Social Research (ICPSR), or a data reference service, all of which would be maintained by the service providers in response to that need. Likewise, many libraries and other organizations are responding to the need for scholars to preserve and make their research data available by developing data repositories or advisory services to connect scholars to disciplinary repositories. Other chapters of this book provide numerous examples of the potential data services that can be provided to meet the needs of scholars and scholars in the making.

In their venerable *Data Basics* text, used to educate generations of data librarians through ICPSR's Summer Program, Geraci, Humphrey, and Jacobs describe another way to think about data services utilizing tiers or levels of service.[2] In this model, data services consist of technology, service providers, and collections, with many different levels of computing, reference, and collections services that a particular institution might provide based on the needs of their users and the capacities of their organization. For example, one library might choose to offer reference service at Tier Two, where staff help patrons identify data by subject; another library might require a Tier Four reference service where librarians help interpret file layouts and codebooks. The levels of service are somewhat hierarchical—in the example above, the Tier Four service would also include the functions from lower tiers—but the book's authors emphasize that service quality is independent of service extent; providing additional levels of service does not necessarily make one service better than another.[3] The *Data Basics* model is user-centric in that it asks the service providers to carefully consider local context and needs, but it also benefits from the expertise of its authors, who are expert data librarians themselves and have years of experience developing and providing data services. As a result, one of this model's strengths is that it identifies and explains the range of specific data services that could be adopted. Bennett expands on the *Data Basics* model using a similar model of service tiers but focuses more on the functions of the data librarian in each tier, ranging from occasional data reference to full curatorial services.[4]

Another service model that resonates in a data services context was described by Elliot Felix of the consultancy firm brightspot in a presentation on library spaces that encourage creativity. This model posits that a space is successful when it provides for five aspects: mindset, skill set, toolset, programs/events, and settings.[5] This model reminds data librarians that providing statistical software or datasets (the toolset) is insufficient without providing users with the skills to use them, which might be done through instruction or consultation on data tools and concepts (skill set). Or, as Thompson and Edelstein aptly describe, "giving a data file to a patron who does not possess the tools and skills needed to analyze it is about as useful as giving a book to someone who cannot read."[6] Additionally, inspiring the right mindset in data users is necessary to help give tools and skills the most impact. A thoughtfully designed, comfortable, welcoming physical space is also important, and events and activities to bring users together ultimately strengthen those users' mindsets and skill sets.

The Studio Model

The word *studio* has a commonly understood meaning, and most people can easily conjure an image of an artist's studio. A *studio model* for academic data services uses the studio—in this case an academic studio for students of art, architecture, and similar pursuits—as a metaphor for planning spaces, staff, and services to support data intensive work. The qualities of this kind of studio are fundamental to the studio model:[†]

- A studio is a place for *creating*. Just as an artist may take a piece of clay and transform it into something new, a student may create a survey, take an existing dataset and analyze it in a new way or combine it with new data, or create a visual representation of data.
- A studio is a place for *learning through iteration*. One rarely, if ever, enters a studio with the expectation of quickly leaving with a finished creation, because the purpose is to experiment, make a mess, and try out different techniques. Sometimes there is an underlying vision at work, a goal, and sometimes there is no particular aim at the outset, but there is nearly always learning that occurs during the process.
- A studio is a place for *self-directed work*. There is no common curriculum, nor is anyone telling users what they should be doing, although there is often help available by request. Users bring their own collection of projects and deadlines to the space, but they come at their own discretion and guide their own work during their stay.
- A studio is a *collective*. The studio is made up of shared resources, not only for reasons of economy, but also to encourage a sense of community among its users. Timm-Bottos and Reilly observed that a studio environment "helped [students] to form connections and relationships with one another, to be more expressive, and to foster the sense that 'we were in this together.'"[7]

† These characteristics of a studio were compiled from a variety of dictionary definitions and encyclopedia entries exploring the studio concept and history. It was also influenced by Mark Hatch's *The Maker Movement Manifesto: Rules for Innovation in the New World of Crafters, Hackers, and Tinkerers*.

- A studio is for work that is *open and public*. Regardless of the particular rules for accessing the space, from the individual's point of view, working in a studio is the opposite of working alone. It is a place where failing in front of others is expected and allowed, which in turn leads to greater innovation and learning.[8] Data-intensive work is more often *not* open—scholars have privacy concerns and mandates, or simply do not want to reveal their unfinished projects—but the ideas of normalizing failure and working among others to encourage creativity are still apropos.

The studio metaphor falls short in at least one critical way: traditional notions of an academic artists' studio do not include the idea of access for all, or the idea that the collective resources and use of the space are available to everyone regardless of affiliation and without barriers. Open and equal access is a central professional value for librarians and many others in higher education support roles, and is certainly part of any library service model,[†] even though it cannot be directly described by the metaphor of a studio.

On a fundamental level, the studio model for academic data services combines space, staff, and resources (including software and library materials) to support data users as creators, learners, and collaborators. For example, many successful data services are made up of staff and resources, or of staff and space, but a key tenet of the studio model is that it emphasizes the incorporation of all three. For example, New York University's Data Services, which is discussed in more detail at the end of this chapter, is made up of data librarians and technologists (staff), access to software, data sources, and training (resources), and an open lab in the library where those people and resources come together (space).

The Studio Model in the Higher Education and Library Landscape

The studio model for academic data services also reflects and stems from several wider trends and themes in higher education and in the practices of librarianship: renewing emphasis on innovative physical spaces, acknowledging the value of informal learning at the collegiate level, participating in the emerging maker movement, encouraging learner-centered education, and fostering development of new literacies.

---

† Admittedly, many academic libraries embrace open and equal access only within a closed community. For example, many restrict access to their buildings or computing resources for those without affiliation to the university, making their resources unavailable to members of the public.

The Value of Physical Space in the Electronic Age

The continual rise and influence of technology and the Web in higher education, through the advent of massive open online courses (MOOCs), synchronous and asynchronous online courses, and flipped classrooms, just to name a few manifestations, has caused anxiety about the future of in-person learning and the traditional college campus experience. The more optimistic view, however, is that there is much to be gained from technology in improving face-to-face learning, and that technology both forces and allows educators to make the in-person aspects, including physical spaces, of higher education more meaningful.[9] Bennett challenges educators, when designing new spaces, to think carefully about what a physical space can provide that a virtual space cannot and suggests that among these are immersive learning, social learning, and collaborative learning.[10] Physical spaces are not obsolete and, on the contrary, must now be designed to intentionally showcase their advantages over virtual spaces.

Spaces for Informal Learning

Along the same lines, informal learning outside the classroom is often just as important to students' academic learning and personal development.[11] Conceptualizing data services as a studio reinforces the importance of informal, self-driven learning and the idea that physical spaces are still important in the age of technology-enhanced education. Libraries have been championing these ideas for more than a decade through the concept of the learning commons, a space designed to enable collaboration, informal learning, and interaction with technology and library resources (including librarians). Sinclair describes the "Commons 2.0" in similar terms and asserts these guiding principles for such spaces: they are open, free, comfortable, inspiring, and practical.[12] Even when not engaged in collaborative activity, students report that being among others and part of a community of people who are working is a source of motivation and inspiration.[13] This "social ambience" factor described by Crook and Mitchell can be important in a space for data activities, too; even if software and resources are available remotely, there is value to being physically present among others who are also engaged in intensive work.[14]

Data Services and Makerspaces

Academic data services can also be compared to and interpreted through the lens of the Maker Movement, whose broader cultural impact has infiltrated higher education and presents a great deal of potential in this context. Those familiar with Hatch's *Maker Movement Manifesto* may have noticed its similarities to the idea of a studio model for data services: makerspaces are places for social and collective learning where experts and novices teach and learn from each other, where resources are shared, and where creating is approached with a spirit of play and enabled by technology.[15] They are safe places for anyone to learn and offer access to "skills that students might not have the confidence or opportunity to pursue otherwise."[16] Burke uses Henry Jenkins' concept of participatory culture to describe makerspaces' role in higher education: students can be creators in addition to consumers, can develop skills at their own pace, and can learn through teaching others.[17] Learning here is personalized, but not merely as a gimmick propagated by commercial learning software salespeople.[18] The studio model for data services has a lot in common with the philosophies of makerspaces, and in reality, many data services labs and spaces could themselves be categorized as makerspaces.

Learner-Focused Education

Another notable trend is the shift in emphasis from teaching to learning over the past quarter century. Learner-focused education emphasizes a constructivist perspective in which students assume more responsibility for their own learning and where a great teacher is defined not by her own qualities, but by the learning of her students.[19]

This shift is evident in the new *Framework for Information Literacy for Higher Education* from the Association of College & Research Libraries (ACRL) division of the American Library Association (ALA), a document meant to guide librarians as they work with others on campus to develop information literacy outcomes for students.[20] This *Framework* is based on the idea of metaliteracy, which "demands behavioral, affective, cognitive, and metacognitive engagement with the information ecosystem" and recognizes students as "consumers and creators of information who can participate successfully in collaborative spaces"; it goes beyond the skills of finding and consuming information and asks students to recognize and develop their own roles in the information landscape.[21] The *Framework* identifies six specific frames that are echoed in a studio model of data services. For example, the "Information Creation as a Process" frame describes the state of understanding that humans construct information in social contexts, and that the many decisions made during that creation process affect the end product. Enabling learners and researchers to interact with data—by collecting and creating it or by analyzing data that already exist—is a textbook example of this frame, since a majority of data work requires constant interpretation, decision-making, engagement, and negotiation with the end goals of the project. Likewise, the frame "Searching as Strategic Exploration," describes the "nonlinear and iterative" nature of scholarship and the requisite "mental flexibility to pursue alternate avenues as new understanding develops"; a data studio's emphasis on supporting creative, iterative exploration is an ideal environment for helping students develop this mindset.

Enabling New Literacies

While librarians have been focusing on information literacy, higher education has concurrently been embracing the idea of "new literacies," and the literacies of the digital age along with visual and quantitative literacy are being considered across the curriculum. Quantitative literacy and information literacy have a lot in common; both focus on finding, retrieving, analyzing, and using, with more emphasis of late on the last two.[22] An example is Carleton College's Quantitative Inquiry, Reasoning, and Knowledge (QuIRK) Initiative, which recognizes that all students, regardless of major or focus, need quantitative reasoning skills to be successful members of society.[23] Carleton College also provides an excellent example of librarians and technologists partnering to support quantitative literacy.[24] Even at institutions that do not have formal cross-curricular initiatives, having data services available to everyone can go a long way to support quantitative literacy development in all students, not just those who are required to take a statistics course. For example, a student who wants to use data or create a visualization for a journalism or biology class, or for an independent project, can access software, training, and assistance to develop those interests regardless of whether his curriculum requires a specific course. Academic libraries are often asked to demonstrate their value to the university's mission,[25] and because the studio model dovetails nicely with these strategic directions for higher education, library data services that embrace it are well positioned to thrive and continue growing with the institution.

Why the Library?

Many librarians have written about the imperatives for establishing data services, about effective environmental scans, and about translating those needs into services,[26] but they have not necessarily addressed the question of why these data services should reside in the library at all. The case for the library has been made effectively for matters related to research data management[27] and for providing access to datasets and data resources that are part of the library's collection. But why would a service that encompasses the other parts of the data lifecycle that are less related to traditional library collections (including survey tools, statistical and textual analysis software, and data visualization) reside in the library? Why not in a department that also teaches courses in data analysis? Why would a traditional "studio" not be housed in an academic department?

Libraries as Connectors

Practically speaking, it is easy to argue that all parts of the data lifecycle can be better served when the services are grouped together, even if multiple persons or departments are providing them. Libraries and librarians serve as natural connectors, linking people and resources, and have always been destinations for self-learning. Most data librarians have strong skills in finding, interpreting, manipulating, and curating data, but librarians do not need to take responsibility for everything on their own. Because of the technical nature of some of these activities, and because providing resources also means providing hardware and software, it is ideal for data services to include support from information technology professionals and many other campus partners.[28] Bennett and Nicholson argue that a successful transaction will also include helping users analyze and use the data, and that librarians may need to seek stronger relationships with other data experts on campus.[29] A fundamental aspect of the studio model for data services is providing space, staff, and resources together, and libraries are inarguably the stewards and providers of intellectual materials on college campuses. The value of locating data services in proximity to these collections and the experts in connecting people to those resources should not be overlooked.

Interdisciplinary, Neutral Space

The other arguments for providing data services in the library return to the tenets of the studio model and the underlying philosophies of librarianship, which point to a welcoming, democratic, interdisciplinary space—and, just as importantly, to the values and skills of the professionals who work there. In their seminal piece, "The Role of the Academic Library in Promoting Student Engagement in Learning," Kuh and Gonyea describe the library as "the physical manifestation of the core values and activities of academic life."[30] The library has long been at the intellectual center of university life, and even though the necessity of visiting a physical library is not what it once was, libraries still command that place metaphorically (and sometimes geographically).

A library is an interdisciplinary space that acts as neutral ground, while at the same time belonging to everyone. A successful library space makes it obvious that everyone is welcome and that there are no prior claims made by individuals or groups that impose on others' sense of ownership; it is a public good for the campus. Walking through the halls of a chemistry building, for example, may be an intimidating experience for a humanist: this space is owned, claimed, and its uses prescribed. Plus, the humanist's trip to the chemistry department is likely an anomaly—it is a break from her normal pattern, and she is not likely to come back without a specific purpose. Spaces for specific community groups are necessary on campus, of course, but stand in contrast to a collective space like a library. Likewise, librarians' interdisciplinary backgrounds can make them ideal providers of interdisciplinary data services that do not preference one discipline over another.[31]

Transcending Disciplinary Differences

Librarians and technologists at universities have a unique ability and, some would argue, mandate, to see the bigger picture on campus and to look for common ground. A scientist might think the concerns of a social scientist are entirely foreign. While a librarian or technologist can understand and respect disciplinary nuances, he or she can also see similarities and when to share knowledge and strategies across disciplines, and identify times when it makes more sense to work together to figure out a path forward. Mooney and Silver describe librarians as "silo crossings, or people in a unique position to see the big picture across campus, while departments and colleges are typically are more focused on their own interests," and note that they can also help the institution avoid costly resource duplication.[32] This is easily apparent when talking about research data management; this concept varies depending on disciplines, sub-disciplines, and sectors. Supporting research data management is a challenge that benefits from taking a broader view to recognize and incorporate the contributions of everyone from NASA to the public opinion polling community.

There are many advantages to providing data services through departmental structures—deep relationships and trust among members, close alignment with disciplinary methods, more control over pedagogy and curriculum, and other reasons—and ideally a university would have some of both types. In a world of limited resources, however, the best impact is achieved through centralized data services, in the library, delivered in partnership with information technology and others.

Case Study: Data Services at New York University

There are plenty of academic data services that fit the studio model described, and many that exemplify it. A small sample of these, all of which have undergone physical space transformations recently, includes Duke University's Data & Visualization Services, which has a new home in The Edge, the Libraries' research commons;[33] Georgia State University's Collaborative University Research & Visualization Environment (CURVE);[34] the StatLab at the Center for Science and Social Science Information (CSSSI) at Yale University;[35] Spatial and Numeric Data Services (SAND) at the University of Michigan Libraries;[36] and the Research Hub at UNC-Chapel Hill Libraries.[37] However, New York University's Data Services is the most fitting case study for this chapter because it was among the first to use the term "studio" to describe its data services and because the metaphor of a studio was intentionally used to guide its development.

Service Overview

Data Services at New York University[38] was formed in fall 2008 to formally amalgamate the data support provided for many years by what was then Information Technology Services (ITS) with that of the Division of Libraries into a new "Data Service Studio." Since its inception, Data Services has been a joint service of the Libraries and NYU Information Technology (NYUIT), with two co-directors (one from each organization) and staff reporting to both. Data Services provides support for the entire data lifecycle, including access to and help with survey, statistical, GIS, and qualitative analysis software, assistance with locating and using data sources, and data management support.[39] These services are provided through one-on-one consultation, workshops, course-integrated instruction, and online documentation and tools, and are housed in a Data Services lab in a prominent location in NYU's main library (although all of the services are also available remotely).[†]

Physical Space

Data Services' physical facility is located in the Research Commons of Bobst Library, the main library at NYU. The Research Commons opened in fall 2012 and co-locates five specialized units: Data Services, the Digital Studio,[40] Digital Scholarship Services,[41] Business & Government Information,[42] and the Coles Science Center.[43] While the space is open to everyone, the renovation planning focused on meeting the needs of graduate students,[44] who make up close to half of NYU's student body.[45] The Data Services lab, the physical space component of Data Services' studio service model, has 26 large-screen Macintosh workstations that all run the Windows operating system, due to the fact that several important statistics and GIS software packages only run on Windows. The lab has no walls dividing it from the rest of the floor, which removes barriers for anyone wanting to sit down and experiment with data software, but also creates challenges when the computers are fully occupied by users who are not using specialized software. This issue is partially alleviated by allowing users to reserve some Data Services computers

† Interestingly, the decision was made in 2012 to drop the word "Studio" from the unit's name, so that the NYU Data Service Studio became NYU Data Services. Although no changes were made to the service model at that time, it was decided that having "studio" in the name implied that Data Services was merely a place, and diminished other elements of the service—consultation, expertise, instruction, collections—that were not dependent upon physical space. This was especially important as NYU was actively expanding its global presence, with new campuses in Abu Dhabi, U.A.E. and Shanghai, China, and a dozen other Global Academic Centers around the world, and the idea was that students and faculty could continue to have access to the services offered in New York. Although its name changed, Data Services continued to utilize a studio model as described here.

ahead of time so that they know they will have a place to work when they arrive. In keeping with the philosophy of the rest of the Research Commons, the Data Services lab is not a silent space—the low-level talking of collaborative work is encouraged—and the furniture is designed for intensive work, with high-end office chairs, access to power at every seat, and a desk footprint large enough to allow the user to spread out and make use of supporting materials like books, papers, and laptops. The lab is staffed for 6-8 hours per day by Data Services consultants and full-time staff, who offer walk-up help with a variety of tools and activities. During hours when the library is open but the lab is unstaffed, the computers are available for data and general computing use. In addition to the lab on the 5th floor, Data Services makes heavy use of a dedicated 10-seat computer classroom on the 6th floor of the library that has the same software as in the lab downstairs. This is where most Data Services workshops are held.

Resources

The specific services provided by NYU's Data Services are designed to support the entire data lifecycle and grew from NYU's long legacy of providing support for statistical software. As a result, Data Services has a list of supported software: quantitative (SPSS, Stata, SAS, R, etc.), qualitative (Atlas.ti, NVivo), surveys (Qualtrics), and GIS (ArcGIS, ERDAS IMAGINE, etc.). It also provides support for locating data and statistics and data management planning, and is actively planning and developing new data repository services. For all of these areas, Data Services offers access to software through the Data Services lab and online through NYU's Virtual Computer Lab; e-mail and in-person consultation on research projects, which often involves multiple appointments; and instruction through an open series of introductory workshops and course-integrated sessions as well as a collection of self-help resources and documentation (such as textbooks and staff-created tutorials). Data Services also works with other librarians to build the library's collection of data resources in the form of database subscriptions and standalone datasets and GIS data products. All of these services and resources are free of charge and available to any member of the NYU community regardless of status or disciplinary affiliations. At the heart of Data Services' approach is the notion that methodological consulting is out of scope: Data Services staff will help a user learn how to perform a chosen statistical method, have a discussion about the pros and cons of certain methods, or provide guidance for further research, but will not decide for a user which method is best or "correct." This is partially out of respect for disciplinary methods and the limitations of staff's knowledge to make appropriate recommendations, but also because of the self-directed learning ethos that guides the service.

Staff

The Data Services staff has grown since 2008 into a team of ten professional staff members plus six to eight graduate student consultants at any given time. The professional staff is made up of two co-managers, three quantitative data/statistics specialists (two full-time and one part-time), one qualitative analysis and surveys specialist, two GIS specialists (one full-time and one part-time), a GIS librarian, and a data librarian. The student consultants are hired from a variety of departments around campus for their skills in software packages and tools. In addition to the core Data Services staff, the service draws heavily on relationships with subject librarians, other technologists (such as those in neighboring Digital Scholarship Services and the Digital Studio), and a few statistical methodology institutes and centers on campus and uses those relationships often to make successful referrals. A typical illustrative example is when a student meets with a Data Services staff member with questions about a project and it quickly becomes clear that the student could benefit from further exploration of the literature of her discipline through a consultation with a subject librarian. The GIS and quantitative consultants often collaborate with the GIS and data librarians when patrons' needs include finding data and analyzing it. The Data Services lab is staffed using an informal triage system: the desk is staffed during open hours with several student consultants who are hired specifically for their statistical or GIS skills, so that one can generally expect to walk up to the desk and be able to get help with any of Data Services' supported software. Student consultants are also trained to recognize more complex questions and anything that would benefit from an in-depth consultation, and can either call full time staff out from their offices or refer the patron to make an appointment. This system allows the full time staff to concentrate on higher-level work by leaving the simpler questions to student consultants. Data Services has also benefited over the years from employing student consultants from a range of programs with a wide variety of experiences and expertise, and their insights have often been the impetus for new or expanded services.

Communicating About the Service

The outreach strategy for Data Services has varied over time, but the general goal is wide exposure with a welcoming and accurate message about the services available, while at the same time avoiding the perception of evangelism. The aim is to respond to the needs of the NYU community, raise awareness and enthusiasm about data tools and resources, and expose community members to needs they might not have considered (such as good data storage practices), while taking care not to impose staff interests or preferences.† This outreach strategy relies heavily on relationships with subject librarians and other colleagues who interact with faculty, word of mouth among users, plus some targeted communications with faculty based on their teaching or research interests.

In recent years, Data Services has worked to build relationships with teaching faculty and instructors to make its instruction program more effective, because learning about data resources and tools is more meaningful when it is contextualized within a course and integrated with a course's overall learning outcomes. At the same time, maintaining the open workshop series is still a priority because it keeps the tools available to anyone (acknowledging that the toolset is not truly available without a skill set to use it), rather than just to those who are enrolled in a course. These workshops frequently attract students, faculty, and staff who have a general interest in data or GIS (without a specific project or goal in mind) and are more willing to attend a workshop "to see what it is all about" than to seek out an appointment with a staff member. The open workshops cater to these patrons and contribute to Data Services' outreach goals of creating a welcoming and wide-reaching service.

Assessment and Looking Forward

Data Services has kept detailed statistics on every patron interaction and workshop since its inception, clearly documenting the growing demand for its services over the years. This documentation has greatly supported the department's growth and addition of new staff members and other resources, and also helps the staff identify trends and respond to them. While Data Services also maintains other mechanisms for gathering patron feedback (especially on workshops), there has been considerably less assessment of patron experience, which would surely be valuable for future planning. Adding and expanding services based on demand worked well in the early days of Data Services, but as it develops services for data management planning and data archiving, for example, it will not be able to rely only on documented demand. These services are critical, but their audience is unlikely to be as large and forthcoming as the audience for statistical software consulting has been. This is because research data management services are generally more complex and less defined, and there is less precedent in this area for faculty seeking data management support and for libraries providing that support. At the same time, Data Services' studio model provides solid infrastructure for developing these and other new services through the combination of staff with a variety of data expertise, a collection of resources, and a welcoming space for consultations, workshops, and self-directed work.

---

† For example, just because a software or tool is supported by Data Services does not mean that it is the right tool to fulfill a patron's needs (e.g. insisting a patron should be using ArcGIS when Google Maps would work better for the students' needs.)

Conclusion

Academic data services are typically seen as research services—conceived and fashioned to support the research needs of faculty and students—but by looking at data services through the lens of the studio model presented here, it is easier to see how they actually bridge the teaching and learning and research functions of a university and help bring them together. The studio model uses the studio as a metaphor to reinforce that data services patrons are creators as well as consumers, that research and learning are inseparable, and that physical space, in conjunction with staff and resources, can still make an impact in today's university. As with all models, the studio model has strengths and weaknesses. Regardless, it is a useful addition to the collection of models that inspire data librarians to plan, rethink, and improve the valuable services they provide—and also a tool to help them articulate that value to their communities.

---

1. For examples, see: Ann Green, "Conceptualizing the Digital Life Cycle," *IASSIST Communique* (blog), June 1, 2006 (8:49 p.m.), http://www.iassistdata.org/blog/conceptualizing-digital-life-cycle.
2. Diane Geraci, Chuck Humphrey, and Jim Jacobs, *Data Basics: An Introductory Text*, 2012, http://3stages.org/class/2012/pdf/data_basics_2012.pdf.
3. Ibid, 106.
4. Terrence B. Bennett, *Research Data Services at Singapore Management University: Engagement Summary Report*, July 1, 2010, http://ink.library.smu.edu.sg/library_research/5: 4–6.
5. Elliot Felix, "Fostering Creativity" (presentation, ACRL 2015 Conference, Portland, OR, March 28, 2015), http://www.slideshare.net/elliotfelix/fostering-creativity-46468132.
6. Kristi Thompson and Daniel M. Edelstein, "A Reference Model for Providing Statistical Consulting Services in an Academic Library Setting," *IASSIST Quarterly* 28, no. 2 (2004): 35.
7. Janis Timm-Bottos and Rosemary C. Reilly, "Learning in Third Spaces: Community Art Studio as Storefront University Classroom," *American Journal of Community Psychology* 55, no. 1–2 (March 2015): 108.
8. Felix, "Fostering Creativity."
9. Audrey Watters, "The Case for a Campus Makerspace," *Hack Education*, February 6, 2013, http://hackeducation.com/2013/02/06/the-case-for-a-campus-makerspace/.
10. Scott Bennett, "First Questions for Designing Higher Education Learning Spaces," *The Journal of Academic Librarianship* 33, no. 1 (2007): 15.
11. For an extensive literature review on this topic, see: George D. Kuh, "In Their Own Words: What Students Learn Outside the Classroom," *American Educational Research Journal* 30, no. 2 (1993): 277–281.
12. Bryan Sinclair, "Commons 2.0: Library Spaces Designed for Collaborative Learning," *EDUCAUSE Quarterly* 30, no. 4 (2007): 5.
13. Charles Crook and Gemma Mitchell, "Ambience in Social Learning: Student Engagement with New Designs for Learning Spaces," *Cambridge Journal of Education* 42, no. 2 (2012): 136.
14. Ibid, 135–136.
15. Mark Hatch, *The Maker Movement Manifesto: Rules for Innovation in the New World of Crafters, Hackers, and Tinkerers*, (New York: McGraw-Hill Education, 2014), 1–2, summarized in John Burke, "Making Sense: Can Makerspaces Work in Academic Libraries?," in *ACRL 2015 Proceedings* (ACRL 2015, Portland, OR: Association of College & Research Libraries, 2015), 497–504, http://www.ala.org/acrl/acrl/conferences/acrl2015/papers.
16. Watters, "The Case for a Campus Makerspace."

17. Burke, "Making Sense," 500.
18. Watters, "The Case for a Campus Makerspace."
19. George D. Kuh and Robert M. Gonyea, "The Role of the Academic Library in Promoting Student Engagement in Learning," *College & Research Libraries* 64, no. 4 (2003): 256.
20. Association of College and Research Libraries, "Framework for Information Literacy for Higher Education," February 2, 2015, http://www.ala.org/acrl/standards/ilframework.
21. Ibid.
22. Terrence B. Bennett and Shawn W. Nicholson, "Research Libraries: Connecting Users to Numeric and Spatial Resources," *Social Science Computer Review* 25, no. 3 (August 1, 2007): 305.
23. Carleton University, "About QuIRK," last modified May 5, 2014, http://serc.carleton.edu/quirk/About_QuIRK.html.
24. Carleton University, "Goals of Research Data Services," last modified July 30, 2014, http://apps.carleton.edu/campus/library/about/data/model/.
25. Megan J. Oakleaf, *The Value of Academic Libraries: A Comprehensive Research Review and Report* (Chicago, IL: Association of College and Research Libraries, 2010): 6.
26. For example, Bennett and Nicholson, "Research Libraries: Connecting Users to Numeric and Spatial Resources."; Minglu Wang, "Supporting the Research Process through Expanded Library Data Services.," *Program: Electronic Library & Information Systems* 47, no. 3 (July 2013): 282–303; Brian Westra, "Data Services for the Sciences: A Needs Assessment," *Ariadne: A Web & Print Magazine of Internet Issues for Librarians & Information Specialists* 30, no. 64 (July 2010): 13–13.; Eleanor J. Read, "Data Services in Academic Libraries," *Reference & User Services Quarterly* 46, no. 3 (2007): 61–75.
27. Carol Tenopir, Robert J. Sandusky, Suzie Allard, and Ben Birch, "Research Data Management Services in Academic Research Libraries and Perceptions of Librarians," *Library & Information Science Research* 36, no. 2 (April 2014): 84–90.
28. For further thoughts on campus collaborations, see: Samantha Guss, "Campus Collaborations for Holistic Data Services" (presentation, Social Sciences Librarians Boot Camp 2013, Medford, MA, June 7, 2013), http://goo.gl/l1b8Vc.
29. Bennett and Nicholson, "Research Libraries: Connecting Users to Numeric and Spatial Resources," 304.
30. Kuh and Gonyea, "The Role of the Academic Library in Promoting Student Engagement in Learning," 256.
31. Wang, "Supporting the Research Process."
32. Hailey Mooney and Breezy Silver, "Spread the News: Promoting Data Services," *College & Research Libraries News* 71, no. 9 (2010): 482.
33. Duke University Libraries, "The Brandaleone Lab for Data and Visualization," accessed January 10, 2016, http://library.duke.edu/data/about/lab.
34. Georgia State University, "About," 2016, http://sites.gsu.edu/curve/about-2.
35. Yale University, "Spaces," 2016, http://csssi.yale.edu/spaces.
36. University of Michigan Library, "Spatial and Numeric Data Services (SAND)," last modified May 6, 2016, http://www.lib.umich.edu/clark-library/services/sand.
37. UNC Libraries, "About the Research Hub," accessed January 10, 2016, http://library.unc.edu/hub/about.
38. New York University Libraries, "Data Services: Home," last modified January 4, 2016, http://library.nyu.edu/dataservices.
39. For more information on Data Services' history, services, and organizational structure, see: http://library.nyu.edu/dataservices; Scott Collard, Matt Zimmerman, Alicia Estes, Gretchen Gano, Frank LoPresti, Heather Stewart, and Jennifer Vinopal, *Report of the Data Services Working Group*; Jenn Stringer, Lynn Rohrs, and Samantha Guss, "What Role Can Peer Benchmarking Play in Planning for the Future of Research and Teaching Technologies?" in *Proceedings of the 2014 Library Assessment Conference: Building Effective, Sustainable, Practical Assessment* (Seattle, WA: Association of Research Libraries, 2014), http://libraryassessment.org/archive/

index.shtml; Jeanine Scaramozzino, Russell White, Jeff Essic, Lee Ann Fullington, Himanshu Mistry, Amanda Henley, and Miriam Olivares, "Map Room to Data and GIS Services: Five University Libraries Evolving to Meet Campus Needs and Changing Technologies," *Journal of Map & Geography Libraries* 10, no. 1 (January 2014): 6–47. doi:10.1080/15420353.2014.893943 ; Jason B. Phillips, Samantha A. Guss, and David M. McGarry, "The NYU Survey Service," "The NYU Survey Service: Promoting Value in Undergraduate Education," *College & Undergraduate Libraries* 18, no. 2–3 (2011): 183–99, doi:10.1080/10691316.2011.577672.; Samantha Guss, Michelle Hudson, Jen Green, and Nicole Scholz, "Data in Common(s): Collaborative Models for Robust Data Support," presentation at the International Association for Social Science Information Services & Technology (IASSIST) (Washington, D.C., 2012), http://iassistdata.org/conferences/archive/2012.

40. New York University Libraries, "Digital Studio: Home," last modified December 8, 2015, http://library.nyu.edu/digitalstudio.
41. New York University Libraries, "Digital Scholarship Services," last modified January 2016, http://library.nyu.edu/research/dss/.
42. New York University Libraries, "Business, Government Documents and Public Policy: Home," last modified January 7, 2016, http://guides.nyu.edu/busdocs.
43. New York University Libraries, "Coles Science Center," last modified January 5, 2016, http://guides.nyu.edu/science.
44. Lucinda Covert-Vail and Scott Collard, *New Roles for New Times: Research Library Services for Graduate Students* (Washington, D.C.: Association of Research Libraries, December 2012), accessed July 22, 2015, http://www.arl.org/storage/documents/publications/nrnt-grad-roles-20dec12.pdf.
45. National Center for Education Statistics. "New York University." *College Navigator*. Washington, D.C.: U.S. Dept. of Education, Institute of Education Sciences, National Center for Education Statistics, July 21, 2015, http://nces.ed.gov/collegenavigator/?q=new+york+university&s=all&id=193900.

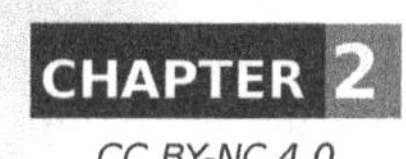

Embedded Options: A Common Framework

Cynthia Hudson-Vitale

EXPERIENCE AND RESEARCH has shown that given the complex nature of research data services, various university units and departments must work together to provide appropriate services to create, manage, store, educate, archive, and preserve research data. Organizationally, this can prove to be a challenge. One viable option for meeting these challenges is the embedded librarian model. In the research data services sense, librarians may be embedded into a faculty-led research group, assisting in creating metadata and managing active data; into the university research office, helping with federal requirements for open data compliance; and into a campus information technology unit providing assistance with big data transfer and data storage issues, to name just a few examples. This chapter provides a common framework that describes the responsibilities and skills of an embedded research data services librarian and then presents various case studies as examples of implementation.

Embedded Research Data Librarian Framework

In general, frameworks serve to provide structure and outline a concept. They provide the scaffolding and common components that describe a system or conceptual schema. The framework for embedded research data services librarians articulates the common skills and responsibilities of the role within the context of location or level of personalized research data services.

Research Data Librarian Responsibilities

The responsibilities and skills expected of a research data services librarian make up a major component of the common framework. A 2003 report titled *Revolutionizing Science and Engineering Through Cyberinfrasctructure: Report of the Na-*

tional Science Foundation Blue-Ribbon Advisory Panel on Cyberinfrastructure was one of the first documents to articulate how new research methods required new technical and social infrastructure to support them.[1] The report highlights the role that digital libraries may play in supporting the development of community data holdings, including the creation of tutorials and documents on data format, quality control, and interchange formatting, as well as tools for data preparation, data fusion, data mining, knowledge discovery, and visualization.

In addition, data information literacy is a useful term to describe a set of skills that data librarians need to provide support and data related services to researchers.[2] These proficiencies include understanding a researcher's culture of practice; data conversion and interoperability; data curation and reuse; data management and organization; data preservation; data processing and analysis; data quality and documentation; data visualization and representation; databases and data formats; discovery and acquisition of data; metadata and data description; and ethics and attribution. As exemplified in the case studies below, many research data services librarians collaborate with faculty in these areas.

Taking the technical skills and requirements of the research data services librarian a step further, another report published by the National Science Board in 2005 expands the role of the data scientist, or data librarian, as having the responsibility to assist researchers with many of their data-related needs throughout the research lifecycle while directly contributing to innovations in data technology and scholarship. This service and research would include helping researchers conduct research using digital data collections; implementing and developing innovative methods and technologies for data storage, visualization, and discovery; and serving as a mentor to those interested in pursuing data related fields and careers.[3]

In sum, these reports and scholarly publications provide research data librarians with a set of services and academic pursuits that are most needed by the domain or practice and the faculty with whom they work. A research data librarian may expect to provide outreach, training, and education around data-related skills (such as file management, analysis, cleaning, visualization, and curation, to name a few), while also applying those skills to faculty, researcher, and library projects and ongoing collaborations.

What it Means to Be Embedded

The other core component of the embedded research data services librarian framework is a common understanding of what is meant by embedded librarianship. In general, to be embedded can take many different forms; it does not necessitate being physically located outside of the library, but does focus on providing a high level of personalized services for a researcher. In this role, the embedded librarian should be located where the users are (either virtually or physically) while actively assessing user needs and creating services to fulfill those needs.[4]

The embedded librarian is a not a new role in the library profession. In 1993 various authors first began to discuss getting outside of the library to provide additional services of value to users in the research setting.[5] More recently, Carlson and Kneale define embedded librarianship as a role that enables librarians to create partnerships with their clientele and apply their information expertise in ways that will have a direct and deep impact on research and teaching.[6] Noticeably absent from this definition is the necessity of being located where the users are; instead, Carlson and Kneale focus on the level and quality of service that an embedded librarian provides. This definition also positions librarians less as service providers and more as collaborators within research groups and to individual faculty, an important reframing of the librarian's role in the research ecosystem.

Carlson and Kneale further outline two modes of embedded librarianship in the research setting that establish these partnerships. The first is a project-based model that involves librarians as collaborators with faculty in a particular research project with defined responsibilities. The second model is programmatic, with a librarian working in an ongoing manner for a research organization to handle various information management tasks. Funding for these types of partnerships can also take many different forms. The embedded librarian may be supported through grant add-ons, co-funded by both the library and the embedded point of service, or even fully funded by the library, with time donated to the embedded service.

Embedded Case Studies

Though an understanding of common research data services and embedded services is helpful, little comparison has been conducted on the common skills and responsibilities of an embedded research data services librarian. To address this gap, embedded research data librarian case studies and examples were mined from the scholarly literature and personal interviews.

Researchers and Research Groups

The embedded data librarian can provide programmatic or project-based services that span the entire research data lifecycle while working with researchers and the research group. These collaborations can develop in a number of ways, but arise predominately through cultivated relationships, grants, and via funded grant add-ons.[7]

The first example provides a programmatic approach to providing embedded research data services at the University of California, Los Angeles. Two librarians worked directly with two distinct research groups to provide a number of data-related services. The first project was funded through the NIH and involved the librarians providing services to improve data management practices within a research group setting. In this role, the librarians provided presentations on best practices for file management and recommended a metadata schema and file/data versioning software (such as Apache Subversion†). The second project was initiated after a researcher attended a university-wide presentation by a librarian about data management practices. For this project, several librarians worked with the research team and led investigations into useful software for data aggregation (such as REDCap‡) and best practices for organizing electronic notebook entries.[8] While not physically located at the research group offices, the librarians regularly attended lab meetings and provided customized solutions to research group data-related challenges.

Customized solutions may also be found in a project-based approach at Washington University in St. Louis. In this instance, a data librarian collaborated with a faculty member in Energy, Environmental and Chemical Engineering to develop and integrate data types into an air quality data catalog. This collaboration was initiated by the librarian and sustained through grant funds for a duration of eight months. The data librarian's activities included grant writing, the registration of data types, the linking of data types to the existing catalog metadata, and the final report writing.[9] Communication was conducted through weekly meetings, Skype chats, and other mechanisms. The librarian did not have dedicated space for working with the faculty in the research lab, but rather offered a high level of service and regular communication to successfully conclude the project.

Clinical Care Group

In the clinical setting, "informationists"§ often subsume research data related services. In this role, they provide clinical care group support for patient health and the training of the next generation of medical practitioners. In 2011 Greyson, Surette, Dennett and Chatterley surveyed 191 Canadian health librarians to determine the most common responsibilities for informationists.[10] They found the top responsibilities included searching literature, attending research team meetings, analyzing, scoping or summarizing literature, providing general reference services and maintaining current awareness for the clinical group. Recently, some clinical informationists have begun formally including research data related services in their practice.

---

† Apache Subversion is an open source versioning control software. It manages files and directories, and tracks changes to them over time.

‡ REDCap (Research Electronic Data Capture) is a secure web application for building and managing online surveys and databases.

§ A term coined by Davidoff and Florence in 2000 to describe the embedded medical librarian.

Beginning in 2012, Informationists at the New York University Health Sciences Libraries provided data-related services to a surgeon-scientist at the NYU College of Dentistry and a protein chemist in a project-based manner. They created an automated literature searching system, introduced tools and workflows for sharing citations, and introduced tools and workflows for sharing data and specimens.[11] To develop the automated literature searching system, the librarians wrote a Matlab program to access the NCBI programming utilities[¶] and then processed the results based upon the clinicians' needs.

Similarly, at Johns Hopkins University, informationists in Welch Library work with faculty in the Department of Radiology and Radiation Oncology as part of a grant-funded project.[12] In this capacity, the librarians provide bibliographic instruction to team members, conduct iterative literature searches, and develop guidelines on data sharing for the larger community. As the project has involved large amounts of literature and text-mined data, the informationists are also implementing a number of data management best practices, software, and tools.

Curriculum and Teaching

The embedded data librarian has also been found providing data-related support in the curriculum and through other training opportunities. According to Shulte, librarians embedded in course curricula have overall positive effects on student learning, specifically writing assignments.[13] While librarians embedding in the curriculum is not a new concept, the skills they are teaching students are new. In addition to, or even instead of, the traditional bibliographic instruction, embedded research data librarians are teaching data information literacy, data science, and data visualization skills.

Purdue University provides a good example of data information literacy skills embedded into an existing course curriculum.[14] Here, librarians partnered with teaching assistants in the School of Engineering to provide data information literacy activities throughout the engineering design cycle. This project was particularly concerned with data management of the code that students produced as part of the course's final project. The librarians were embedded in the course by regularly attending class sessions and holding customized workshops on data management skills.

At Weil Cornell Medical College, a librarian co-taught a course that introduced students to data mining and computational analysis in health informatics.[15] In addition to creating a resource guide, the librarian taught various R skills and computational methods, including such topics as support vector machines,

---

¶ NCBI programming utilities are a group of eight programs that allow stable access and querying of the databases that make up Entrez.

Monte Carlo method, Naïve Bayes and Adaptive Boosting.[†] Rather than stand-alone workshops on skills related to data information literacy, the librarian integrated those skills within the data science sessions she was teaching. This allowed the students to implement best practices while conducting course related assignments.

Examples of librarians co-teaching or leading data related courses may also be found at Washington University in St. Louis, where a Geographic Information Systems (GIS) Data Librarian has been added to the program faculty[16] for the International and Area Studies (IAS) department. In this role, the librarian teaches GIS courses and workshops and collaborates with other IAS faculty to conduct GIS research. Within the GIS courses the librarian includes data information literacy skills and practices. The librarian also actively attends faculty meetings and oversees the GIS curriculum for the department.

University Research Office

The role of the data librarian in the university research office can take many forms including providing and analyzing institutional author data to assist Research Offices with determining federal funding compliance and providing training and education in data management best practices. At the University of Oregon, the data management librarians partner with the Research Compliance Services to provide data management instruction as a component of the Responsible Conduct in Research Education program for graduate students in Biology, Psychology, Human Physiology, Geology, and Planning, Public Policy and Management.[17] Data librarians are also alerted when a faculty member applies for a federal grant requiring a data management plan. This alert allows the librarians to reach out and offer assistance in reviewing the data management plan and other data related services.[18]

Additional Examples

In addition to the organizational units described above, which may be found at many institutions, embedded opportunities exist in other Centers and multi-university projects.

---

† These topics are computational algorithms and machine learning models. Support vector machines are models that conduct supervised learning to analyze data, recognize patterns, classify objects, and conduct regression analysis. The Monte Carlo evaluation is a computational algorithm that conducts repeated random sampling to obtain numerical results in three main areas: optimization, numerical integration, and generating draws from probability distribution. Naïve Bayes is a family of machine learning probabilistic classifiers. Adaptive Boosting is an optimization algorithm.

Biomedical Informatics Service Providers

The Center for Biomedical Informatics (CBMI) at Washington University in St. Louis is currently collaborating with a data librarian to provide reproducible research services for their clinical trial and bio-specimen databases and search queries. Using the outcomes and recommendations of the Research Data Alliance working group on Data Citation: Making Dynamic Data Citable,[19] the data librarian is responsible for the phased implementation and management of a data citation initiative that will serve to make the CBMI databases, queries, and code reproducible and persistent. This collaboration began as a time donation, but the work has proven useful, and thus turned into a grant-funded project in little more than a year's time. With the grant funding, the aims and outcomes have expanded into improving the CBMI research reproducibility. In this example, the data librarian physically locates herself at the CBMI, where she has dedicated space for conducting her work.

Research/Data Communities

Data-related needs are not limited to just an individual team or unit on campus; often, they are a domain and discipline need. It therefore makes sense for data librarians to also heavily involve themselves in the research and data communities that are developing data-related recommendations and procedures that many of the faculty may adopt.

For example, the Sediment Experimentalist Network (SEN), an EarthCube Research Coordination Network (RCN), has included a data librarian from the University of Minnesota on its steering committee.[20] RCN grants serve to bring together domain researchers to collaboratively address discipline-specific issues in a virtual manner. Many data librarians have played various roles in these grants. For the SEN, the librarian provides expertise in data management planning, community education, and metadata development.[21] To be successful in this capacity it is important for the embedded research data librarian to attend all available meetings and conference calls. Additionally, the scope and extent of the expertise the data librarian will provide should be made explicit.

Conclusion

Various opportunities exist for data librarians to embed themselves into the academic scholarship within their home institutions, research domains, and data process communities. The case studies above offer examples of research data librarian embedded options that range significantly along a spectrum of ease of implementation (see Figure 2.1).

Figure 2.1. Spectrum of Initiating and Implementing Embedded Services

Embedded Options	**Low Barrier** → **Resource Intensive**
Securing Funding	
Grant Supported	
Time Donated	
Cultivating University Relationships	
E-mail Faculty/Research Office	
Attend University/Department Receptions	
Chat/E-mail about Research Data Services Regularly	
Embedded Services	
Provide DIL Instruction in the Classroom/Lab/Office	
Provide Data Science Instruction in the Class/Lab	
Provide Data Science Services	
Recommend Practices for Data Management	
Act as Data Manager for Lab	
Set up RO DMP Alerting Service	
Review Faculty DMP's with Research Office	
Assessing Services	
Develop a Model to Assess Services	

Providing embedded research data services is not without challenges, though, especially when it comes to scalability. The services that each of the librarians in the case studies provide are incredibly specialized, tailored to the needs of the embedded location, and incredibly time consuming. Rather than supporting the research and teaching of an entire department, they are only reaching a handful of faculty, at most.

Additionally, for many in the university research community (faculty, graduate students, and post-docs), metadata and data information literacy skills are not understood to be essential to conducting research. Thus, the time and effort that are needed for proper data management and outreach to be successful is sometimes lacking.

Some university libraries are also calling on subject liaisons to develop data-related skills to scale up the embedded data model. However, these librarians will need additional training and free time from other responsibilities to support research data. For many subject liaisons, the question of how to balance traditional librarian activities with data-related activities requires further exploration.

Future research in this area should focus on the impact that the embedded research data librarian model has had upon research and teaching. Data and information that determines if the level of tailored support provided through the embedded research data services model is of enough value to warrant a continued involvement is significantly lacking. To make an informed decision about the viability of this role, a mechanism of evaluation needs to be developed and implemented. Additional metrics of how the embedded research data services model impact compares to the traditional model impact, also do not yet exist. If embedded librarianship is to be understood as an advantage over traditional librarianship, benchmarks need to be established and points of comparison further explored.

Ultimately, to have significant impact and show value to library users, McCluskey finds the embedded librarian model needs to shift from one of support and collaboration, to one of knowledge creation itself.[22] She asserts that the work embedded librarians conduct should reflect or build upon the practices of the librarian community. It is through the drive to improve the data librarian 'practice' that true embedding takes place.[†]

---

1. Daniel Atkins (chair) *Revolutionizing Science and Engineering Through Cyberinfrastructure: Report of the National Science Foundation Blue-Ribbon Advisory Panel on Cyberinfrastructure*, National Science Foundation (2003), 42.
2. Jacob Carlson, Lisa R. Johnston, and Brian Westra, "Developing the data information literacy project" in *Data Information Literacy: Librarians, Data, and the Education of a New Generation of Researchers*, eds. Jake Carlson and Lisa R. Johnston (West Lafayette: Purdue University Press, 2015).
3. National Science Board. *Long-Lived Digital Data Collections: Enabling Research and Education in the 21st Century.* (National Science Foundation, 2005), 27, accessed April 30, 2015 http://www.nsf.gov/pubs/2005/nsb0540/.
4. David Shumaker and Laura Ann Tyler, "Embedded Library Services: An Initial Inquiry into Practices for Their Development, Management and Delivery," paper presented at the Special Libraries Association Annual Conference, Denver, Colorado, 2007.
5. Tom Davenport and Larry Prusak. "Blow up the Corporate Library," *International Journal of Information Management* 13, no. 6 (1993): 405–412.
6. Jake Carlson and Ruth Kneale, "Embedded librarianship in the research context: Navigating new waters," *College and Research Libraries News* 72, no. 3 (2011):167–170, accessed March 1, 2015 http://crln.acrl.org/content/72/3/167.full.
7. Lisa Federer, "Embedded with the Scientists: The UCLA Experience," *Journal of eScience Librarianship* 2, no. 1 (2013): 6–7, doi: 10.791/jeslib.2013.1039.
8. Vessela Ensberg, Personal Interview, April 24, 2015.

---

† I would like to thank all of the librarians who allowed me to interview them for this article, especially Vessela Ensberg, Lisa Johnston and Jennifer Moore. Additionally, Lauren Todd and Jennifer Moore were invaluable in providing their feedback and comments on this chapter.

9. "RDA grant" *DataFed.net*, February 25, 2015, http://datafedwiki.wustl.edu/index.php/2015-02-25:_RDU_Project_-_DataFed_Metadata_Stack.
10. Devon Greyson, Soleil Surette, Liz Dennett and Trish Chatterley, "You're just one of the group when you're embedded': report from a mixed-method investigation of the research-embedded health librarian experience," *Journal of the Medical Library Association*, 101, no. 4 (2013): 287–297.
11. Alisa Surkis, Aileen McCrillis, Richard McGowan, Jeffrey Williams, Brian L. Schmidt, Markus Hardt, and Neil Rambo, "Informationist Support for a Study of the Role of Proteases and Peptides in Cancer Pain," *Journal of eScience Librarianship*, 2, no. 11 (2013): 35–40.
12. Victoria H. Goode and Blair Anton, "Welch Informationists Collaboration with the Johns Hopkins Medicine Department of Radiology,"*Journal of eScience Librarianship*, 2, no. 1 (2013): 16–19.
13. Stephanie Schulte, "Embedded Academic Librarianship: A Review of the Literature," *Evidence Based Library and Information Practice*, 7, no. 4 (2012): 122–138.
14. Jake Carlson and Megan Sapp Nelson, "Addressing Software Code as Data: An Embedded Data Librarian Approach," in *Data Information Literacy: Librarians, Data, and the Education of a New Generation of Researchers*, eds. Jake Carlson and Lisa R. Johnston (West Lafayette: Purdue University Press, 2015).
15. Daina Bouquin, "New Experiences with Teaching—Computational Methods in Health Informatics" (blog), June 17, 2014, http://dainabouquin.com/teachingcompmethods/.
16. Jennifer Moore, Personal Interview, April 30, 2015.
17. University of Oregon, "Responsible Conduct of Research," accessed May 15, 2015 http://orcr.uoregon.edu/content/responsible-conduct-research.
18. Brian Westra, "Developing Data Management Services for Researchers at the University of Oregon," in *Research Data Management: Practical strategies for Information Professionals*, ed. Joyce M. Ray, (West Lafayette: Purdue University Press, 2014).
19. Research Data Alliance, "Data Citation WG," accessed May 15, 2015, https://www.rd-alliance.org/group/data-citation-wg.html.
20. EarthCube, "SEN," accessed May 15, 2015, http://earthcube.org/group/sen.
21. Lisa Johnston, Personal Interview, July 11, 2015.
22. Clare McCluskey, "Being an embedded research librarian: supporting research by being a researcher," *Journal of Information Literacy*, 72 no. 2 (2013): 4–14.

CHAPTER 3

Data Reference:
Strategies for Subject Librarians

Bobray Bordelon

FINDING STATISTICS HAS long been a major component of most librarians' jobs. However, microdata† assistance is new to many. While most researchers are typically trying to obtain summary statistics, published aggregates may not provide each of the desired characteristics, much less a complex array of demographics. Data reference allows the researcher access to the possibility of finding responses to a given question for the desired population using microdata. For example, survey respondents are often asked gender, age, income, and geography, and survey microdata allows for the production of tables broken down by these factors. Due to privacy restrictions, a researcher may not be able to get to the precise desired level of detail (for example, age may be given in broad categories rather than exact years of age), but the possibilities of getting more detail are much greater with microdata than with aggregates. The tools for locating the proper dataset are often not part of a reference librarian's regular arsenal of tools. As a subject liaison in business, economics, and finance for a quarter of a century, I have always had statistical reference as a primary job duty. I had dabbled in microdata prior to its becoming a focus in 2004, and I am primarily self-taught. This chapter will offer tips for either the data librarian who needs to help subject liaisons discover data in their area or for subject liaisons to gain knowledge on their own.

† "Microdata files are those that contain information on individuals rather than aggregate data. The U.S. Census Bureau's "Summary Files" contain aggregate data and consist of totals of individuals with various specified attributes in a particular geographic area. They are, in a sense, tables of totals. The Bureau's PUMS (Public Use Microdata Sample) files, however, contain the data from the original census survey instrument with certain information removed to protect the anonymity of the respondent." From "Glossary of Social Science Terms," Inter-university Consortium for Political and Social Research, accessed June 12, 2015, http://www.icpsr.umich.edu/icpsrweb/ICPSR/support/glossary.)

While librarians have become involved in data reference at an increasing rate, responsibility for data is often concentrated in the hands of a single individual or a small group. A data librarian can provide a broad level of expertise on data, keep abreast of changes in the field, fill in topical gaps not covered by a specific subject expert, and serve as a go-to reference, but subject expertise is what makes the subject librarian so valuable. Subject librarians should understand the practices, methodology, and critical players of the field they represent and be able to link the literature of the field with the data. It is critical that subject specialists answer data questions just as they would answer other questions in their field. That does not mean subject librarians or even data librarians will be able to take the user from the identification of a dataset and finding appropriate variables to helping with the analysis. Keeping up with the statistical packages is a full time job, and in an ideal situation the data librarian and perhaps the subject librarians would have some basic familiarity with a statistical package (such as SPSS or R) but experts would help with analysis and statistical packages. However, many institutions have only one person to help with both the data reference and statistical analysis, which makes the subject librarians even more critical for their depth of subject knowledge.

To be successful in today's environment, subject specialist librarians need to have deep subject knowledge, traditional finding and organizing skills, and knowledge of the data, methodology, and major data archives[†] in their discipline. Librarians who lack these skills are increasingly being left behind. For the experienced librarian, this often means no longer being able to adequately serve one's faculty and students, which leads to sitting on the sidelines and the position possibly not being replaced when vacated. New library and information science graduates have always faced a myriad of new concepts to learn that were not part of their education, but are increasingly being asked to hit the ground running with knowledge of data as well as the traditional skills. Data reference is detective work, and many of the skills employed in traditional reference are applicable. Unfortunately, many of the traditional skills such as cataloging and conducting a general reference interview are increasingly being excluded from library school curriculums. Traditional skills such as digging through books to look for obscure facts are similar to the skills needed to find data variables in codebooks.[‡] In the past, data librarians only

† "A data archive is a site where machine-readable materials are stored, preserved, and possibly redistributed to individuals interested in using the materials." Taken from "Glossary of Social Science Terms," Inter-university Consortium for Political and Social Research, accessed June 12, 2015, http://www.icpsr.umich.edu/icpsrweb/ICPSR/support/glossary.)

‡ "Generically, any information on the structure, contents, and layout of a data file. Typically, a codebook includes: column locations and widths for each variable; definitions of different record types; response codes for each variable; codes used to indicate nonresponse and missing data; exact questions and skip patterns used in a survey; and other indications of the content of each variable. Many codebooks also include frequencies of response. Codebooks vary widely in quality and amount of information included." Taken from "Glossary of Social Science

had a title, an abstract, and subject headings to begin the process of locating an appropriate dataset. The librarian had to manually search through a printed or PDF codebook to find the questions asked in a survey as well as counts or frequencies of how many people answered each question. Today, metadata, or data describing data, is increasingly being coded to the variable or question level. Those who excel at traditional reference questions that require deep digging into databases and indices can also answer data reference questions as long as they keep in mind data-specific issues such as sample size, population, and methodology.

The call for librarians to be involved with data is not new. In an article originally submitted in 1989 and published in 1991, Deborah Rinderknecht stated that non-bibliographic databases "should not be ignored by the library that is seeking to maintain its role as the chief disseminator of information to its research community."[1] A quick look through the IASSIST[§] Jobs Repository shows that even positions that do not have data in the title are routinely requiring data skills.[2] While several library and information science programs are now beginning to offer tracks for "big data," few offer a regular course on research data. While big data, or unstructured data that is not easily read by statistical packages, can provide valuable insight through its large numbers of responses, the demographic characteristics that researchers often seek are typically not present. Traditional research data on human subjects tend to be more highly structured, contain demographics, and be scientifically produced.

Supporting Data in the Library

Luckily there are many resources available to help the new librarian, the seasoned librarian taking on new data responsibilities, or the librarian wishing to further develop his or her skills and knowledge. Subject librarians need a firm grasp of the literature and its organization, major thinkers, and research methodologies in their field. These aspects in the past formed the core of a subject librarian's responsibilities, but this is no longer enough. This chapter will provide fifteen tips for supporting data in the library.

Start with Familiar Topics

For a first exposure to data, start with topics that are not technical and are familiar. You should examine the scope of the study, the sample sizes, questions asked, and

---

Terms," Inter-university Consortium for Political and Social Research, accessed June 12, 2015, http://www.icpsr.umich.edu/icpsrweb/ICPSR/support/glossary.)

§ The International Association for Social Science Information Services & Technology is an international organization of professionals working in and with information technology and data services to support research and teaching in the social sciences.

demographic breakdowns. This section describes a few user-friendly sources for getting started. You can demonstrate how sources such as these are easy to use, can answer a large variety of questions, and be useful to everyone from a freshman needing a quick table to the senior faculty member wanting to do complex analysis.

As an example, in 2007, a former data librarian at New York University saw interest from subject librarians in both the social sciences and the arts and humanities about data. She wanted to expose them to data that they could all identify with and not be burdened with technical jargon or many unfamiliar concepts. She invited me to speak with her subject librarians in my capacity as the director of the Cultural Policy and the Arts National Data Archive (CPANDA†). At the time it was one of the few archives making all data available in both the common statistical packages of the time (SAS, STATA, and SPSS) as well as in Survey Data Analysis (SDA) format that allowed a user to perform cross tabulations and simple analysis. All of the data in the archive dealt with arts and culture, so participants could look up personal areas of interest such as music, art, and theater and explore.

A similarly accessible option is the widely subscribed to Roper Center Public Opinion Archives, which houses many familiar polls from news and other sources. It is the largest repository of public opinion and many of its datasets are available in an easy to use format, with pre-set demographic cross tabulations available with a quick click. In addition, the *General Social Survey* is the go-to source for sociologists, but is also a fun source to explore since it covers so many topics of public opinion. It is also available in SDA format (http://www3.norc.org/GSS+Website). Moreover, the Pew Research Center (http://www.pewresearch.org) provides easy to read reports, data, and discussions of the methods used to collect their data on a wide variety of subjects. Examples include journalism, Internet, science, and technology, and social trends.

Finally, the Inter-university Consortium for Political and Social Research (ICPSR) (http://www.icpsr.umich.edu/), a member based organization and the largest social science data archive, is most widely known to researchers in the social sciences and covers a wide variety of topics. Users can search by specific variables, conduct subject searches, discover literature that has used data held in the archive, and browse by broad topic.

Know the Terminology

Once you see that data can be fun, the more serious steps begin. It is critical that you know the major terminology in your field. We are all accustomed to having questions come to us that contain unfamiliar terms. However, there are major concepts that form the core of a discipline. The easiest way to break the confidence of

† In 2016, CPANDA is in its final stages of moving to the National Archive of Data on Arts & Culture (http://www.icpsr.umich.edu/icpsrweb/NADAC).

the researcher is to be unfamiliar with the major disciplinary concepts. Several sources can provide guidance for terminology in specific disciplines. The prefatory pages of the International Monetary Fund's *International Financial Statistics* are a go-to source for economics and help researchers understand that they should not just pick the first item that looks relevant among variables with similar names. For example, economists regularly request statistics on foreign direct investment, but the IMF divides foreign direct investment into direct investment and portfolio investment. You need to understand the differences between the two, the direction of the flows, and what is included in each component.

To assist users, many statistical agencies maintain metadata pages. While the researcher may think that they only want the numbers, knowing how the agency defined the terms as well as details of how the numbers were collected is critical. Some databases such as the OECD iLibrary (http://www.oecd-ilibrary.org/) have extensive metadata with each dataset, but that is rare.

Just as you need to be familiar with the basic terminology of your fields and the basic terminology of libraries, you should also know basic statistical terms. While the methods employed differ somewhat by discipline, the major statistical terminology cuts across fields. ICPSR maintains a "Glossary of Social Science Terms" (http://www.icpsr.umich.edu/icpsrweb/ICPSR/support/glossary) and the Social Science Research and Instructional Council produces a useful glossary (http://www.csub.edu/ssric-trd/glossary.htm) to help researchers with statistical terminology.

Look at Major Journals in the Field(s) You Represent

Focus on the data and methodology sections of the major journals in your field. This will show what data are commonly used, how researchers describe the data, and some of the different uses of datasets. Each field tends to have core journals that are quantitative and regularly feature rigorous methodological sections. Databases such as *Scopus* and *Web of Science* can be used to find the top ranked journals in each discipline, such as *American Economic Review*, *American Political Science Review*, *American Sociological Review*, *Demography*, and *Journal of Finance*. In general the primary publications of the major association representing the field are often of the highest quality. Moreover, an increasing number of journals are starting to have provisions that data or the program files be deposited with the organization.[3]

It is also useful to look through the *Annual Review* (http://www.annualreviews.org) subscription series in your discipline and closely related disciplines. The Annual Review series now covers almost fifty areas in a wide range of the social sciences and the sciences.[‡] Some date back to the 1970s, while a few were only

‡ Areas include economics, environment and resources, financial economics, law and social science, organizational psychology and organizational behavior, political science, psychology, public health, resource economics, sociology, statistics and its application, and many others.

recently introduced. These serve as incredibly useful literature reviews, will often point to data in a field, and help to discover the major scholars in a given area.

Look at the Research of Your Own Researchers

Look up your own faculty's publications using the major indices in your discipline such as *ECONLIT*, *International Political Science Abstracts*, or *Sociological Abstracts*, or more general citation sources such as *Web of Science* or *Scopus* and focus on the data and methodology sections. This is an easy way to see what your faculty are using, allowing you to find areas to seek out additional data for your collections and to suggest new sources for the faculty to use in future research. See if there are popular datasets within your discipline being used at your institution. If this is the case, these might be good ones to examine first. Examine the demographics and other characteristics your researchers are seeking. Attend faculty lectures and PhD defenses. While the content may be technical and esoteric, it is a great way to see what current research your clientele is engaged in and the types of methodological questions that can create challenges. This will also give you a glimpse into whether they are largely using secondary data or gathering their own data, and what types of analysis are being conducted.

Examine the Source Notes and Footnotes of Statistical Compilations

ProQuest Statistical Abstract of the United States and other major statistical compilations are helpful not just for their summary statistics. They provide an easy way to break into data because most librarians use statistics regularly. Knowing how the statistics were derived and from what sources will provide a deeper understanding of the statistics and allow you to recommend sources for further refinement. See what sources are used as the underlying data. Do not forget the specific topical abstracts such as *Health United States*, *Sourcebook of Criminal Justice Statistics*, and *Digest of Education Statistics*. When working with students, inform them that the table can lead to the original source, which may have more precise data. The compilations will also show the most heavily used resources in a specific subject area.

The various historical compilations such as Palgrave's *International Historical Statistics* can be particularly helpful for tracking sources over time and the notes can often be helpful in tracking down collected data. The notes will often say when a specific data point was first collected and describe changes in detail over time.

As an example, Table 48 of the 2014 edition of *Health United States* provides summary statistics for vision limitations among adults aged 18 and over by selected characteristics (age, sex, age and sex, race, Hispanic origin and race, education, percent of poverty level, Hispanic origin by race and Hispanic origin, geographical region, and if one is in a metropolitan area) for the United States for select years between 1997 and 2013 (see Figure 3.1). While this table is very useful, if a patron needs education by race or some other cross-tabulation not provided, then you can turn to the source note to find that the data was derived from the *National Health Interview Survey*. Knowing the source, you can then turn to the original data and questionnaire to obtain the desired cross-tabulation. The footnotes provide the actual question asked, discuss margins of error, and describe how some of the summary categories were grouped together.[4]

Figure 3.1. Example Table from *Health United States*

Table 48 (page 2 of 2). Vision limitations among adults aged 18 and over, by selected characteristics: United States, selected years 1997–2013

Updated data when available, Excel, PDF, more data years, and standard errors: http://www.cdc.gov/nchs/hus/contents2014.htm#048.

[Data are based on household interviews of a sample of the civilian noninstitutionalized population]

	Any trouble seeing, even with glasses or contacts[1]									
Characteristic	*1997*	*2000*	*2005*	*2007*	*2008*	*2009*	*2010*	*2011*	*2012*	*2013*
Percent of poverty level[2,7]	Percent of adults									
Below 100%	17.0	12.9	15.3	15.0	16.7	14.3	14.8	14.2	13.7	15.6
100%–199%	12.9	11.6	11.5	13.0	14.2	11.1	12.2	11.5	10.9	11.2
200%–399%	9.1	8.8	8.9	9.4	11.3	8.0	9.0	8.7	7.9	7.6
400% or more	7.3	7.1	6.9	7.8	7.8	5.7	6.4	6.0	6.1	6.4
Hispanic origin and race and percent of poverty level[2,4,7]										
Hispanic or Latino:										
Below 100%	12.8	11.0	13.6	13.4	12.9	12.2	10.8	13.9	13.1	13.1
100%–199%	11.2	9.4	8.8	11.1	11.3	8.1	10.8	9.6	10.0	10.6
200%–399%	8.1	9.2	8.2	7.2	10.2	9.0	8.9	8.3	6.8	7.4
400% or more	*8.1	10.5	8.0	10.6	7.5	*4.6	5.3	5.1	7.8	9.0
Not Hispanic or Latino:										
White only:										
Below 100%	17.9	13.1	16.2	16.3	19.5	13.4	16.8	14.4	14.5	17.7
100%–199%	13.1	12.0	12.7	14.2	15.6	12.1	12.6	12.3	11.7	11.8
200%–399%	9.2	9.2	9.0	10.3	11.5	8.3	8.8	9.0	8.5	7.8
400% or more	7.3	7.0	6.9	7.7	7.9	5.8	6.7	5.9	6.0	6.4
Black or African American only:										
Below 100%	17.9	13.6	16.0	15.1	16.9	17.8	15.8	15.5	13.7	15.3
100%–199%	16.0	12.9	11.3	14.0	14.5	11.7	14.9	12.3	11.3	11.4
200%–399%	9.3	7.7	9.7	7.3	9.8	8.1	12.0	8.5	6.8	8.0
400% or more	7.7	8.3	6.4	6.9	7.4	5.6	6.6	8.6	6.4	6.7
Geographic region[2]										
Northeast	8.6	7.4	8.1	8.1	9.3	7.3	7.8	7.6	6.4	7.4
Midwest	9.5	9.6	9.7	10.3	10.7	8.2	9.1	8.7	8.7	9.0
South	11.4	9.2	9.8	10.1	12.4	8.7	10.6	9.4	9.1	8.9
West	9.7	9.9	8.6	10.5	10.2	8.6	8.0	9.1	8.9	9.1
Location of residence[2,8]										
Within MSA	9.5	8.5	8.6	9.6	10.6	8.2	8.6	8.6	8.2	8.4
Outside MSA	12.0	11.1	11.7	11.4	12.5	9.0	11.6	10.3	9.8	10.6

* Estimates are considered unreliable. Data preceded by an asterisk have a relative standard error (RSE) of 20%–30%. Data not shown have an RSE greater than 30%.
- - - Data not available.
[1]Respondents were asked, "Do you have any trouble seeing, even when wearing glasses or contact lenses?" Respondents were also asked, "Are you blind or unable to see at all?" In this analysis, any trouble seeing and blind are combined into one category.
[2]Estimates are age-adjusted to the year 2000 standard population using five age groups: 18–44 years, 45–54 years, 55–64 years, 65–74 years, and 75 years and over. Age-adjusted estimates in this table may differ from other age-adjusted estimates based on the same data and presented elsewhere if different age groups are used in the adjustment procedure. See Appendix II, Age adjustment.
[3]Includes all other races not shown separately and unknown education level.
[4]The race groups, white, black, American Indian or Alaska Native, Asian, Native Hawaiian or Other Pacific Islander, and 2 or more races, include persons of Hispanic and non-Hispanic origin. Persons of Hispanic origin may be of any race. Starting with 1999 data, race-specific estimates are tabulated according to the 1997 *Revisions to the Standards for the Classification of Federal Data on Race and Ethnicity* and are not strictly comparable with estimates for earlier years. The five single-race categories plus multiple-race categories shown in the table conform to the 1997 Standards. Starting with 1999 data, race-specific estimates are for persons who reported only one racial group the category 2 or more races includes persons who reported more than one racial group. Prior to 1999, data were tabulated according to the 1977 Standards with four racial groups, and the Asian only category included Native Hawaiian or Other Pacific Islander. Estimates for single-race categories prior to 1999 included persons who reported one race or, if they reported more than one race, identified one race as best representing their race. Starting with 2003 data, race responses of other race and unspecified multiple race were treated as missing, and then race was imputed if these were the only race responses. Almost all persons with a race response of other race were of Hispanic origin See Appendix II, Hispanic origin; Race.
[5]Estimates are for persons aged 25 and over and are age-adjusted to the year 2000 standard population using five age groups: 25–44 years, 45–54 years, 55–64 years, 65–74 years, and 75 years and over. See Appendix II, Age adjustment.
[6]GED is General Educational Development high school equivalency diploma. See Appendix II, Education.
[7]Percent of poverty level is based on family income and family size and composition using U.S. Census Bureau poverty thresholds. Missing family income data were imputed for 1997 and beyond. See Appendix II, Family income; Poverty; Table VI.
[8]MSA is metropolitan statistical area. Starting with 2006 data, MSA status is determined using 2000 census data and the 2000 standards for defining MSAs. For data prior to 2006, see Appendix II, Metropolitan statistical area (MSA) for the applicable standards.

NOTES: Standard errors are available in the spreadsheet version of this table. Available from: http://www.cdc.gov/nchs/hus.htm. Data for additional years are available. See the Excel spreadsheet on the *Health, United States* website at: http://www.cdc.gov/nchs/hus.htm.

SOURCE: CDC/NCHS, National Health Interview Survey, sample adult questionnaire. See Appendix I, National Health Interview Survey (NHIS).

Read Statistical Briefs

While many countries have a central statistical agency that collects and disseminates data, the United States has a much more decentralized approach and uses many statistical agencies that are housed in various governmental departments. The primary statistical agencies of the United States, such as the Census Bureau and the Bureau of Labor Statistics, often conduct surveys and provide accessible reports of findings in the form of statistical briefs and reports. While each tends to focus on a specific topic, these go a step further than the statistical abstracts and area great way to find out about sources, methodology, dataset segmentation, and potential challenges.

For example, the Census Bureau issues a series of guides covering education, employment, families and living arrangements, health, housing, income and poverty, and population. A series of reports collectively form the *Current Population Report* series (http://census.gov/library/publications.html), and the *American Community Survey Data Briefs* (http://www.census.gov/acs/www/library/by_series/acs_data_briefs) are a complementary series. The Bureau of Labor Statistics issues a series of statistical reports on labor and consumer prices entitled *Issues in Labor Statistics* (http://www.bls.gov/opub/opborder.htm#1b). For education topics, the National Center for Education Statistics issues *Statistical Analysis Reports* (http://nces.ed.gov/pubsearch/). For health, see *Data Briefs* from the National Center for Health Statistics (http://www.cdc.gov/nchs/products/databriefs.htm) and publications by topic from Center for Disease Control and Prevention (http://www.cdc.gov/publications).

Look at ICPSR Usage at Your Institution

The Inter-university Consortium for Political and Social Research (ICPSR) traces its origins back to 1962 as the Survey Data Archive and began with twenty-five member institutions.[5] Today there are 750 member institutions including consortiums, and each ICPSR institution has a representative.[6] It is becoming increasingly common for the primary data specialist and ICPSR representative to be in the library. The 2014 ICPSR Membership Survey indicated 54% of its official representatives worked in libraries; in 1988 that number was 23%. The most common task among all official representatives was to find data (95%).[7] If you are the ICPSR representative, ask your subject librarians if they would like to receive periodic reports about usage in their area. As stated earlier, while the number of ICSPR representatives who are located in the library continues to grow, this is not the case in all institutions. If the ICPSR representative is not in the library, contact that person to ask for usage statistics for your department. While users are not required provide their department in their account setup, most will supply this information.

Quite a bit can be learned from the most heavily used datasets in a discipline. See what types of questions are in the codebooks of the corresponding datasets. Discover how the data are broken down by key variables. Commonly requested variables are race, ethnicity, age, marital status, educational attainment, occupation, and income. In addition, examine the lowest geographic level in the public use dataset. While respondents are often asked for an exact address, or at least city or ZIP code, exact geography is typically not made available in order to preserve respondents' privacy. It is rare for geography below the state level to be revealed in the public use version of a dataset. Often a full version is restricted[†] and requires special clearance to obtain access.

Use the ICPSR Bibliography of Data-Related Literature and Other Similar Bibliographies

The ICPSR Bibliography (http://www.icpsr.umich.edu/icpsrweb/ICPSR/citations/index.jsp) allows you to find what data has been used in publications through a keyword search. Note this tool does not search abstracts or full text. It is primarily searching for words in the journal citation. Search results will link to the ICPSR data that was used, but be aware that other data could be used in the research that is not in ICPSR. ICPSR's Bibliography is also useful to see what research has been conducted using a specific dataset. This is particularly helpful for researchers building upon the work of others or trying to find untapped areas with a dataset.

In addition to ICPSR, many of the producers of the more heavily used datasets maintain bibliographies of publications that have used their data. The National Center for Education Statistics tracks major publications for many of their most popular datasets (http://nces.ed.gov/bibliography). The Bureau of Labor Statistics maintains a similar bibliography for its heavily used *National Longitudinal Survey* series (http://www.nlsbibliography.org). The Minnesota Population Center at University of Minnesota compiles a bibliography for its IPUMS series (https://bibliography.ipums.org), and the *Demographic and Health Surveys* have a select bibliography (http://www.dhsprogram.com/publications/index.cfm).

Know the Long-Running Series in Your Field

Most researchers want time series, ideally longitudinal,[‡] and they often want to

† For more information about restricted data, see chapter in this volume by Jennifer Darragh called "Restricted Data Access and Libraries."

‡ "In survey research, a study in which the same group of individuals is interviewed at intervals over a period of time... Note that some cross-sectional studies are done regularly. For instance, the General Social Survey and the Current Population Survey: Annual Demographic File are conducted once a year, but different individuals are surveyed each time. Such a study is not a true longitudinal study. An example of a longitudinal study is the National Longitudinal Survey of Labor Market Experience, in which the same individuals have been followed over time." Taken from "Glossary of Social Science Terms," Inter-university Consortium for Political and Social Research, accessed June 12, 2015, http://www.icpsr.umich.edu/icpsrweb/ICPSR/support/glossary.)

examine the impact of policy changes over time, the impact that changing demographics have had on a particular topic, or shifts in public opinion. Find out which major ongoing datasets exist in your area. For example in education, the *National Education Longitudinal Study of 1988* (https://nces.ed.gov/surveys/nels88) has long served as the gold standard for following individuals (first interviewed in the base year of 1988) through their education and later career choices. It is important to be aware though that most datasets are not longitudinal. Many datasets are single studies, or repeated cross-sectional studies (observing a new "cross-section" of individuals each time the study is repeated). A cross-sectional dataset allows a researcher to examine individuals with similar characteristics over time, but not the same individuals at different points in time.

Examine Data Holdings

If your institution's data service has web pages or a catalog listing and describing data, examine those and incorporate appropriate sources into your subject-based research guides. Also look at the data web pages of other institutions, keeping in mind that unless the source is free or part of a subscription your institution has, you may not be able to access the data. However it is still useful to know what exists. A few examples include Princeton University (http://dss1.princeton.edu), UCLA (http://dataarchives.ss.ucla.edu/da_catalog/da_catalog_index.php), and Cornell University (https://ciser.cornell.edu/ASPs/browse.asp). Examining holdings of other institutions can also serve as a collection development source.

Partner with Other Subject Librarians

Research is often interdisciplinary. Learning about the major datasets in another discipline can be very helpful; there are often other substantive questions that are not the primary focus of the dataset. An example is religion. Public Law 94-521 prohibits the United States Census Bureau from collecting data on religious affiliation in its demographic surveys or decennial census on a mandatory basis.[8] For data on religion in the U.S. post-1950s, you either must turn to a religious survey from a private organization or some other non-federal source.[9] The Association of Religion Data Archives (ARDA) (http://www.thearda.com) provides many surveys that focus primarily on religion. However, researchers often want detailed demographics and ties to education, labor, or health. It is important to look for less obvious surveys. The *American National Election Study* (http://www.electionstudies.org) has many questions on religion as does the *National Longitudinal Study of Adolescent Health* (http://www.cpc.unc.edu/projects/addhealth). Reading just the description of these datasets, one would not know each has detailed religion sections.

The best way to learn is to teach. Have mini-sessions with other librarians focusing on what major datasets cover and some questions one might not think of that could be answered with a given dataset. Include elements such as years covered, alternative titles, preceding titles, scope, sample size and makeup, how segmented, lowest level of geography in the public use version, location of documentation, and how to find major publications that have used the data. Give examples of questions that have been answered with a given dataset by either using your own experiences or the literature.

Create Comparison Charts

Comparison charts allow researchers and librarians to quickly discover the major differences among datasets in a specific field. They can also be used to highlight items from surveys that may not be the obvious surveys for a subject but may be useful. In the following example for health data, you can quickly determine which surveys include marital status, education, and other variables. These charts can save time for the researcher as well as the librarian and provide an easy way for the librarian to summarize the characteristics of commonly used datasets. Table 3.1 includes some major USA health surveys, reporting age, gender, race, diagnosis, and procedures.†

Finally, look for the less obvious. Requests for data on China are common yet there are few microdata surveys available for that nation. As an example, when looking for income and employment data on China, expand your search beyond Chinese labor surveys. Look at surveys not directly related to those areas emanating out of China as well as more general surveys that include China. Surveys to consider include *China Health and Nutrition Survey* and the *World Values Survey.*

Attend Training and Webinars

There are some excellent training programs available, such as one started through the Data Liberation Initiative (DLI) in Canada and many offerings through ICPSR. The DLI in Canada is a peer-to-peer training program for data librarians.[10] ICPSR offers a week-long biennial workshop called "Providing social science data services: strategies for design and operation" as part of its ICPSR Summer Program in Quantitative Methods of Social Research series, as well as many workshops that go into detail on specific datasets and methods.

For most librarians, though, webinars are the most convenient means of obtaining ongoing knowledge in small chunks. Many organizations offer free webinars to either the general public or to their members. While I am only listing

---

† The complete guide can be found at http://libguides.princeton.edu/healthdata/healthdatacompare.

Table 3.1. Comparative Major Microdata Health Sources

Survey	Dates	Lowest Geography	Constituents	Payment Source	Marital Status	Income/ Education/ Occupation	Duration of Visit or Waiting Time
National Health Interview Survey	1963+	4 regions; Urban vs. Rural	Civilian, noninstutionalized population sample	Insurance, Social Security?	Yes	Yes	Estimate
Medical Expenditure Panel Survey	1977, 1980, 1987, 1996+	4 regions; Urban vs. Rural	Subsample of prior year's NHIS.	Yes	Yes	Yes	Yes
National Ambulatory Medical Care Survey	1973-1981, 1985, 1989+	4 regions; Urban vs. Rural	Sample of outpatients in physician's offices	Yes	No	Median household income for patient's zip code/No/No	Yes
National Hospital Medical Care Ambulatory Medical Survey	1992+	4 regions; Urban vs. Rural	Sample of patients selected from emergency & outpatient departments of hospitals.	Yes	No	Median household income for patient's zip code/No/No	Yes
National Hospital Discharge Survey	1964+	4 regions.	Sample of hospital discharges	Yes	Yes	No	Yes
National Health & Nutrition Examination Survey	*1959+*	*4 regions; Urban vs. Rural*	*Civilian noninstitutionalized population sample*	*Insurance, Social Security?*	*Yes*	*Yes*	*N/A*

a few that offer consistently excellent webinars, many government departments, data organizations, and vendors offer webinars on a regular basis.

- ICPSR (https://www.youtube.com/user/ICPSRWeb) offers webinars that are free to members of subscribing institutions. Recent topics have included data on education, suicide, addiction, health, elections, midlife development, drug use, addiction, and the arts. Other topics have included the legal and policy landscape for data, building restricted use data services, and overviews of various topical archives.
- Association of Public Data Users (http://apdu.org/events/webinars) webinars are free to staff from member institutions; a nominal fee is charged for non-members. Recent topics have included data for the 1940 census, pensions, special districts, health, and federal government spending.
- Roper IPOLL has had recent webinars introducing their services, using IPOLL, and accessing datasets.
- The North Carolina Library Association has a free series called "Government Resources: Help I'm an Accidental Government Information Librarian" (http://www.nclaonline.org/government-resources/help-im-accidental-government-information-librarian-webinars). Data topics have included the census, economic indicators, the *American Community Survey*, United States Department of Agriculture, education, international development, and the National Archives.
- The United States Bureau of the Census has regular webinars that are free to everyone. Recent data topics have included the *American Community Survey*, wealth inequality sources, and alternative questionnaires.

Read Compilations and Data Guides

While few handbooks exist that provide overviews of sources of microdata, there are some excellent ones. The best one that provides a broad overview of many areas is Lynda Kellam and Katharin Peter's *Numeric Data Services and Sources for the General Reference Librarian.* This book includes data definitions, information on supporting statistical and numeric data services, reference and instruction for data services, a look into the lives of various data librarians, and annotations for major sources for statistics and data on a variety of topics coming from different areas of the world. Julia Bauder's *The Reference Guide to Data Sources* is also very useful, providing a mixture of statistics and microdata descriptions in a wide variety of fields. Hopefully more specialized ones covering a field in-depth will be published. The two best are: Sarah Boslaugh's *Secondary Data Sources for Public Health: A Practical Guide* and Tom McNulty's *Art Market Research: A Guide to Methods and Sources.*

Join Relevant Organizations

Even if data are only a small part of your job, you can learn from others with similar duties. Two organizations that are at the data forefront are the International Association for Social Science Information Services & Technology (IASSIST) and the American Library Association's (ALA) Association of College and Research Libraries' (ACRL) Numeric and Geospatial Data Services in Academic Libraries Interest Group (DIG).

IASSIST's membership cost is low and even if you never attend a conference, the listserv alone is worth the membership. Members include the heads of national data archives around the world, producers of surveys, and many academic librarians. Anyone can freely read the articles in its journal *IASSIST Quarterly* and many of the presentations from recent conferences are posted on the organizational website (http://www.iassistdata.org).

DIG (http://www.ala.org/acrl/aboutacrl/directoryofleadership/interestgroups/acr-igngdsal) was established in September 2009 and confirmed at the 2010 ALA Midwinter Conference. Its primary activities have been discussion forums of emerging issues in data librarianship. It is free to join for ACRL members.

The fifteen strategies outlined above are ways to get started gaining familiarity with the data and methodology of your subject area. Before you can begin to answer data reference questions effectively, subject expertise combined with at least a basic knowledge of key datasets and methodology is critical. There are many other ways to become more proficient at answering data questions and the most important element is experience, so get started! The purpose of this chapter was to offer some practical advice on techniques and tools to become more familiar with data. Like most things in life, the more practice you have the better you become.

---

1. Deborah Rinderknect, "Nonbibliographic Databases: Determining Levels of Service," *RQ* 30, no. 4 (Summer 1991): 528.
2. International Association for Social Science Information Services & Technology, "Jobs Repository," accessed January 20, 2016, http://www.iassistdata.org/resources/jobs/all.
3. MIT Libraries, "Data Management. Journal Requirements," accessed January 20, 2016, https://libraries.mit.edu/data-management/share/journal-requirements/.
4. National Center for Health Statistics, "Health, United States, 2014, accessed January 20, 2016, http://www.cdc.gov/nchs/data/hus/2014/048.pdf.
5. Inter-university Consortium for Political and Social Research, "Membership in ICPSR. History," accessed January 20, 2016, http://www.icpsr.umich.edu/icpsrweb/content/membership/history/index.html.
6. Inter-university Consortium for Political and Social Research, "ICPSR Annual Report for 2013–2014," accessed January 20, 2016, http://issuu.com/icpsr/docs/annualreportfy2013_14final v2.
7. Linda Detterman, ICSPR Director, Marketing and Membership, e-mail message to author, March 18, 2015.
8. United States Census Bureau, "Does the Census Bureau have data for religion?," accessed June 12, 2015, https://ask.census.gov/faq.php?id=5000&faqId=29.

9. Pew Research Center, "A Brief history of religion and the U.S. Census," accessed January 20, 2016, http://www.pewforum.org/2010/01/26/a-brief-history-of-religion-and-the-u-s-census.
10. Wendy Watkins, Elizabeth Hamilton, Ernie Boyko, and Chuck Humphrey, "Creating a national peer-to-peer training program for data librarians in Canada," *IASSIST Quarterly* 28, no. 2–3 (Summer/Fall 2004): 17–23.

Further Reading

Bauder, Julia. *Reference Guide to Data Sources*. Chicago: ALA Editions, 2014.

Boslaugh, Sarah. *Secondary Data Sources for Public Health: A Practical Guide*. Cambridge; New York: Cambridge University Press, 2007.

Kellam, Lynda M. and Katharin Peter. *Numeric Data Services and Sources for the General Reference Librarian*. Oxford: Chandos Publishing, 2011.

McNulty, Tom. *Art Market Research: A Guide to Methods and Sources*. Jefferson, North Carolina: McFarland & Company, 2014.

Further Reading

CHAPTER 4

The Data Management Village: Collaboration among Research Support Providers in the Large Academic Environment

Alicia Hofelich Mohr, Lisa R. Johnston, and Thomas A. Lindsay

DATA MANAGEMENT ENCOMPASSES the practices and people that acquire, control, protect, deliver, and enhance the value of data throughout the research lifecycle.[1] Done well, data management requires that these practices and people be connected throughout the *entire* research lifecycle. However, much of this work takes place in researchers' own offices or labs or with the help of specialized support offices on campus, who only directly interact with researchers at single points in their projects. In academic libraries, a data management specialist may only interact with researchers at the beginning and end of a project, assisting with the creation of a data management plan (DMP) and preservation of the data when the research is completed. This poses a challenge when trying to help researchers integrate best practices into their workflows throughout the planning, collection, and analysis stages. Most libraries are focused on providing broad, public access to the content under their stewardship, and given this mission, libraries alone may not be able to offer all of the data services that our researchers need (for example, dark archives for sensitive or private data). Therefore, given the diverse nature of research data and the distributed support researchers may seek throughout their project, universities need a well-connected, distributed way to support data management; it is a service that "takes a village."

In this chapter, we will describe efforts at the University of Minnesota (U of M) to build our data management village, the "village" being a useful metaphor for our community of connections between researchers and staff and the infrastructure of referral networks across campus units. Part 1 of the chapter provides an overview of some of the key offices on our campus and describes why they may be useful members of a data management village at any institution. Part 2 is an in-depth description of a collaboration between the University Libraries and the College of Liberal Arts (CLA) at the U of M that began in 2013. We describe how the collective and complementary skills of our offices provide researchers with support across much larger portions of the research lifecycle than either unit could provide alone.

Background and Context

Before we discuss what this partnership looks like in terms of collaborations and services, we should describe the context that led to these two groups coming together. While there are necessarily many players in a data management village, some may be willing to contribute more than others. This has a lot to do with university context, job roles, funding, and specific priorities set by the college or university. For example, offices that deal with highly structured, high-demand regulatory tasks, such as grants administration or human subjects oversight, may not have the bandwidth to commit to a more in-depth partnership. On the other hand, offices that work closely with researchers supporting data collection/analysis, IT, or grant-writing likely encounter needs for data management support at times in the research process where they can impact a researcher's practices, and may have more flexibility to engage in collaborative work.

Research Support Services, housed in CLA's technology office, has historically supported data collection and data analysis for faculty and graduate students. As a result of the university's push for traditional IT services to be more centralized, CLA's IT division transitioned out of desktop support and invested in specialized services for research and teaching. As part of this shift, Research Support Services expanded in 2013 to include a full-time research position devoted to developing and providing data management support for the college. A data librarian was appointed chair of the search committee, and the job description involved seeking out and forming collaborations across the university.

The University Libraries have provided support for data management for many years through training, DMP consultations, and an informational website (http://lib.umn.edu/datamanagement). In early 2014, the Libraries formed a data management and curation working group charged to establish formal data management services and develop an institutional data repository, the Data Repository for the University of Minnesota (DRUM; http://z.umn.edu/DRUM). The team was led by one of the authors (Johnston), and members included librarians, archivists, and IT experts from across the libraries; unlike prior Libraries initiative groups, the team also included an expert from outside the Libraries, the new CLA data manager (Hofelich Mohr). Meeting regularly, the working group offered structured, long-term interactions for forming these services and allowed them to shape and be shaped by services Research Support Services was providing.

Several other factors also contributed to the growing emphasis on data management. The Libraries started a university-wide Research Data Management Community of Practice in June 2013 to bring people together and foster conversations around data management. The community of practice now hosts monthly presentations and discussions around issues such as data management needs, data storage, security, visualization, access, archival, and sharing. The group consists largely of service providers from IT, the libraries, colleges, the data security office, and the Office of the Vice President for Research, as well as researchers. Now in its third year, it has provided opportunities to connect with other service providers (and potential village members) and build referral relationships.

Collaborative projects and open conversations such as these have enabled those of us developing data management services to identify and connect potential members of a data management village. The result has been increased opportunities for more formal collaborations, such as participating in communities of practice tasked with updating and communicating new policy changes around data security, and consulting on the development of a new secure data storage service. For Research Support Services and the University Libraries, these interactions have led to service-level collaborations, where together we can offer a suite of services that support researchers wherever they are in the research process.

Part 1: The Data Management Village

We started our search for potential members of our data management village by looking to service providers who assist researchers across the research lifecycle and across the various levels of the university. While university-wide offices may have been the most obvious places to look, we realized that it was important to also include departments and individual colleges, as researchers may encounter these sources first. Although this review process was similar to conducting an environmental scan,[2] it was more focused on identifying service providers, rather than existing data types or data services. In a 2014 review, we focused primarily on social sciences, in part because of the vast number and diversity of departmental resources that could exist university-wide, but also because Research Support Services specializes in social science research support.[3] Below we describe the offices that may be good members of a data management village at other institutions, based on what we found on our campus.

Collegiate Grant Consultants

Subject-specific grant consultants are located in individual colleges or departments, and work closely with researchers on finding, writing, and submitting grants. In CLA, almost all of our DMP consultations come to us as referrals from the college's grant consultants. In a University with a high demand for DMP consultations, grant consultants may be a great resource for providing initial consultation and referral to data management specialists.

Collegiate Research Deans

Research deans are good resources for connecting researchers to services; they are aware of the research climate in their colleges, know the researchers, and typically sign off on all grant applications that come from their colleges. In CLA, we have found our Research Associate Dean to be a valuable advocate for our services and have received considerable guidance and advice from him on the specific needs of the college. Research deans can also help foster connections between other university offices, such as the grants administration office and the researchers within the college.

Commercialization Office

Technology or business commercialization offices can guide researchers on how to share their data/materials for wide research use and validation, without precluding the possibility of commercialization later on. The commercialization office can help researchers explore options, including data use agreements and licensing, and offer practical guidance, such as providing a permanent link to a questionnaire in a manuscript rather than including it in the publication, which could give the journal copyright to the instrument.

Copyright Librarian/Legal Counsel

Copyright librarians and/or legal counsel are knowledgeable not only about sharing sensitive data that fall under legally protected categories (student grades, health-care provided data, etc.), but also data that may face other kinds of legal restrictions, such as copyright. This is especially important when researchers are using data or materials that they did not generate, or when they are thinking about how to best share their produced data or materials while still retaining copyright or intellectual property rights. As specific policies on intellectual property, copyright, and data ownership vary by institution, copyright librarians and legal counsel are important resources for education on these topics.

Data Security Offices

Data security offices know the security policies and restrictions for various kinds of storage solutions and additionally create or contribute to university-wide policies on secure data practices. With data security requirements increasingly defined by US federal granting agencies, there are opportunities to work with these offices to enact policies that make sense for research data, which often differ from the categories used to determine security risks for more administrative non-research university data.

Grants Administration Offices

In contrast to collegiate grants consultants, grants administration offices are central units where researchers are required to submit their grants before the university officially submits them to the granting agency. Typically, these offices receive grant applications late in the submission process and are more focused on whether all parts of the application are present, rather than the whether the content is strong. However, they can be a good resource for information about which grant agencies are funding research at the university and which researchers have had successful grant applications.

Institutional Review Board (IRB)

The IRB, or research ethics board, approves all human subjects research at the university. Because these offices typically require researchers to specify how data will be secured, stored, and maintained, decisions that are reported to this office can have important impacts on later sharing and archiving. Data management professionals need to openly communicate with the IRB administrators to ensure that good practices in each domain are understood by both sides, especially when trying to balance data accessibility and preservation with the protection of participant information. It is also important for curators to understand what the researchers promised to the IRB and their participants before developing or accepting a data submission for sharing or archiving.

Information Technology (IT) Professionals

IT professionals are another good route to researchers who are in the planning phase, since researchers may contact IT as they budget funds for servers, storage, or other customized technology needs. In colleges or departments, IT professionals are often well aware of their researchers' needs; centrally, IT professionals run secure storage, supercomputing centers, and other resources for research.

Library

Libraries can serve as a neutral party to connect key players across an institution and to direct researchers to services across an institution. Their open access digital archiving services, such as an institutional repository, are often available to researchers for sharing and preserving their research data. In addition to this dissemination role, libraries offer specialized skills that are not present elsewhere on campus and are crucial to data management, especially pertaining to metadata creation and cataloging, curation, access and reuse, and archiving and preservation.

Office for Research

A university's Office for Research creates research policy, provides administrative support, and sets the agenda for university research. Often the office for sponsored projects and the IRB are located within this office, and potentially other research support offices; for example, at the U of M, the Supercomputing Institute and the Informatics Institute are housed under this office.

Research or Survey Support Offices

Offices that provide data collection services have a unique opportunity to improve data management practices by ensuring that data collected meet expectations for good data stewardship. These offices directly support the development and implementation of faculty research projects rather than administrative or institutional research. While these offices may exist at many different levels of the university, the closer they are to the researcher, the more likely these offices are to have discipline-specific knowledge and to be able to help integrate best practices into researchers' workflows.

Statistical Consulting Offices or Statistics Departments

While statistical consulting offices are a valuable resource in analysis, connecting researchers with statistical consultation at earlier points in the lifecycle can be valuable in establishing quality data practices from the start. For example, the consultants can help researchers establish and document decisions about sample size and planned analysis, and they can help promote reproducible data practices during analysis. They may also be a good resource for the statistical knowledge needed for de-identification or assessing disclosure risk for a dataset prior to sharing.

Part 2: Life in the Village: A Partnership in Data Management

Although identifying crucial resources and people at a university is an important step in assembling a data management village, it alone is not enough. To achieve the benefits of a distributed model for research data management support, it is critical to trust members of the village to be committed collaborators and not just a passive referral network. However, Tenopir and colleagues[4] found that outreach and collaboration with other data service providers is uncommon among academic research libraries in data services. The rest of this chapter will describe an in-depth collaboration between two members of our village, Research Support Services and the University Libraries, illustrating how we are attempting to move beyond a passive referral network and towards a partnership in providing distributed services.

In Figure 4.1 we illustrate our collaborative effort to provide data management services to our researchers across the research lifecycle, from the planning of their research project to the archiving of their data. At various points within the lifecycle researchers may need different levels of support and seek out different services. While the following overview describes an idealized situation of how a researcher might seek out data management support, in reality, we see different researchers in a variety of places and meet the needs they come with at the time. By having support set up at each point of the lifecycle, we are best able to reach people wherever they are in the process.

Figure 4.1. The Data Life-Cycle

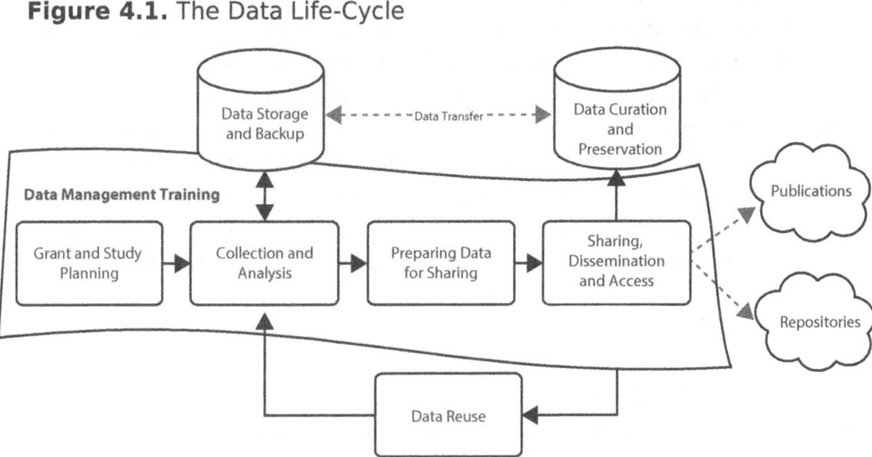

Visualizations, such as this, of the path that data take may help define the roles and responsibilities of members in your "data management village."

Data Management Training

Like their counterparts at most universities, researchers and PIs at the U of M take mandatory training in issues such as data security, ethical treatment of human subjects, and orientations to university policies on data retention and transfer.[5] However, most researchers do not have available training options in other skills and issues, such as data management best practices, data ownership, de-identification techniques, or digital preservation concerns.[6] To help address this need, the University Libraries have been offering drop-in workshops and non-credit courses in data management topics since 2009. These sessions have reached over 800 faculty, staff, and students with an emphasis on discussion-based exercises and hands-on, active-learning activities.

The library workshop session on "Creating a Data Management Plan for Your Grant Application" has been taught to faculty and researchers since 2010, when the NSF announced that they would begin requiring DMPs for all grant applications. The session creators have determined that this content is best taught by two co-instructors, one data management specialist and one disciplinary specialist;[7] this approach lends itself well to collaboration among campus units. For example, one pair of co-instructors includes a social sciences librarian and the CLA data management specialist for researchers in the social sciences. Here the focus of the content can point to resources and best practices within the discipline with experts who understand the nuances of data management and sharing relevant to the audience.

The student-focused workshops at the U of M have been evolving over the years to meet the urgent needs of those who are most often asked to handle the day-to-day workload of managing research data: graduate students. To introduce students to data management topics, the University Libraries developed a "Data Management Course" that has been taught online and as a hybrid online and in-person 5-week class[8] for five semesters since 2012. The online course is open to anyone who wishes to partake in the video-based content and download a data management plan template for their own data (http://z.umn.edu/datamgmt15). This open educational content can also be embedded in our campus partner websites for asynchronous and time-of-need learning.

Grant and Study Planning

One of the most common needs for data management support involves assistance with DMPs,[9] which are required for researchers applying for funding from a variety of federal and private agencies. With increasing requirements for federal data to be managed and shared,[10] this need is likely to increase. Researchers may need broad education on what is required in a DMP, provided through University Libraries workshops or web resources, or specific consultation for questions related to their current grant proposal. Even if a researcher is not required to submit a DMP, she may need consultation on other aspects of study planning, such as IRB applications, file format plans, metadata schemes, or collection methods, all of which may impact the ease of sharing or archiving their data later on.

Both Research Support Services and the Libraries offer individual consultation and DMP review, which allow researchers to take different routes to these services. We work collaboratively, using the same DMP checklist created by the libraries and sharing information when a unique grant or requirement is encountered. DMP consultations can not only help researchers write a strong DMP tailored to their project, but also connect them to the university and college resources needed to execute their plan. This is where a well-connected data management village can be very beneficial. For example, a project collecting highly sensitive data may require custom storage from IT; projects using university survey or statistical services will need tools for secure data transfer to these groups; and projects planning to deposit data in the institutional repository need to make sure such a plan is feasible. In addition to DMP consultation, the Libraries also consult on metadata schemes and file formats, and Research Support Services consult on collection methods and IRB submissions, encouraging researchers to not thwart opportunities for sharing or preserving data with overly restrictive language in their IRB documents.

Storage and Backup

Securely storing and backing up research data are critical steps in ensuring the longevity of the data.[11] While many universities offer multiple storage options, researchers often store and backup data using external hard-drives or other external media,[12] which may not be secure and are vulnerable to theft and failure.[13] Therefore, data managers need to be well connected to and aware of IT and Data Security offices to provide researchers with guidance as they plan storage and backup strategies. Despite not offering this as a direct service, both Research Support Services and the Libraries consult with researchers on storage and backup options that are provided centrally.

Although much of this service involves referral to IT, many questions about tools or security may actually have deeper issues of workflow at their core. For example, if a researcher is having trouble identifying a way to share a sensitive, personally identifiable dataset with colleagues, the question may not necessarily be best addressed by finding the right tool (which may or may not exist), but rather by thinking through the workflow and where de-identification occurs. It may be possible to not collect identifiers with the data in the first place or to de-identify the data and not share the linking information. This may lead to a less expensive and less risky solution to the problem, benefiting both the researchers and the university.

Collection and Analysis

Although the U of M provides some centralized tools for data collection, and many colleges provide additional services, most researchers are not aware of the options available to them.[14] Adding to the complexity, the U of M has central tools for survey design (e.g., Qualtrics), central offices for institutional or administrative surveys (e.g., Office of Measurement Services), and department or college offices for discipline-specific survey design (e.g., Social and Behavioral Sciences Laboratory, Minnesota Center for Survey Research). Researchers and data managers alike may not be aware of all, or indeed any, of these services, making it challenging to incorporate all relevant offices in planning discussions around DMPs or human subjects protections. However, this is an important step, as data collection practices may inadvertently violate promises made, or might render data documentation much more difficult than needed.

In the last few years, we have brought many of these data collection services together, and our data management village has allowed us to clarify needs, expectations, and best practices. By helping researchers identify specific collection and analysis needs during the earliest planning discussions, and connecting them to the relevant service providers before DMPs and IRB protocols are submitted, we can often avoid later challenges from overly-restrictive protocols or unrealistic plans for data management.

Not all members of the village are directly involved in the various data collection and analysis processes. However, when service providers know how their services may affect or be affected by preceding or following stages, they are able to prevent unnecessary problems for the researcher. For example, while University Libraries staff are unlikely to be directly involved with the collection and analysis details of a project, their knowledge of how data should best be preserved or shared can help shape decisions on file formats used in collection to ensure they will be sustainable over the long-term. Even within collection and analysis, coordination among providers allows prioritization of analysis goals during data collection, and integration of good data management practices from the start. The village approach also means that data can be documented during collection and analysis to meet expectations for later sharing. For example, Research Support Services is working to provide scripts, codebooks, and enhanced variable-level metadata along with data collected from all self-response surveys to meet data-sharing expectations for the Libraries' data repository.

Preparing Data for Publishing and Sharing

Many of our recent user-needs assessments have shown that researchers want additional support in preparing data for sharing.[15] As there are many considerations when preparing data depending on the type, sensitivity, and reasons for sharing, support for this is provided collaboratively by the Libraries and Research Support Services. Data preparation is an undertaking that requires considerable time, effort, and expertise, and a data management village can help reduce the burden on any individual office to accomplish it. A researcher needs to consider the different options for sharing, such as a repository that provides restricted data sharing, a more open repository with a de-identified version of the data, or both. The Libraries offer consultation and training on these options, as well as templates for documentation and information about negotiating data licensing when sharing.

Research Support Services provides consultation to help de-identify data and to examine possible concerns from direct or indirect identifiers. While software is available to automate checks of identifying numeric codes (Social Security numbers, credit card numbers, ZIP codes, etc.) and other regularly occurring patterns, it will not detect unique combinations of indirect identifiers or other data or documentation that may be linked to produce unique identifiers. This kind of consultation requires discipline-specific knowledge, understanding of the sample and population, and analysis of the dataset to identify unique or small-count cross-sections.[16] A data specialist from Research Support Services and a library staff member might meet with a researcher to ask about his goals for sharing, help identify the best home for the data, and guide him through the needed preparation.

At the University of Minnesota, this has been one of the most successful areas of collaboration between our two groups. We believe this is due to a variety of reasons. First, data sharing is an emerging area that, until recently, many researchers have not had to think about as part of their research process, and therefore one where they are likely to need assistance. Second, this area is within both the Libraries' and college's missions and a clear part of data management service, giving both our groups equivalent motivation. Finally, because data preparation requires disciplinary expertise as well as knowledge of general dissemination avenues, the Libraries and the college can jointly provide best practices for preparing data for sharing.

Data Sharing, Dissemination, and Access

Researchers are faced with increasing requirements to share the underlying data from their research. These include new mandates from federal funding agencies to comply with the Office of Science and Technology Policy (OSTP) guidelines on public access to data,[17] journal requirements to provide access to data,[18] and institutional policies for data management that include appropriate long-term archiving.[19] All of these pressures are combined with the individual's goals as a scholar to create better transparency for her results and allow others to discover, use, and cite her work.

Our data management village helps researchers provide broad access to their data through a digital repository called the Data Repository for the University of Minnesota (DRUM, http://z.umn.edu/DRUM). DRUM was developed as a joint collaboration between the Libraries and Research Support Services to meet specific needs related to dissemination and access to data. In addition, DRUM provides the mechanisms for proper citation of data (e.g., a digital object identifier, or DOI, is generated for every dataset) and additional indexing services to disseminate the data beyond the university.

Because sharing data in an institutional data repository is just one avenue our researchers may take to comply with their requirements and meet their goals, we also provide consultations for individuals to help them find the most appropriate place or method to share. Many offices at the U of M provide options for sharing data less broadly. For example, researchers may use our institutional Google Drive to share data by request with other users and potential research collaborators. By keeping aware of various options and solutions that exist across the university, we can help meet the variety of needs researchers may have.

Data Curation and Preservation

In our village, we have found that partnerships for curating and preserving research data are important for two reasons. First, not all research data should be made open and available through the broad data access mechanisms described above (which the libraries might provide) and therefore may require special storage services to protect data for the long-term (which the college might provide). Second, all data should be curated before archiving regardless of the destination; this is a task that "takes a village," given the diversity and size of potential datasets.

Defining what curation means for a particular dataset also requires a village. Our criteria for curation were jointly developed by information experts, curators, digital preservation specialists, and data management staff in a 2013 pilot of data curation services, and are published online.[20] To preserve the data long-term, it is important to understand whether the dataset is appropriately described and documented to remain useful over time, who is responsible for questions about the data, how long the data should be retained, and whether the data are valuable enough to be preserved indefinitely through potentially costly digital preservation techniques. Before any actions are taken to archive or preserve the data, these questions should be well understood by all parties.

Though still in development, in time this model might allow the curators and data storage providers to work together to create a safe, redundant, long-term digital archive for the data and actively manage it over the course of the data's life expectancy, using techniques such as access controls and digital preservation guidelines. Once a workflow for curation has been established, the process of curating a dataset will also require input from the researcher, data managers, data collection offices, and others to capture all relevant information.

Reuse

The fundamental principle of data management is the potential for reuse.[21] Therefore every aspect of the research data lifecycle must be employed with reuse in mind. Reuse of data comes in many forms and for many purposes, such as validating the results in a published paper, mining the data for new results, asking different questions, combining data with other sources to create a new dataset, or simply allowing the data author to revisit and understand his data years later. Given the diverse nature of data reuse, services to aid researchers in data discovery should benefit from the diverse and varied perspectives of the data management village. For example, updating and collaborating with partners on data indexes and guides offered by the library can help researchers find and make better use of existing data.

Understanding the benefits of reuse might also help researchers create better-described data. This includes the ability for data custodians to track the use and the impact of the data.[22] Impact can be tracked through the number of citations to the dataset, often most easily done when the dataset is granted a persistent URL, such as a DOI. Data citation formats are increasingly gaining acceptances in professional societies, such as the American Chemical Society journals,[23] or through guidance of citation standards, like the APA citation style for data.[24] Collaborative data villages can use subscription-based services, such as DataCite.org, to mint DOIs for datasets from their institution. This service should be backed by trusted storage and preservation protocols to prevent any DOIs from breaking or degrading over time if the data were to move from location to location. Our library uses these services for DRUM; however, we have not fully utilized the citation tracking features of the service to demonstrate impact.

Another mechanism for tracking the impact of reuse might be through monitoring requests to the data, either through mediated access or digital download counts for the dataset, or through altmetrics. As web statistics for the number of times a dataset is downloaded are problematic due to bots and malicious gaming of the system,[25] we might implement other ways to assess quality. Alternatives include follow-up surveys to data requestors or implementation of online shopping tools, such as rating systems or customer reviews, in a data repository. These are ideas that our data village should explore and implement with the combined resources of experts from a variety of campus units.

Conclusion

Overall, supporting researcher needs in data management has been a major focus at the U of M. Many campus players have come together to advance the goals of promoting and supporting good practices; specifically, CLA and the University Libraries have established more formal collaborations. Although environments vary across campuses, we emphasize the importance of reaching out across organizational and college boundaries and believe this is key for supporting diverse data management needs (see Table 4.1 for takeaways and lessons learned). While the collaborations described here might be considered among the more developed partnerships, there is still much work to be done. One of the main challenges that we face is scale: there are many moving parts at a large, distributed university such as the U of M. Therefore, learning about all the services, people, offices, and initiatives on campus, and attempting to connect and fill gaps (rather than replicate work) is a large, ongoing task for the service providers.

Table 4.1. Takeaways and Lessons Learned from Our Experiences

Suggestions for starting a "Data Management Village" on your campus

- Connect with other people on campus interested in data management through groups dedicated to discussing these topics (such as informal communities of practice). Start a group like this or join existing groups on campus.
- Research community-based groups at your institution. Are there ways to connect to existing groups already focused on issues relevant to data management, such as IT or security?
- Think about collaboration from the start. Write collaboration into new positions and have interviewees meet with diverse candidates across the university. If possible, have interdisciplinary search committees. One of the best ways to be better connected is to have never experienced disconnection.
- Consider bringing in cross-campus experts for workshops and courses. For example, involve IT or a Data Security office in presentations on data storage and backup. You will make connections with their office and everyone will learn about the available options.

Researchers have an even greater challenge: to be aware of and easily navigate these distributed resources. This is where the strength of the village can be felt. With enough awareness of services both within the village and among researchers, we hope to keep researchers at the center and provide seamless support for data management around their workflows and across the research lifecycle. Our work so far has reaped rewards by elucidating research support options and by providing a way to conceptualize and advance services as part of a coordinated approach to university support for research data management. As a data management village, service providers who are otherwise disconnected come together to provide researchers with a broader range of services than each could provide alone.

1. Research Data Alliance, "DAMA Dictionary of Data Management," *Mapping the Data Landscape 2011 Summit; TBS Information Management Glossary (BC Government Information Resource Management)*, 2011, http://smw-rda.esc.rzg.mpg.de/index.php/Main_Page.
2. Michael Witt, Jacob Carlson, D. Scott Brandt, and Melissa H. Cragin, "Constructing Data Curation Profiles," *International Journal of Digital Curation* 4, no. 3 (2009): 93–103, doi:10.2218/ijdc.v4i3.117; Heather Coates, "Building Data Services from the Ground up: Strategies and Resources," *Journal of eScience Librarianship* 3, no. 1 (2014): 52–59, doi:10.7191/jeslib.2014.1063.
3. Alicia Hofelich Mohr and Thomas Lindsay, "It Takes a Village: Strengthening Data Management through Collaboration with Diverse Institutional Offices.," (presentation at the *International Association for Social Science Information Services & Technology* Annual Conference, Toronto, ON, 2014), doi:http://dx.doi.org/10.6084/m9.figshare.1390629.
4. Carol Tenopir, Robert J. Sandusky, Suzie Allard, and Ben Birch, "Research Data Management Services in Academic Research Libraries and Perceptions of Librarians," *Library & Information Science Research* 36, no. 2 (2014): 84–90, doi:10.1016/j.lisr.2013.11.003.
5. Office of the Vice President for Research, "Core Curriculum: Research Education & Oversight," *University of Minnesota*, 2015.
6. Jacob Carlson, Michael Fosmire, C.C. Miller, and Megan Sapp Nelson, "Determining Data Information Literacy Needs: A Study of Students and Research Faculty," *Portal: Libraries and the Academy* 11, no. 2 (2011): 629–57, doi:10.1353/pla.2011.0022.
7. Lisa Johnston, Meghan Lafferty, and Beth Petsan, "Training Researchers on Data Management: A Scalable, Cross-Disciplinary Approach," *Journal of eScience Librarianship* 1, no. 2 (2012): 79–87, doi:10.7191/jeslib.2012.1012.
8. Lisa Johnston and Jon Jeffryes, "Data Management Skills Needed by Structural Engineering Students: Case Study at the University of Minnesota," *Journal of Professional Issues in Engineering Education and Practice* 140, no. 2 (2013), doi:10.1061/(ASCE)EI.1943-5541.0000154.
9. Rebecca Reznik-Zellen, Jessica Adamick, and Stephen McGinty, "Tiers of Research Data Support Services," *Journal of eScience Librarianship* 1, no. 1 (2012): 27–35, doi:10.7191/jeslib.2012.1002; Alicia Hofelich Mohr, Steven Braun, Carolyn Bishoff, Josh Bishoff, and Lisa Johnston, "Understanding Researcher Needs in Data Management: A Comparison of Four Colleges in a Large Academic American University" (presentation at the *International Association for Social Science Information Services & Technology* Annual Conference, Minneapolis, MN, 2015).
10. John P. Holdren, "Memorandum for the Heads of Executive Departments and Agencies: Increasing Access to the Results of Federally Funded Scientific Research" (Washington, D.C., 2013), doi:10.4135/9781483300672.n99.
11. Clifford Lynch, "Big Data: How Do Your Data Grow?," *Nature* 455, no. 7209 (2008): 28–29, doi:10.1038/455028a.
12. Katherine G. Akers and Jennifer Doty, "Disciplinary Differences in Faculty Research Data Management Practices and Perspectives," *International Journal of Digital Curation* 8, no. 2 (2013): 5–26, doi:10.2218/ijdc.v8i2.263; Hofelich Mohr et al., "Understanding Researcher Needs in Data Management: A Comparison of Four Colleges in a Large Academic American University."
13. Brian Beach, "How Long Do Disk Drives Last?," *Backblaze*, last modified November 12, 2013, https://www.backblaze.com/blog/how-long-do-disk-drives-last/.
14. Hofelich Mohr et al., "Understanding Researcher Needs in Data Management: A Comparison of Four Colleges in a Large Academic American University."
15. Ibid.
16. Federal Committee on Statistical Methodology, *Identifiability in Microdata Files*, last modified July 5, 2002, https://fcsm.sites.usa.gov/files/2014/04/CDAC-Ident.pdf.
17. Holdren, "Memorandum for the Heads of Executive Departments and Agencies: Increasing Access to the Results of Federally Funded Scientific Research."

18. Paul Sturges, Marianne Bamkin, Jane H.S. Anders, Bill Hubbard, Azhar Hussain, and Melanie Heeley, "Research Data Sharing: Developing a Stakeholder-Driven Model for Journal Policies," *Journal of the Association for Information Science and Technology*, 2014, 1–17, doi:10.1002/asi.23336.
19. University of Minnesota, "Research Data Management: Archiving, Ownership, Retention, Security, Storage, and Transfer" (Minneapolis, MN: UWide Policy Library, 2015).
20. Lisa Johnston, "A Workflow Model for Curating Research Data in the University of Minnesota Libraries: Report from the 2013 Data Curation Pilot," *University of Minnesota Digital Consevancy*, 2014, 1–87, http://hdl.handle.net/11299/162338.
21. National Research Council, *Preparing the Workforce for Digital Curation* (Washington, D.C.: The National Academies Press, 2015).
22. National Research Council, *For Attribution—Developing Data Attribution and Citation Practices and Standards: Summary of an International Workshop* (Washington, D.C.: The National Academies Press, 2012).
23. American Chemical Society, *The ACS Style Guide: Effective Communication of Scientific Information*, ed. Anne M. Coghill and Lorrin R. Garson (New York, NY: Oxford University Press, 2006).
24. American Psychological Association, *Publication Manual of the American Psychological Association* (Washington, D.C.: American Psychological Association, 2009).
25. Kirk Hess, "Discovering Digital Library User Behavior with Google Analytics," *Code{4}Lib Journal* 2012, no. 17 (2012): 1–10, http://journal.code4lib.org/articles/6942.

CHAPTER 5

The Data Librarian in the Liberal Arts College

Ryan Clement

FOR DECADES, RESEARCH universities and libraries have been developing services and support for working with administrative, research, and government data. These services have grown in response to the massive amounts of data researchers in these institutions work with. Typically, the support includes data management planning, data analysis consultation, software instruction and support, and data discovery and acquisition. More recently, smaller liberal arts colleges have begun to develop their own data services and support. These programs are often modeled on the programs in larger research-intensive institutions, a common pattern from past developments in library services. This model has served liberal arts libraries well, allowing them to take advantage of advances from the universities, where larger budgets and staff sizes tend to make innovation easier. In developing these data services, though, the liberal arts data librarian needs to not only look to the large research university for inspiration, but also needs to focus on what makes the liberal arts experience unique, and how this affects the development of data services.

Liberal arts college faculty may not generate data of the same size as faculty at larger institutions, but they are still generating and using a lot of data. Between 1997 and 2006, over half of the top fifty baccalaureate-granting institutions graduating eventual science and engineering doctorate recipients, proportionate to size, were liberal arts institutions.[1] Often the "liberal arts" are thought to be non-technical disciplines. It is clear, however, that liberal arts colleges are graduating science and engineering students, who both collect data and work with secondary data. Liberal arts programs in the social sciences and humanities are also recognizing the importance of data to their work.

This chapter will first briefly look at what makes the liberal arts college in the United States unique, not only in mission but also in typical organization and structure. With the wide variety of programs in the liberal arts, it is difficult to develop a definition of "the liberal arts"; instead of a strict delineation, I will base this discussion on the outline Hugh Hawkins offers: "A four-year institution of higher education, focusing its attention on candidates for the B.A. degree ... an institution resistant to highly specific vocational preparation and insisting on a considerable breadth of studies ... [that hopes to develop] interests and capabilities that will enrich both the individual learner and future communities."[2] With this foundation, I will then turn to several areas of interest for those developing data services for the liberal arts college library: how to structure and staff data services, collection development for data collections, and data management and curation. Each of these areas can be of greater or lesser importance, depending on the particular institution. There is a considerable amount of heterogeneity amongst liberal arts institutions, and unique campus concerns must always be taken into consideration when building new services. This heterogeneity, along with the great breadth of topics that fall under the umbrella of data services, means this chapter cannot be exhaustive. However, it can hopefully serve to highlight the need for data services, and unique approaches to these services, on the liberal arts campus.

The Structure and Organization of the Liberal Arts College

A number of different types of institutions could fall under the "liberal arts college" heading above. What makes these organizations unique? First and foremost, as seen in both Hawkins's definition and Robert Birnbaum's discussion of "the collegial institution" in *How Colleges Work: The Cybernetics of Academic Organization and Leadership*, the liberal arts institution is one that values a breadth of curriculum as opposed to a number of highly specialized fields of study (or vocational training).[3] Students that pursue a degree even in a highly technical field such as biochemistry, or econometrics, are commonly expected to meet diverse distribution requirements. As an example, at Reed College in Portland, Oregon, students must fulfill distribution requirements across all academic divisions of the college, including physical education, and even have a "breadth requirement" that requires further coursework outside a student's home division in addition to the other distribution requirements.[4] Curricular breadth, as well as curricular depth within a student's chosen major, is a hallmark of the liberal arts institution.

Liberal arts institutions may have library and information technology departments that have been merged to some degree, or they may be completely separate departments on campus. Typically the liberal arts institution will not have more than one information technology department, though, unlike many research institutions. In addition, liberal arts institutions may have some sort of student services department, offering writing help and other tutoring, outside of the other supporting departments. No matter the degree to which these departments have been merged, the typical liberal arts institution is small in both size and number of support departments, allowing for greater communication both inter- and intra-departmentally. This communication is perhaps the most important cultural marker of the liberal arts institution—students, faculty, and staff tend to migrate to such institutions because of the opportunity for communication and relationship building, which sets these schools apart from similarly sized comprehensive universities or small research universities.

Unlike at large research libraries, library work at the liberal arts college tends to be almost exclusively focused on the institution's curriculum. Most activities, from collection development to library instruction, are tied to this curriculum. This often means the faculty has a greater say in the activities of the liberal arts library than at a larger research institution. For this reason, it is of the utmost importance that librarians at liberal arts institutions develop and maintain particularly strong relationships with faculty from across the institution.

While the primary focus for faculty in a liberal arts college is typically on advising and teaching students, faculty do conduct research. They are typically both consumers and producers of data, though in many cases these datasets are smaller than those being produced and consumed in larger research labs. There are, of course, examples of big data being used in smaller liberal arts environments, as well as smaller data being used at larger research universities. On average, though, the data produced and used a liberal arts institution tend to be more manageable (at least in terms of size), but also quite diverse.[†]

Finally, these institutions normally have a very low student-to-faculty ratio, with median of 1:13,[5] allowing faculty to be heavily involved in working with undergraduate students not only in the classroom, but also in the field and in the lab. Science and social science labs in liberal arts colleges tend to employ undergraduate students in many of the same roles that typically go to graduate students or post-doctoral researchers in larger institutions. Students in these positions are often given the opportunity to not only work on faculty data, but also to produce original data of their own. This type of close relationship between faculty, particularly those conducting research, and students, who are learning to conduct their own research, creates a unique opportunity to teach undergraduates about working with data at a high level.

---

† Throughout this chapter, the terms "big data" and "small data" will be used in a quite general sense. As a general rule of thumb, "big data" can be taken to refer to anything in the multi-terabyte and larger range, usually highly unstructured, while "small data" can be anything from several megabytes to many gigabytes of data, usually structured.

Structure and Staffing of Data Services in the Liberal Arts College

Structure and staffing of data services programs at any institution are an important consideration. The breadth of expertise that can fall under the purview of "data services" makes it unlikely that any one person could cover all practices for all disciplines. This is especially true at small liberal arts institutions, where librarians often have to strike a special balance between the generalist and specialist sides of their positions. In addition to working with data, a data librarian at a liberal arts college may also have duties including liaison work, shifts at the reference or circulation desk, general information literacy instruction, and other digital scholarship tasks. Unlike those at other small institutions, where librarians also maintain such diverse job functions, these functions are all extremely high-touch at the liberal arts institution, where students, faculty, and staff all come with the expectation of close relationships. Considering the various demands these relationships make on a liberal arts librarian's time, it makes sense to pursue a *distributed model* for data services staffing.

In this distributed model, no one staff member is responsible for all aspects of data services or all disciplines that may use data in their research. Each staff member has an area(s) of expertise, and a place in the data. Faculty and student researchers interact with different team members throughout a research project, but behind the scenes, the team coordinates efforts and communicates internally about hand-offs from one stage to the next. Below in Table 5.1 is an example of the staffing at a hypothetical college:

Table 5.1. Hypothetical Staffing Model with Related Services

Staff Member	Services
Science Librarian	Data Discovery
Data Services Librarian	Data Management
Student Support Tutor	Fundamental Statistics Help
Instructional Technologist I	Data Analysis Software Consultation
Instructional Technologist II	Web-based Data Visualization Help
Science Librarian	Data Citation Assistance

Each team member has a stage in the process at which they provide the primary support. In addition to allowing the team members to accomplish their other job duties and best use their particular expertise, this makes the model highly flexible. In the case above, perhaps the researcher was a biology student. When an economics faculty member asks for assistance, the team can easily be reconfigured. For instance, by switching out the Science Librarian for the Social Science Librarian (and hopefully dropping the need for fundamental statistics help), the team has easily been reconfigured to best meet the needs of another user.

Another advantage of the distributed model is that it works equally well whether or not the IT and library departments are merged in a particular institution. As long as the data services team performs outreach and presents themselves *as a team* to faculty and students, users needing assistance can come to see them as such, irrespective of their various departmental affiliations.

This need to present the data services team as a unified team in outreach brings up the main disadvantage of the distributed model: it requires a great deal of coordination, communication, and trust amongst the various members. When a researcher comes to the data services team for assistance, they should feel as though they are being escorted through the research process, so that each handoff from team member to team member makes sense.[†] Not only does the process need to be properly communicated to the researcher, but team members also need to be communicating behind the scenes about what has already been tried or accomplished—the researcher should not need to repeat requests unnecessarily. To this end, all members of the team need to trust in each other's expertise, as well as fully understand what that expertise means. Ideally, each team member should also have some degree of training in conducting a reference interview, so that no matter which team member is contacted first, this person can appropriately assess the researcher's data needs and provide an effective referral for the researcher.

These disadvantages may be magnified somewhat on campuses where IT and the library are not merged. Due to the cultural, political, and sometimes even spatial differences between different departments in some non-merged organizations, it can require a great deal of work to get a data services team to work together in *a unified fashion*, rather than as a collection of disparate staff. However, in the long run, these efforts will be rewarded by satisfied researchers who recommend the data services team to their students and colleagues.

Data Collection Development for the Liberal Arts

Although data and statistical information have been collected by libraries for a long time, just like any other form of recorded information, this collection has often been done in the absence of clearly defined policies.[6] Many aspects of collecting data can fall easily in line with a wider institutional collection development policy. However, there are enough differences in the collection of data that any institutional policy should have, at the very least, a separate section on data address-

† Again, remember the importance of high-touch relationships at the liberal arts institution.

ing these issues.[7] Some of these issues include restricted access data, single-user licenses, third-party aggregation of publically accessible data, and data preservation and storage. The effect of each of these issues on collecting data will be discussed in this section. While many of these points may also apply to the non-liberal-arts institution, the typically loose nature of policy documentation at many liberal arts schools makes this an important discussion.

Many liberal arts library collections are driven, at least in part, through faculty input. These collections are tightly tied into both the institution's curriculum and researchers' specific interests. This collaboration between liaison librarians and faculty can work quite well in purchasing monographs, serials, and subscriptions to library databases, but it falls apart somewhat when it comes to purchasing and/or licensing datasets. Again, this dynamic reinforces the need for a well-articulated policy for data collection development at the liberal arts institution.

Restricted Access Data†

Some human subjects data, because of their highly confidential nature, are restricted in their accessibility. Often, a public-use version of the data will be created, with the confidential information recoded or removed. However, the original version of the data are often of great interest to researchers because of the greater ability to perform innovative investigations. In these cases, researchers must agree to certain conditions and procedures in order to gain access to these data.

At a small liberal arts college, while it is possible to assist researchers in meeting the conditions and procedures for access, it is often not possible to collect and store such restricted data for the long term, even when it has been generated by local researchers. Instead of trying to manage these data in a local repository, it is advisable to maintain memberships in data repositories, such as the Inter-university Consortium for Political and Social Research (ICPSR), which have the ability curate, store, and provide safe and confidential access to these restricted data for researchers who request it.

Single-User Licenses

Many highly specialized datasets, which may be of interest for a particular class or research project, can also be extremely restrictive in their licensing agreements. As an example, the *Corpus of Global Web-Based English*, which is a valuable dataset for computational linguists, restricts institutions that purchase a multi-user academic license to only providing access to those faculty and graduate students affiliated with a particular campus (i.e., users at another campus in a multi-campus institution can-

† For more information about restricted data, see the chapter in this volume by Jennifer Darragh called "Restricted Data Access and Libraries."

not use the data).[8] There are also a number of specific restrictions on the use of the data that each user must be made aware of before using the data. This requires oversight from the data services librarian, coordination with Collection Services, and infrastructure for ensuring compliance with the restrictions. While liberal arts institutions usually need not worry about single-campus restrictions, they need to plan for negotiating undergraduate access when adding such items to their collection.

Still more restrictive data licenses exist where only an individual researcher is to be given access to the data. Unlike a single-user e-book license, this means that *only that specific researcher* can *ever* access the data. This is most likely outside the collection development practices of most liberal arts libraries, but it is a case that should be addressed, if possible, in a collection development policy for data. Researchers should be made aware that they will need to seek funds from their home department, or include such funding in grant proposals, if they need access to these datasets.

Third-Party Aggregation of Public Data

As interest in data collection has grown in libraries, so too has vendor interest in providing value-added access to publically available data. Many products now exist that aggregate public data sources (such as data from the United States government) and provide improved browsing and searching interfaces for such data. Some third-party aggregators will also provide access to the data in various formats, or allow specialized subsetting of large datasets.

In developing a data collection development policy, it is important to balance the convenience of such services with the goal of teaching students to find, obtain, and evaluate data. If in certain cases (such as a class on statistical methodology) it would be beneficial to have a certain type of data centralized with an easy-to-use interface, purchasing access to such third-party products can make sense for the library.[‡] However, in other cases a user may request that the library pay for access to one of these products when she simply does not want to do the searching (or do not want to pay a research assistant to do it). In these cases, it is helpful to have a clear policy in place, as well as having a data librarian who can help train research assistants to search for data. These sustainable research data skills will serve the research assistant, the researcher, and the library better in the long term, as well as advancing the teaching mission of the college.

Data Preservation and Storage

Today, many of the sources of data and statistics that a library collects are stored and preserved by third parties, both public repositories and vendors. However, in some cases, libraries will need to purchase a dataset in the form of a digital file that

‡ Examples of such products include ProQuest International Datasets, CQ Press Voting & Elections Collection, and Social Explorer.

they will need to host and preserve themselves. If the institution has a data repository, and can restrict access to individual files in this repository, then storing and preserving these files is much easier. In the case that the institution does not have a data repository, though, this becomes a more complicated question.

Most of the best practices and guidelines related to data storage and preservation are applicable across all types of institutions. There is little in this area that is unique to liberal arts institutions; I recommend that those interested look to the widely available literature on this topic. To get started, the "Best Practices" section of the DataONE website, as well as the "Preservation" section of the ICPSR's website, are both highly recommended.[9,10]

Data Management and Curation

The National Institutes of Health (NIH) were the first federal agency to require data management and data sharing plans from their grant applications, starting in 2003.[11] This policy did not affect many liberal arts institutions, however, as most of them do not have health sciences programs; even for those that do, the NIH only required these plans from applicants seeking more than $500,000 in costs per year, a large amount even for some health-sciences-exclusive institutions. When the National Science Foundation (NSF) issued their own data management planning and sharing requirements to take effect January 2011,[12] liberal arts colleges (and institutions of all types that rely on grant funding) began to take more notice. When the White House Office of Science and Technology Policy issued a 2013 memorandum requiring the heads of *all* federal funding agencies to develop policies for requiring data management and sharing plans,[13] it became clear that data management planning and sharing were here to stay. Researchers and the libraries and IT departments that support them needed to tackle this issue, no matter how large or small the institution, if they wanted to continue to receive grant funding.

While some liberal arts colleges had data services programs prior to these increased demands for accountability from funding agencies, they rarely covered areas such as data management and curation. These areas were the purview of large research institutions, whose researchers were gathering datasets so large that managing them and describing them became difficult to do through traditional means. It did not seem imperative for liberal arts colleges, with relatively smaller data collections and a focus on teaching undergraduates, to fully engage with the world of data management and curation. Data discovery, manipulation, interpretation, and analysis—these topics were seen as more important for undergraduates to learn. Even as data management instruction for undergraduates has grown, it is often still offered at research universities rather than liberal arts colleges.[14] While data management and curation have become important components of data services at any institution that relies on grant funding, it has also started to become clear that, from a sustainability point of view, these topics need to become part of an instructional program that trains future researchers in these skills themselves.

While it has not yet become a common data service in liberal arts colleges, training in data management and curation *should* become an important component of these programs. Not only do undergraduates in liberal arts colleges often work with faculty on research and assist in grant-funded projects requiring data management planning and compliance, but many of these undergraduates will go on to pursue graduate degrees, often requiring them to take on more significant responsibility for data management, both within a lab in which they work and in their own research. Of the top fifteen baccalaureate-origin institutions for recipients of science and engineering doctorates from 2002–2011, when considered by institution-yield ratio, eight are small liberal arts colleges.[15] As the training ground for a number of our future researchers and scholars, liberal arts schools would be doing them a disservice to make them wait until they get to a graduate institution to learn about data management and curation. These rich and complex topics deserve to be integrated into *all* levels of higher education.

What do liberal arts undergraduates need to know about data management and curation, and how should we deliver this instruction to them? If we take the broad view that data management and curation encompass all of the practices surrounding the collecting, organizing, documenting, sharing, and preserving data, we can see several opportunities for integrating these topics into the liberal arts curriculum, particularly in the sciences and social sciences, but even in the humanities as well.

Collecting and Organizing

Often in classes where students are taught data analysis or statistical methodologies, their instructors give them pre-scrubbed and organized datasets in the interest of saving them time and allowing students to concentrate on learning analytic techniques. This makes sense, to some degree, but also puts the students at a disadvantage. When they start doing their own research, such as for a final paper or an undergraduate thesis, they may need to collect and organize the data themselves. When students are first tasked with organizing their own data, whether collected themselves or not, they often approach the task with a variety of non-standard solutions, sometimes following inscrutable logic.[16] Several types of exercises could help with this issue, such as giving students detailed directions for collecting and organizing the data, instead of giving them a premade dataset. Another exercise that can teach students about the large differences in data organization is to give them an unorganized dataset (cutting out the collection step), as though they had just been handed it by another researcher, and then have them devise their own organizational scheme before proceeding to the analysis, visualization, and presentation steps.[17] Sharing their process can highlight the need for standardization and communication in labs and other collaborative environments. Learning how to logically organize files (and document that organization) is a skill that all undergraduates can easily learn, and one that will serve them well in their work beyond data, too.

Documenting

Librarians sometimes struggle with talking to non-librarians about metadata, particularly in avoiding the use of jargon. Anecdotal evidence suggests that some librarians would rather scholars not create final, study-level metadata for their own scholarly products. However, the reality is that with the increase in public data repositories allowing self-deposit, as well as the increase in collaborative research, many researchers are *already* creating their own metadata, for better or worse. Some faculty may think that metadata is a topic that students do not need to know about, or that they already know what it is and how it works.[†] It is important in pushing back against these claims to use learning outcomes, which are more meaningful for non-librarians, and to avoid the use of jargon. Example learning outcomes include "using disciplinary metadata standards," and "explaining why metadata is important."[18] Instead of talking about "metadata," particularly when talking to undergraduates, librarians can use the phrase "contextual details needed to make the dataset meaningful to others."[19]

Card-sorting exercises can be particularly helpful for teaching about the importance of standardized metadata and also can serve to open up conversations about why metadata standards are so important for increasing understanding.[20] For example, the instructor can give students cards with a number of items that are familiar to their discipline, or are generally familiar (e.g., fruits and vegetables), and have them sort them into categories of their own devising. Students can then discuss how they sorted their items and try to figure out how other groups performed their sort. This can then lead into a discussion of metadata standards and controlled vocabularies, and their importance for long-term searchability and access.

Sharing and Preservation

This final topic under the umbrella of data management and curation is often seen as too complex for undergraduate students. To be sure, data sharing is a complex subject, encompassing the above practices of organization and documentation, as well as intellectual property issues, ethical considerations (especially with human subjects data), and disciplinary cultural practices. Data preservation is also a

† The author has heard both of these claims: the former, in reference to an attempt to talk about evaluating a repository's quality based on metadata quality, and the latter accompanied by the claim that "they know all about that after the NSA thing."

complex topic, involving the practices of the broader world of digital preservation, as well as the tricky prospect of appraising the future value of research data. Preservation, in particular, is one of the areas where faculty themselves have difficulty both evaluating the importance of the practices, as well as knowing how to teach students about these topics—both the faculty and students interviewed as part of the Data Information Literacy Project rated "data preservation" as the least important topic to teach students.[21] Despite this complexity, liberal arts institutions are some of the most promising venues for teaching undergraduates about data sharing and preservation.

As discussed above, a high proportion of students graduating from liberal arts institutions go on to advanced study after earning their baccalaureate. This fact, when coupled with the high involvement of liberal arts undergraduates in faculty research (as well as their own original research) means that there is not only ample *reason* for teaching liberal arts undergraduates about data sharing and preservation, but ample *opportunity* to do just that. While it is true that graduate study is where students are taught how to become members of their disciplinary culture, this enculturation also takes place at a significant level at the undergraduate level in a liberal arts environment. Despite, or perhaps because of, the lack of vocational training at liberal arts institutions, students are often being trained in the "vocation" of becoming a scholar. Working closely with faculty in the classroom, the lab, or the studio, as well as learning how this work of scholarship can affect the larger world for better or worse—these are some of the hallmarks of a liberal arts education. Learning about using data as a scholarly product, with real value beyond its original purpose, can help students working with data to learn other ways to place themselves into the scholarly conversation. Learning about the preservation of data can help students to learn that materials beyond the journal article and the monograph can have real value and need to be preserved as part of the cultural record (even if they are never the ones who have to preserve it in practice). Thinking about data being preserved and shared for the long term can also help students to do better data management work in the longer term, similar to what Char Booth and Char Miller have argued about other undergraduate work and open access publishing.[22] When you are thinking that another scholar, or another student, may read or use your work, it makes the whole scholarly enterprise much more real in a way that few frameworks can.

Conclusion

The development of data services programs for liberal arts colleges is a project still in its infancy, and there are many questions for liberal arts data librarians to answer. In such environments, innovation is very important, but sometimes carries more risk than in a large research institution. Being able to fail and recover from failure is a privilege for those institutions with the resources (e.g. staff, time, money) to do so. As they do in many other areas, liberal arts libraries look to these larger institutions for ideas and infrastructure, but they must do so with a careful eye to their unique communities and circumstances. Just because something works in a larger institution does not mean it can scale down to your particular institution. On the flip side of this, just because something does not work in a larger institution does not mean it cannot work in a liberal arts college. Collaboration, whether with students, with faculty, or with other colleges, can allow a culture of data information literacy to flourish in the liberal arts environment in special ways that may be constrained in larger organizations. One of the long-standing goals of the liberal arts program is the holistic development of a better-informed and more critical citizenry. Providing data services and data information literacy instruction is an essential part of continuing this mission in the twenty-first century.

---

1. Victor E. Ferrall Jr., *Liberal Arts at the Brink* (Cambridge, Mass. ; London: Harvard University Press, 2011), 22.
2. Hugh Hawkins, "The Making of the Liberal Arts College Identity," in *Distinctively American: The Residential Liberal Arts Colleges*, ed. Steven Koblik and Stephen R. Graubard (New Brunswick, U.S.A: Transaction Publishers, 2000), 23.
3. Robert Birnbaum, *How Colleges Work: The Cybernetics of Academic Organization and Leadership* (San Francisco: Jossey-Bass, 1991), 85–104.
4. Reed College, "The Educational Program," *Reed College Catalog*, accessed April 26, 2015, http://www.reed.edu/catalog/edu_program.html.
5. Institute of Education Sciences, National Center for Education Statistics, "Integrated Postsecondary Education Data System Provisional Release Data" (U.S. Department of Education, 2013), http://nces.ed.gov/ipeds/datacenter/Default.aspx.
6. William H. Walters, "Building and Maintaining a Numeric Data Collection," *Journal of Documentation* 55, no. 3 (1999): 271–87.
7. Ibid.
8. Mark Davies, "Restrictions on the Use of the Copora," *Full-Text Corpus Data: Based on 450 Million Word COCA Corpus and the 1.9 Billion Word GloWbE Corpus*, accessed April 26, 2015, http://corpus.byu.edu/full-text/restrictions.asp.
9. DataONE, "Best Practices | DataONE," accessed August 8, 2015, https://www.dataone.org/best-practices.
10. Inter-university Consortium for Political and Social Research, "Digital Preservation at ICPSR," accessed August 8, 2015, http://www.icpsr.umich.edu/icpsrweb/content/datamanagement/preservation/index.html.
11. National Institutes of Health, "NIH Data Sharing Policy and Implementation Guidance," accessed April 27, 2015, http://grants.nih.gov/grants/policy/data_sharing/data_sharing_guidance.htm.
12. National Science Foundation, *Proposal and Award Policies and Procedures Guide* (Washington, D.C.: National Science Foundation, 2010).
13. John Holdren, "Memorandum for the Heads of Executive Departments and Agencies: Increasing Access to the Results of Federally Funded Scientific Research," February 22, 2013, http://www.whitehouse.gov/sites/default/files/microsites/ostp/ostp_public_access_memo_2013.pdf.
14. Yasmeen Shorish, "Data Curation Is for Everyone! The Case for Master's and Baccalaureate Institutional Engagement with Data Curation," *Journal of Web Librarianship* 6, no. 4 (October 2012): 263–73, doi:10.1080/19322909.2012.729394; Yasmeen Shorish, "Data Information Liter-

acy and Undergraduates: A Critical Competency," *College & Undergraduate Libraries* 22, no. 1 (January 2, 2015): 97–106, doi:10.1080/10691316.2015.1001246.

15. Mark K. Fiegener and Steven L. Proudfoot, "Baccalaureate Origins of US-Trained S&E Doctorate Recipients," *Arlington, VA: National Science Foundation, National Center for Science and Engineering Statistics*, 2013, http://nsf.gov/statistics/infbrief/nsf13323/nsf13323.pdf.
16. Jacob Carlson, Michael Fosmire, C. C. Miller, and Megan Sapp Nelson, "Determining Data Information Literacy Needs: A Study of Students and Research Faculty," *Portal: Libraries and the Academy* 11, no. 2 (2011): 629–57, doi:10.1353/pla.2011.0022.; Nicole Vasilevsky and Jackie Wirz, personal communication.
17. Nicole Vasilevsky, Jackie Wirz, Robin Champieux, Todd Hannon, Bryan Laraway, Kyle Banerjee, Chris Shaffer, and Melissa Haendel, "Lions, Tigers, and Gummi Bears: Springing Towards Effective Engagement with Research Data Management," *Scholar Archive*, December 1, 2014, http://digitalcommons.ohsu.edu/etd/3571.
18. Mary Piorun, Donna Kafel, Tracey Leger-Hornby, Siamak Najafi, Elaine Martin, Paul Colombo, and Nancy LaPelle, "Teaching Research Data Management: An Undergraduate/Graduate Curriculum," *Journal of eScience Librarianship* 1, no. 1 (February 14, 2012): 48, doi:10.7191/jeslib.2012.1003.
19. Ibid.
20. Mike Kuniavsky, *Observing the User Experience: A Practitioner's Guide to User Research* (San Francisco, CA: Morgan Kaufmann Publishers, 2003), 192–199.
21. Carlson et al., "Determining Data Information Literacy Needs"; Jake Carlson, Jake, Lisa Johnston, Brian Westra, and Mason Nichols, "Developing an Approach for Data Management Education: A Report from the Data Information Literacy Project," *International Journal of Digital Curation* 8, no. 1 (June 14, 2013): 204–17, doi:10.2218/ijdc.v8i1.254.
22. Char Booth and Char Miller, "Open Access as Undergraduate Pedagogy," Blog, *Library Journal*, (March 26, 2014), http://lj.libraryjournal.com/2014/03/opinion/backtalk/open-access-as-undergraduate-pedagogy-backtalk#_.

CHAPTER 6

Teaching Foundational Data Skills in the Library

Adam Beauchamp and Christine Murray

UNDERGRADUATE STUDENTS OFTEN struggle when first asked to locate and evaluate data for use in their own research projects. These skills are often given scant attention in social science curricula that emphasize statistical formulas and software when teaching quantitative methods. Librarians have a unique opportunity to help students develop their data literacy skills, but our existing data services may not be enough. In our eagerness to connect libraries and scholars through data management services, librarians risk leaving behind the data novices. The same outreach and instruction approaches used to teach data skills to seasoned researchers may not be successful with an audience of beginners, nor are they guaranteed to translate well across disciplines. At the same time, we cannot simply provide datasets to these students, relegating them to the role of data consumer as librarians do the work to locate and provide access to data. Librarians working with students in the social sciences can bridge this gap between data consumption and data research expertise through information literacy instruction. Teaching students the skills needed to identify, locate, and evaluate existing datasets is an excellent way to develop students' data literacy skills and jumpstart their transition from being passive consumers of data to becoming active participants in quantitative research. This chapter offers a pedagogical framework and three sample lessons designed to integrate basic data literacy into information literacy instruction for students in the social sciences who are new to quantitative methods and data analysis.

Data Literacy Challenges in the Social Sciences

Introductory courses in quantitative analysis in the undergraduate social science curriculum frequently focus on statistical formulas and software packages. In order to focus on these skills, instructors omit the task of finding context-appropriate data by providing students with a suitable dataset, often one that has acquired canonical status in that discipline. While this approach ensures students have data with variables rich enough to support the statistical methods of the course, it also hides from view an integral step in authentic quantitative research. The Data-Driven Learning Guides published by the Inter-university Consortium for Political and Social Research (ICPSR) take a similar approach, providing lesson plans for exercises that guide students through applying analytical skills like cross-tabulation or comparison of means to predetermined datasets like the American National Election Studies (ANES) or Monitoring the Future.[1] Similar approaches can also be found in the disciplinary pedagogical literature, as in an assignment using the decennial U.S. Census to analyze community demographic trends in an introductory sociology course, or in another using the World Development Indicators to examine claims about globalization.[2] Such exercises are an essential step in training the novice social science researcher in using data from these influential studies but do not teach students the full range of data skills they will need to conduct their own research. The identification and location of datasets is glossed over in curricula that focus on statistical inference methods and software.

Empowering undergraduates to conduct their own quantitative data analysis is increasingly within librarians' reach considering the variety of downloadable data now available and the relative ease of use of the statistical packages included on many campus computers. Yet, librarians should be mindful that linking data novices to sources of data requires more than a technical solution. Unfortunately, we cannot just hook up the correct virtual pipes and let the data flow; simply providing access to data is not enough. Students must make a cognitive leap from analyzing a dataset provided to them to identifying and locating an appropriate dataset to answer a research question of their own.

Teaching this process in a classroom setting poses challenges that may not arise in the one-on-one reference encounter or research consultation. In a classroom, each student may have a different research question, making it difficult to anticipate the variety of specific challenges students may encounter. Partly this is because of the heterogeneous nature of datasets, which are presented in a variety of file formats and methods of access that complicate their use. Furthermore, data do not fit seamlessly into search tools developed around published scholarly materials, such as library catalogs, article indexes, and, most recently, discovery layers. While there are tools useful for finding data within certain disciplines—for example, Federal Reserve Economic Data (FRED) provides access to thousands of time-series datasets from many sources—they are nowhere near as comprehensive as bibliographic tools like WorldCat. When navigating the world of data, therefore, students must develop their own search strategies in order to make up for this deficiency in the available search tools.

In Search of a Data Literacy Pedagogy for Data Novices

The library literature is strangely silent on teaching undergraduate students the primary data literacy skills that advanced researchers and librarians themselves use to identify, locate, and evaluate statistics and datasets—abilities that are prerequisite for students becoming active participants in quantitative research. Instead, discussions of data literacy in librarianship tend to focus on either data reference skills for librarians or data management services designed for expert researchers. With regard to the former, the data reference literature supplies librarians with a wealth of data resources useful for answering reference questions and assisting researchers but usually assumes a central role for the librarian in identifying and providing access to data.[3] This approach may leave students in a passive, consumer role, relying on *librarians'* data literacy skills rather than developing their own abilities to identify and evaluate datasets. Alternatively, Kristin Partlo uses data reference as a teaching opportunity, helping to develop students' data literacy through modeling, structured worksheets, and dialogue to empower data novices in the learning process.[4]

The literature on data management, on the other hand, tends to focus on the needs of expert researchers who have already mastered the skills of data discovery and analysis. Librarians' involvement in data management has expanded beyond its original emphasis on science research and requirements for federal grants, but instruction and outreach in this area are largely based on the data information literacy competencies developed within this expert scientific context.[5] Most recently, Yasmeen Shorish has invited us to include undergraduates in our data management instruction but suggests we use the same curricula, modules, and outreach methods designed for advanced researchers.[6] This assumes undergraduates already possess the same basic data literacy skills we expect of expert researchers and may not account for disciplinary differences. In sum, there appears to be a pedagogical gap between data reference and data management services. Librarians and their social science faculty partners need to develop pedagogical strategies for teaching data novices the primary data literacy skills needed to thrive in quantitative social science research.

Librarians may find inspiration for a new pedagogy of data literacy from the scholarship of teaching and learning in two seemingly disparate disciplines. First, from the data-intensive field of statistics education, the work of Cobb and Moore suggests that before we ask data novices to identify and locate relevant datasets, we should first ensure that students have some experience with data analysis—the reverse order of operations typical of undergraduate research assignments. Cobb and Moore's data analysis will be familiar to information literacy librarians, as it focuses on asking questions about the data, critically examining the context of their collection and presentation, and developing hypotheses about the underlying phenomena the data describe.† Learning to interpret and critically evaluate existing data are easier skills than trying to operationalize abstract concepts into measurable variables and control for bias while designing an experiment or imagining data yet to be collected. Once students have learned to recognize the potential value and inherent limitations of any given dataset, they can then appreciate the need for careful design and collection techniques and be able to think ahead to their analytical needs when planning for and implementing a data collection project.[7]

A second inspiration for data literacy instruction comes from history education. Sam Wineburg studied the different ways in which experts (historians) and novices (students) read primary source texts, the most common data format in the humanities. The experts engaged this textual data critically, considering the author's purpose, intended audience, and historical context, while the students read for basic comprehension, as they had been taught to do in primary and secondary schools. Based on these findings, Wineburg called on history instructors to teach the analytical heuristics of historians, and more importantly, to apply these techniques to primary sources to promote the critical interpretation of history.[8] Mastering these techniques must almost certainly precede students' ability to imagine relevant primary source materials for a historical question (i.e., hypothesis) and then locate them on their own.

Both the statistical and historical pedagogies outlined here begin with what librarians will recognize as information literacy. While a librarian's experience, like a historian's, is most often with textual sources, numeric data files require the same critical evaluation as the products of scholarly and popular publishing. Further, disciplines fundamentally shape the data they analyze, as do the bureaucratic structures that frequently collect and disseminate data. The students' search for data will be incoherent without some idea of how and why data come into being; teaching about data, therefore, must counter what Ribes and Jackson call the "commodity fictions of data." Independent, skilled student researchers understand that data are not an undifferentiated resource ready to be tapped online, as the common phrase "raw data" may imply, but rather data are produced in scholarly and political contexts.[9] The lessons that follow aim to keep that relationship in the foreground.

Thus, with these pedagogical models to guide us, we present three lesson plans that we have used in one-shot library instruction sessions to help students develop their data literacy skills and make the transition from passive data consumers to creative data scholars. While the lessons were not developed as a sequence, and in fact have been used in different disciplines at three different universities, together they suggest a scaffolded approach. Lesson One introduces the value of secondary data analysis and data search skills through the more familiar search

---

† These analytical skills are not the same as statistical inference, which Cobb and Moore treat separately and are beyond the scope of this chapter.

for scholarly literature. Lesson Two adds critical evaluation to students' developing repertoire of data skills. Finally, Lesson Three challenges students to identify their own data needs to solve a research problem, an act of scholarly imagination that not only opens the door to more sophisticated secondary data analysis, but may also encourage expert research design practices and foster a readiness for data management services. Based on the needs and existing skills of any group of learners, these lessons can be adapted individually or in sequence to any librarian's local community in order to enhance the data skills of students in a wide range of disciplines.

Lesson One: Discovering Data through the Literature

Our first lesson was created for a sociology research methods class at Bates College that covers a range of methodologies, both quantitative and qualitative. In the year we describe here, the class focused on attitudes toward immigrants among receiving communities, and the library instruction aimed at introducing them to quantitative datasets in a general way. The session was not tied to a specific assignment in this course but was intended to get students thinking about how they might use quantitative datasets for their senior theses, which they are required to write the following year. The lesson accomplished this goal with an activity emphasizing the relationship between datasets and other scholarly literature. In short, students began with a bibliography of journal articles based on quantitative methods, then located the data on which the articles were based.

The lesson also had an ancillary goal, developed by the course instructor and the librarian with the larger learning outcomes of the course in mind, of socializing students in the use of secondary data. For some disciplines, such as economics, the necessity of using data collected for another purpose is relatively obvious. Most students will intuitively grasp that they cannot calculate a nation's gross domestic product themselves. While they may not be specifically familiar with the Bureau of Economic Analysis, it probably will not surprise them that they would have to obtain data from some other entity in order to analyze their topic. However, for disciplines such as sociology that commonly employ techniques such as the sample survey, it is entirely possible for students to collect their own data with tools like SurveyMonkey or Qualtrics. Designing and deploying a local survey is a great learning experience for students, but there are a few drawbacks, mainly that their samples are often limited to acquaintances, and thus their findings have limited generalizability. By instead using a nationally representative dataset collected for another purpose, often by a government agency or research center with far more extensive resources than an undergraduate could muster, students can learn a great deal about sample surveys by example. Unfortunately, some undergraduates may dismiss using someone else's dataset as less authentic than collecting their own. This lesson is intended to counter that notion by showing students that use of secondary data is a standard practice is sociology and other social sciences.

In this lesson, the librarian introduced secondary datasets by approaching the data search problem through the scholarly literature.† The lesson began with a demonstration using an assigned reading. Students had all read, prior to class, a literature review on attitudes toward immigration that is particularly rich in citations to quantitative studies. One of these citations, for Schildkraut's *Americanism in the 21st Century*,[10] was based on a nationally representative survey archived in ICPSR. The librarian demonstrated how to find the survey data in ICPSR and how to interpret the ICPSR study description page and all the important information found there, including study methods, universe, variables, and means of access. At this time, the librarian facilitated a discussion on the advantages and pitfalls of secondary data, including issues of data access and confidentiality, sample size, timeliness, and generalizability of findings.

Next, pairs of students each received a different citation taken from the bibliography of the literature review, all of which were based on quantitative data archived in ICPSR. The librarian challenged them to find the dataset analyzed by the cited article using ICPSR's Bibliography of Data-Related Literature. Once they had found the dataset, students were asked to determine the following information relevant to evaluating the dataset for potential use, and then share their findings with the group:

- What is the universe of the study?
- When were the data collected?
- Are there any restrictions on accessing the data?
- Which variables are related to immigration?

Though some students struggled with the specialized vocabulary of survey methodology, they were all able to quickly locate the data, reinforcing the connection between published research and the data that underlie it.

This exercise was intended to model the experience of entering a topic through an extensive literature review or bibliography, identifying the key datasets related to the topic, and considering how these datasets might be used in their own research, potentially opening up possibilities for when they tackle their own senior theses. While this lesson's focus on existing data risked encouraging what Schrodt describes in "Seven Deadly Sins of Contemporary Quantitative Political Analysis" as "sloth" (reanalyzing over-used datasets again and again instead of seeking out novel or emerging sources of data),[11] for data novices, secondary data analysis provides a valuable opportunity to learn how experts structure and use data, enhancing the sophistication of undergraduate research.

---

† This is an adaptation of a lesson plan created by Rachel Barlow and available via ICPSR, called Exploring Data through the Research Literature (http://www.icpsr.umich.edu/icpsrweb/instructors/edrl/index.jsp).

Lesson Two: Evaluating Datasets

Our second lesson was designed to support an introductory demography course at the University of Pennsylvania in which students, for their final paper, were asked to analyze data of their own choosing. Because the students had varying levels of quantitative ability—some had taken statistics, some struggled with constructing tables and charts—the actual analysis could be more or less sophisticated, but they were all required to locate relevant data and use them in support of an argument, even if it was only to make an illustrative cross-tabulation. Because students had to choose their own datasets out of a pool of potential datasets vaster and more varied than can be introduced in a single session, the librarian's goal was to teach students strategies for locating data as well as for evaluating and understanding them. In this lesson, the entrée to the data was not the scholarly literature, but rather the sources of data, often government bureaucracies and intergovernmental organizations (IGOs) in this discipline.

To begin the discussion, the librarian asked students to imagine themselves as researchers in search of data to answer a research question, which they would in fact become by the end of the semester. As a data search strategy, they were instructed to ask of their topic, who cares? In other words, which organizations care enough about this topic to collect data about it, as well as have the not-insignificant resources and authority to do so? Students were encouraged to think of government agencies, national statistical offices, and intergovernmental organizations that frequently collect and disseminate population data.

After this discussion, the bulk of the class time was devoted to an activity examining actual data available online from the IGOs and governments discussed above. In a way, the direction is flipped compared with the previous lesson. Instead of progressing from a research question to a data source, the students were given a data source and asked to devise possible questions that could be asked of it. Small groups of students were given an information sheet on a potentially useful dataset from a government agency or IGO, such as the World Bank World Development Indicators, the World Health Organization Global Health Observatory, or the National Center for Health Statistics CDC Wonder. All of the datasets have some mechanism for exploring and analyzing the data online without having to download large, complex files. The information sheet included a URL and a set of questions for students to investigate by visiting the website for the data and exploring the documentation. These questions included:

- How do you describe what data are available?
- What trends, health disparities, or spatial patterns could you investigate using these data?
- Why do you think these data were collected by this organization?

The class session concluded with a group discussion of their findings. Because each dataset had been assigned to more than one group, students were able to comment on and enlarge upon each other's observations. During the discussion, the librarian redirected the students to the data documentation in response to vague or uncertain responses, underlining the importance of thoroughly understanding the dataset before analysis.

In this activity, students were given some ideas about likely data producers and directed to a selection of commonly used demographic datasets, but those students who did not choose to use these selected datasets in their projects had to make the leap themselves between their topics and other potential sources of data. In these instances, students were encouraged to seek out an in-depth consultation so the librarian could assist them. However, by requiring students to consider potential data sources and explore what data are available, the assignment positioned the students to better formulate research questions, identify data, and carry out an analysis.

Lesson Three: Operationalization

Our last sample lesson was designed for a research analysis class in sociology at Tulane University. Students in this course learn the basics of statistical inference, from simple hypothesis testing to linear regression models, and they often use prepackaged data from the *General Social Survey* and SPSS statistical software to practice these techniques. For the final project, however, students must develop a research proposal that uses existing quantitative data to test a hypothesis relevant to sociology. Students are free to select any dataset so long as it is both accessible to them and appropriate to the research question. In support of this goal, the librarian collaborated with the instructors to create a library instruction session that would teach students how to first break down their research questions into measurable variables and then to identify potential sources of the desired data.

The library session began with an open discussion about the collectors and disseminators of data that might be of use to sociologists. When asked, students considered the questions of who collects data and whether or not they make their data available to the public. Students in this class have already had at least three other sociology courses, so they were generally able to identify government agencies, NGOs, scholars, and private businesses as the typical collectors of data. After a group discussion on why each entity might collect data, the librarian asked students to imagine whether or not these data would be made available to a wider audience, including themselves. Students described a wide spectrum of data sharing or sequestering motives, from government agencies who are often required to share information with citizens except when individual privacy or national security are at stake, to private businesses which likely collect data to support the profit-making endeavor and would prefer to keep this information hidden from potential competitors.

With the class primed to consider the array of potential data collectors and disseminators, the librarian moved to the more challenging learning objective, the ability to identify measurable variables that will illuminate a given research question, commonly known as operationalization. Gerhan offers librarians some guidance on how to operationalize a question received at the reference desk, and while he hints at ways to engage the user in the process through the reference interview, his focus is primarily on the librarian's ability to deliver a data source deemed appropriate for the user.[12] His advice, however, is readily adaptable to a classroom setting, and with a well-chosen active learning method, students can learn to operationalize problems themselves. Students should also understand that there is no one correct way to operationalize a problem. Different approaches to measuring a phenomenon are often at the heart of scholarly debates, and learning to operationalize is an important skill for students to be able to gather evidence and contribute their own ideas to these conversations.

With the sociology students at Tulane, the librarian provided a sample research question that had been a topic of discussion in the local news: gentrification. To practice operationalizing this phenomenon, the librarian invited students to work in groups and come up with a list of measurable variables that could be used to study the extent and nature of gentrification in New Orleans, Louisiana. After allowing for adequate time, during which the librarian and the course instructor circulated to provide support as needed and noted how students' teamwork supported each other's learning, the groups shared their variables with the class while the librarian compiled a master list on the board. Students successfully identified the standard demographic variables that could be used to measure gentrification, as well as other indicators such as changing housing values, the types of businesses in a neighborhood, and, as a humorous suggestion, the number of hipsters that could be observed over a given period of time. The librarian suggested that the classification of hipster would also need to be operationalized.

With a list of variables on the board, the librarian asked students to connect each variable with a potential source, recalling the discussion that opened the library session. Most of the demographic information was correctly associated with government sources, in particular the U.S. Census. For housing values, which the Census only provides in aggregate by tract or block group, students suggested the real estate industry for more granular data, although this presented a problem of accessibility. With guidance, the students eventually noted that the city government would need the value of individual homes in order to assess and collect property taxes, and the librarian was happy to demonstrate the city government website that provides this information.

The remainder of the library session was given over to students to work on their own research projects, during which the librarian and instructor circulated to provide support as students attempted operationalizing on their own. Students were also encouraged to refer back to the relevant scholarly literature on their topic when they struggled to identify a relevant data source—a reminder of skills students learned in a pre-requisite course, but also reminiscent of the first lesson plan discussed in this chapter. Based on observations during the library session and students' responses to a one-minute paper asking what they had learned in the session, it appeared that students seemed to grasp the concept of operationalization, and many were successful in identifying relevant variables for their projects. This was then confirmed by follow-up conversations with the instructor on how well students integrated the lesson into their subsequent class discussions, and by students' final projects, which mostly demonstrated successful attempts at operationalizing their research questions.

Conclusion

The three lesson plans offered here represent our efforts to support students as they make the often difficult transition from data consumer to data scholar. By juxtaposing the information skills of our data novices with the expert practices of social science researchers, we identified the range of abilities and dispositions students needed to develop and created learning experiences focused on those areas, data discovery and evaluation in particular. This pedagogical approach seems to have anticipated the Association of College & Research Libraries' new *Framework for Information Literacy in Higher Education*, the early drafts of which were released while we were testing these lesson plans in the classroom. Each "frame" under this new rubric for information literacy outlines the knowledge practices and dispositions of information experts. Librarians in their local contexts are afforded the flexibility to develop learning objectives and teaching strategies most appropriate to their learners and institutions.[13] Additionally, as demonstrated here, the *Framework* can be adapted to particular disciplinary practices and specialized forms of information.

In Lesson One, we used the scholarly literature to show students how researchers often use existing datasets to explore a variety of research questions. Opening students to the possibilities of secondary data analysis in their own research not only models the modes of inquiry common to social science research, but also reinforces the notion of quantitative scholarship as a collaborative endeavor, suggestive of the conversational metaphor of the ACRL *Framework*. In Lesson Two we focused on the evaluation of datasets, considering the authoritative sources of data relevant to the social sciences and the resources necessary to collect data about large populations. While seemingly simple, the evaluation of existing data engages with multiple frames of information literacy, including the nature of authority, the processes by which datasets are created, and the value datasets carry in the cost of their creation and dissemination and in their utility to myriad research questions. Finally, in Lesson Three we asked students to more fully engage in research as inquiry, challenging them to transform their questions into executable research projects. Each of these three lessons engages with some or all of the frames under the new ACRL *Framework for Information Literacy for Higher Education* to assist students in their development of expert research practices in the social sciences. Librarians are well suited to tackle this task by taking the best practices of data reference services and translating them into the library classroom through sound pedagogy, collaboration with faculty, and a bit of creativity. By harnessing the increasing number of datasets available to students in their library collections and for free online, librarians can help students gain confidence with numeric information sources, build their information literacy and analytical skills, and take an active role in the scholarly enterprise.

---

1. Inter-university Consortium for Political and Social Research, "Data-Driven Learning Guides," *ICPSR Resources for Instructors*, accessed April 25, 2015, https://www.icpsr.umich.edu/icpsrweb/instructors/biblio/resources.
2. Amy M. Burdette and Kerry McLoughlin, "Using Census Data in the Classroom to Increase Quantitative Literacy and Promote Critical Sociological Thinking," *Teaching Sociology* 38, no. 3 (2010): 247–57; Bhavani Arabandi, Stephen Sweet, and Alicia Swords, "Testing the Flat World Thesis: Using a Public Dataset to Engage Students in the Global Inequality Debate," *Teaching Sociology* 42, no. 4 (2014): 267–76.
3. Popular textbooks for reference courses in library school often include a section on government statistical sources. See, for example, Richard E Bopp and Linda C Smith, *Reference and Information Services: An Introduction* (Santa Barbara, Calif.: Libraries Unlimited, 2011). For an excellent source specific to statistics and data, see Lynda M. Kellam and Katharin Peter, *Numeric Data Services and Sources for the General Reference Librarian*, Chandos Information Professional Series (Oxford: Chandos Publishing, 2011). See also, David R. Gerhan, "When Quantitative Analysis Lies behind a Reference Question," *Reference & User Services Quarterly* 39, no. 2 (1999): 166–76; Elizabeth Stephenson and Patti Schifter Caravello, "Incorporating Data Literacy into Undergraduate Information Literacy Programs in the Social Sciences: A Pilot Project," *Reference Services Review* 35, no. 4 (November 13, 2007): 525–40, doi:10.1108/00907320710838354; Karen Hogenboom, Carissa M. Holler Phillips, and Merinda Hensley, "Show Me the Data! Partnering with Instructors to Teach Data Literacy," in *Declaration of Interdependence: The Proceedings of the ACRL 2011 Conference, March 30–April 2, 2011, Philadelphia, PA* (ACRL 2011, Philadelphia, PA: Association of College and Research Libraries, 2011), 410–17, http://www.ala.org/acrl/conferences/confsandpreconfs/national/acrl2011papers.
4. Kristin Partlo, "The Pedagogical Data Reference Interview," *IASSIST Quarterly* 33/34, no. 4/1 (2009): 6–10.
5. Javier Calzada Prado and Miguel Ángel Marzal, "Incorporating Data Literacy into Information Literacy Programs: Core Competencies and Contents," *Libri: International Journal of Libraries & Information Services* 63, no. 2 (June 2013): 123–34, doi:10.1515/libri-2013-0010; Jacob Carlson, Michael Fosmire, C. C. Miller, and Megan Sapp Nelson, "Determining Data Information Literacy Needs: A Study of Students and Research Faculty," *Portal: Libraries and the Academy* 11, no. 2 (2011): 629–57, doi:10.1353/pla.2011.0022; Jian Qin and John D'Ignazio, "The Central Role of Metadata in a Science Data Literacy Course," *Journal of Library Metadata* 10, no. 2–3 (2010): 188–204.
6. Yasmeen Shorish, "Data Information Literacy and Undergraduates: A Critical Competency," *College & Undergraduate Libraries* 22, no. 1 (January 2, 2015): 97–106, doi:10.1080/10691316.2015.1001246. The data management instruction designed specifically for undergraduates is described in Richard Ball and Norm Medeiros, "Teaching Integrity in Empirical Research: A Protocol for Documenting Data Management and Analysis," *The Journal of Economic Education* 43, no. 2 (April 1, 2012): 182–89, doi:10.1080/00220485.2012.659647.

7. George W. Cobb and David S. Moore, "Mathematics, Statistics, and Teaching," *The American Mathematical Monthly* 104, no. 9 (November 1, 1997): 815–16, doi:10.2307/2975286.
8. Samuel S. Wineburg, *Historical Thinking and Other Unnatural Acts: Charting the Future of Teaching the Past*, Critical Perspectives on the Past (Philadelphia: Temple University Press, 2001), 63–88.
9. David Ribes and Steven J. Jackson, "Data Bite Man: The Work of Sustaining a Long-Term Study," in *Raw Data Is an Oxymoron*, ed. Lisa Gitelman (Cambridge, Massachusetts: MIT Press, 2013), 147–66.
10. Deborah Jill Schildkraut, *Americanism in the Twenty-First Century : Public Opinion in the Age of Immigration* (New York: Cambridge University Press, 2011).
11. Philip A. Schrodt, "Seven Deadly Sins of Contemporary Quantitative Political Analysis," *Journal of Peace Research* 51, no. 2 (March 1, 2014): 287–300, doi:10.1177/0022343313499597.
12. Gerhan, "When Quantitative Analysis Lies behind a Reference Question."
13. Association of College & Research Libraries, "Framework for Information Literacy for Higher Education," 2015, http://www.ala.org/acrl/standards/ilframework.

CHAPTER 7

Technical Data Skills for Reproducible Research

Harrison Dekker and Paula Lackie

> *The fact that raw data is rarely usable for analysis without significant work is a point I try hard to make with my students. I told them "do not underestimate the difficulty of data preparation." When they turned in their projects, many of them reported that they had underestimated the difficulty of data preparation.*
>
> *~ David Mimno, Assistant Professor, Computer and Information Science, Cornell University.*[1]

STATISTICIANS NICHOLAS HORTON, Benjamin Baumer, and Hadley Wickham state that "statistical educators play a key role in helping to prepare the next generation of statisticians and data scientists," but "there are barriers and time costs to the introduction of reproducible analysis tools and more sophisticated data-management and -manipulation skills to our courses."[2] The time-consuming nature of data preparation, a precursor to reproducible research, is not just an issue in the introductory curriculum. Professional data scientists also report "spending most of their time … turning data into a usable form rather than looking for insights."[3] Given their research experience and the allocation of precious time and attention in courses, it is not surprising that faculty members are wary of losing focus on the richness of the analytic process by diving too deeply into the time-consuming and distracting processes of data preparation. However, this avoidance undervalues the benefits of understanding the unique characteristics of the data before jumping into the analysis stage. As a result, novice researchers rarely have a chance to systematically learn about the essentials of data preparation before they are faced with applying the necessary principles in their own research.

While one traditional role for data librarians is to assist researchers by collecting, locating, and recommending appropriate data resources, the data service provider (often a data librarian with additional technical data experience) can offer equally important services to help researchers bridge the gap between acquiring and analyzing their data. These data professionals must field a wide range of research questions and a wider range of data analysis and formatting issues with the ultimate goal of reinforcing reproducible research practices. Filling this niche can be especially rewarding, largely due to the high degree of creative problem solving that it requires.

A fundamental characteristic of the technical data preparation component of data services is that unlike statistical methodology, which lends itself to traditional instructional methods (i.e., in which foundational skills are taught and new ones progressively layered on, thus gradually building the researcher's set of tools), the ability to "wrangle"† well develops more organically. As in the maxim "that which doesn't kill you, makes you stronger," data preparation skills are strengthened as the wrangler grapples with a wider range of "messy" data problems.

As data services providers, we frequently observe one common source of messy data: idiosyncratic data management practices. With experience we can anticipate when and how these unique data preparation processes will become problematic for researchers and alert them to these probabilities. Since "reproducibility is collaboration with people you don't know, including yourself next week,"[4] getting researchers started early with best practices facilitates the diffusion of reproducible research practices.

To develop best practices, novices generally need to learn from experts. In this case, because the norms of record keeping (i.e., documentation) are often not taught in the curriculum, data services professionals with expert knowledge will find themselves in that sweet spot in what Everett Rogers calls "the diffusion of innovations," the place in the cycle also known as the "take off point" where change agents have the greatest impact on the adoption rate of an innovation.[5]

Data services professionals can increase the adoption rate for conducting reproducible research by modeling best practices and filling the data preparation instruction gap.

So what are these best practices? And how can they be classified? In short, they represent a systematic approach to managing and documenting all components of the research process such that a project may be set down by one researcher and picked up by another, who will not only be able to make sense of it but also be

† With the dramatic pace of development in data science, the vocabulary surrounding it has not yet settled and several terms relate to overlapping aspects of the work. Data wrangling here refers to the gathering and managing of disparate data sources and file types, but it can also include wrangling individual variables. Data science is the whole set of skills necessary to extract knowledge from data, usually from disparate sources.

able to completely replicate the scholarship as presented.[‡] These principles need to be applied to all stages throughout the entire lifecycle of that research. To itemize best practices, we can look at an ideal, generic research project and separate it into stages. At each of these stages and for all layers of the work there needs to be the following basic best practices components: 1) metadata and other documentation; 2) file naming and format consistency; and 3) a deliberate strategy for organizing and backing up files.

The Basics of Best Practices

We begin with **metadata and other documentation**: the plain language description of where all data resources and specific variables came from and what they mean. It is important that this information be gathered as, or if possible before, the data are collected. This includes the proper, full citations for each data resource (especially in secondary research) as well as any related details about the variables. Although this step is basic, novice researchers eager to get into the analysis stage often overlook it as superfluous. It is not until they need to describe their datasets and provide adequate citations in their research papers that novices realize how difficult, time consuming, and sometimes impossible it is to compile this information after the fact. In practice, this process is similar to managing standard footnotes and bibliographies in traditional research as references are collected and used, but novices do not know to apply these techniques to working with data. For the data support professional, advising on these forms of documentation in a timely fashion is the easiest and most basic step in supporting researchers working with data.

Additional documentation can be in readme[§] files, comments and annotations in code files, and ideally, in an additional project research journal. A research journal is a simple record of potential hypotheses with initial justifications, thoughts about primary or secondary resources, and a place to track search strategies. The journal helps a researcher to discover the aspects of her research that she does not yet understand. It is especially useful for novice researchers to maintain a research journal in which they track their progress in language that is meaningful to them. For faculty working with research assistants, reviewing the research journal can lead to cleaner and more rapid uptake by assistants new to the project. As novices mature through their research project and practice as researchers in general, they

‡ Because of the increase in service demands on faculty is often correlated with a degradation in their research time, the person most likely to pick up where they left off is themselves, sometimes after years of hiatus. Changes in demands on faculty should be a powerful motivator for adopting best practices in reproducible research over less-documented idiosyncratic research processes.

§ By convention, a readme file is a small documentation file describing the contents of other files in the same directory or project and assigned a name like README.txt, READ.ME, README.1ST, etc.

will develop the expertise to recognize which aspects are most useful to record and in the associated expert vocabulary.

Next is clarity and consistency in **file naming conventions and formats.**[6] Naming a file *Final* is rarely accurate or useful; a better choice would be *TITLE_*submitted_to_*X*_on_*DATE.pdf.*[†] The same is true for writing code; Data.sps is not as useful as Merge_code_for_NES2012to14_12June2015.sps. Meaningful file names are another form of metadata useful to the original researcher or others attempting to make sense of a project at some later point in time, particularly when files have been moved out of the context in which they were created.

There also needs to be clarity and consistency in **file organization** (e.g., box.com or a local drive for working copies), and only one location (with verified backups) for the authoritative version. We are particularly fond of Git and GitHub for documentation, code, and sometimes even the papers.[‡] Being diligent about following through with documented file locations is especially important when working in groups.

The last component is a **backup strategy**, to recover from immediate file corruption with minimal loss of work time, as well as file snapshots, to allow for the ability to backtrack in a process and recover some specific content that had been removed. Ideally this strategy will include a definition of when these materials may be safely discarded as well. Note that some services provide a file recovery option, but these are not infallible. For instance, with a free Dropbox account, if an error occurs but is not noticed within the 90-day recovery window (e.g., from one term break to the next) it is not possible to use that avenue for file recovery. In another example, with Google Drive it is important that the Principal Investigator retain full ownership and not just editing ability for all related files. Research assistants come and go, and if a Google account is deleted, there is no way to recover any Google Drive files that person *owned.*

Advanced Best Practices: Working with Code Files

The premise behind these best practices for file management and documentation apply when working within code files as well. We recommend that novices especially comment (i.e., annotate) *in plain language* within the code file what the code does, what inputs are required, when the code was written, and by whom the code was written. Explaining what it is they are writing in code will facilitate their own reuse as well as contribute to the process of learning to code and to conduct repro-

---

† For milestone versions of the research and outcomes the files should be in at least two formats: PDF and the format of the editable version.

‡ Note that best practice for the data file/s involve one additional step, storing a read-only copy of original data files before any cleaning or transformation steps have taken place.

ducible research. In addition to commenting, it is also good practice for users to become aware of the style guides for each code language.[7]

> *Good style is important because while your code only has one author, it will usually have multiple readers, and when you know you will be working with multiple people on the same code, it's a good idea to agree on a common style up-front.*
>
> ~ Hadley Wickham, Chief Scientist at RStudio, Inc.[8]

These sorts of practices are a few of what some, like author Scott Long, call *data workflow practices.*[9] The ability to develop and apply good workflow is contingent on a variety of factors. For one, researchers must follow a set of best practices like those outlined earlier, which allow them to record as much of their data manipulation and analysis processes as possible. Writing well-annotated code files (as opposed to utilizing only a click-based interface) is the most efficient way to document the research process. For another, it is critical that researchers see these skills within the larger context of an overall ethos of reproducibility. Data service professionals can reinforce the ethos by reminding researchers that will benefit from reproducible practices. The immediate benefits will be measurable in terms of improvements to their productivity, for instance by making it possible to reconstruct the logic of a past data workflow. Additionally, researchers can be reminded that a possible long term benefit of reproducible practices is an improvement to their academic reputation because these practices facilitate replication of their work by others. Working with reproducibility in mind addresses directly the replication crisis in social science research.

Mitigating the Replication Crisis through Use of Best Practices

---

> *There is a replication crisis throughout research. When subjected to independent scrutiny, results routinely fail to stand up. We are starting to accept that there will always be glitches and flaws. Slowly, as a consequence, the culture of science is shifting beneath everyone's feet to recognize this reality, work with it, and create structural changes or funding models to improve it.*
>
> ~ Ben Goldacre, Senior Clinical Research Fellow, University of Oxford.[10]

While there is alarm over the "replication crisis" in research, this has encouraged pragmatists into action. Some of this has been facilitated in the United States by the addition of required data management planning or data sharing for certain federal grants and academic publishers as well as widespread training activities initiated by leading research data archives and professional associations worldwide.† On the curricular level, efforts like the Teaching Integrity in Empirical Research (TIER) project at Haverford College freely provide their curricular protocols for a thorough approach in training for "complete replicability."[11] As is noted on the TIER website:

> The guiding principle is that the information included in the documentation of a statistical study should be complete and transparent enough to allow an interested third party to easily and exactly reproduce all the steps of data management and analysis that led from the original data files to the results reported in the paper. By contrast, among most academic journals that maintain on-line repositories of documentation for the empirical studies they publish, the requirement is just that authors submit the processed data (after cleaning, merging, etc.) used for analysis, and computer code with commands that generate the results in the paper from the processed data. This standard of "partial replicability" leaves the steps needed to transform the original data files into the files used for analysis entirely undocumented.[12]

The TIER research framework is broadly useful both as a guide for students as well as a framework for developing curricular support materials by faculty or data support professionals. The main elements of the documentation specified by the TIER protocol include:

- **Keep a read-only copy of all the original data** files in from which any data used in the study were extracted. In some cases, it is necessary also to save metadata with coding or other information explaining how to interpret the data in the original files.
- **Maintain metadata files** containing additional information a user would need to understand the data, such as variable definitions, units of measurement, coding schemes, and sampling methods.
- **Provide all commented command files** (i.e., code) necessary to construct the final dataset(s) used for analysis, and finally to generate all the statistical results—the numbers reported in text, tables and figures—

† Join the international organization *IASSIST Data* to tap into this robust and growing community. (http://iassistdata.org).

presented in the paper. These files will include all the original instructions needed to both access the data in the original files and process it as necessary (cleaning, merging, defining new variables, etc.). Also include a readme file that gives instructions for using the data and command files to replicate the results reported in the paper.‡

While basic, these steps are rarely practiced. There are rational reasons for this. The researcher may be unclear on the utility of documentation or code for her own use or underestimate the amount of trial and error effort necessary to complete the data preparation process. These tendencies to skip documentation steps in the service of expediency provide another opportunity for timely intervention by a data service professional.

It is common for novices not to realize how frequently data preparation steps must be re-done due to data changes or discovered problems. In other cases, they are new to the conventions of coding and do not realize the ease with which commands can be saved and reused. This problem is compounded when in their preparatory courses they choose use a spreadsheet package for analysis or a statistics package that steers them towards menu driven operations. Reproducibility is hindered by the immediacy of less technical "simplified" but opaque processes.

Technical Components of Data Preparation

To provide basic technical assistance, a data services professional should be familiar enough with the common components of technical documentation to interpret and explain to a researcher. For novice researchers or more experienced ones who are expanding their research to unfamiliar domains, the expertise of a librarian who has experience with a broad range of documentation can be critical in determining whether they will be able to use a particular dataset. On a more technical level, this documentation is often essential for understanding what steps are needed to process the data in a statistical package.

In the social sciences, an example of technical documentation that almost always accompanies a published dataset is the statistical codebook. The lack of stan-

‡ Corporate software trademark rules as well as open source logic generally reinforce the best practice of including notation that indicates precisely which version of which software, with which add-ons, produced the results (e.g. "the suggested citation for the Stata 14 software is StataCorp. 2015. Stata Statistical Software: Release 14. College Station, TX: StataCorp LP." http://www.stata.com/support/faqs/resources/citing-software-documentation-faqs/). Some academic communities include code for citing the specific versions and packages used in the analysis. See, for example: http://astrostatistics.psu.edu/su07/R/html/utils/html/citation.html. Details about the software used are integral to complete replicability.

dardization in layout and content can make codebook interpretation a challenge for both novice and experienced researchers. Still, a codebook can generally be relied upon to provide standalone documentation of such technical details as the layout, structure and content of a dataset. In terms of subject matter, the codebook can provide critical information such as whether it is a sample or population; a list of variable names and labels; the values assigned to categorical variables and the corresponding value labels (e.g. 1 = "Male," 2 = "Female"); and how missing values are represented. All of these are important when using the data in a statistical software package. Codebooks may also contain other types of information of importance to researchers. For instance, in survey research, the codebook will usually contain the original text of the survey questions as well as details on how the survey was conducted and the sampling methodology employed. A codebook often includes a data dictionary, a kind of census of the basic elements of the data file (or files in a database). This includes the basic characteristics of each variable, the relationships to other variables (often called "fields" in programming), and their format.

The following example taken from the 1993 *Indonesian Family Life Survey*[13] demonstrates some of the challenges inherent in codebook interpretation (see Figure 7.1). The excerpt at first glance may seem cryptic, but it contains critical details about the file layout. Without this information (or an accompanying complete script file in an accessible code language), the original data are useless.

Figure 7.1. Codebook Example

```
-----------------------------------------------------------------------------
Variable  Loca  Len   Deci  For   Class  Variable Label
Name      tion  gth   mals  mat          Value    Label
-----------------------------------------------------------------------------
AR22       188    2     0     N      S   PRIMARY ACTVTY DURING PAST WEEK
                                         values:  value  label
                                                      1  WORKING/EARNING INCO
                                                      2  JOB SEARCHING
                                                      3  ATTENDING SCHOOL
                                                      4  HOUSEKEEPING
                                                      5  RETIRED
                                                      6  OTHER, SPECIFY

                                         ranges:  lower    upper
                                                      1        6
                                                     96       99
```

- In the first column is the Variable Name (AR22), which serves as a unique identifier for this set of information in the dataset. The variable name is the key to finding and using these data after the dataset has been successfully loaded into a statistics package and for locating other relevant metadata in the codebook or other documentation sources.†

† Note that clever novices will soon learn to modify the variable names to suit their work, but it is wise practice to retain the originally assigned variable name so that it can be tracked throughout the codebook and other documentation. It is also helpful for reproducibility.

- The second, third, and fourth columns (Location, Length, and Decimals), provide important metadata about the actual layout of this variable in the original data file. In this case, the original data file is in a *fixed width* format. The location (188 characters from the left), length (2 characters wide) and decimal field (no decimal places) are essential for writing code to import (or to read) the variable into a statistical package. This is because in a fixed width file, there is nothing in the file to delimit (separate) each variable from the next within the original data, which may include numbers or text.
- The fifth column (Format) tells us that the variable is intended to be numeric (N), so if we find any non-numeric character in this variable, there is a problem with the file that needs to be sorted out before any useful analysis may be started.
- The sixth column (CLASS) is a variable that only has relevance to the program used to prepare the dataset and is irrelevant to most analysis, a detail documented elsewhere in the codebook.
- The seventh and eighth columns (Variable Label and Value Label) do not follow the pattern set in the previous columns and instead stack the information horizontally: Variable Label = "PRIMARY ACTIVITY DURING PAST WEEK" and value label = the plain text explanation for what each assigned value means (e.g. 1 = WORKING/EARNING INCO). It may be helpful to note that formatting issues like this are not unusual.

Although all of the information has utility, the variable label is the portion in which the researcher is most interested. It provides a longer description of the variable than the Variable Name, which in this example actually provides no descriptive information. Most statistical software packages allow the variable label and the equally important value labels to be stored and associated with a specific variable name when the dataset is saved in the native format of that package. Importantly, without a dataset saved in native format and without a script for assigning this information to the data set, the codebook is the only source for assigning meaning to the numbers.[‡]

Providing assistance with codebook interpretation is an experience that all data librarians are likely to encounter given the popularity of data archives like the Inter-university Consortium for Political and Social Research (ICPSR) and the UK Data Archive, which bundle codebooks with virtually all their published datasets.[14] One bad habit that a service provider should be mindful of is the tendency of researchers to completely bypass the codebook, like most of us bypass software

‡ Often there is an associated "data dictionary" as well. The standards as to what each of these metadata resources provide are inconsistently followed and/or differ among communities of practice.

manuals, and expect to "open the file" and be able to ascertain by "looking at the data" whether it will be suitable for their analysis. A timely intervention in this scenario is another opportunity to teach basic documentation reading skills and simultaneously assess the researcher's level of expertise and future need for assistance.

Another common and potentially more challenging interaction for data professionals comes when a researcher requires assistance with data acquired from a less curated source where the documentation is not as neatly bundled with the data. Examples of these are acquisition of under-documented data from another researcher or from online databases such as *Social Explorer*, *World Development Indicators* or *Datastream*. These latter systems allow a researcher to extract particular variables and other subsets from a large database system through a user-friendly interface. To a certain extent, these systems eliminate the need for some types of technical documentation, such as file structure characteristics. The extracted data are typically saved in a spreadsheet or comma-delimited format and thus easy to open and inspect in a familiar software package like Microsoft Excel. But it is not uncommon to encounter situations requiring more documentation in order to, for instance, answer questions about the source of the data or interpret certain variables. This type of "metadata sleuthing" will be familiar territory for an experienced librarian.

It is tempting to think that once a researcher has her data "in hand" and has sufficient documentation to enable its use, the data professional's job is done. In practice, the opposite is often the case; the creative work of data preparation has just begun and so has the potential need for assistance. Following are descriptions of useful technical skill areas for supporting researchers working with data. When providing this type of assistance, it is important that data professionals resist the urge to prepare the data for the researchers and consider the long-term value of educating researchers about reproducible practices by assisting them in doing this work themselves.

To this end, particular emphasis should be placed on writing code. Researchers should be encouraged to learn to use commands, rather than relying solely on graphical user interfaces, to perform data preparation and analysis. All the major statistical software packages, namely SAS, SPSS, Stata, and R, allow or require the use of commands. To promote reproducibility, all commands used to accomplish a task or a series of tasks should be saved in a file, (or *script*), which can then be processed by the statistical software package. Each package has its own command language, and while becoming proficient enough to provide assistance in multiple languages may seem a daunting task at first, by focusing on a narrow set of the most commonly used skills—like the ones outlined below—and by identifying useful sources of help, it is a surprisingly achievable goal.

Conversion

It is common practice for data archives, such as ICPSR, to distribute data in multiple formats. The most basic is an archival format (like ASCII) provided with a script for loading (i.e., *opening*, or *reading*) the file into their preferred software. Data archives may also provide the data in any number of statistical package formats, making it easy for researchers to simply open the file in the package of their choosing. This, however, is the best-case scenario. In other cases the researcher's data may be provided with appropriate metadata, but the data file is in a format that is incompatible with the required analysis software. There are as many variations to this problem as there are file types, so it is not possible to provide a comprehensive set of solutions here.

Most conversion issues can be solved by using the Stat/Transfer software package. This extremely flexible and simple application should be available to every data services professional and is relatively inexpensive. There are no clear open source alternatives, although open source programming languages often used for data wrangling, like R, Python, and Perl, have the capability of opening and processing a wide range of file formats. This type of solution requires the user to know how to write code, which even with these skills will take significantly longer than Stat/Transfer.

While software tools are an important aspect for data conversion, another equally important aspect is knowledge of various file formats. Novice users often routinely open files by double clicking them. This approach typically works only when a file is saved in a proprietary format, the software in question is loaded on the machine, and file associations are set up correctly, which may not be the case for obscure data formats. Therefore, a fundamental concept to teach users is to open data files from the application menus, or better still, from commands or a command script written in the language used by the statistics package.

In summary, when a user asks for assistance with file conversion, the initial assumption should not be that they will need to use a separate application to do the job. Generally, the file extension identifies whether it belongs to a known proprietary software. If the extension is unfamiliar, an online resource like the Wikipedia "List of file formats" page (https://en.wikipedia.org/wiki/List_of_file_formats) should help identify the software with which it can be opened. If it is not an identified format, a next step is to try to open the file with a programming text editor like Sublime or Textmate, or to view the first few lines with a command line utility like "head" or "less" on a Mac or Linux machine or "more" on Windows. When the associated documentation fails it is often possible to discern the format of the data (assuming that it is not in an unreadable binary format) by looking for clues in the file itself. Another approach is to examine accompanying script files, to sort out any codebook-like information such as variable names and datatypes.

Importing

As indicated above, importing data is sometimes an alternative to converting data. Generally speaking, importing data into a statistical package means that the data are being read from a format other than the package's native format. Virtually all statistical software can import (*or read*) data from standard text formats like comma delimited or fixed width,† and many include the ability to import data saved in the native format of some other statistical packages.

The import process is often managed via a wizard, in packages using a graphical user interface, or via scripted commands. Scripted import commands often require the user to specify various command options. For instance, an import command usually has a way to specify that the first line of the data file contains variable names, or that the file should be read starting from a line other than the first one. Reading the documentation is the key to understanding the various options available and how to use them. Inspecting the contents of a file with a programming editor or command line tool before trying to import it is another best practice, especially when the file is assumed to be in ASCII format.

The code-approach to importing data is preferred for several reasons: it nudges a user towards a replicable workflow; it facilitates her own record keeping; and it helps her understand the workings of the research process. If a file is opened via code which is then saved to a research process directory, there is an exact record of which file was opened, where it was saved, and what command parameters were required to open the data file.

One last best practice with importing data worth mentioning is *patience*; depending on file size and other factors, the initial import of a file can take anywhere from several seconds to several hours. Data users will sometimes report that they attempted to load a large file and it "crashed" their computer. It is important to ascertain details like the amount of system memory (RAM) available, the size of the file, and whether the software they were using has any file size restrictions in order to rule out the possibility that they simply did not wait long enough.

Validation

Once the data file is in place it is time to look at the individual variables. Since it is common for data services professionals to provide assistance to novice users who are loading a dataset for the first time, this is an ideal time to remind them that there are important validation steps to consider before they plunge into analysis. Validation is

† A *comma-delimited* file refers to a file with the extension .csv (comma separated values—where each piece of information is separated from the next by a comma.) Fixed width data require a codebook or some basic programming to separate the raw numbers into separate variables (or fields). These data will be in the most basic ASCII format and the extension is likely to be .txt.

accomplished by running basic descriptive analyses on all of the relevant variables. At a minimum, variables should match what is reported in the documentation. Basically, the goal is to determine if the researcher actually has the data that they think they have.

While there are some essential components of variables that are common across academic disciplines, these components are not always identified by the same terms. Regardless of the vocabulary used, there are still some basic characteristics of variables that are fundamental to statistical analysis. This list is roughly in order of their level of importance.

1. Data types

The most fundamental distinction between data types is whether the variable is numeric or string (text). If numeric, a second step involves specifying the specific type of numeric variable. There are three basic numeric variable subtypes (continuous, ordinal, and categorical), but the names for these categories vary by disciplinary norms.

A note about numeric variable subtypes:

Continuous (i.e., interval or scale, and ratio, which has a definitive 0 point) variables are most easily characterized by the conceptual notion that the intervals between each possible measured point are consistent. (The distance between 1 and 2 centimeters is the same as the distance between 20 and 21 centimeters.) Interval variables have the highest explanatory power in statistics.

Ordinal variables are merely variables where the values are in a specific order. Think of a Likert scale (e.g. 1=never, 2=rarely, 3=occasionally, 3=often, 4=very frequently) where the value of 4 is more than the value of 1, but is it exactly 4 times more? Ordinal variables can provide some inference to the direction in a relationship between variables.

Categorical (or nominal) variables are values that might as well be randomly assigned. Think of a variable "color" where 1=blue, 2=purple, 3=brown, or a zip code variable. Computing the average is meaningless on a categorical variable. Categorical variables can only indicate whether a relationship exists between variables that is more or less likely than random chance.

Dummy Variables: a special case variable type where the only two values possible are 1 and 0. In this case, a categorical or ordinal variable may be converted to a kind of continuous variable by splitting the relevant values into separate variables where 1=*it is* and 0=*it isn't.*

Type assignment is one step in this process. It refers to setting the appropriate data type for each variable in a data set. The codebook is important to this process because it should list the proper variable type for each variable. The codebook is not infallible, however, as some data providers will simply supply an unedited software-produced data dictionary that includes inaccurately assigned data types, or for various reasons the data do not match what is defined in the codebook. Verification that a variable is what it is expected to be can be accomplished through a simple univariate analysis for each variable of interest.

Another important data type is date. When date variables are read from a file, in most cases they are interpreted as strings (e.g., "8/19/2015" or "19 August 2015"). Fortunately, a common feature of statistical software is the ability to convert strings containing consistently formatted dates into a date data type. Whenever possible, these conversions should be made to ensure that dates will sort properly and that the data will be compatible with other date-specific functionality. Note that date types are capable of containing a time component as well, but it is not required.

In some cases, particularly when data pass through Excel on their way to a different data analysis program, the data type can be incorrectly assigned and the data may even be modified from the original format. This can be difficult to identify without careful validation of all of the data types, since a single number among thousands could be auto-modified from a number to a string (text), and that will typically convert the entire variable type into a string format (even if it looks like it is all numbers) that is unsuitable for most statistical analysis. For instance, Table 7.1 shows Excel auto-convert examples:

Table 7.1. Examples of Auto-converted Data in Excel®

Data as entered	**Auto-converted by Excel®**	**Effect on data**
44:45	44:45:00	Converts to timestamp with special formatting (hh:mm:ss)
8-3002	Aug-02	Converts into a "date" with text that replaces the original data

When unexpected character values are discovered in a variable, the researcher must determine whether this is an error (messy data) or whether the value has some significance. Again we refer to the codebook for clarity. If there is no codebook it is even more important to examine each variable individually to assure that all values within each variable fall within the expected range. Data outside the expected range may be errors, intended "missing" values, or outliers, which are valid data with values that could skew the analysis because they are dramatically outside the norm.

All of this activity may be classified as *data cleaning* and is best managed through writing code. While some data cleaning is possible within statistical packages, it is often too cumbersome to be practical. An alternate approach is using a program designed for this process (e.g., OpenRefine and Colectica's free Excel add on), though careful documentation is essential to ensure reproducibility. For more efficient data cleaning and transformation work, the Python programming language is recommended because it is a powerful and relatively simple programming language.

A note about missing values:

Missing values may be assigned by the software or programed by the researcher. The key is in recognizing which variables may need to have missing values identified. An example is a missing value indicator such as "N/A" in a variable that is otherwise all numbers. In this case, it may be necessary to convert the "N/A" values into something outside the range of expected values for that variable and then label these as "missing" from within the statistical package. It is conventional to use 9, 99, and 999 as missing values as long as these are well outside the expected range of the valid data.

With survey analysis in particular, there are usually instances of values that may be important to some research but not always relevant. For instance, gender may be recorded as: 1 = male, 2 = female, 3 = other, 9 = refused to answer. Most researchers will want only the values for 1 and 2 and should probably use the statistical program to label the values 3 and 9 as "missing." Other researchers will be specifically interested in the individuals whose genders are not clearly identified. In that case they might choose to select only the cases whose values are 3 or 9 in the gender variable, or they could set the values of 1 and 2 to "missing."

2. Naming and labeling

When working with novice researchers who are either creating their own data from original research or synthesizing it from multiple sources, an important role of the data services professional is to encourage users to either create codebooks or to at least use practices consistent with codebook standards. Examples of these practices are creating short variable names that do not include special characters (i.e., $ or %) as well as longer, more descriptive variable labels, and assigning and saving value labels for all non-interval variables. Researchers should be encouraged to do this in code whenever possible, as opposed to doing it via menu-based operations as writing and preserving the code makes the process easily reproducible. In addition, the code can serve as a substitute for a more robust codebook or as a short-list for the researcher, since it is usually interpretable even to someone who is not familiar with the programming language in which it was written.

3. Restructuring

Data users often need to perform some sort of restructuring to a dataset before they begin analysis. Two common forms of restructuring **are subsetting** and **reshaping**. Subsetting involves making the dataset smaller by reducing the number of variables (columns) or the number of observations (rows). Subsetting is a relatively basic operation that can be learned and taught to a user quickly, and it is important because it reinforces fundamental concepts of working with data in a statistical programming language.

Novice users are generally more comfortable thinking of their data in a visual way, but subsetting goes better if the user can think of it from a programmer's perspective. Columns are identified by variable names, rather than by visually locating them and manually doing something to them. The same applies to rows, but in the case of rows there is another level of abstraction. Rows are not identified by name or position, but by characteristics of the variables they contain. So, for instance, a researcher interested in analyzing characteristics of the elderly will most likely want to subset her data to contain only observations about people over a certain age. This type of subsetting (or filtering) is generally done through constructing a logical expression in code, rather than sorting and deleting as one might do in a spreadsheet.

Reshaping involves restructuring the data to match the format required to conduct a particular type of analysis. In the following example from the *World Development Indicators* database (http://databank.worldbank.org/data/home.aspx), row subsetting and reshaping are necessary to get data from Table 7.2 (the original format) into an extract where a specific unit of analysis is isolated. In this example *Series.Name* describes the unit of analysis for these data. The goal is to create a subset showing the percentage growth of a country's GDP over time, and the extra variables are dropped. To get there, a preliminary restructuring step brings us to Table 7.3, where the rows are subsetted to contain only the *Series.Name* of "GDP growth (annual %)."

Table 7.2. Initial Data from World Development Indicators

Country.Name	**Series.Name**	**2008**	**2009**
Cyprus	Population density (people per sq. km of land area)	116.5680736	118.0252165
Cyprus	GDP growth (annual %)	3.626616209	-1.666159464
Czech Republic	Population density (people per sq. km of land area)	134.4285178	135.1965825
Czech Republic	GDP growth (annual %)	2.71095557	-4.841785296
Germany	Population density (people per sq. km of land area)	235.5221782	234.9396374
Germany	GDP growth (annual %)	1.052109101	-5.637953129

Table 7.3. First Extract Based on Series.Name

Country.Name	**Series.Name**	**2008**	**2009**
Cyprus	GDP growth (annual %)	3.626616209	-1.666159464
Czech Republic	GDP growth (annual %)	2.71095557	-4.841785296
Germany	GDP growth (annual %)	1.052109101	-5.637953129

In Table 7.3, the data of interest are spread across three columns, each one containing values for a different year. While this may be a convenient form for some purposes, it actually limits the possibilities for analysis. This is because a key attribute of the data, year, is unavailable in this format. In order to remedy this, an operation known as reshaping must be performed. Table 7.4 shows the data in its reshaped format. Notice that there are two new variable names, *year* and *GDP. Growth.*

Table 7.4. Final Extract

Country.Name	**Year**	**GDP.Growth**
Cyprus	2008	3.626616209
Czech Republic	2008	2.71095557
Germany	2008	1.052109101
Cyprus	2009	-1.666159464
Czech Republic	2009	-4.841785296
Germany	2009	-5.637953129

In most statistical software packages this type of operation can be performed quickly and efficiently with only a few commands. Figure 7.2 shows the R code used to create Tables 7.2–7.3.

Figure 7.2. R Code Example for Generating Tables 7.2–7.3

```
# load some additional package and the original Table 1 data file
library(dplyr)
library(tidyr)
df <- read.csv("../original_data/Table1.csv")
# filter out the GDP growth rows and display the data frame (Table 2)
df <- filter(df,Series.Name=="GDP growth (annual %)")
# reshape and create Year and GDP.Growth variables
df <- gather(df,Year,GDP.Growth,X2008:X2010)
# clean the leading 'X' from Year
df$Year <- substr(df$Year,2,5)
# save Table 3
write.table(df, file = "../generated_data/table3.csv", sep = ",")
```

Getting Started

Given the rise of publicity related to all things data, a host of organizations support individuals motivated to improve their technical skills. In this rapidly evolving landscape it is impossible to create a comprehensive list of resources, but there are three complementary approaches to building and maintaining technical data skills:

- **In-person or online classes**. Data preparation is *not* typically taught in traditional academic courses (e.g., Computer Science or Statistics departments). Fortunately, there exist new online options like Coursera (https://www.coursera.org/course/getdata) and School of Data (http://schoolofdata.org/courses/#IntroDataCleaning).
- **One-off workshops**. In academia, this is the most common way to teach these skills. If an institution does not offer these types of classes, the non-profit organization Software Carpentry (https://software-carpentry.org/) or its affiliate Data Carpentry (https://datacarpentry.org/) has an international network of trained instructors available to teach on-site.
- **Self-directed learning**. This works best when working on an actual research project. Countless books exist, but the web is the most up-to-date resource. To start with, here are two highly recommended resource sites: The UCLA Institute for Digital Research and Education (IDRE) (https://idre.ucla.edu/) and StackOverflow (http://stackoverflow.com/). Resources of this type are growing at a refreshing pace!

Conclusions

> *An article about computational results is advertising, not scholarship. The actual scholarship is the full software environment, code and data, that produced the result.*[15]
>
> ~ Johnathan Buckheit and David Donoho, Stanford University.

Data service professionals play a key role in assisting and instructing researchers in good reproducible practices. A key element of this argument is that data service professionals engage with researchers at points in the research process where data wrangling assistance is often needed. Despite this, there are obstacles to success, even when the data service professional possesses the right skills to do the job. If the goal of the data services professional is to take on an expanded role, it may take time to develop a reputation as a trusted service provider, particularly when not affiliated with a particular academic discipline. The specific approach should depend on the needs of the institution, in particular on whether other service providers are available. One successful model is to partner with an instructor who grasps the potential benefits of a data service professional's involvement with her students' research projects. Such benefits include the use of more interesting data sources, the application of reproducible research methods, and a higher proportion of instructor time spent with theoretical or methodological questions rather than data manipulation. Another type of "easy win" is to offer workshops on reproducible research for beginning graduate students or undergraduate thesis writers. This approach works well when it catches novices at their points of need.

A potential impediment to success, particularly for those who must make a case for additional training or for investment in software or hardware, is the institutional perception about what is in scope for the data service professional's position. The following points can help make an effective case to administration for investing in a role for data services professionals:

- The fundamental importance of reproducible research to academia
- The benefit of reducing the impact of time-consuming data wrangling questions for the faculty
- The opportunity to instill the sense that providing robust data services is analogous to good citation practice
- Data preparation is not emphasized elsewhere in the curriculum
- Data preparation is a form of information literacy for data.

If on the fence about adding technical data skills to their skill sets, the data services professionals should remember, working with data is "the sexiest job of the 21st century!"[16] But more to the point, data wrangling is a creative endeavor that is both rewarding and an essential component of a robust data service. By imparting better data manipulation and management skills to our scholars, we empower them as learners and researchers.

---

1. David Mimno, "Data carpentry," *David Mimno* (Blog), August 19, 2014, http://www.mimno.org/articles/carpentry/
2. Nicholas J. Horton, Benjamin S. Baumer, and Hadley Wickham, "Setting the stage for data science: integration of data management skills in introductory and second courses in statistics." *arXiv* preprint, February 1, 2015, arXiv:1502.00318.
3. Sean Kandel, "The Sexiest Job of the 21st Century is Tedious, and that Needs to Change." *Harvard Business Review*, April 1, 2014, https://hbr.org/2014/04/the-sexiest-job-of-the-21st-century-is-tedious-and-that-needs-to-change/.
4. Jake Vanderplas. Twitter post.
5. Everett Rogers, *Diffusion of Innovations,* (New York, NY: Simon and Schuster, 2003).
6. The MANTRA research data management training toolkit from has some suggestions on file and folder naming conventions. Research Data MANTRA online course http://datalib.edina.ac.uk/mantra by EDINA and Data Library, University of Edinburgh is licensed under a Creative Commons Attribution 4.0 International License.
7. See, for instance, Google's R Style Guide: https://google-styleguide.googlecode.com/svn/trunk/Rguide.xml or Hadley Wickham's R Packages Style Guide: http://r-pkgs.had.co.nz/style.html.
8. Hadley Wickham "Style Guide," from "Introduction to Data Analysis," Rice University Fall 2012, accessed on May 18, 2015, http://stat405.had.co.nz/r-syle.html
9. Scott Long, *The Workflow of Data Analysis Using STATA*, (College Station: Stata Press, 2009).
10. Ben Goldacre, "Scientists Are Hoarding Data And It's Ruining Medical Research," last modified 22 July 2015, http://www.buzzfeed.com/bengoldacre/deworming-trials.
11. Richard Ball and Norm Medeiros, "Teaching integrity in empirical research: A protocol for documenting data management and analysis," *Journal of Economic Education*, 43 no. 2 (2012): 182–189.
12. Haverford College, "Project TIER: About," accessed on May 18, 2015, http://www.haverford.edu/TIER/about/.
13. Christine E. Peterson and Deborah Wesley. *The 1993 Indonesian Family Life Survey: Appendix C, Household Codebook, Book I Subfiles (Household Characteristics)*, DRU- 1195/4-NICHD/AID, RAND, 1995, accessed May 18, 2015, http://www.rand.org/content/dam/rand/pubs/drafts/2007/DRU1195.4.pdf, 73.
14. For a more detailed examination of codebooks and more example of variable level detail, visit the ICPSR, "What is a codebook," accessed May 18, 2015, http://www.icpsr.umich.edu/icpsrweb/NAHDAP/support/faqs/2006/01/what-is-codebook.
15. Jonathan B. Buckheit and David L. Donoho, "Wavelab and Reproducible Research," in *Wavelets and Statistics* ed. Anestis Antoniadis and Georges Oppenheim, (New York, NY: Springer, 1995), 59.
16. Thomas H. Davenport and D.J. Patil, "Data Scientist: The Sexiest Job of the 21st Century," *Harvard Business Review Magazine* 2012, http://hbr.org/2012/10/data-scientist-the-sexiest-job-of-the-21st-Century/ar/1.

CHAPTER 8

Restricted Data Access and Libraries

Jen Darragh

WHILE THERE ARE multitudes of freely-available data sources available for public use out there on the Web, thanks in part to the Open Data movement as well as advances in technology, sometimes these data are not quite detailed enough to answer specific research questions; for example, those that have a narrow geographic focus, require detailed medical information, include illicit behaviors, or include information on minors, or possibly even all those together. In some cases, that can be a bit of a "tough luck" situation, where a researcher may instead need to collect data on her own. In others, these more detailed versions of the data exist, but access is restricted due to confidentiality laws and requirements. This chapter focuses on the latter situation, with special attention on the process for acquiring these types of data and how the academic library can assist with this process.

Restricted-use data are defined here as data that are released only under stringent conditions due to a high level of unique variable granularity. Even with direct identifiers (such as names and addresses) removed, the data present an elevated risk of deductive disclosure. Releasing the data as restricted-use allows researchers to have access to data that would likely not be shared for secondary analysis otherwise. An example of the granularity in question often includes some combination of the following:

- Multiple demographic details (age, race, sex, veteran status, income, employment, education)
- Linkable variables (education transcript data, test scores, health insurance information)
- Specific geographic data (smaller than state, province or region-level)
- Compromising personal information (HIV status, mental health diagnoses, criminal record information, and illicit behaviors)

When this type of granularity is available in the data, it becomes more likely that a person could deduce the identity of a study participant, just by knowing some specific information about that person and then matching that information to variables within the data. In order to diminish the likelihood that someone could accidentally (or purposefully) deduce the identity of a research participant, the data are restricted from public release. Restricted-use data can be generated by government and non-profit agencies, as well research teams and individual researchers. The data are often hosted or provided by the source (e.g. Census Research Data Center) or through a third-party (such as the UK Data Archive or ICPSR). We will touch upon some of these datasets later on in the chapter, but some common options include the National Longitudinal Study of Adolescent to Adult Health (Add Health), the Health and Retirement Study (HRS), and the Early Childhood Longitudinal Study (ECLS) Birth and Kindergarten Cohorts. The process for obtaining restricted-use data varies widely across providers, and researchers wishing to access the data must usually meet several criteria.

This chapter focuses on the qualifications that researchers must typically meet and indicates how and where the library and librarians may assist researchers in the restricted-use data acquisition process. Each of the numbered items in the following list will be covered in greater detail. The chapter will close with a discussion of three service models that libraries could explore and potentially adopt in order to support restricted-use data acquisition.

Restricted-Use Data Researcher Qualifications

1. Researcher must have a Ph.D. and be employed by an institution that supports/vouches for the researcher and her project.
2. Researcher must demonstrate a need for the restricted-use data by providing a project proposal (varying in length).
3. Researcher must obtain IRB approval for her project for which the restricted-use data are needed.
4. Researcher must be able to prevent unauthorized physical and electronic access to the data by meeting specific security standards.
5. Researcher must be able to obtain an authorized signature from the employer to bind the organization and the researcher to the agreement.
6. Researcher must communicate with the data provider regarding any changes to the initial agreement (adding/removing staff, changing location of personnel or data) and track those changes.
7. Researcher may need to submit publications and presentations to the data provider for disclosure review prior to formal presentation or submission for publication.
8. Researcher must be mindful of any deadlines pertaining to agreement renewals or dissolution.
9. Researcher must be able to securely wipe all traces of the data from any computing system and return or destroy all media when the agreement expires.

Before We Begin...

Restricted-use data are provided under formal agreement between the data provider and the researcher and, often, his institution (more on this later). It is a legal agreement, and therefore it is essential that the researcher and his team understand expectations in order to be compliant with the agreement as penalties can be severe.[1] All paperwork should be read fully and the researcher should seek clarification on anything that is ambiguous, both from the data provider and the research office at the home institution. Ideally, the principal investigator should make sure that all members of the research team understand the terms of the agreement in plain language. Many mistakes can be mitigated by reducing human error through proper training. In addition, restricted-use data agreements can be called contracts, DUAs (data use agreements), licenses, and NDAs (non-disclosure agreements). While the nomenclature may vary, the principles and practices described within and the legally binding nature are generally similar.[2]

Researcher Must Have Ph.D.

In nearly all circumstances, the researcher requesting restricted-use data must already have obtained a doctoral degree. The Ph.D. requirement can be discouraging to graduate students who want to work with restricted-use data for their dissertations or theses. In most circumstances, a graduate student needs to have a faculty member request restricted-use data on her behalf. The faculty member should be someone actively engaged with the student, and both willing and able to oversee her work while assuming full responsibility for her conduct utilizing restricted-use data. In some cases, a faculty member with an existing data use agreement for the desired dataset could be an option for the student to pursue (in most cases, adding an additional user is fairly straightforward), but again, that faculty member is responsible for that student's involvement with the data. In addition, graduate students should typically only request restricted-use data for a long-term project such as a dissertation or thesis. It can take at least one month, (usually longer) for the data access request to be granted. The librarian could assist with explaining these terms to graduate students seeking to acquire restricted-use data. If the student is asking for restricted-use data for a semester-long class project, suggesting a public-use version of that dataset or a public-use dataset with similar variables would be advisable. For example, if the student is attempting to write a mock grant proposal, perhaps she could do preliminary analysis with the public-use data and come to some conclusions that could potentially be supplemented with findings from the restricted-use data "if funded."

Researcher Must Provide a Project Proposal

Proposals vary in length depending on the data provider. They can be as short as a brief paragraph and up to several pages long. Researchers are typically on their own when crafting proposals as they are the ones who can explain their specific needs for the restricted-use data and how it will be analyzed. The components generally required include the hypothesis, restricted-use variables needed from the dataset, and analysis plan. If multiple datasets are requested, or if multiple users on the license will be working on different projects, then proposals specific to the datasets and to the individual data user would need to be provided. For example, the Centers for Medicare and Medicaid do not allow new projects to be initiated on data already held under agreement without a formal reuse request being filed and approved.[3]

Researcher Must Have IRB Approval

Often the proposed project and/or the restricted-use data protection plan must be reviewed by the researcher's Institutional Review Board (IRB) and be approved prior to obtaining restricted-use data. In the U.S., an Institutional Review Board is required by law to review any research that involves human participants to protect them from potential harms.[4] Public-use data (such as web-accessible Census data) are typically exempt from IRB review; restricted-use data, because it is not publicly released, is subject to expedited review in most cases.[5] When in doubt, researchers should always consult with the institution's IRB for clarification, as some want to review all research regardless of data type. Most IRBs have helpful documentation available to assist researchers with the review process.[6]

Depending on the library's involvement with the restricted-data use project, there may be a need for a librarian to be listed as a project staff member on the IRB application (e.g., the librarian is the data custodian). Before being included as a staff member on an IRB application, the librarian will often have to take and pass a formal training course(s) in human subjects' research protection (the IRB will indicate what training is required). The librarian should review proper procedures as they pertain to restricted-use data with the IRB office prior to application submission to ensure that the application does not end up in a bottleneck. One way to avoid bottlenecks is for the researcher or project manager to provide to the IRB all materials that are being submitted in support of the request for restricted-use data. If applicable, a memo or cover letter briefly explaining what each of the documents is for, and what they pertain to, is helpful.

Researcher Must Be Able to Secure the Data

Perhaps the most daunting part of a restricted-use request is determining where the data can be securely stored and accessed. There is no agreement across data providers as to what provides the best security. Some providers, such as the Institute of Education Sciences (part of the U.S. Department of Education), will only allow data to be housed on a stand-alone (that is, non-networked) computer in a locked room that only authorized personnel may access (this can be problematic when it pertains to custodial staff).[†7] Others, such as the Health and Retirement Study, will allow data to reside on a secure server, but with multiple technical requirements and specifications that must be met.[8] A researcher's ability to secure the data ultimately determines whether or not the researcher will be able to obtain access to the data. Some universities, such as Cornell University, provide centralized, secure data access solutions for any affiliated researcher.[9] However, this is not the norm. There may be research centers or institutes at certain universities that will support restricted-use data (acquisition and storage) for those associated with the center, but in most instances researchers and research teams must fend for themselves.[10]

Researcher Must Have Support from His/Her Employer

Obtaining access to restricted-use data generally requires that the data provider and the receiving organization enter into a legally binding agreement (license, contract, DUA, etc.). While the researcher and his team are included as parties in the agreement, the binding signature comes from someone who has the authority to sign for the receiving organization. The appropriate university signatory is typically someone at a high level in research administration, which could be the Office of Sponsored Programs or Office of Research, a school's Dean's Office, or university legal counsel, depending on the institution. Universally, an academic department head is not an appropriate signatory. It is worthwhile for anyone supporting inquiries about restricted-use data to know who the appropriate parties or entities on campus are who would review and sign-off on data use agreements.

Researcher Must Communicate Any Changes in Environment or Staffing to the Data Provider

This area is often where mistakes are made. It is important to understand that any changes to the research environment or staffing must be communicated back to the data provider in a timely fashion. In most cases, anything that is a change to the original agreement must be communicated to and approved by the provid-

† The author has found that using a CPU cage (e.g., http://www.cnet.com/products/adjustable-locking-wire-cpu-cage-black/) or a removable hard drive that can be locked up when not in use are the only ways to satisfy data provider requirements when a room must be accessed by custodial staff or other non-project personnel.

er before the change can actually be made. In addition, these changes should be tracked to avoid any confusion in the event that the data provider opts to perform a site visit to check adherence to terms in the data use agreement. These changes can include any of the following:

1. Change in office location for any team member. Researchers often forget that "working from home" is typically not allowed at all, or must be approved in advance. Using VPN to log into a machine on campus is not the same as working in the office.
2. Changes in computing. Are desktop computers being added? Does someone need to use a laptop? Does that laptop have to be secured? Is the project changing servers? Where is the server located?
3. Adding staff to or removing them from the project.
4. Changing the scope of the original project or starting a new project using the data. A request to reuse data for a new project may be needed if it deviates substantially from the original project. Errors occur here when faculty allow graduate students to use the data for dissertations, but the dissertation abstracts were never shared with the data provider.

A good rule of thumb is that when there is a question about what is permissible, the researcher should ask the provider before making any type of change. Even if something seems trivial, it is better to ask than risk being tagged non-compliant, which could result in not only losing access to the data, but could also be detrimental to an academic research career.

Researcher May Need to Submit Publications and Presentations for Disclosure Review

Some data providers require that they be acknowledged in any publications based on the data[11] and that any potential publications or presentations based on the data be submitted for review prior to submission to journals or presentations at conferences.[12] These requirements can often be buried in lengthy agreements, so it is important that the researcher make note of any of these requirements and ensure that her team is made aware of them in a prominent way (post a notice on the project computer, post on a project wiki, etc.). It could be worthwhile to have the researcher designate one person as the coordinator of all publishable output.

Researcher Must be Mindful of Any Deadlines Pertaining to Agreement Renewals or Dissolution

Researchers and their staff need to be mindful of when restricted data use agreements will expire. The time period for how long a researcher may possess and analyze restricted-use data varies across providers, though typically it is a period between one and five years. Data providers typically send prompts via email prior to expiration, but having an internal tracking system for the agreement, be it calendar reminders, prominent file folder, or an actual database, is beneficial. This is especially true if there is a finite window of time during which the researcher must inform the provider about intent to renew the agreement (if allowed). The renewal period may be shorter than the original analysis period. Some data providers appear to allow perpetual renewal as long as all terms and access conditions are met, but others can require termination after a set number of renewals.

Researcher Must Be Able to Securely Wipe All Traces of the Data from Any Computing System and Return or Destroy All Media When the Agreement Expires

What may be retained by the researcher once the agreement expires can differ, but all providers will require that the original restricted-use dataset be returned or destroyed. Returning the data may require use of a certified courier service (e.g., FedEx); even if it is not required, having some sort of certification that the data package gets to its final destination is a good idea. Destruction of the original data can be done by physically (CD/DVD shredder) or by degaussing (external hard drive or data tape). The data provider often has a preferred method listed in the agreement, but if not, there are resources online to consult, and local IT support can also provide advice. If the researcher is allowed to keep de-identified files or statistical code, there may be some conditions under which that information must be stored. The computing environment (server or personal computer) on which the working copy of the data was stored and analyzed must also be "wiped" in some fashion. This could involve reformatting the hard drive, using a secure erasure program, or both. Working with local IT support is paramount at this step to ensure compliance with provider guidelines.

Determining Library Support

If you have read up to this point, it is safe to say that you have realized that obtaining access to and managing restricted-use data is neither a simple nor quick process. It is a significant investment in both time and effort, and can involve many players. Academic libraries can assist in this process at different points and at different levels. The appropriate level of support depends on available human and financial resources both inside and outside the library. The purpose of this final portion of the chapter is to assist librarians and library managers with proposing and developing a service model appropriate for the institution.

Environmental Scan

Before looking at what the library can do, it is a good idea to look at what services already exist at the university level and what the process would be to obtain restricted-use data without library involvement. The lowest (but still useful) level of support is to be able to direct researchers to services that they may not know exist. At some institutions, this may be the only restricted-use data support that can be offered. Where centralized services do not exist, a concierge that is aware of all the right people and places to seek help from on campus is invaluable. Questions the library should consider include:

1. How are requests for restricted-use data handled in IRB applications?
2. How do grant or research administration offices treat restricted-use data contracts and licenses?
3. Who are the appropriate people to sign contracts and licenses?
4. Are there any departments that currently host restricted-use data? What is the environment or equipment available? Who are the parties that made this possible?
5. Are there any IT personnel at the department/school/institution level that have experience working with restricted-use data parameters? What have they created?
6. What are the departments or schools most likely to have researchers working with restricted-use data? Who has helped those researchers?
7. For available services, who is eligible to use it?

Stakeholder Needs Assessment

After scanning the institution's environment to determine what is or is not available, it is time to determine what services are desired, feasible, and sustainable. Schedule time to chat with potential stakeholders; stakeholders would include faculty and graduate students from various social, behavioral, or health sciences disciplines, as they are the most likely to encounter restricted-use data. Suggestions for questions to pose during this meeting include:

1. Have you ever encountered a restricted-use dataset when searching for data to analyze?
2. What did you do when you realized the dataset had access restrictions? What steps did you take?
3. Were the restricted-use data the best or only option for your research?
4. Were you successful in obtaining the data or did you abandon the dataset and go with a public-use option or choose to collect your own data?
5. What was the most frustrating aspect of this experience? What would have made obtaining restricted-use data easier for you?

Developing a Service Framework

After speaking with various stakeholders, a picture should emerge as to what level of service is desired. It is beneficial to prioritize each potential service from the most immediately feasible (meaning resources readily available) to the least (needing to add resources). Once the list is prioritized, a service framework will begin to emerge. While addressing desired need versus service level, the following questions should be answered:

1. Does the library have space it can dedicate for a researcher to work securely?
2. Does the library need to make modifications to the space such as providing locking furniture (e.g. CPU cage, data safe, or locking cabinets)?
3. Can the library provide ID card swipe access? ID card access is more efficient than physical keys (nothing needs to be returned/recovered from the researcher), but expensive.
4. How many researchers can the space accommodate? Is it possible for researchers to share space (impacts the amount of paperwork filed with each provider)?
5. Does the library have adequate local IT support (expertise and time) in order to develop and maintain the computing environment needed? Servers require far more customization and monitoring than non-networked computers.
6. Does the library have a designated staff member who can oversee the operation of the room? This includes developing security plans, being a part of a data use agreement, ensuring compliance with data provider, university-wide and library-specific policies. Does this staff member have a back-up? How many staff should be involved? Do staff schedules or duties need to be modified?
7. What are the actual financial costs of staff time (librarians and IT staff), space modifications, and equipment to maintain the desired level of service?

Once the framework is completed, the library will have something tangible to present that addresses faculty needs while also taking into account associated costs. When discussing restricted-use data services with library administration, any potential risks in addition to service benefits should also be addressed. Some potential risks that should be taken into account:

1. Specialized knowledge: How many staff fully understand this process? Is there a backup support staff member?
2. User error: While there are technical and physical safeguards that can be applied, the onus is still on the user to follow proper protocol. This is perhaps the largest risk, as it takes a fair amount of staff time to oversee protocol. More enforcement, such as weekly meetings with each project or staging surprise inspections, takes more time and effort.

3. The data provider changes policies and paperwork: New versions of security plans or agreement documents may be required, and in some instances requirements on data storage and access may become more stringent. IT support will need to anticipate and respond to potential changes.
4. University-level sanctions for non-compliance: Some providers will freeze access to restricted-use datasets for all researchers at the university even if only one person makes a mistake.
5. Technology changes: Machines break and IT staff can change. Do you have contingency plans? Do you have funds for continued maintenance? Technology can be a significant investment. The more machines, systems and staff, the higher the risk.
6. Inspections: Some data providers can show up un-announced to inspect the work environment. Do you have a plan in place for when this occurs?

Policies and Procedures

The potential for user error is a large risk when investing in restricted-use data services. While researchers generally do not intend to violate terms of agreements, it can be difficult to remember all the various caveats listed in lengthy agreements. This is where coming up with "common sense" rules and reminding all users of these rules (at least annually) is beneficial. The lead researcher and the library should agree upon these rules. The library should develop a responsible restricted-use data policy that all persons using the library's services must sign and adhere to. In developing this policy it is important to seek input from library administration as well as university research administration, and possibly general counsel as well. This policy should be reviewed with users of the service (at least) annually. As part of this policy, faculty who are supervising the research of students are held responsible for their students' conduct. As an example, assume that the library is offering both space as well as technology support. Here are some for language to include in the policy based on that level of service:

1. This is a work space dedicated for working with restricted-use data. Please do not invite non-approved personnel into this space.
2. Never assume it is permissible to take any data out of the restricted-use data room.
3. Read all guidelines for storing and disposing of output.
4. Retrieve any printouts promptly.
5. Never assume you can use a VPN. For some providers you have to be specific about your location when working with the data.
6. Do not bring unapproved hardware into the restricted-use data room (e.g. extra monitor, thumb drives, DVD burner, etc.).

7. If anything changes with your project, such as a change in staff, change in proposed project, project is over, etc., communicate those changes back to the library and to the data provider as soon as possible.
8. Your output will not be vetted. Read all guidelines for publishing results from your analyses.

Parting Thoughts

At the time of this writing, academic library services for supporting restricted-use data acquisition are sparse and are primarily limited to consultation and referral.[†] Academic libraries can definitely provide valuable support for restricted-use data acquisition and use, but due diligence is required in order to determine what level of support can be sustainably offered. Risks need to be assessed and weighed with the perceived benefits. Any users of the service have to be properly trained in order to avoid errors that, while small, could have serious repercussions. Libraries and librarians should stay nimble; as with any library service, what is offered may change over time based on need and available resources. The restricted-use data landscape is always shifting, and involves many small details. Keeping projects organized utilizing electronic tracking or physical files[‡] with contact information, key dates, contacts, specialized requirements, etc. is essential. Finally, the skills that librarians and library staff can acquire through supporting restricted-use data are likely to become increasingly valuable as more research data sharing requirements emerge.[13]

---

1. Health and Retirement Study, "Requirements for Receiving Restricted Data from HRS," *Health and Retirement Study: A Longitudinal Study of Health, Retirement, and Aging*, accessed April, 16 2015 http://hrsonline.isr.umich.edu/index.php?p=resappreq#reqsanct.
2. Population Studies Center, "Contracts Database," *Data Use Agreement [DUA] Portal*, accessed July 2, 2015 http://www.psc.isr.umich.edu/dis/data/restricted/rdc/.
3. Centers for Medicare and Medicaid, "Re-Use of Data," *DUAs*, accessed July 2, 2015 http://www.cms.gov/Research-Statistics-Data-and-Systems/Computer-Data-and-Systems/Privacy/DUAs.html.
4. Department of Health and Human Services, "46.107 IRB membership" *Code of Federal Regulations: Title 45 Public Welfare: Department of Health and Human Services: Part 46 Protection of*

---

† Based on anecdotal knowledge, conversations and presentations at the International Association for Social Science Information Services and Technology (IASSIST) 2015 Annual Conference, and a Web-search for university libraries and restricted-use data. Library Websites that provide information about restricted data support include Johns Hopkins University (this author's employer), MIT Libraries, Penn State Libraries, Rutgers University Libraries, University of Virginia Library, and University of Wisconsin-Madison Libraries. There may be more academic libraries offering some consultative/referral support on an as-needed, informal basis.

‡ The chapter author recommends both formats.

Human Subjects, accessed July 2, 2015 http://www.hhs.gov/ohrp/humansubjects/guidance/45cfr46.html#46.107.

5. Department of Health and Human Services, "Human Subjects Research (45 CFR 46)," *Code of Federal Regulations: Title 45 Public Welfare: Department of Health and Human Services: Part 46 Protection of Human Subjects*," accessed April 16, 2015 http://www.hhs.gov/ohrp/humansubjects/guidance/45cfr46.html#46.101.
6. Johns Hopkins Homewood Institutional Review Board, *Navigating the Homewood Institutional Review Board (HIRB): A Primer for Students, Faculty Members Acting as the PI of a Student Initiated Project, and Individuals New to Human Participants Research*, accessed April 16, 2015 http://web.jhu.edu/Homewood-IRB/images/forms/Navigating%20the%20HIRB%20FINAL.pdf.
7. National Center for Education Statistics, "Chapter 3, Section 3.5: Computer Security Requirements," *Restricted Use Data Procedures Manual*, accessed April 15, 2015 http://nces.ed.gov/statprog/rudman/chapter3.asp#3.5.
8. Health and Retirement Study, *The Restricted Data Environment: Issues Relating to Network-Connected Clients*, accessed April 12, 2015 http://hrsonline.isr.umich.edu/sitedocs/rda/RestrictedDataEnvironment.pdf.
9. Cornell Institute for Social and Economic Research. "What is CRADC?," *CISER Secure Data Services: CRADC*, accessed April 15, 2015 http://ciser.cornell.edu/cradc/what_is_cradc.shtml.
10. Hopkins Population Center, "Data Services," *Hopkins Population Center HPC Associate Services*, accessed April 16, 2015 http://web.jhu.edu/popcenter/hpc_associate_services/data_services/index.html.
11. Carolina Population Center, "What acknowledgment should be included in each written report or other publication based on analysis of data from Add Health?," *Add Health: National Longitudinal Study of Adolescent to Adult Health: Questions About Add Health*, accessed April 12, 2015 http://www.cpc.unc.edu/projects/addhealth/faqs/addhealth/index.html#what-acknowledgment-should-be.
12. National Center for Education Statistics, "Chapter 3: Security Procedures," *Restricted Use Data Procedures Manual*, accessed April 15, 2015 https://nces.ed.gov/statprog/rudman/chapter3.asp#adpm.
13. National Institutes of Health, "NIH Sharing Policies and Related Guidance on NIH-Funded Research Resources," *National Institutes of Health Grants and Funding*, accessed April 16, 2015 http://grants.nih.gov/grants/sharing.htm.

PART II

Data in the Disciplines

CHAPTER 9

Supporting Geospatial Data

Nicole Scholtz

GEOSPATIAL DATA AS a subcategory of data has its own peculiarities, tools and approaches. A working definition of geospatial data is *data containing information about location and geometry on the earth that describe or model features or characteristics*. In this chapter, I will introduce the range of options for providing data services that support finding and using geospatial data, the ways in which geospatial data are different from other kinds of data, and the associated challenges of working with geospatial data. This material is not exhaustive, but should be seen as an overview to tempt the data librarian into further interest in the geospatial. The data librarian dealing with geospatial data is challenged to develop a service model that fits the context of her campus, while also cultivating the specific expertise necessary for dealing with the geospatial in that context.

Designing Library Services to Support Geospatial Data

Information is the currency of the library. As this book demonstrates, academic libraries increasingly approach data as simply another form of information that needs to be grappled with, and they are developing a variety of services suited to the complex needs of data users. Treating geospatial data as a subtype of data can provide a useful framework for developing geospatial services. Other framings, which look at geospatial services as an extension of map librarianship, geography liaisonship, the IT unit, or technology training exist and are well covered in the library literature, but approaching geospatial library services from the data perspective sheds new light on these services. The recent article "Map Room to Data and GIS Services: Five University Libraries Evolving to Meet Campus Needs and Changing Technologies" provides an excellent introduction to what are termed GIS and data services, an overview of the library literature, and in-depth descriptions of programs at five different academic libraries.[1] In the same special issue of the *Journal of Map and Geography Libraries*, dedicated to the past and future of geospatial information, "Maps & GIS Data Libraries in the Era of Big Data and Cloud Computing" takes a computing-oriented approach to the topic of geospatial data services in libraries.[2] Ann Holstein's summary of an ARL survey of geographic information and technologies in academic libraries gives a snapshot of current services, a comparison with activities in 1997, and recommendations for building a service based on the existing literature.[3] Finally, Eva Dodsworth's *Getting Started with GIS: A LITA Guide* provides another perspective and recommendations for providing GIS-related services in library contexts, with many detailed tutorials and specific resources.[4] Each of these recent publications is a valuable resource for anyone delving into geospatial data service provision. By keeping data at the center of the following discussion of geospatial data service design, I hope to provide something slightly different.

Implementing a library-based service that supports the use of geospatial data requires careful consideration of the context of the institution. Are there many researchers working on spatial problems? Is GIS taught in courses, either from a research perspective or in a professional program? Is there a geography department and to what degree does it influence the institutional geospatial context? Are any advanced courses taught that relate to spatial statistics? How widely available is proprietary software (such as ArcGIS for Desktop), and is there an institutional level license, or is proprietary software only available in specific locations, or not at all? Are there units embedded in schools, departments, IT units, centers, or elsewhere that provide some geospatial data services? The answers to these questions will help frame potential services.

Potential users of geospatial data services will range from the most novice to expert, and the needs vary tremendously across these populations. Google Maps, the excellent map-based visualizations at *The New York Times*, and the ubiquity of GPS in smartphones are just some of the factors that can introduce users to the potential of maps and geospatial data and inspire them to start seeing potential connections to their research or studies. At the other end of the spectrum are those in the field of Geographic Information Science (GI Science), who are developing new spatial analysis techniques that are deeply abstract. No data service can or should serve all potential users at an institution equally, and it is important to think about the range of users and the different possibilities of how to serve them. Excellent case studies that explore this range are available in the article by Scaramozzino et al.[5]

What types of services can be offered? A service can help patrons with any or all of their needs for finding, accessing, storing, subsetting, converting, creating and modeling, editing, visualizing, citing, and analyzing geospatial data. There are processes that are highly specific to geospatial work, such as geocoding addresses and georeferencing maps. Services may be provided through consultations, email reference (though the asynchrony and technological challenge may be particularly cumbersome with geospatial data), open workshops, course-based instruction sessions, and guides. A service may include acquiring existing geospatial data for collections, which will include specialized work such as licensing, providing access, creating geospatial metadata, and preservation issues peculiar to the myriad formats of geospatial data. A service provider may create and update guides to accessing geospatial data as relates to specific disciplines important to the institution, or specific to the geographic region in which the institution resides, or on other locally relevant topics. A service can provide tutorials for working with particular visualization techniques, types of data, specific datasets, kinds of analysis, or other common scenarios encountered. A service may support licensing or contracts for proprietary or subscription tools and attendant activities, such as creating accounts for users and distributing software and licenses.

Over the course of a year, any geospatial data or map-related service provider may be asked by faculty or students to produce static maps for publication (or perhaps even interactive maps) or to host spatial data on a server. Service providers should anticipate this and decide whether they are going to do this production type of work, and if so, whether they will charge. Production services, which are distinct from consultation because the service provider is actually producing work, such as analysis, clean data, or a hosted website, can quickly become resource intensive, in terms of staff time and/or infrastructure (for hosted projects).

The geospatial data reference interview is important to discerning the needs of the patron. Many patrons will start with an uninformative inquiry such as "I want to make a map." Almost any discipline will have a researcher who might make use of geospatial data and tools, which have many different uses. Some patrons may have a purely visualization-related need. They might want a static map for a publication or an image to display some data visually, or they could require a dynamic visualization—perhaps something that allows interaction with filters, shows an animation of change over time, or even displays multiple layers at different levels of zoom. Others may be working with spatial data to produce metrics or outputs to analyze in non-spatial ways, perhaps using more traditional statistical analyses. Other patrons may be doing spatial analysis procedures (such as spatial regression) that have an essential geospatial element and yet produce outputs or metrics that cannot be visualized on a map at all. Still others may be planning to collect data and want advice on equipment or modeling or what elements to include in a grant proposal. During direct work with patrons, the service provider will learn to recognize the degree of spatiality of the researcher's needs. Something may appear to be a spatial need, but not actually be, and vice-versa. The librarian can listen for keywords that refer to spatiality or maps or the above-referenced tools or techniques or formats or concepts, and follow up with questions to determine how geospatial a problem it is.

Many newer users of geospatial data will focus on a tool, a specific need, or want to know a series of steps. As librarians, we know that information seeking and the research process are bigger than just knowing where to click to find the right article. We can frame geospatial data in the context of other data and information, while also assisting with their special nature. For example, many patrons new to the field of geospatial data may think of this area as something exotic and strange, and may be intensely focused on file formats and finding data they imagine must exist. It is important to remind them of the classic approaches to finding data that involve thinking about who would produce such data, considering related data that might meet their research need, and then being open to finding formats that may not meet their initial expectations.

On the other hand, a large number of decisions go into any project using geospatial data—for instance, when creating a thematic map visualization of median income by census tract in a particular metro area. What year should the data reflect? What median income measure exactly should be used? What projection should be used? What kind of output is needed—a static image, and if so, what size? What classification method will be used in coloring the values? What will the legend say? How will the data be cited? What other information will be displayed to show context, (e.g. water bodies, state boundaries, main roads)? What labels should be on the map? And for each answer to these questions, how is the decision actually implemented in the particular tool or software being used? The questions required vary based on the intended use of the geospatial data and the potential for mistakes increases as we move from visualization into spatial research methods and analysis. The librarian may also have a role in steering a patron who is a novice to GIS to a tool like Social Explorer, which allows the patron to generate a map (although with limited customization and output control) without spending significant resources learning GIS. The librarian may help patrons consider their needs, their existing abilities, their future research, their timeline for a project, and their interest and desire to explore a new domain.

How does the data librarian develop and maintain expertise on geospatial topics? Formal coursework in GIS can be a strong foundation for working with geospatial data and tools. There are many relevant online tutorials, open educational resources, books, and in-person training opportunities, and the service provider will need to visit these resources regularly to keep developing knowledge and skills. Geospatial data tools and techniques are so vast that any given project may become a new area of exploration for the service provider. It can be easy to simply react to the needs at hand, rather than proactively choosing which tools and techniques to support. Many of the resources for learning are very tool-based, and the better resources integrate with tools and help with transferable knowledge. It is important to understand specific topics such as georeferencing historic maps[†] and

† Georeferencing is the process of assigning coordinates to an image so that it can be used in a system that can make use of that information. For example, a georeferenced historic map of Paris could be overlaid with other geospatial data layers such as current highways and demographic information.

geocoding addresses[‡] both on a tool level and a conceptual level as technologies change around these common activities.

Geospatial Data as a Subtype of Data

Academic libraries have long been full of paper geospatial materials in the form of maps and atlases, and frequently have one or more specialists to assist patrons with these materials. Digital corollaries range from providing access to digital scans of paper materials, to purchasing born-digital maps and atlases, to supporting campus needs around geospatial data and technologies such as Geographic Information Systems (GIS). Services related to geospatial data vary widely between institutions, and the home for such activities in a library might be in or adjacent to a map collection, government information or government documents collections, a data services department, or in a combined unit or elsewhere. In considering geospatial data a subtype of data and then framing services in relation to broader ideas about data services, we can find a different perspective that enlarges the possibilities of geospatial service provision and leverages the thoughtful work of data professionals.

What are the characteristics of geospatial data that require specialized services? Perhaps it is better to start by looking at what geospatial data have in common with other forms of data. Geospatial data can be collected through administrative or research activities. Many geospatial data are produced through government activities, but they are also produced by researchers and corporations, and increasingly also through crowdsourced mechanisms. All data are a structured representation of the world (either observed or modeled), whether that representation derives from survey data or scientific instruments or simulation outputs, and geospatial data are no different. A point file that shows the locations of oak trees in a city is a representation of those trees, as is a high-resolution aerial image that shows the tree canopy clearly. Both spatial models will allow us to gain an understanding of the trees in the context of the space they inhabit. Geospatial data, especially aerial images, sometimes feel very real to a viewer and it is important to remember that these data are still merely models or representations of the world and that necessary simplifications are built into these models. A given dataset may store a specific type of object, such as the locations of secondary schools, or a broader collection of items, such as locations of all organizations providing education-related services, or something somewhere in-between. The geospatial rendering of a specific dataset is called a layer, and multiple layers usually go into making up a visualization, or map. Spatial analysis techniques also frequently make use of multiple

‡ Geocoding is the process of assigning coordinates or other location information to some not-yet-spatial information. The most common kind of geocoding involves taking a table of addresses and finding latitude and longitude for each address.

datasets. Like other data, geospatial data have a temporal aspect that is important. A dataset may describe a point or range in time, or include multiple points in time within the same data, and a data user must pay attention to what time period is represented and how time is modeled in the data. Analytic techniques for dealing with temporal aspects of geospatial data are still in development.

Geospatial data can be divided into two major subtypes: vector and raster.

Figure 9.1. Vector and Raster Models of the Same Features

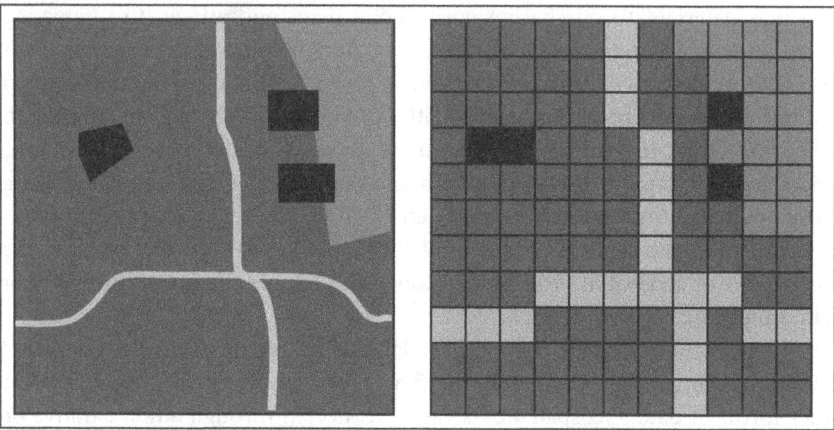

Vector representations can be points, lines or polygons, in which coordinates define the locations or vertices of these features. A vector data layer will typically be only one of these (e.g., a set of points representing hospitals). Each object will also have attribute data associated with it (e.g., the number of hospital beds, and the number of surgeries performed in 2013 and in 2014). The data format will encode the geometry (the point coordinates, or line or polygon vertices) and typically also has some fields with values. Some data formats can also store the coordinate reference system information. Different vector data formats actually handle the geometry and value encoding differently. For example, a GeoJSON version of a point file describing tree locations and their estimated age and species will store the attributes, geometry, and coordinate reference system in text within the same file. The same data represented in a shapefile format will have attribute data in the DBF file, the geometry in the SHP and SHX files (and potentially others), and the coordinate reference system in the PRJ file. These files are viewed in concert as a single shapefile by a tool capable of consuming this format. Different formats have different possibilities and limitations, including scalability and what tools are available to consume and convert them. There is no single best format, but rather the one most appropriate to a tool, visualization technique, analysis or conversion.

Raster data describe the space differently, and instead carve up a given space into a grid of equal sized units (usually squares) with values that are assigned to each unit. Values can be numeric or categorical, and some formats allow for a number of values to be associated with each grid cell. As with vector formats, each raster format has constraints built into it that the data creator should consider when selecting an appropriate format. In both vector and raster data, values such as strings, integers, floating point numbers, and other typical data types can be stored. Both vector and raster data types can be incorporated into database structures.

An object in the world can be modeled as either vector or raster data, and there are benefits and limitations to each. Some objects are more efficiently modeled as raster data for storage purposes, (e.g., elevation values), but may be easier to interpret visually as vector data, (e.g., contour lines), because it is more common to see such information represented in its vector form. The elevation raster and contour lines for an area describe essentially the same thing, and interchanging between them is possible, but information is lost in the translation. Different visualization and analysis techniques are available for raster and vector data.

Geospatial data have further peculiarities that the service provider will need to understand in order to provide effective service. It is critical to understand the scale and resolution for which a geospatial dataset is produced and the ways that affects what can be done with the data. Coordinate reference systems (CRSes), or spatial references, are perhaps the most challenging aspect of working with geospatial data, and it is important to develop a good understanding of them. This topic is too complex to cover in its entirety here, but there are many good sources available online and in print for the interested reader.

Formats of geospatial data vary tremendously. A very common vector format is the shapefile. Other vector formats include coverages, ESRI geodatabase feature classes, GeoJSON, KML, GML, Spatialite, PostGIS, and more. Raster formats include IMG (ERDAS IMAGINE), ESRI grid, GeoTIFF, netCDF, ASCII, and an even broader array than exist for vector data; supporting raster formats requires being able to quickly learn about previously unseen formats. Spatial data users need to also be familiar with tabular data formats and database concepts. As with other data, the form by which a geospatial dataset is accessed may not be the best form for using it, nor is it likely a good long-term storage format. For example, a large amount of the vector data freely available for download comes as a zip file containing a shapefile. This is a decent dissemination format, and arguably good for preservation as well. The format is stable, open, widely understood, and many tools can make use of it. It is also inefficient for space and tool usage and does not scale well for larger datasets; an advanced user would likely convert the shapefile to a more robust modern format for use in a specific context, such as an ESRI geodatabase feature class if making use of ArcGIS products.

The tools of the geospatial data user range from GIS tools that are very specific to kinds of analysis or kinds of data, to those GIS tools that are broader in approach, to tools more typically used for other kinds of data or analysis but which have some possibilities for handling geospatial data either built in or available through plugins or libraries (e.g. R and MATLAB). Proprietary desktop software packages such as ESRI's ArcGIS for Desktop dominate the landscape, but open source tools are in active and increasing development. These tools can handle a wide range of activities with geospatial data, from displaying to converting to analyzing. Historically these tools were more desktop-based and relied on Graphical User Interfaces (GUIs), but programmatic-style tools are coming into use. QGIS is an increasingly popular desktop GIS software package that is essentially a GUI on top of a set of programmatic tools, including the Geospatial Data Abstraction Library (GDAL), which can also be used independently of QGIS. ArcGIS for Desktop implemented Python as a way to automate processes in 2004, an interesting integration of proprietary software with a programmatic open source language access point.

Mapping services based online are proliferating, and while at first these were focused primarily on visualizing data and sharing map content, they are increasingly being used for data creation and analysis. Tools such as ArcGIS Online and CartoDB are in rapid development and have a low bar for entry, and they are structured in terms of what they allow and how they are accessed. Lightweight tools for highly customizable interactive online display of content, such as the specifically map-oriented leaflet.js, or the visualization tool that involves some mapping-related features D3.js, have been developed in recent years. These tools have strongly shifted creators' ability to display map content interactively and have raised the bar for what a map-based visualization should be able to do, as patrons frequently come in with examples from *The New York Times* and want to be able to make something as seamless and interactive. This is a rapidly shifting area which geospatial services may be challenged to support effectively.

Some important trends have interesting developments related to geospatial data. Crowdsourcers contribute to geospatial data in OpenStreetMap (OSM) and other projects, and in the context of geospatial data, crowdsourcing is often referred to as Volunteered Geographic Information (VGI). Zook et al. provide an excellent overview of this topic as well as discussion of a specific application to the Haitian Earthquake Crisis.[6] Many citizen science initiatives have a deeply geospatial element, enabled by mobile technologies that easily incorporate location in data collection by using GPS. Open data movements are particularly relevant to geospatial data because many geospatial data are government-produced information. Cultural and legal frameworks for sharing government data vary widely from place to place, and open data movements are responsible for the availability of more and more geospatial data each year.

Conclusion

Geospatial data services require service providers with specific expertise in geospatial data, but the degree of that expertise will vary with the depth of services offered. It is possible to offer a wide range of services, and as with other library services, the specific services offered should not be merely in response to gaps that exist. Geospatial data services are offered at a wide range of institutions, from the large ARL libraries surveyed by Holstein to liberal arts colleges and community colleges. Geospatial data services must reflect the campus context, fit with other services both in the library and other campus units, and support the mission of the library and institution.

---

1. Jeanine Scaramozzino, Jeanine, Russell White, Jeff Essic, Lee Ann Fullington, Himanshu Mistry, Amanda Henley, and Miriam Olivares, "Map Room to Data and GIS Services: Five University Libraries Evolving to Meet Campus Needs and Changing Technologies," *Journal of Map & Geography Libraries: Advances in Geospatial Information, Collections & Archives* 10, no. 1 (April 2014): 6–47, doi:10.1080/15420353.2014.893943.
2. Daniel Goldberg, Miriam Olivares, Zhongxia Li, and Andrew G. Klein, "Maps & GIS Data Libraries in the Era of Big Data and Cloud Computing," *Journal of Map & Geography Libraries: Advances in Geospatial Information, Collections & Archives* 10, no.1 (April 2014): 100–122, doi:10.1080/15420353.2014.893944.
3. Ann Holstein, "Geographic Information and Technologies in Academic Libraries: An ARL Survey of Services and Support," *Information Technology and Libraries* 34, no. 1 (March 2015): 38–51, doi:10.6017/ital.v34i1.5699.
4. Eva Dodsworth, *Getting Started with GIS: A LITA Guide* (New York: Neal-Schuman, 2012).
5. Scaramozzino et al., "Map Room to Data and GIS Services: Five University Libraries Evolving to Meet Campus Needs and Changing Technologies."
6. Zook, Matthew, Mark Graham, Taylor Shelton, and Sean Gorman, "Volunteered Geographic Information and Crowdsourcing Disaster Relief: A Case Study of the Haitian Earthquake," *World Medical & Health Policy* 2, no.2 (July 2010), doi:10.2202/1948-4682.1069.

CHAPTER 10

From Traditional to Crowd and Cloud:

Geospatial Data Services at GMU

Joy Suh

THE PRODUCTION AND distribution of geospatial data† has changed considerably in the past ten years. Academic libraries in the United States have managed digital geospatial data as part of their collections since the beginning of the distribution of the Census Bureau's TIGER Files in the early 1990s, later followed by other digital geospatial data distributed by authorized government agencies.‡ These geospatial data require the use of Geographic Information Systems (GIS), a powerful tool that stores, views, analyzes, and visualizes data associated with geospatial data. Providing GIS services and the technology (predominately ESRI's ArcGIS) therefore has been part of many academic libraries' geospatial data services. In the past few years, geospatial data has been rapidly produced and disseminated by non-government entities or by individuals. Volunteers and citizens have generated crowdsourced geospatial data, which a field often referred to as volunteer geographic information (VGI).[1] For instance, users can update roads and buildings through open source mapping applications such as Open Street Map (OSM) using Web 2.0 technology. Crowdsourcing allows users to geotag spatial information to posts harvested from microblogs such as Twitter, which is referred to as ambient geographic information (AGI).[2] As geospatial data become more ubiquitous and GIS technology becomes more Web and open source software based, academic libraries face new opportunities and challenges in adapting to these dynamic changes.

---

† Geospatial data refers as data that identifies the location of objects (natural and man-made features) on the Earth. It also calls spatially reference data (XY coordinates) or GIS data.

‡ Examples of this type of data include the USGS DEM and DOQQ files, and NASA's Landsat satellite images.

A recent article by Scaramozzino et al. captures an overview of GIS and data services across five university libraries in the areas of collection, consultation, instruction, and course support including computing facilities.[3] In comparison, the GIS service provided at George Mason University is a distinctive example of an academic library extending its service to meet the emerging need to harvest geospatial data generated by social media networks and data mining for GIS applications that had not been previously offered by academic libraries.

This chapter describes the experience at George Mason University (referred to as "Mason") and highlights the adaption of the library's services to the trends and changes in geospatial data and GIS technology. It begins with a brief review of the GIS environment at Mason, describes the evolution of GIS service practices with the transition from government documents and maps to data services, and presents examples of current practices in harvesting Twitter data collection and Web mapping. This chapter ends with a discussion of the possible incorporation of user-generated geospatial data into the current GIS service at Mason and anticipated future services.

GIS Landscape of Mason

Located near Washington D.C. and founded in 1972 as a formal independent university out of the Northern Virginia Branch of the University of Virginia, George Mason University has been one of the most rapidly growing universities in the nation. It was named as the top national university to watch by *U.S. News & World Report* in 2008[4] and was the first university in the nation to offer a doctoral degree in Information Technology in 1985. Enrollment is currently more than 33,000, making it the largest university in the State of Virginia, with students enrolled in 88 undergraduate and 127 graduate degree programs including Law across eleven colleges. Mason has campuses in Fairfax, Arlington, and Manassas, Virginia and one international branch campus in Song-Do, South Korea.[5] Each campus has distinctive academic programs not replicated elsewhere; for instance, the Arlington campus includes the Public Policy graduate school, the Conflict Analysis and Resolution program, and the School of Law, while Prince William campus includes the School of Bioinformatics and Bioengineering. The majority of the university's students are from Virginia; however, the student population is diversified both geographically and ethnically, with students from all 50 states and 130 countries. While full-time undergraduates make up the largest student group, part-time graduate and undergraduate students account for nearly half of the population.[6]

The Department of Geography and Geoinformation (GGS) in the College of Science located on the Fairfax campus leads GIS research at Mason. The department offers Bachelors, Masters, and Doctoral degrees in Geography, GIS, Earth Systems, and Geoinformation Sciences including three graduate certificates (GIS, Geointelligence, and Remote Sensing). It also offers one graduate certificate in Environmental GIS and Biodiversity Conservation jointly with the Department of Environmental Science and Policy and Smithsonian Mason School of Conservation.[7] It is known as the premier department in the Washington, D.C. metropolitan area since many federal employees are in the degree program. The program offers several different GIS courses including Web and Cloud Sourced GIS. Many faculty and students in GGS and in the College of Science have been affiliated with campus research centers supported by grants and contracts from federal agencies.[8] Several research centers and their geospatial data portals are nationally known. For example, the Center for Spatial Information Science and Systems (CSISS) maintains GeoBrain (http://geobrain.laits.gmu.edu/), a Web-based catalog for NASA's EOS and USGS DEM data, and CropSCape (http://nassgeodata.gmu.edu/CropScape/), a geospatial data portal to retrieve USDA's annual cropland layers. The Center for Earth Observing and Space Research (CEOSR), the Center of Intelligent Spatial Computing for Water/Energy Science (CISC), and the Center for Computational Data and Statistics in the College of Science provide cutting-edge research related to spatial computing and analysis of large datasets in the areas of natural hazard, disaster management, hurricane tracking, water and energy.[9]

GGS facilities include several labs equipped with high-end computers and software. ArcGIS (available through a university site license) and other open source GIS packages such as GRASS and Quantum GIS (QGIS), PostgreSQL, and GeoExt are extensively used. GGS and the affiliated research centers are well connected with computer clusters provided by the Office of Research Computing for big data analysis and computing.[10] Many faculty members are interested in using Twitter data mining to explore possible patterns of social interactions on political topics such as the Affordable Care Act ("Obamacare") over space and time. GeoSocial Gauge (http://geosocial.gmu.edu), a Web interface to explore peoples' social and political views using live stream data, was developed by a team in GGS and has been recognized as a pioneer work on harvesting geospatial intelligence for social media data.[†]

There has been growing use of GIS in teaching and research outside of GGS at Mason. The Graduate School of Public Policy in Arlington campus was the first to offer GIS courses (one for introductory level of GIS and another for spatial statistics). It was soon followed by the departments of Civil Engineering, Environmental Policy, and Global and Community Health. Recently many students, especially research assistants from Government, Education, Social Work, Criminology and History, have used GIS to handle their faculty research projects. In 2015, more than 200 individuals were involved in a GIS Day event hosted by GGS held on the Fairfax campus. Student interest in learning GIS from across academic disciplines, along with strong GIS research activities lead by GGS in geoinformatics and spa-

† The project was awarded in 2012 by the U.S. Geospatial Intelligence Foundation (USGIF) for their pioneering work on harvesting geospatial intelligence for social media data.

tial data computing and analysis, brings an increasing demand for geospatial data, software, and technical support that has been centrally accommodated by the libraries' GIS service.

Evolution of GIS Services at Mason

Government Documents and Maps: 2002–2010

From the beginning, GIS library services were under the Government Documents and Map unit, which was part of the Reference Department in Fenwick Library on the main campus. Starting in 2002 the government documents librarian (the author) started to build a GIS program at Mason Libraries[11] ("the libraries") part-time with the help of one half-time graduate student assistant (GRA) and a small lab with two workstations to access software (running ArcView software at that time).

A major component of the libraries' GIS service was data collection. The libraries acquired spatial and numeric datasets from a variety of sources. As a federal and Virginia State depository library, the libraries naturally received USGS topographic maps and digital geospatial data including Census data on CD-ROMs and DVDs. Because of the relatively short history of the university, the libraries lacked historical map collections. The libraries purchased census data with added geographical data based on census tracts, such as the Neighborhood Change Databases (NCDB), through commercial vendors such as Geolytics Inc. The libraries also purchased several Northern Virginia county GIS datasets that were not freely available. During this period, collecting local county GIS data (vector and raster-based format) on CD-ROMs and making them accessible to users efficiently was a major task. In 2007, the librarian, with help from the GRA, developed a designated Web server to access the restricted local county GIS data collection online (called the "library geodata server).[12] This is a file-based system where users can browse the titles of the collection and download individual layers through an authentication process on or off campus. During this period, data that had initially been provided in tangible format such as CD-ROMs became available online. Many state and federal agencies provided geospatial data clearinghouses and open data repositories to access their downloadable data. The libraries added commercial databases (i.e. SimplyMap and Social Explorer), which offer cloud based data and mapping applications together to create maps without having GIS skills. Major duties for the librarian became creating a library guide (http://infoguides.gmu.edu/gis) to list these online downloadable data sources and creating tutorials to help users use the resources.

Another major role of the libraries' GIS staff was outreach across campus. The librarian offered GIS drop-in workshops in a library lab with three high-end computers. She promoted the workshops in a targeted fashion via a listserv of the chairs of the departments such as Political Science, Criminology, Social Work and Sociology that did not yet have GIS courses, but had students and faculty who might need GIS skills for research. Students interested in learning GIS could attend the one-and-a-half hour long drop-in workshops alternating every other week in the libraries during regular semesters. The introductory level of the GIS workshop covered geospatial data structure (vector and raster data) and major geospatial data resources, basic concepts of GIS, and skills to create a simple thematic map using census demographic data in the most current version of ESRI ArcGIS. Later, the librarian added workshops on geocoding† and georeferencing‡ and intermediate levels of GIS (covering spatial analysis tools). These workshops helped students do the following: identify a spatial data format to use and major resources to discover and access data; build knowledge and skills in manipulating spatial data (such as importing data to software, joining two tables based on a common uniquely identified attribute field, converting one projection to another); and present data as a map. Most of all, students acquired the knowledge and skills to recognize that any data associated with locations can be analyzed and displayed as a map in GIS. These two-hour drop-in workshops offered a useful venue to increase spatial literacy and the awareness of the libraries' GIS service on campus.

Class-integrated instruction was another form of outreach. The librarian visited classes that were conducting GIS-related assignments. For example, in an undergraduate geology class the librarian showed students how to download image data (raster) using the "Seamless Viewer" site offered by the USGS repository and how to import and use them in GIS. The librarian also demonstrated a step-by-step procedure on how to download 2000 Census data using American Factfinder for community demographic mapping and how to join the census data with a census tract GIS boundary files and make a thematic map in an undergraduate social work class. A collaborative project subsequently was born, with several members on the campus placing the instruction steps online using multimedia tools.[13]

Participating in annual GIS Day events at Mason was another important form of outreach. The libraries hosted this annual event jointly with the Department of Geography as a partnership starting in 2002. Since then, the library staff has demonstrated various GIS tools, such as Google Fusion Tables, and presented new library GIS services such as the geodata server through this event.

Another major role of the service was reference and consultation. During this period, the librarian had reference desk hours under the Fenwick reference department and individual research consultations based on appointments for finding data and creating maps using desktop ArcGIS and Google Earth. The most

---

† Geocoding is the process of converting address data into location point data with their longitude and latitude information.

‡ Georeferencing is the processing of assigning georeferenced information (longitude and latitude) on a scanned image maps.

frequent assistance provided during this period was for geocoding addresses, georeferencing, converting data to other formats (e.g., converting KML to shape files), and joining census data with boundary GIS files.

Data Services Group: 2011–Present

In fall 2010, the libraries created a Data Services Group (DSG) under the Digital Programs and Systems Departments that combined the existing government documents and GIS services with the statistical consultant services that had been under the Resources and Collection Management department and added the new position of Data Librarian. In addition to managing the DSG, the new position assumed the role of providing e-research management services related to the data lifecycle and collecting a variety of datasets to support teaching and research on campus. The shift represented the changing landscape of library services at Mason by integrating existing data-related services such as GIS and statistical consultation into one group, and the addition of a new data position responded to the emerging need of E-research data management and curation services in academic libraries.[14]

After some three years of preparation and adjustment, the DSG currently has three full time staff: one data librarian, one geospatial resource librarian, and a data and research consultant. Each position has its own specialization: the data librarian focuses on numeric and statistical data; the geospatial resources librarian focuses on geospatial data and GIS; and the data research consultant on data analysis and research methods. The group manages a dedicated computer lab (six workstations) staffed by two graduate research assistants (one for GIS and another for Statistical and Qualitative Analysis) housed in Fenwick Library in Fairfax. The group serves as a central point to provide any help that is needed for finding, acquiring, and using statistical, geospatial, and qualitative data as well as providing data collection, data management, outreach, and software support across campuses.[15] The group has provided data management training to graduate students and faculty members on campus through the annual Virginia Data Boot Camp since 2014[16] and conducted in-house data management training sessions for subject librarians in 2014. Within this group, the geospatial resources librarian serves a broader role encompassing geospatial data management and curation and is closely aligned to the area of e-research, in addition to further developing the existing GIS service program.

Currently, data access is mostly online except for a few commercial CD-ROMs that have single user licenses (e.g., NCDB by Geolytics, Inc.). Accessing geospatial data became easier as more open data repositories and geospatial data catalogs were developed by states and academic libraries covering a wider variety of topics.[17] The libraries are adding more commercial databases such as the Data Planet Statistical Insight, Statista, China GeoExplorer, Landscan Global Archive, and PolicyMap in addition to the existing Social Explorer and SimplyMap databases. Recently, the leading proprietary GIS vendor, ESRI, began requiring that member organizations share their open data to the public via ArcGIS Open Data. This is part of a larger trend of increased data sharing by a diverse range of organizations. Keeping the GIS InfoGuides (http://infoguides.gmu.edu/gis) frequently updated to include all of these diverse geospatial data resources has become increasingly important for users looking for geospatial data and GIS resources at Mason.†

The libraries maintains a Web server which contains 108 gigabytes data of Northern Virginia county-level GIS data collected over the last 10 years for those who need historical county GIS data that are not all available online yet. This is still a file-based system to browse the data files. In the future, user access will be improved through a keyword or topic search interface. The in-house server will also be moved to a cloud-based system.

Outreach to promote the services has been continually accomplished through class integrated instruction, GIS workshops, and the annual GIS Day event. As a result of class integrated sessions, several students attended the library GIS workshops to learn more about the technology. Since not many classrooms are equipped with GIS software such as ArcGIS due to specific system requirements, teaching GIS in regular classrooms for those departments that do not have labs is a barrier to outreach in classroom instruction. ArcGIS is accessible through the Virtual Computing Lab, but it is too slow to access and often crashes.

The librarian has recently offered more advanced level GIS workshops including open source GIS alternatives, such as Quantum GIS (QGIS). This reflects the fact that more students have been looking for open source alternatives that they can use after graduation (without purchasing a costly ArcGIS individual license). Moreover, several graduate courses in GGS have integrated the use of QGIS into their course.

The workshops added in the last two years include: Introduction to QGIS (open source GIS), Harvesting Geotagged Twitter Data using Python and Twitter APIs, Python for ArcPy, and Web-based Demographic Data and Mapping, in addition to existing introductory and intermediate GIS workshops (a list and descriptions are available: http://dataservices.gmu.edu/workshops/gis). These workshops are held in a small lab that can accommodate a maximum of six people. The average GIS workshop attendance per session has been three people in the past two calendar years. Figure 10.1 provides the GIS attendances by majors or departments during the 2014-15 academic calendar year.

† The GIS infoguide has been one of the top five visited sites among the Libguides provided at the Libraries in the past five years.

Figure 10.1. GIS Workshop Attendance by Department Affiliation, 2014–15 Academic Year

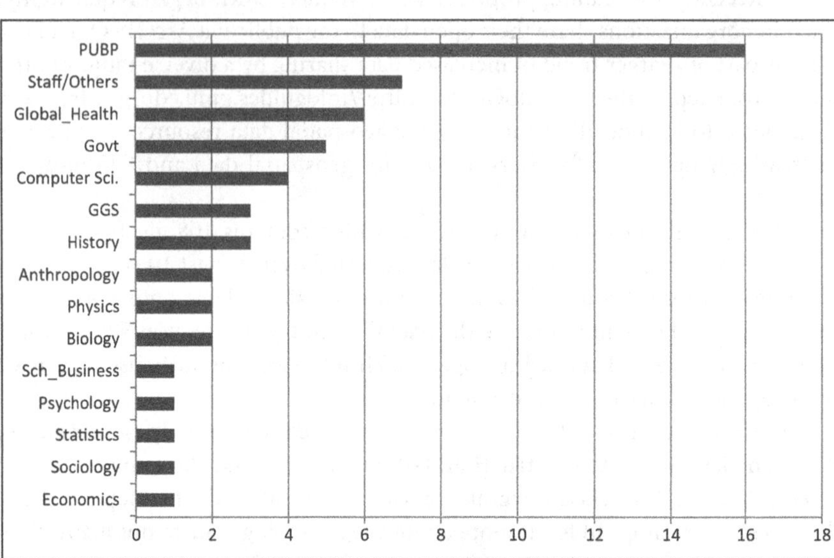

Seventy percent of the attendees are graduate students. These students are from a variety of disciplines, although Public Policy still accounts for about 25 percent. This reflects the strong outreach the librarian provides to Public Policy students (including going to the Arlington campus twice a semester to teach workshops and provide consultation for those students).

Most individual consultations are GIS project based that often requires follow-up appointments from an initial project appointment. A typical initial consultation is to determine whether a student has a research question and is able to identify dependent and independent variables for the research. Next the librarian needs to identify whether the student understands geographical data (based on a level of geography such as census tract) and the associated topical data (such as population) that are needed to map and analyze using GIS. In addition, the consultation is geared to the student's GIS analysis requirement and necessary output for data presentations (print or interactive web mapping). Once a student acquires or creates the necessary datasets, the next appointment often involves assistance in cleaning datasets for use in GIS and displaying data to complete the project.

Depending on the users' levels of proficiency with GIS, the level of assistance varies. Most of the GGS students only need help with looking for geospatial datasets, while non-GGS students need help in finding or creating datasets, cleaning datasets, and working with GIS software to visualize data. These non-GGS students often lack the basic knowledge and skills that are currently covered by the libraries' GIS workshops including:

- Creating a spreadsheet or a geodatabase file based on a level of geography
- Joining a table of data to a layer table of data based on a common attribute that can be found in both table
- Geocoding

The librarian often encourages these students to take an appropriate GIS workshop in order to learn the skills to complete their own projects. Under limited circumstances, the librarian or the GRA provide advanced assistance, such as data cleaning or creating maps to help complete a project. If there is a project that requires unrealistic demands on the staff's time or is beyond their knowledge and skills, they refer to someone on the campus network for further consultation. The librarian has often been proactive about identifying future service needs for students on campus. For instance, if the same types of questions are asked or services are needed repeatedly, the librarian has tried to provide in-house guides or tutorials (http://infoguides.gmu.edu/gis/tutorials) with the assistance of the GRA. The following section highlights two examples of the most recent GIS services offered at Mason in which the demand was identified through project consultations.

Examples of Current Practices

Harvesting Twitter Data and Visualization

The ability to geotag social media in the past few years allows for easier visualization of data over geographic space. Unlike other social-microblogs, Twitter allows their users to access Twitter's global stream of Tweet data with their Streaming API.[18] Geolocation based off of the user's allowed GPS location and its content, or "tweets," provides an effective way of visualizing a topic along space and time. Academic researchers have been increasingly using crowdsourced information and social media data to improve routing and navigation services[19] and in geoinformatics.[20] These data are often perceived as a part of big data since these data possess three characteristics: volume (large scale of data storage and processing), data variety (different type and format), and velocity (fast rate of new data acquisition).[21] A special issue of the *Journal of Map and Geography Libraries* discusses the evolution of real-time crisis mapping as impacted by open source software and social networks, the contributions of these maps to managing various disasters such as the Haiti and Libya cases, and crisis mapping as a new curriculum in academics.[22] Many public and non-public agencies provide tools to collect crowdsourcing data and crowd mapping to aid their decisions and actions.[23] For example, the National Geospatial Intelligence Agency provides a tool, "GeoQ," to collect crowdsourcing data to assess damages over large areas.

In early 2014 an adjunct faculty member in the Department of Criminology was one of the first individuals on campus who approached to the

Libraries to ask for help with harvesting Twitter data and visualizations. Her objective was to make a map of drug-related crime in Mexico using official statistics, but she also wanted to visualize Twitter data on a map in order to understand and analyze crime patterns. After exploring several tools and available resources at the libraries, she and the librarian decided to use NVivo Ncapture software. First, they searched the words “crime” AND “Mexico” AND “drug” on Twitter. They captured the results, opened them with NVivo Ncapture and saved them in .xls. Figure 10.2 shows Twitter data collected by NVivo Ncapture in .xls format.

Figure 10.2. Example of Twitter Data Collection with NVivo NCapture

E1 fx Time

	A	B	C	D	E	F	G	H	L	M	N	O	P	Q	R
1	Row IC	Tweet ID	Usernan	Tweet	Time	Tweet Typ	Retweeted By	Number	Location	Web	Bio	Number of Tweets	Number of Followers	Number Following	Coordinates
2	1	49233849§	OCCRP	RT @OCCF	7/24/2014 12:00:	Retweet	KieranBeer	2		http://t.co/UB2pc8b4	Organized Crime & C	1849	2725	1070	
3	2	49232808§	OCCRP	RT @OCCF	7/24/2014 11:18:	Retweet	srubenfeld	2		http://t.co/UB2pc8b4	Organized Crime & C	1849	2725	1070	
4	3	49232362§	OCCRP	2 men sent	7/24/2014 11:01:	Tweet		2		http://t.co/UB2pc8b4	Organized Crime & C	1849	2725	1070	
5	4	491350084	retaketh	@DanaPeri	7/21/2014 6:32:4	Tweet		0	Deep in th		Constitutional Conse	18787	2940	2127	
6	5	49128995§	conexio	50 casas lu	7/21/2014 2:33:4	Tweet		0			Conexion Nacional e	1378	81	203	
7	6	49122756§	retaketh	@KatiePav	7/21/2014 10:25:	Tweet		0	Deep in th		Constitutional Conse	18787	2940	2127	
8	7	490607414	Siete24	RT @Siete	7/19/2014 5:21:3	Retweet	lopezsiete24	1	México, C	http://t.co/8X9SU3W	7/24 'La Verdad en Ti	203890	32957	1842	+19.42847-099.12766/
9	8	49060290§	Siete24	Demolerán	7/19/2014 5:03:4	Tweet		1	México, C	http://t.co/8X9SU3W	7/24 'La Verdad en Ti	203890	32957	1842	+19.42847-099.12766/
10	9	490602902	emanuel	Demolerán	7/19/2014 5:03:4	Tweet		0	México, C	http://t.co/8X9SU3W	Un contador de cuen	21771	873	1843	+19.42847-099.12766/
11	10	490313321	ErickCU	#narcobloq	7/18/2014 9:52:5	Tweet		0	Corregido		Mis princesas	5811	36	181	+20.5084-100.43606/
12	11	490312811	Damian	#narcobloq	7/18/2014 9:50:5	Tweet		0	Playa del		Le cerré las puertas	5500	145	174	+20.6274-087.07987/
13	12	490311031	Blanco_	#narcobloq	7/18/2014 9:43:5	Tweet		0	El Marqué		Sigo siendo la peque	5955	230	178	+20.65854-100.27444/
14	13	490310981	Ama_yr	#narcobloq	7/18/2014 9:43:4	Tweet		0	Tequisqui		E sabor mas rico es	6081	216	178	+20.5225-099.89167/
15	14	49030949§	RobertA	#narcobloq	7/18/2014 9:37:4	Tweet		0	Huimilpan		La esperanza nunca	6102	227	183	+20.43317-100.32323/
16	15	490309207	Alexand	#narcobloq	7/18/2014 9:36:3	Tweet		0	Isla Mujer		El ruido de tus zapat	5593	225	176	+21.27101-086.89904/
17	16	49030878§	Marcos	#narcobloq	7/18/2014 9:34:5	Tweet		0	Cozumel		De que te sirven esa	5516	222	163	+20.501-086.94598/
18	17	49030855§	Mencha	#narcobloq	7/18/2014 9:34:0	Tweet		0	Tolimán,C		Los cachorros son ta	5991	272	178	+20.91168-099.94568/
19	18	49030842§	DaniaTr	#narcobloq	7/18/2014 9:33:3	Tweet		0	Cancún		Me da tanto gusto q	5408	219	175	+21.17429-086.84656/

They had to go through some necessary clean up before using the data in GIS. For example, the column “coordinates” of the table in Figure 10.2 needed to be split into two columns for latitude and longitude, and those tweets with no coordinates needed to be removed.

Collecting Twitter data from Nvivo NCapture turned out to be inefficient for creating a large dataset with live stream data. Twitter’s search results only display tweets posted in the preceding five days from the current time of the search. To collect more than five days’ worth of tweets, the search must be run again after the original five days have elapsed to get sufficient data.

They needed an alternative way to harvest tweets by geographic area, containing specific word(s), and limited to those data where the user provided their location information (referred to as “geotagged tweets”). A student taking the course on Web-based GIS (GGS 692) asked the librarian for help with harvesting Twitter data. The librarian, with help of the GRA, provided a Python script that used Twitter APIs. Working with this script requires using the Tweepy application and API keys from a Twitter account.† The script feeds live stream data tweeted while the program is running, allowing users to choose a particular time and a time duration to capture live stream data for their needs.

In fall 2014, the libraries started to offer GIS workshops on harvesting Twitter data and visualizing it in GIS, as well as a step-by-step tutorial that included the Twitter data harvesting Python script.[24] Figure 10.3 is a screenshot of the visualization of the geotagged "ebola" Twitter data collected using the script from 4:00 pm on November 4 until 5:00 am on November 5, 2015 (with the generated total of 908 tweets).

Figure 10.3. Visualization of Twitter Data on Ebola in ArcGIS Online

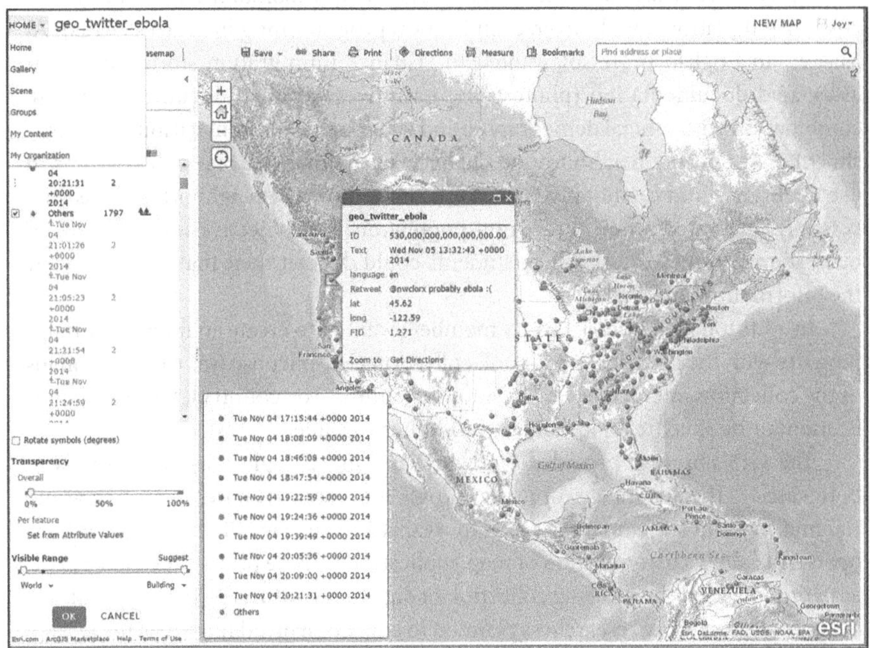

Once the data are exported into GIS formats, such as shape files, the data can be explored and analyzed with GIS spatial query and analysis functions, such as aggregating point data based on a census geography level, mining data based on attribute values, and even animating the tweet event over time.

The libraries has its own tool to help our users collect live stream tweets with location information by keyword (a topic) and geographic area. This provides en-

† The data output of this script is in .csv format rather than the JSON format that is originated from Twitter. Anyone can easily import this file to any GIS software.

hanced support to research and teaching on campus, as this demand for social media data searching is anticipated to grow on campus. In the future, online tools that easily harvest Twitter data based on more customized criteria may become available. However, until one is found, the in-house developed tool will continue to serve as an effective mean to this end.

Interaction Web Maps: Cloud Based GIS

Instead of creating digital maps using desktop GIS software, more researchers are turning to interactive Web mapping interfaces with the fast development of Web-based GIS technology. It offers users many advantages over desktop GIS, such as the ability to view and share maps globally, use and maintain data easily, and a customized platform with diverse application programming interfaces (APIs). At Mason, an English professor wanted to visualize immigration stories and their associated documentation (photos, oral narratives, scanned documents, etc.) in combination with official demographic and economic data from various dates that show how a specific neighborhood changed over time. Her research goal was to use qualitative and quantitative data to illustrate how the neighborhood has successfully integrated a new immigrant population. Her objective was to create an open source framework in which students could deposit their materials and view the information interactively.

In addition, two library faculty members wanted to create an interactive mapping site with the libraries' artist book collection. The purpose was to display maps of the collection interactively by locations of authors (by country), by year of publication, or by specific topic, language, or other variable.

The GIS librarian provided Google Drive and Google Mashup tutorials in both cases.[25] The advantages of using Google tools are that base maps such as aerial imagery and street maps are already available from the cloud server, and their open APIs allow customization of map applications. These projects needed a server in order to feed the growing collection of data in the future. As it turned out, the on-going datasets the researchers planned to collect involved huge files (especially with narrative-interview data collected by the classroom environment) that required a large server. Although the libraries could not support this endeavor fully, the use of Google Fusion Tables and Google Mashup provided a proof of concept for visualizing data interactively on a web-mapping interface.

Better alternatives to the Google products, however, are emerging now, such as Leaflet (an open source platform using OpenStreetMap as a base map) and ArcGIS Online. More recent developments in ArcGIS Online include advanced functionalities without the need to use APIs. Students can easily make a map by uploading their data or using data or maps generated or shared by others with the public. Students can save their own projects in the ArcGIS online server and use various web application templates to publish or host their own web mapping sites. In theory, the library can use ArcGIS online as a surrogate institutional repository for students and faculty GIS projects as long as it keeps a site license with ESRI. There is, however, still an issue that prevents campus-wide promotion of the availability of ArcGIS Online. Mason's site license for ESRI software allows a limited number of user accounts and service credits, and individual users need to request their own account with the GIS manager who organizationally resides in GGS. Because of this access limitation associated with ArcGIS Online, the libraries are using the online product cautiously and will continue to direct students to use other open source Web Mapping Sources (i.e. CartoDB, Google Drive, etc.) until ESRI broadens this usage policy. As the ability to create maps in a cloud-based GIS will no doubt continue to become progressively more sophisticated, the libraries is looking forward to providing more Web-based GIS services, especially in the humanities fields.

Future Directions

The evolution of GIS service at Mason since 2002 illustrates how the libraries have responded to the growing demand for the service on campus and how the service itself has also quickly adapted to new demands, such as harvesting social media data, providing access to open source software, and creating interactive maps.

Given the recent growth of this user-generated geospatial data—either from crowds participating in collaborative projects (VGI) or from georeferenced content shared by social media network sites (AGI)—the demand for GIS services in academic libraries will no doubt continue to increase in a dynamic and more complex geospatial environment. GIS librarians are now positioned to take advantage of opportunities to expand existing GIS services with emerging types of geospatial data.

One opportunity is to create a section of an existing information guide that focuses on key resources and tools for user-generated geospatial data. Existing collection development policies can also include this type of data as part of the libraries' geospatial data collection. Library instruction sessions and workshops can include instruction on how to extract data from cloud-based networks, clean datasets, collect geospatial data using mobile devices, and import the result to online GIS applications such as ArcGIS online and Google Fusion Tables. Libraries can also facilitate a designated workstation in a secure place to support users who harvest live stream data, a process that can sometimes take more than several days, and help users locate possible cloud-based storage sites for saving the resulting datasets.

Although the opportunities discussed above provide an excellent potential for improving and evolving current services, there is something more that could be done beyond this. This is in the area of data curation, which has not been practiced at Mason due staffing constraints. A recent article by Bishop suggests that data curation for geospatial data generated by users is an important emerging role for GIS librarians.[26] Since the value of user-generated geospatial data is unpredictable and there are also issues of authority (unaffiliated users), precision, and accuracy with this type of data, as discussed in recent literature,[27] the best practices for data curation of this type of data may be similar to that of the e-research data management that many academic libraries are already currently practicing. Since many librarians are being asked to provide data management support to researchers as part of the researchers' funding requirements, there is no doubt that librarians will need to include new and emerging geospatial data types in their research data management and curation services.

Since developing and maintaining an institutional data repository along with e-research data management is one of the important missions for the DSG at Mason, the group will implement Mason Dataverse on the Dataverse network to preserve and share data generated by Mason faculty, staff, and students.[28] Coming in the future we will provide data curation for geospatial data in accordance with the geospatial metadata standard guided suggested by the Federal Geographic Data Committee (FGDC). Mason's Dataverse will provide a new place for researchers at Mason to deposit, access, share, and preserve their geospatial data, in turn enhancing research efficiency and accessibility of geospatial data.

Based on these experiences, the most important librarian aptitudes and abilities for providing good geospatial data services include the following:

- guiding users in identifying relevant geospatial data (vector vs. raster data types)
- teaching users to use various GIS software tools to transform, analyze, and display geospatial data
- curating and/or cataloging geospatial data using the FGDC metadata for discovery and reuse
- monitoring awareness of campus data needs
- continuously updating technical skills to meet users' emerging needs and demands
- building partnerships and collaborative relationships with partners both within and outside their institutions

All of these are vital and will empower geospatial librarians at other academic and research libraries to excel in their multiple roles within the dynamic and rapidly evolving world of GIS and Web technology.

---

1. Goodchild refers to this type of data as "Voluntary Geographic Information" (VGI). Michael F. Goodchild, "Citizens as Sensors: The World of Volunteered Geography," *GeoJournal*, 2007: 211–221.
2. Stefanidis et al. refers this type of geographic data generated by social media called to as "Ambient Geographic Information" (AGI). Anthony Stefanidis, Andrew Crooks, and Jacek Radzikow-

ski, "Harvesting Ambient Geographic Information from Social Media Feeds," *GeoJournal* 78 (2): 319–338. doi: 10.1007/s10708-011-9438-2.

3. Jeanine Scaramozzino, Russell White, Jeff Essic, Lee Ann Fullington, Himanshu Mistry, Amanda Henley, Miriam Olivares, "From Map Rooms to Data Services: Five University Libraries Evolving to Meet Campus Needs and Changing Technologies," *Journal of Map and Geography Libraries* 10, no. 1 (2014): 6–47, http://dx.doi.org/10.1080/15420353.2014.893943.
4. George Mason University, "About Mason," last modified 2016, http://about.gmu.edu/history-and-tradition/.
5. George Mason University, "2014–2015 Facts & Figures," last modified December 2014, http://irr.gmu.edu/FastFacts/.
6. George Mason University, "Degrees Awarded," accessed January 5, 2016, https://irr2.gmu.edu/index.cfm?activePage=degree&subLink=Degree.
7. George Mason University, "Geography and Geoinformation Science," accessed January 5, 2016, https://cos.gmu.edu/ggs/academic-programs/; "Graduate Certificate in Geographic Information Sciences," accessed January 5, 2016, https://cos.gmu.edu/ggs/academic-programs/graduate-certificate-in-geographic-information-sciences/; Mason Office of Continuing Professional Education (OCPE) located in Prince William Campus also offers a GIS certificate program for business and professional community.
8. George Mason University, "Research," accessed January 5, 2016, https://cos.gmu.edu/ggs/research/.
9. George Mason University, "Research: Research Centers," accessed January 5, 2016, https://cos.gmu.edu/about/research/#centers.
10. George Mason University, "Mason Office of Research Computing," last modified June 19, 2015, http://orc.gmu.edu/.
11. George Mason University, "University Libraries," accessed January 5, 2016, http://library.gmu.edu.
12. George Mason University, "Library Geo Data Server," accessed January 5, 2016, http://librarygeodata.gmu.edu.
13. George Mason University, "GIS & Geospatial Data," accessed January 5, 2016, http://dataservices.gmu.edu/resources/gis; Joy Suh, "Integrating Library's GIS Skills into Undergraduate Courses," (presentation at the ALA Annual Conference, Anaheim, CA, 2008); Michael Wolf-Branigin, Joy Suh, and Star Muir, "Applying Census Data for Small Area Estimation in Community and Social Service Planning," *Journal of Applied Statistical Methods* 8, no. 1 (2009): 299–305.
14. Minglu Wang, "The new role of academic libraries," (presented at ACRL Biennial Conference, 2013), http://www.ala.org/acrl/sites/ala.org.acrl/files/content/conferences/confsandpreconfs/2013/papers/Wang_AcademicLibrary.pdf.
15. George Mason University, "Welcome to Data Services," accessed January 5, 2016, http://dataservices.gmu.edu.
16. Old Dominion University, "Virginia Data Management Boot Camp," last modified May 5, 2015, http://guides.lib.odu.edu/VADMBC/.
17. Christine Kollen, Cynthia Dietz, Joy Suh, and Angela Lee, "Geospatial Data Catalogs: Approaches by Academic Libraries," *Journal of Map & Geography Libraries* 9, no. 3 (2013): 276–295, doi:10.1080/15420353.2013.820161
18. Twitter, "The Streaming APIs," accessed May 20, 2015, https://dev.twitter.com/streaming/overview.
19. Mohamad Bakillah, Johannes Lauer, Steve H.L. Liang, Alexander Zipf, Jamal Jokar Arsanjani, Amin Mobasheri, and Lukas Loos, "Exploiting Big VGI to Improve Routing and Navigation Services," in *Big Data: Techniques and Technologies in Geoinformatics*, ed. Hassan A. Karimi (Boca Raton: CRC Press, 2014).
20. Arie Croitoru, Andrew Crooks, Jacek Radzikowski, Anthony Stefanidis, Ranga R. Vatsavai, and Nicole Wayant, Geoinformatics and Social Media: New Big Data Challenges

21. Michael R. Evans, Dev Oliver, Xun Zhou, and Shashi Sekhar, "Spatial Big Data: Studies on Volume, Velocity, and Variety," in *Big Data: Techniques and Technologies in Geoinformatics*, ed. Hassan A. Karimi (Boca Raton: CRC Press, 2014).
22. See *Journal of Geography and Map Libraries* 8, no. 2 (2012).
23. Office of Science and Technology Policy, "Fact Sheet: Empowering Students and Others through Citizen Science and Crowd Sourcing," last modified March 23 2015, https://www.whitehouse.gov/sites/default/files/microsites/ostp/citizen_science_backgrounder_03-23-15.pdf.
24. See the tutorial, "Harvesting Geo-tagged Twitter Data," last modified December 10, 2015, http://infoguides.gmu.edu/gis/tutorials.
25. See Google Fusion and Mashup tutorials, "Creating Web Maps," last modified December 10, 2015, http://infoguides.gmu.edu/gis/tutorials.
26. Bradley Wade Bishop, Tony H. Grubesic, and Sonya Prasertong, "Digital Curation and GeoWeb: An Emerging Role for Geographic Information Librarians," *Journal of Map & Geography Libraries* 9, no. 3 (2013): 276–295, doi:10.1080/15420353.2013.817367.
27. Stephane Roche, Eliane Propeck-Zimmermann, and Boris Mericskay, "Geoweb and Crisis Management: Issues and Perspectives of Volunteered Geographic Information," *GeoJournal* 78, no. 1 (2013): 1–20, doi: 10.1007/s10708-011-9423-9; David J. Coleman, "Volunteered Geographic Information in Spatial Data Infrastructure: An Early Look At Opportunities and Constraints," (presented at GSDI Conference, Singapore, 2010), http://www.gsdi.org/gsdiconf/gsdi12/papers/905.pdf.
28. George Mason University, "Start Archiving Your Data," accessed January 5, 2016, http://dataservices.gmu.edu/mars.

Further Reading

Baker, Robert. "Universities for Ushahidi: A Curriculum for Crisis Mapping." *Journal of Map & Geography Libraries* 8, no. 2 (2012): 173–76. doi:10.1080/15420353.2012.656834.

Blatt, Amy J. "Using GIS in Emergency Management in Chester County, Pennsylvania." *Journal of Map & Geography Libraries* 8, no. 2 (2012): 163–72. doi:10.1080/15420353.2012.662472.

Fu, Pinde. *Getting to Know Web GIS*. Redlands, CA: ESRI Press, 2015.

Meier Patrick. "Crisis Mapping in Action: How Open Source Software and Global Volunteer Networks Are Changing the World, One Map at a Time." *Journal of Map & Geography Libraries* 8, no. 2 (2012): 276-295. doi:10.1080/15420353.2012.663739.

Ziemke, Jen. "Crisis Mapping: The Construction of a New Interdisciplinary Field?" *Journal of Map & Geography Libraries* 8 no. 2 (2012: 101-117.

CHAPTER 11

Qualitative Research and Data Support:

The Jan Brady of Social Sciences Data Services?

Mandy Swygart-Hobaugh

THOSE FAMILIAR WITH *The Brady Bunch* television show, which aired in the United States from 1969-1974 but lives on via syndicated reruns and streaming services, are likely also familiar with the episode in which middle daughter Jan laments the fact that her older sister always receives accolades while Jan languishes in her shadow: "Marcia, Marcia, Marcia!" she cries in despair.[1] In the world of social sciences, qualitative researchers are often similarly overshadowed by their quantitative colleagues, with "Statistics, Statistics, Statistics!" perhaps echoing through their heads.

The abounding literature spanning various social sciences, continents, and decades points to a continuing divide between quantitative and qualitative research.[2] Despite the politics that often pits quantitative researchers against qualitative ones, many social sciences researchers continue to employ qualitative research methods, as they recognize its merits for nuanced, contextualized study of social life.[3] Likewise, social sciences researchers trying to bridge this divide are increasingly turning to triangulated mixed methods (i.e., a combination of quantitative and qualitative data analysis) as an arguably more robust research approach when contrasted to using one method or type of data in exclusion of the other.[4] The National Science Foundation's offering a specific grant for "Strengthening Qualitative Research through Methodological Innovation and Integration" and funding the recently launched Qualitative Data Repository illustrates the legitimacy of qualitative research in the United States academy.[5] Moreover, several established and developing European qualitative data archives such as the UK Data Service's QualiBank, the Irish Qualitative Data Archive, and the Finnish Social Science Data Archive point to a demand for reuse of qualitative data for secondary analysis.[6] Social sciences graduate programs commonly require qualitative methods courses along with those on quantitative methods, thus ensuring that qualitative research will continue to flourish in academia.

Qualitative research is and likely will remain a core methodology in the social sciences. Consequently, academic librarians providing data services in the social sciences should offer services to qualitative researchers on their campuses as well as quantitative ones. But is this the case in practice? Do social sciences librarians devote their primary attention to quantitative researchers over qualitative researchers? What qualitative data support services are social sciences librarians currently offering? And is there room for expansion of qualitative data support services provided by social sciences librarians?

The current library science literature on data support services reflects a predominantly quantitative focus. The major texts describing data services provisions in academic libraries, *Numeric Data Services and Sources for the General Reference Librarian* and *Data Basics: An Introductory Text,* focus on quantitative/numeric data services.[7] While several articles discuss the challenges of archiving qualitative data for long-term preservation and sharing and reuse, all of these articles are focused on European countries, with Louise Corti of the UK Data Archive, who is to be commended for her dedication to qualitative data, writing several.[8] Fifteen of these articles appeared in a special Fall 2010 issue of *IASSIST Quarterly (IQ),* a publication of the International Association for Social Science Information Services & Technology (IASSIST), in which the editor noted that while "in the beginning of IASSIST data was equivalent to quantitative data," more digital archives are beginning to recognize the value of qualitative data for secondary research, thus implying that qualitative has moved out from under the shadows of quantitative data to some degree.[9]

While the present literature is valuable in terms of addressing the challenges of archiving qualitative data for long-term access and reuse, it needs to be buttressed by work describing the current practices and future possibilities for academic social science librarians—particularly those in public services, subject liaison, or dedicated data services positions—to expand qualitative data support on their campuses to span the various stages of the research data lifecycle. This chapter undertakes that task by first giving an overview of the context of qualitative data and the resulting support needs of qualitative researchers at various stages of the research data lifecycle. The current state of qualitative data support services in social sciences librarianship is then explored by reporting on (1) an analysis of social sciences data librarian job postings, (2) a survey of social sciences librarians, and (3) an examination of online research guides describing qualitative data support services presently offered by social sciences librarians. Finally, this chapter concludes with recommendations for how social sciences librarians might embark on the expansion of their qualitative data support services.

Qualitative Data and the Support Needs of Qualitative Researchers across the Research Data Lifecycle

Demarcating what constitutes qualitative data is not an easy task. Corti offers a "simple definition" of qualitative data as including "any research material that is collected from studying people ... unless it has been transformed into numerical values ... in which case it becomes quantitative."[10] Corti also lists materials that are likely to first come to mind when thinking of qualitative data in the social sciences: "Such data include interviews—whether in-depth or unstructured, individual or group discussion—fieldwork diaries and observation notes, structured and unstructured diaries, personal documents, or photographs."[11] The list grows longer when consulting the 2014 *Sage Handbook of Qualitative Data Analysis,* which in addition to Corti's items adds news media, visual and audiovisual representations (still images, video, film/movies), sounds, and virtual/cyberspace data.[12] Denzin and Lincoln offer an "initial, generic definition" that melds both what materials might constitute qualitative *data* as well as the question of what does it mean to *do qualitative research*:

> Qualitative research is a situated activity that locates the observer in the world. It consists of a set of interpretive, material practices that make the world visible. These practices transform the world. They turn the world into a series of representations... At this level, qualitative research involves an interpretive, naturalistic approach to the world. This means that qualitative researchers study things in their natural setting, attempting to make sense of, or interpret, phenomena in terms of the meanings people bring to them. Qualitative research involves the studied use and collection of a variety of empirical materials—case study; personal experience; introspection; life story; interview; artifacts; cultural text and productions; observational, historical, interactional, and visual texts—that describe routine and problematic moments and meanings in individuals' lives.[13]

Drawing from these definitions, *any* material becomes qualitative data if researchers choose to analyze it as such—using their chosen analytical framework, they interpret and extrapolate nuanced, contextualized meaning from materials to better understand and describe social phenomenon in non-quantified ways.

Given these amorphous definitions of what constitutes qualitative data, delineating distinct, standardized support needs for qualitative researchers across the different stages of the research data lifecycle proves challenging. Using Corti, Van den Eynden, Bishop, and Woolard's overview of "typical activities undertaken in the research data lifecycle" as a foundation, what follows are proposed qualitative data support services that most readily lend themselves to social sciences librarians' knowledge and expertise.[14]

Discovery and Planning

At this stage of the research data lifecycle, social sciences librarians can support qualitative researchers by collecting and helping them find secondary resources for designing qualitative research studies and collecting original qualitative data. Similarly, librarians can provide instruction to researchers on how to find existing archived qualitative data for secondary analysis (e.g., data from the UK Data Archive's QualiBank, the Qualitative Data Repository at Syracuse University, or other repositories collecting qualitative data), point researchers to library print or digital collections and databases that contain materials for potential qualitative analysis (e.g., special collections, oral histories, newspaper databases, legislation and policy collections, etc.), and assist them in finding and collecting other digital, audiovisual, or print materials for qualitative analysis. In the realm of data management planning, librarians can consult qualitative researchers regarding best practices for documenting their research process (e.g., the parameters for the accession or collection of their data, their coding scheme development,[15] the iterations of their analysis process, developing and generating memos/reports/outputs from qualitative research software programs) to provide the necessary context for reuse of their data for secondary analysis by other researchers but also to gather evidence to strengthen the validity of their own findings.[16]

Data Collection

While traditionally librarians do not have a large role in the data collection stage of the research data lifecycle, there are possibilities for providing support services in this area. For example, librarians can collect or help qualitative researchers find secondary resources for data collection methods and refer them to resources for data collection (e.g., available online survey programs for collecting open-ended qualitative data). Likewise, in addition to consulting qualitative researchers regarding best practices for documenting their research process, librarians can consult on creating keyword/subject term metadata, guided by Data Documentation Initiative (DDI) standards for qualitative data documentation, to facilitate discovery of the data should it be archived for reuse by other researchers.[17]

Data Processing and Analysis

As with data collection, librarians traditionally have not played a large role in the data analysis stage of the research data lifecycle. However, there is potential for librarians to expand their roles in this area. For instance, librarians can pool resources for available transcription services on campus or in the community as well as available transcription software. Librarians with training in using qualitative data analysis softwares (e.g., NVivo, Atlas.ti, Dedoose, etc.) or digitization of textual and visual materials can provide instruction on data entry and digitization of qualitative materials to facilitate ease of analysis. Likewise, librarians with training in qualitative data analysis software can provide training on using it for data analysis and producing research outputs, reports, and visualizations to facilitate interpretation of the data. Similarly, librarians can collect or help qualitative researchers find secondary resources for best practices in data entry, transcription, digitization of qualitative data, and analyzing and interpreting qualitative data. Librarians can assist researchers in finding qualitative research publications that can serve as examples for them to model when writing their methods and findings. If researchers are using secondary sources for analysis, librarians can aid them in properly attributing the origin of the qualitative data used in their research study.

Publishing and Sharing

At this stage of the research data lifecycle, librarians can help researchers identify the best archive or repository in which to deposit their qualitative data and work with them to prepare the data and documentation for deposit to optimize reusability and discoverability, using DDI standards for qualitative data documentation. As qualitative researchers typically do not see the value of their data for reuse by others, librarians can explain to their campus researchers why depositing their qualitative data not only benefits other researchers but also themselves, as reuse demonstrates their own scholarly impact. Moreover, librarians can promote the qualitative data generated by their campus researchers by distributing announcements via listservs, blogs, and social media that encourage others to reuse the data for secondary analysis and for teaching qualitative data analysis.

Long-Term Management

Librarians can consult researchers regarding what file formats they should save or convert their qualitative data to for optimal long-term accessibility. Librarians can also act as mediators between the researchers and the campus information technology units to ensure the backing up and long-term storing of their data. Additionally, libraries with institutional data repositories can store the researchers' data for open-access in perpetuity.

Reusing Data

In this final stage of the research data lifecycle, librarians can promote to faculty and particularly to graduate researchers the merits of secondary analysis of qualitative data (e.g., less costly and less time consuming than collecting own data, applying new perspective to data can produce unique insights).[18] Librarians can help faculty teaching qualitative research methods to find existing qualitative data for teaching students about the kinds of qualitative data that are relevant to their disciplines or for analysis exercises. Librarians with training in qualitative data analysis software can train students on the logistics of coding for their analysis exercises.

As the above examples illustrate, many of the potential support activities for qualitative researchers are similar to those for quantitative researchers. Because many social science librarians are increasingly being tasked with inserting themselves into the various stages of the research data lifecycle to support quantitative researchers, so too is there potential for support across these stages for qualitative researchers. Gauging from the research literature and sessions at conferences addressing social sciences data support, social sciences librarians continue to focus primarily on quantitative data support.[19] But is this definitely the case in practice?

Current Qualitative Data Support Practices amongst Social Sciences Librarians

This section presents exploratory findings from (1) an analysis of social sciences data librarian job postings, (2) a survey of social sciences librarians, and (3) an examination of online research guides describing qualitative data support services presently offered by social sciences librarians. It concludes with a summary of answers to two questions:

- Do social sciences librarians devote their primary attention to quantitative researchers over qualitative researchers?
- What qualitative data support services are social sciences librarians currently offering?

IASSIST Job Postings Analysis

Content analysis of library job postings is a common methodological approach for assessing characteristics of the library profession.[20] This exploration of qualitative data support expectations in job postings focused on postings from the IASSIST job repository. IASSIST is an "international organization of professionals working with information technology and data services to support research and teaching in the social sciences" and a key professional organization for social sciences librarians tasked with data services support on academic campuses.[21] The IASSIST job postings repository compiles job descriptions posted to the IASSIST members' email listserv (iasst-l) from 2005 to the present and thus provides a logical collection for exploratory analyses.[22] The initial data collection included all the job postings from the years 2005–2014 for a total of 270 job postings; those that were not academic library positions (e.g., government and non-profit positions, academic researcher positions or other academic positions outside of the library, etc.) were then excluded, resulting in a dataset of 148 academic library job postings.

The following information was compiled from the job postings with corresponding fields: Job Title, Posting Year, Required Skills, Preferred Skills, and Job Description. The dataset was imported into NVivo qualitative data analysis software. NVivo was used to analyze the textual data by using word frequency queries and text search queries to mine the textual data for patterns; the qualitative-focused postings were also read and coded at themes (or NVivo "nodes"). The methodological approach of using word frequency and targeted text searching drew in part from Xia and Wang's text mining research method used to explore the competencies and responsibilities of social science data librarians in IASSIST job postings from 2005–2012.[23]

A word-frequency query of the text fields (Job Title, Required Skills, Preferred Skills, and Job Description) was used to count the top 200 words grouped by stemmed endings (e.g., the count for "statistics" included the counts for "statistic," "statistical," etc.). Not surprisingly, the top five most frequently occurring stemmed word groupings in descending order were variations of "data" (1641 counts), "library" (1023 counts), "research" (1023 counts), "services" (960 counts), and "managing" (580 counts).† No qualitative terms or qualitative software (e.g., qualitative, NVivo, Atlas.ti, etc.) made it to the top 200 most frequent words list. However, the following quantitative terms and statistical software appeared: "statistics/statistical" (127 counts, 58th rank); "numeric/numerical" (102 counts, 76th rank); "quantitative" (62 counts, 147th rank); and "SPSS" (47 counts, 186th rank).

Targeted text search queries across the text fields of Job Title, Job Description, Required Skills, and Preferred Skills were used to explore the explicit mentions of qualitative and quantitative expectations in the job postings. The NVivo text search query feature allows for use of Boolean search strategies to find instances of terms in textual data. The following searches were coded into thematic nodes (see Table 11.1): (1) *Qualitative*—postings including qualitative terms, common qualitative data analysis software (NVivo, Atlas.ti, QDAMiner, Dedoose, MAXQDA), and/or abbreviations commonly used to indicate computer assisted qualitative data analysis software (CAQDAS) or qualitative data analysis (QDA); and (2)

† While the context of the frequent occurrences of variations of the word "managing" was not investigated, it is likely that this frequent appearance reflects the increasing expectations of data management amongst data librarian positions, as was found by Xia and Wang when analyzing the IASSIST job postings from 2005-2012.

Quantitative—postings including quantitative terms and/or common quantitative analysis software (SPSS, SAS, Stata, R).

Table 11.1. Text Search Queries and Corresponding Coded Theme Nodes for Quantitative/Qualitative Terms in Job Postings

Coded Theme Nodes:	Text Search Queries (Boolean Logic):
Qualitative	qualitative OR CAQDA* OR QDA OR NVivo OR QDAMiner OR "QDA Miner" OR MAXQDA OR Dedoose OR Atlas.ti OR "Atlas ti"
Quantitative	quantitative OR statistic* OR numeric* OR SPSS OR SAS OR Stata OR "R"

After these text search query results were coded as either *qualitative* or *quantitative,* the number of job postings that mentioned qualitative expectations and those mentioning quantitative were tallied. Of the 148 postings, 83 (56.1%) explicitly mentioned quantitative expectations while only 22 (14.9%) mentioned qualitative expectations, and all of the 22 postings mentioning qualitative also mentioned quantitative expectations. The remaining 65 (43.9%) postings did not explicitly mention either qualitative or quantitative expectations.

As a measure of the nature of qualitative data support expectations within the 22 postings, job postings containing qualitative terms were coded based on the different types of expectations using themes informed by Xia and Wang's synthesized research data lifecycle model of data support services types.[24] The following groupings were created for the 22 postings:

- *Data Analysis*—Fifteen (68.2%) listed desired experience and/or expectations of supporting qualitative data analysis, frequently referring specifically to qualitative data analysis software support and to NVivo and Atlas.ti software most often.
- *Data Discovery*—Seven (31.8%) mentioned data discovery activities.
- *Data Sharing/Preservation/Management*—Six (27.3%) listed expectations for facilitating the collecting, managing, and archiving of qualitative data produced by the academic institution's researchers for long-term preservation and reuse by other researchers.

Survey of Qualitative Data Support Practices

An online survey of social sciences librarians further explored the current state of qualitative data support in comparison to that for quantitative. The survey asked respondents about (1) expectations regarding their supporting researchers' qualitative and quantitative data needs; (2) the types and frequency of quantitative and qualitative data support they provide; and (3) their thoughts regarding the relevance of qualitative as compared to quantitative data for the future of data support services. An invitation to participate in the survey was distributed via eight email listservs targeting academic librarians and social science data services professionals.† The quantitative data were analyzed using SPSS and Excel analysis software, and the qualitative data again using NVivo qualitative data analysis software.

One hundred and twelve participants completed the survey (see Table 11.2 for the breakdown of participants by job type). Ninety-nine (88.4%) of the participants worked in the United States, eight (7.1%) in Canada, and five (4.5%) in Europe. Sixty-eight (60.7%) reported working in doctoral-granting universities, 23 (20.5%) in master's colleges or universities, fifteen (13.4%) in baccalaureate colleges, two (1.8%) in associate colleges, one (0.9%) in a special focus institution, with the remaining three (2.7%) either not reporting or reporting "not sure" regarding their institution's analogous Carnegie classification.[25]

Table 11.2. Survey Participants by Job Type

TOTAL PARTICIPANTS:	**112**
Social Sciences Librarians	
Data Services Librarians with responsibilities to the social sciences	23
Social Sciences Librarians with explicitly defined data services responsibilities	10
Social Sciences Librarians without explicitly defined data services responsibilities	60
Subtotal:	93
Other Participants	
Non-librarians with data services responsibilities to the social sciences	11
Others (7 non-social sciences academic librarians, 1 PhD Student)	8
Subtotal:	19

The analysis of the closed-ended questions regarding expectations and type or frequency of data support includes only the 93 participants who indicated that they were social sciences librarians, as the primary aim was to gauge the current data support practices amongst specifically social sciences librarians. The analysis of the participants' open-ended thoughts regarding the quantitative/qualitative divide includes comments by all 112 survey participants, to provide a broader perspective.

† Email listservs: IASSIST (iasst-l); Association of College & Research Libraries (ACRL) Anthropology & Sociology Section (anss-l); ACRL Information Literacy Instruction Discussion (ili-l); ACRL University Libraries Section (uls-l); ACRL Women and Gender Studies Section (wgss-l); American Library Association (ALA) Library and Information Technology Association (lita-l); ALA Reference and User Services Association (rusa-l); and Northern Arizona University's Business Information (buslib-l).

The survey asked participants to report on expectations of supporting qualitative and quantitative data as denoted in their job description for their current position (see Figure 11.1). The majority reported not having explicit expectations for either quantitative or qualitative data support; however, more participants reported expectations for quantitative data support than for qualitative. To examine whether there was a statistically-significant relationship between the type of data services responsibilities (quantitative or qualitative) and its being listed in the participants' job description, a chi-square test of independence was performed using the data displayed in Figure 11.1. A significant relationship† was found, indicating that participants were significantly more likely to report expectations for quantitative data support than for qualitative in their current job description.

Figure 11.1. Data Support Services Expectations in Job Description

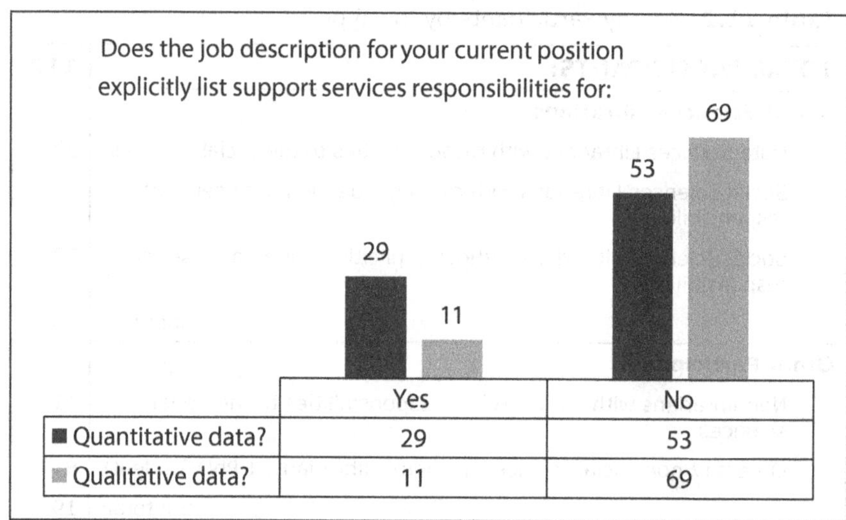
Does the job description for your current position
explicitly list support services responsibilities for:
29
11
53
69

	Yes	No
■ Quantitative data?	29	53
■ Qualitative data?	11	69

Note: X^2 (df=1, N=93) = 10.1752, $p < 0.01$. Sixteen participants who responded "don't know" and six who responded "N/A" were excluded from the analysis as missing data; however, the chi-squared test statistic remained significant with their inclusion.

The survey also asked participants to report the frequency in a typical semester of consultations and/or instruction sessions related to seven distinct types of data support activities for both quantitative and qualitative data:‡

† Chi-square value of 10.1752 is significant at the $p < 0.01$ level for 93 observations and 1 degree of freedom.

‡ The construction of the above data support activity types was informed by Geraci, Humphrey, and Jacobs's "levels of [data] reference service," Xia and Wang's synthesized data lifecycle model, the UK Data Archives "research data lifecycle," and the author's experiences of providing data services support.

- Finding existing data sources
- Software training for analyzing data
- Constructing and/or understanding data files
- Visualizing data
- Collecting new/original data
- Analyzing data
- Data management, sharing, and/or curation of data

Figures 11.2–11.8 reflect the participants' reported frequency of the seven data support activities. The overwhelming majority of participants reported engaging in finding existing data sources for both quantitative and qualitative data (see Figure 11.2) as compared to all the other types of data support activities (see Figures 11.3 through 11.8), echoing Xia and Wang's findings that "social sciences data professionals are still performing traditional primary services in the stages of data discovery."[26] A chi-square test of independence examined whether there was a statistically-significant relationship between the type of data (quantitative or qualitative) and participants' reported frequency in providing consultations/instruction on finding existing data sources (see Figure 11.2). There was a significant relationship,[§] suggesting that participants were more likely to report providing support for finding existing quantitative data sources than for qualitative.

Figure 11.2. Frequency of Consultations/Instruction on Finding Existing Quantitative and Qualitative Data Sources

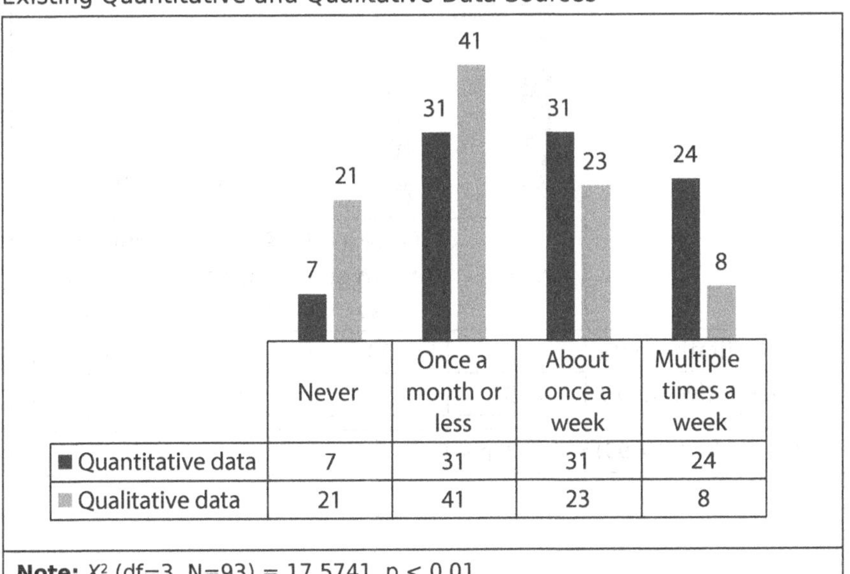

	Never	Once a month or less	About once a week	Multiple times a week
■ Quantitative data	7	31	31	24
■ Qualitative data	21	41	23	8

Note: X^2 (df=3, N=93) = 17.5741, p < 0.01.

§ Chi-square value of 17.5741 is significant at the p < 0.01 level for 93 observations and 3 degrees of freedom.

To examine whether there was a statistically-significant relationship between the type of data (quantitative or qualitative) and participants' reported frequency in providing consultations/ or instruction for the remaining data support activities (see Figures 11.3–11.8), the data were collapsed for "once a month or less," "about once a week," and "multiple times a week" into one category of "provided support" to perform chi-square tests of independence comparing that collapsed data category with the "never [provided support]" data category.[27] For the software training data support activity, there was a significant relationship,[†] suggesting that participants were more likely to provide support for software training for analyzing quantitative data than for qualitative (see Figure 11.3). No significant relationships were found for the remaining data support activities (see Figures 11.4–11.8 for the chi-square statistics and p values), suggesting there was no significant difference between participants' providing these data support activities by type of data (quantitative or qualitative).

Figure 11.3. Frequency of Consultations/Instruction on Software Training for Analyzing Quantitative and Qualitative Data

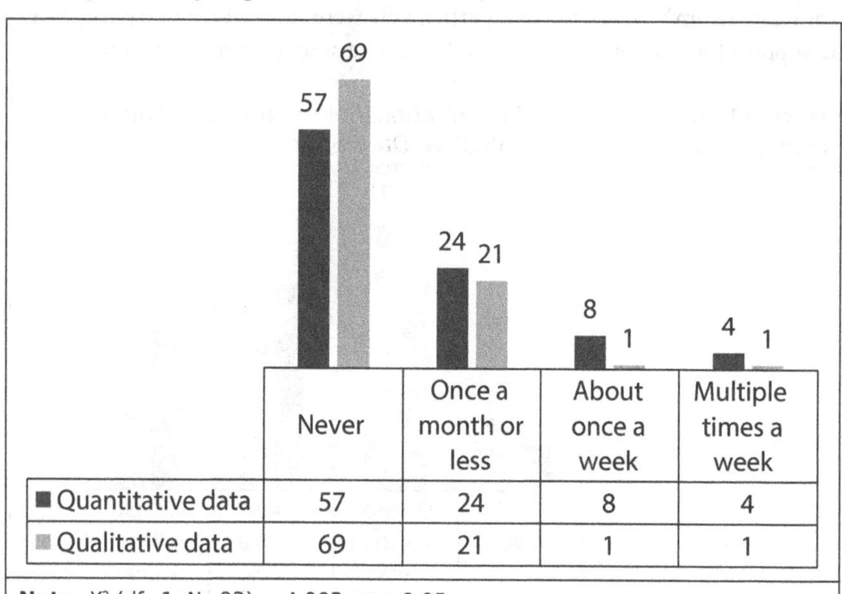

Note: X^2 (df=1, N=93) = 4.002, $p < 0.05$.

† Chi-square value of 4.002 is significant at the $p < 0.05$ level for 93 observations and 1 degree of freedom.

Figure 11.4. Frequency of Consultations/Instruction on Constructing and/or Understanding Quantitative and Qualitative Data Files

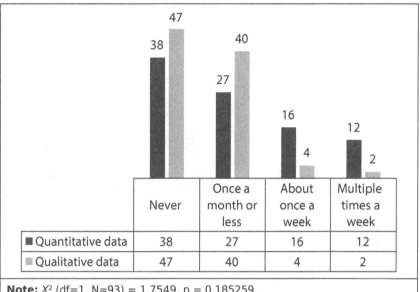

	Never	Once a month or less	About once a week	Multiple times a week
■ Quantitative data	38	27	16	12
■ Qualitative data	47	40	4	2

Note: X^2 (df=1, N=93) = 1.7549, p = 0.185259.

Figure 11.5. Frequency of Consultations/Instruction on Visualizing Quantitative and Qualitative Data

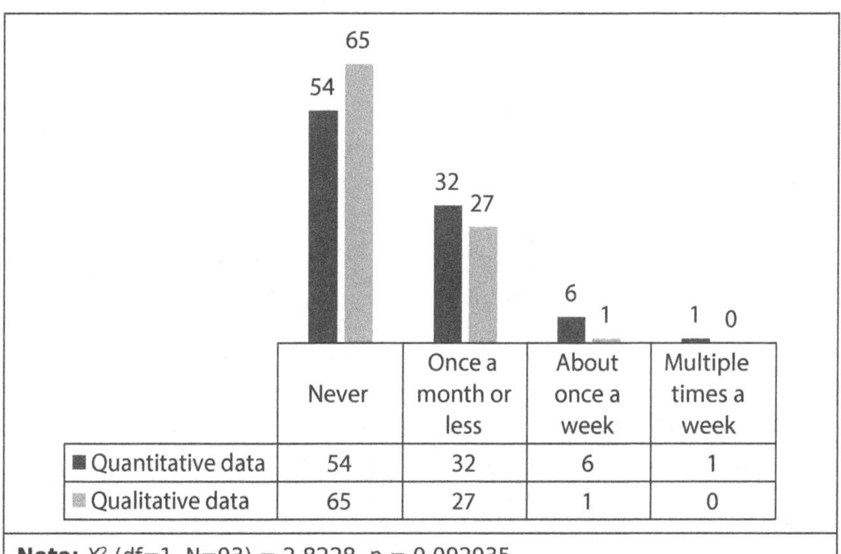

	Never	Once a month or less	About once a week	Multiple times a week
■ Quantitative data	54	32	6	1
■ Qualitative data	65	27	1	0

Note: X^2 (df=1, N=93) = 2.8228, p = 0.092935.

Figure 11.6. Frequency of Consultations/Instruction on Collecting New/Original Quantitative and Qualitative Data

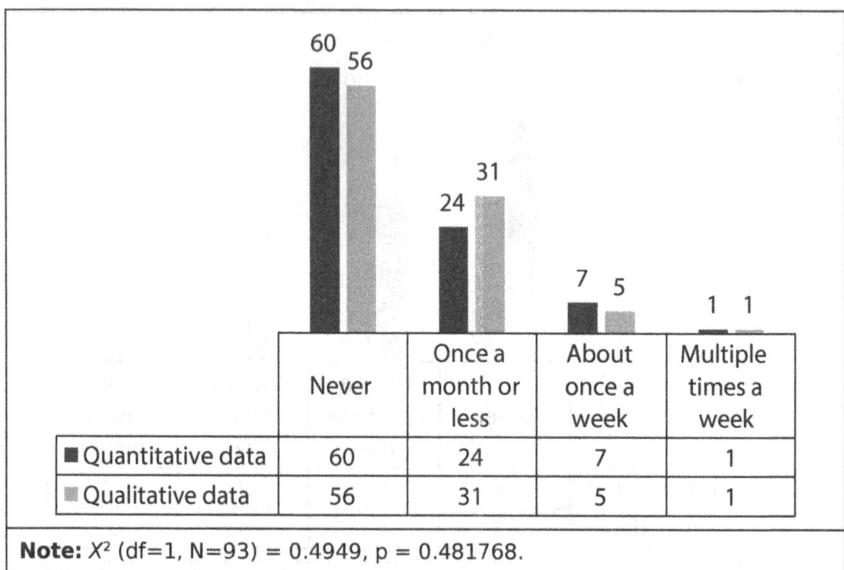

	Never	Once a month or less	About once a week	Multiple times a week
■ Quantitative data	60	24	7	1
■ Qualitative data	56	31	5	1

Note: X^2 (df=1, N=93) = 0.4949, p = 0.481768.

Figure 11.7. Frequency of Consultations/Instruction on Analyzing Quantitative and Qualitative Data

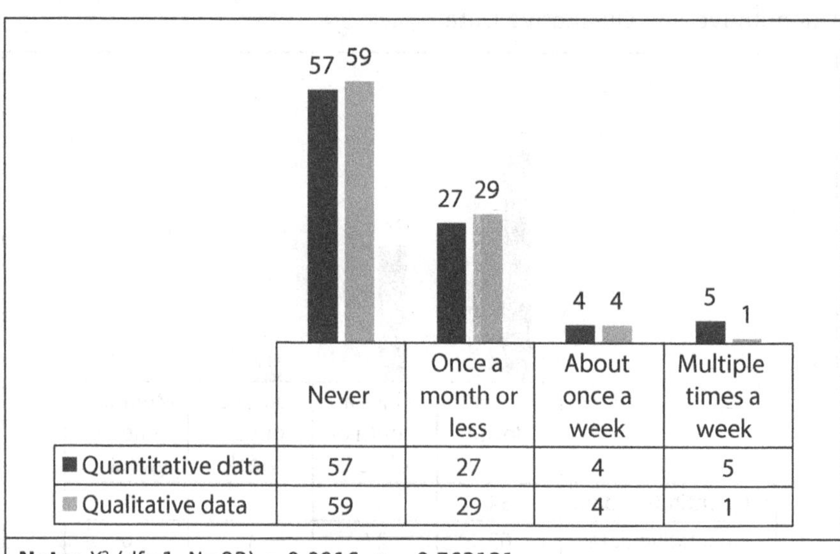

	Never	Once a month or less	About once a week	Multiple times a week
■ Quantitative data	57	27	4	5
■ Qualitative data	59	29	4	1

Note: X^2 (df=1, N=93) = 0.0916, p = 0.762121.

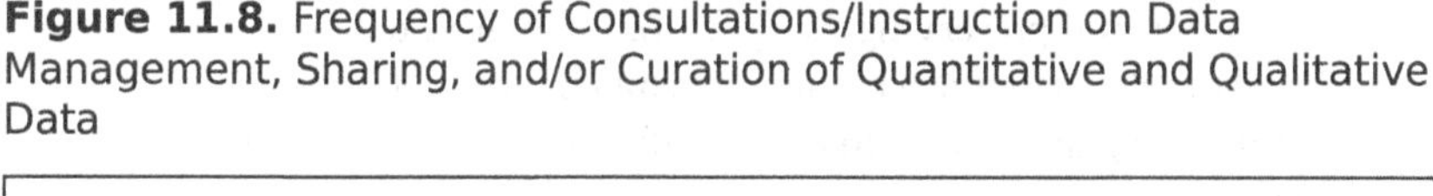

Figure 11.8. Frequency of Consultations/Instruction on Data Management, Sharing, and/or Curation of Quantitative and Qualitative Data

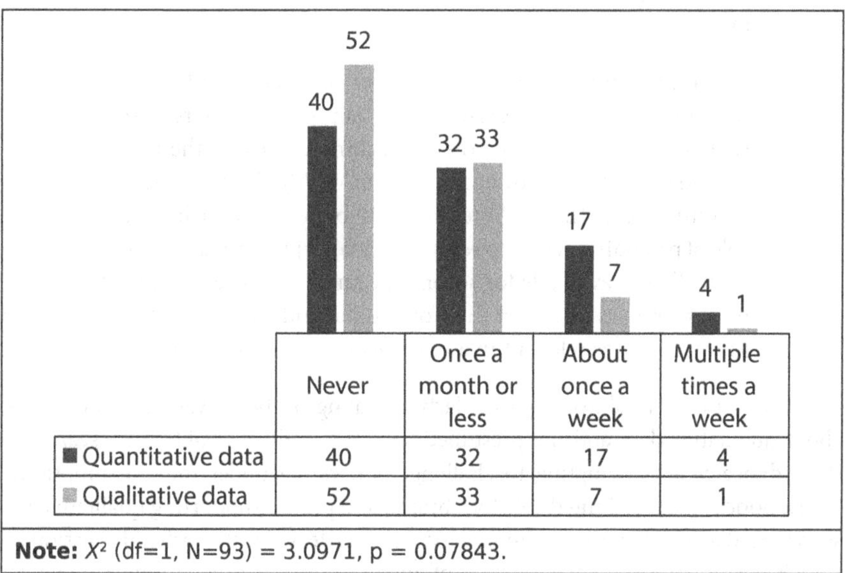

	Never	Once a month or less	About once a week	Multiple times a week
Quantitative data	40	32	17	4
Qualitative data	52	33	7	1

Note: X^2 (df=1, N=93) = 3.0971, p = 0.07843.

Among the 112 participants' open-ended thoughts† regarding the quantitative/qualitative divide, almost all unequivocally stated that supporting both quantitative and qualitative data was important. A recurring theme was that data support services should be guided by the local needs of the institution's researchers, and thus the primary focus for data support should be either quantitative or qualitative, depending on the predominant need. Many of the respondents openly acknowledged that quantitative data probably gets more attention at present, some again indicating that this often reflected the specific needs of an institution. Some alluded to a uniqueness of qualitative data that did not lend itself to or posed specific challenges to traditional roles of data support, as the following excerpts exemplify:

> One of the big problems, of course, is the wide divergence in types of qualitative "data" as well as the methodologies used for analyzing them.

> Quantitative data has historically been better supported, with systems in place for data collection, analysis, and now sharing,

† Respondents reviewed this material and gave consent to include their excerpted answers.

> curating, and preserving. Support for qualitative data is not as well developed, largely because it is much more heterogeneous, and setting up systems to de-identify and share it is a difficult task.

> My impression is that qualitative research is often less dependent on technology/software than quantitative research, therefore I see less demand for assistance. Further, the use of secondary data/data in archives is more highly developed in quantitative methods, therefore fits in better with the librarian role of providing access to resources, while qualitative data [are] typically not available for secondary analysis, more dependent on researchers to collect their own data, and consequently the librarian is less relevant in a reference/access to data role.

The last excerpt above is particularly revealing of the prevailing assumptions about qualitative data and the presumed support needs of qualitative researchers that advocates are attempting to challenge. Operating under these assumptions, the respondent sees a limited role for librarians to play in supporting qualitative researchers' data needs across the research data lifecycle, while the earlier discussion in this chapter demonstrates a wide array of possible qualitative data support activities.

A few participants' responses reveal a sense that support for quantitative data does indeed hold a "privileged" status and that qualitative data "often gets the short shrift" in comparison, as these excerpts illustrate:

> Right now it seems like quantitative services are privileged and I would like to see that change.

> Given that my institution …was established with the conviction that qualitative research often gets the short shrift in the social sciences in terms of explicit methodological and data management training (even though they are the most widely used type of data on their own, not to mention as the underlying information for all quantitative data), I believe that supporting qualitative research is of utmost importance.

> Traditional qualitative data projects (such as doing a lot of interviews and reporting on the results) are not valued in many departments, so it's easier to get broader support for quant [*sic*] support/analysis positions.

> We have a high demand for both in our social sciences areas but because the STEM [science, technology, engineering, and

> math] areas are better funded and focus on the quantitative side we have more software and infrastructure to support quantitative.

Some participants pointed to an anticipated upswing in the need to support qualitative data services as mixed-methods and qualitative research increases on their campuses. A handful of respondents pointed to the increasing digitization of qualitative sources and thus the ability to *quantify* this data for statistical analysis as the impetus for increasing demand for "qualitative" data support services.

Several respondents pointed to the possibility for librarians, given the proper training and provided with the needed resources and infrastructure, to seize the opportunity to fill this dearth of support for qualitative research on campuses and thereby create a particular "niche" for themselves. These excerpts give examples of how this could happen or already is happening in some libraries:

> We do have a Data Centre which has always dealt with helping researchers with quantitative data, and they wanted nothing to do with supporting the qualitative tools, so that is why we (Reference dept.) took it on. Our demand has grown to the point where we are going to shortly have 4 people able to offer support.

> Hugely important and relevant and, I think, largely unfulfilled. I've seen a lot of people doing this type of work without tools, and that's a big place where libraries/IT groups can have an impact.

> Qualitative researchers need just as much if not more support than quantitative researchers. I say this because both undergrad [*sic*] and grad [*sic*] students are being taught qualitative research methods by older faculty who may not be as familiar with and/or actively using various qualitative data software/tools such as NVivo, Atlas.ti, Dedoose, etc. There are also amazing visualization capabilities now available to qualitative researchers, including ArcGIS and other mapping applications. These researchers, who may not be as technologically savvy as quantitative researchers (although this is a gross and perhaps mistaken generalization) may need an introduction to these tools as well as training on how to use them. Moreover, data management is just as important for qualitative researchers, many of whom may not think of their research products as "data" and therefore requiring management and/or planning.

As the above excerpts illustrate, these respondents saw the most potential for librarian-provided support services in the area of computer-assisted qualitative data analysis software (CAQDAS) with one respondent indicating success in filling this gap in support on campus.

Online Research Guides Describing Qualitative Data Services

Online research guides can be examined as virtual indicators of what types of services/resources librarians are offering.[28] Thus, to further explore the current practices of qualitative data support amongst social sciences librarians, online research guides focused on social science researchers' qualitative data needs were examined.† Two methods were used to identify guides: (1) a keyword search for "qualitative" in Springshare's *LibGuides Community* database, limiting to academic institutions; and (2) a Google search as follows: qualitative librar* data OR analysis OR method* OR research site:.edu.[29] After reviewing results from these searches, 53 relevant guides were collected in a Zotero library to then use the Zotero "tags" feature to tag the guides with the types of qualitative data support activities demonstrated.‡ The constructed tags were guided in part by the activities and resulting support needs described earlier in this chapter, but new tags emerged from the review of the research guides when warranted.

Of the 53 total guides, eighteen (34.0%) were general qualitative research guides with no discipline specified, fifteen (28.3%) were created for specific qualitative methods courses, eleven (20.7%) were dedicated computer assisted qualitative data analysis software (CAQDAS) guides, eight (15.1%) explicitly targeted individual or multiple disciplines, and one (1.9%) was a data management guide with recommendations on managing/sharing qualitative as well as quantitative data.§ Within the guides targeting specific qualitative methods courses or specific disciplines, the following social science disciplines appeared, listed in descending order of frequency of occurrence: sociology (8); education (7); psychology (4); political science (4); anthropology (3); communications (2); public health (2); social work (1); and criminal justice (1).

Gauging from the types of support activities represented, graduate student and other novice qualitative researchers were the primary target audience of the reviewed guides. Several guides integrated some teaching of concepts related to qualitative research: thirteen (24.5%) provided some basic definition of what con-

† Because survey participation predominantly originated from the United States, the online research guide sample was limited to U.S. institutions.

‡ Zotero (https://www.zotero.org/) is an open-source reference management system.

§ See the accompanying web site (https://databrarianship.wordpress.com/) for the list of guides.

stituted qualitative research; six (11.3%) contrasted qualitative with quantitative research; and two (3.8%) discussed the typical structure of a qualitative research article. The most popular activity, demonstrated in 33 (62.3%) guides, was linking to secondary resources for qualitative researchers to consult for designing their research and analyzing their data; this manifested often as links to catalog records for print and electronic books, qualitative-focused journals, websites, or video tutorials. Similarly, fifteen (28.3%) guides provided strategies on keyword/subject searching, Library of Congress call number classification searching/browsing, and/or using database search limiters to hone in on books or articles using qualitative research methodologies. While linking to or providing strategies for identifying secondary resources for consultation regarding research design/methods and analysis were common, pointing to existing data source materials for original qualitative analysis was comparably sparse: seven (13.2%) guides linked to newspaper databases, four (7.6%) provided links for film and/or television sources, four (7.6%) provided links to print or digital archives for primary historical sources, three (5.7%) linked to policy, legislation, or government sources, and only three (5.7%) of the guides linked to data repositories. Among the eleven dedicated computer assisted qualitative data analysis software (CAQDAS) guides, five (45.5% of 11) indicated that librarians were available for consultations or training workshops on the software, while the remaining six (54.5% of 11) did not explicitly indicate as such. Similarly, among the eight guides that were not CAQDAS-dedicated but did contain links to information or training resources for CAQDAS, only one (12.5% of 8) indicated that consultations and training workshops were available, while the remaining seven (87.5% of 8) did not specify as such.

Summary of Findings

Do social sciences librarians devote their primary attention to quantitative researchers over qualitative researchers? The findings suggest an affirmative answer to this question. The majority (56.1%) of the IASSIST job postings identified expectations for quantitative data support while only 14.9% of the postings mentioned qualitative data support. The survey participants' job descriptions were more likely to include support expectations for quantitative data over qualitative, and the participants were more likely to report that they provided support for finding existing quantitative data sources and for quantitative analysis software training. Why does this predominance of quantitative data support over qualitative persist? A handful of survey participants alluded to quantitative research's "privileged" status on campuses and described qualitative research as "not valued" and possibly "get[ting] the short shrift." Some participants also commented that providing qualitative researchers with traditional support services—namely, assisting with data discovery—was comparatively difficult due to the heterogeneity/diversity of qualitative data and methods and the presumed lack of availability of secondary data sources. However, several survey participants emphasized that while supporting all researchers was important, the individual institution's needs should drive data support services. For example, if the institution is dominated by qualitative researchers, data support efforts should primarily be focused there.

What qualitative data support services are social sciences librarians currently offering? The findings do not provide a clear-cut answer to this question and sometimes contradict each other. For example, 68.2% of the 22 IASSIST postings mentioning qualitative data listed support of computer assisted qualitative data analysis software (CAQDAS) as an expectation. But both the survey results and the online research guides suggest that very few librarians are offering CAQDAS support. As another contradictory example, only 31.8% of the 22 IASSIST postings mentioning qualitative data listed data discovery support expectations, and few online research guides linked to resources for finding existing qualitative data or materials for original data analysis. Yet 77.4% of the survey participants reported providing support on finding existing qualitative data sources, which seems to contradict the other findings. However, it is possible that survey participants interpreted this question to include activities such as helping researchers find secondary resources to consult for qualitative research design and analysis. With this alternative interpretation, 77.4% of survey participants reporting this type of support activity is then echoed by 62.3% of the online research guides providing secondary sources on qualitative research design and analysis.

Qualitative Data Support—Recommendations for an Expanding Future

Based on these exploratory findings, it appears there is room for expansion of qualitative data support services provided by social sciences librarians. Many of the potential qualitative data support activities across the research data lifecycle discussed earlier in this chapter were not represented in the job postings, survey responses, or online research guides. Therefore, below are some recommendations for key areas in which social sciences librarians might expand their qualitative data support services, drawing from these exploratory findings as well as examples from the author's institution, Georgia State University Library.

Qualitative Data Analysis

There is great potential for social sciences librarians to expand their qualitative data support activities to include support for computer-assisted qualitative data analysis software (CAQDAS). For example, Georgia State University Library's

NVivo support librarian offers a twice-monthly NVivo workshop series as well as custom workshops for qualitative methods classes across the social sciences, provides one-on-one consultations to graduate and faculty researchers, and maintains an online guide that pools various NVivo help resources and FAQs.[30] In the year 2014, 65 (approximately 74%) of the NVivo support librarian's 88 data services consultations involved NVivo support, thus illustrating that it has become a core part of her data services support activities.

Qualitative Data Discovery

Providing instruction sessions, consultations, and online research guides directing researchers to archived qualitative data for secondary analysis as well as to print and digital resources for potential qualitative analysis is a definite growth area for support. Graduate students are a key target group for these services, as they are often in a position of having little time or funds to invest in collecting original qualitative data in the form of in-depth interviews and ethnographies and thus are searching for alternatives. For example, when the Sociology Librarian meets with the new graduate students each fall in the proseminar course, she introduces them to potential materials for qualitative analysis for their theses and dissertations, including qualitative data archives, relevant Special Collections archives, and library print, audiovisual, and digital collections and databases.[31]

Qualitative Data for Teaching and Learning

Social sciences librarians can provide support for teaching and learning qualitative methods in a variety of ways. As was illustrated in several of the online research guides, social sciences librarians can help students find secondary resources to aid their learning about qualitative methodologies. Likewise, social sciences librarians can assist faculty who are seeking existing qualitative data for source materials to teach students about relevant qualitative data and analysis methods in their disciplines. For example, Walter Giesbrecht, a Data Librarian at York University in Toronto, received such a request from a criminology professor teaching a qualitative methods course: the professor wanted to introduce his students to interview transcripts and other material typical of the kind of qualitative research criminologists might perform.[†] Similarly, a public health professor teaching qualitative methods asked that the Georgia State University Library's NVivo support librarian find qualitative data relevant to public health issues for her students to use for an NVivo coding exercise.

† Walter Giesbrecht, e-mail message to iasst-l listserv, February 3, 2015.

Qualitative Data Management and Sharing

One survey respondent astutely reflected that "data management is just as important for qualitative researchers, many of whom may not think of their research products as 'data' and therefore requiring management and/or planning." Social sciences librarians could play an important role in promoting awareness to qualitative researchers of the importance of managing their data for potential reuse as well as for buttressing their own findings with thorough documentation of their research process. Just as many social sciences librarians are providing data management support to quantitative researchers in terms of assisting in creating metadata and data documentation for ease of sharing and discoverability and are recommending archives/repositories and file formats for long-term preservation, they should also be ready to offer these services for qualitative researchers. The Georgia State University Library's Data Management Advisory Team has been approached several times by researchers writing data management plans that involve qualitative data and, as a result, has compiled resources on an online research guide to address archiving qualitative data.[32]

Conclusion

Is qualitative research support the Jan Brady of social sciences data services? Drawing from the review of the literature and the presented exploratory analyses, at present it very well may be. Before enthusiastically embarking on expanding qualitative data support services to bring it out of the shadows, an environmental scan exploring the following questions will help to gauge if there is, in fact, a *need* for such services:

- Do campus social sciences departments/programs offer qualitative research methods courses?
- Are faculty and graduate researchers engaging in qualitative research?
- Are those qualitative researchers inclined to (or required to) deposit their data in repositories for reuse?
- Is qualitative data analysis software available to researchers on campus, and, if so, is no one providing training/support for those using it?

If the answers to the above questions are affirmative, it likely is safe to conclude that there is a need for qualitative data support services on a campus. Furthermore, as one participant in the survey described, when much of the campus is invested in supporting quantitative researchers, social sciences librarians might carve a successful niche for themselves in serving the qualitative researchers that are perhaps being neglected. And, just as her mom advised Jan Brady to "find out what you do best, and then do your best with it," perhaps qualitative research support is a particular place for social sciences librarians to shine.[33†]

---

† The author would like to thank Jingfeng Xia and Minglu Wang for sharing their 2005-2012 IASSIST job postings dataset.

1. "The Brady Bunch: Marcia, Marcia, Marcia!—YouTube," accessed April 12, 2015, https://youtu.be/w2fXs3bf-p0.
2. Kevin Buckler, "The Quantitative/Qualitative Divide Revisited: A Study of Published Research, Doctoral Program Curricula, and Journal Editor Perceptions," *Journal of Criminal Justice Education* 19, no. 3 (November 2008): 383–403; Erica Burman, "Minding the Gap: Positivism, Psychology, and the Politics of Qualitative Methods," *Journal of Social Issues* 53, no. 4 (Winter 1997): 785–801; Rachel Lara Cohen, Christina Hughes, and Richard Lampard, "The Methodological Impact of Feminism: A Troubling Issue for Sociology?" *Sociology* 45, no. 4 (August 2011): 570–86; Aaron Cooley, "Qualitative Research in Education: The Origins, Debates, and Politics of Creating Knowledge," *Educational Studies* 49, no. 3 (June 5, 2013): 247–62; Norman Denzin and Michael Giardina, *Qualitative Inquiry and the Politics of Evidence* (Walnut Creek, CA: Left Coast Press, 2008); Daniel DiSalvo, "The Politics of Studying Politics: Political Science Since the 1960s," *Society* 50, no. 2 (April 2013): 132–39; Scott Jacques, "The Quantitative-Qualitative Divide in Criminology: A Theory of Ideas' Importance, Attractiveness, and Publication," *Theoretical Criminology* 18, no. 3 (August 2014): 317–34; Agnieszka Leszczynski, "Quantitative Limits to Qualitative Engagements: GIS, Its Critics, and the Philosophical Divide," *Professional Geographer* 61, no. 3 (August 2009): 350–65; Wendy Luttrell, "Crossing Anxious Borders: Teaching across the Quantitative–Qualitative 'Divide,'" *International Journal of Research & Method in Education* 28, no. 2 (October 2005): 183–95; Jill Morawski, "Our Debates: Finding, Fixing, and Enacting Reality," *Theory & Psychology* 21, no. 2 (April 2011): 260–74; Keith Morrison, "Challenging the Qualitative–Qualitative Divide: Explorations in Case-Focused Causal Analysis," *International Journal of Research & Method in Education* 37, no. 3 (August 2014): 344–46; Erwin Neuenschwander, "Qualitas and Quantitas: Two Ways of Thinking in Science," *Quality & Quantity* 47, no. 5 (August 2013): 2597–2615; Kaya Yilmaz, "Comparison of Quantitative and Qualitative Research Traditions: Epistemological, Theoretical, and Methodological Differences," *European Journal of Education* 48, no. 2 (June 2013): 311–25; Noga Zerubavel and Alexandra L. Adame, "Fostering Dialogue in Psychology: The Costs of Dogma and Theoretical Preciousness," *Qualitative Research in Psychology* 11, no. 2 (April 2014): 178–88.
3. Arthur P. Bochner, "Between Obligation and Inspiration: Choosing Qualitative Inquiry," *Qualitative Inquiry* 18, no. 7 (September 2012): 535–43; Burman, "Minding the Gap"; Cohen, Hughes, and Lampard, "The Methodological Impact of Feminism"; Cooley, "Qualitative Research in Education"; Denzin and Giardina, *Qualitative Inquiry and the Politics of Evidence*; Evan S. Lieberman, "Bridging the Qualitative—Quantitative Divide: Best Practices in the Development of Historically Oriented Replication Databases," *Annual Review of Political Science* 13, no. 1 (June 2010): 37–59; Luttrell, "Crossing Anxious Borders"; Yasuhiro Omi, "Tension Between the Theoretical Thinking and the Empirical Method: Is It an Inevitable Fate for Psychology?" *Integrative Psychological & Behavioral Science* 46, no. 1 (March 2012): 118–27; Donald E. Riggs, "Let Us Stop Apologizing for Qualitative Research," *College and Research Libraries* 59, no. 5 (1998): 404–5.
4. William L. Benoit and R. Lance Holbert, "Empirical Intersections in Communication Research: Replication, Multiple Quantitative Methods, and Bridging the Quantitative-Qualitative Divide," *Journal of Communication* 58, no. 4 (December 2008): 615–28; Julia Brannen, "Mixing Methods: The Entry of Qualitative and Quantitative Approaches into the Research Process," *International Journal of Social Research Methodology* 8, no. 3 (July 2005): 173–84; Dydia DeLyser and Daniel Sui, "Crossing the Qualitative-Quantitative Divide II: Inventive Approaches to Big Data, Mobile Methods, and Rhythmanalysis," *Progress in Human Geography* 37, no. 2 (April 2013): 293–305; Omar Gelo, Diana Braakmann, and Gerhard Benetka, "Quantitative and Qualitative Research: Beyond the Debate," *Integrative Psychological & Behavioral Science* 42, no. 3 (September 2008): 266–90; Linda Hantrais, "Combining Methods: A Key to Understanding Complexity in European Societies?" *European Societies* 7, no. 3 (September 2005): 399–421; Morawski, "Our

Debates"; Mansoor Niaz, "A Rationale for Mixed Methods (Integrative) Research Programmes in Education," *Journal of Philosophy of Education* 42, no. 2 (May 2008): 287–305; Anthony Onwuegbuzie and Nancy L. Leech, "On Becoming a Pragmatic Researcher: The Importance of Combining Quantitative and Qualitative Research Methodologies," *International Journal of Social Research Methodology* 8, no. 5 (December 2005): 375–87; Daniel Sui and Dydia DeLyser, "Crossing the Qualitative-Quantitative Chasm I: Hybrid Geographies, the Spatial Turn, and Volunteered Geographic Information (VGI)," *Progress in Human Geography* 36, no. 1 (February 2012): 111–24; Charles D. Yeager and Thomas Steiger, "Applied Geography in a Digital Age: The Case for Mixed Methods," *Applied Geography* 39 (May 2013): 1–4.

5. "SBE SES Sociology Strengthening Qualitative Research through Methodological Innovation and Integration," accessed July 24, 2015, http://www.nsf.gov/sbe/ses/soc/sqrmii.jsp.
6. "Finnish Social Science Data Archive (FSD)," accessed August 6, 2015, http://www.fsd.uta.fi/en/; "Irish Qualitative Data Archive," accessed August 6, 2015, http://iqda.ie/; "QualiBank," accessed July 24, 2015, http://discover.ukdataservice.ac.uk/QualiBank; "Qualitative Data Repository," accessed July 24, 2015, https://qdr.syr.edu/.
7. Lynda M. Kellam and Katharin Peter, *Numeric Data Services and Sources for the General Reference Librarian* (Oxford: Chandos Publishing, 2011); Diane Geraci, Chuck Humphrey, and Jim Jacobs, *Data Basics: An Introductory Text*, 2012, http://3stages.org/class/2012/pdf/data_basics_2012.pdf.
8. Piotr Binder and Piotr Filipkowski, "Data Sharing and Archiving Qualitative and QL Data in Poland," *IASSIST Quarterly* 34/35, no. 3/1–2 (2010): 71–76; Libby Bishop and Bren Neale, "Sharing Qualitative and Qualitative Longitudinal Data in the UK: Archiving Strategies and Development," *IASSIST Quarterly* 34/35, no. 3/1–2 (2010): 23–29; Jurate Butviliene and Tomas Butvilas, "Exploring Qualitative Longitudinal Research and Qualitative Resources," *IASSIST Quarterly* 34/35, no. 3/1–2 (2010): 67–70; Tomáš Čížek, "Archiving Qualitative and Qualitative Longitudinal Social Sciences Data In the Czech Republic," *IASSIST Quarterly* 34/35, no. 3/1–2 (2010): 36–37; Louise Corti, "Progress and Problems of Preserving and Providing Access to Qualitative Data for Social Research—The International Picture of an Emerging Culture," *Forum Qualitative Sozialforschung / Forum: Qualitative Social Research* 1, no. 3 (December 31, 2000), http://www.qualitative-research.net/index.php/fqs/article/view/1019; Louise Corti, "Qualitative Archiving and Data Sharing: Extending the Reach and Impact of Qualitative Data," *IASSIST Quarterly*, no. Fall (2005): 8–13; Louise Corti, "The European Landscape of Qualitative Social Research Archives: Methodological and Practical Issues," *Forum Qualitative Sozialforschung/Forum: Qualitative Social Research* 12, no. 3 (2011), http://www.qualitative-research.net/index.php/fqs/article/view/1746; Louise Corti, Annette Day, and Gill Backhouse, "Confidentiality and Informed Consent: Issues for Consideration in the Preservation of and Provision of Access to Qualitative Data Archives," *Forum Qualitative Sozialforschung / Forum: Qualitative Social Research* 1, no. 3 (2000), http://www.qualitative-research.net/index.php/fqs/article/view/1024; Judit Gárdos and Gabriella Ivacs, "Qualitative Longitudinal Research and Qualitative Resources," *IASSIST Quarterly* 34/35, no. 3/1–2 (2010): 64–66; Jane Gray and Aileen O'Carroll, "Qualitative Research In Ireland: Archiving Strategies and Development," *IASSIST Quarterly* 34/35, no. 3/1–2 (2010): 18–22; Gry-Hege Henriksen, Maria Bakke Orvik, and Trond Pedersen, "Mapping Out Qualitative Data Resources in Norway," *IASSIST Quarterly* 34/35, no. 3/1–2 (2010): 47–49; Anne Sofie Fink Kjeldgaard, "Archiving and Disseminating Qualitative Data in Denmark," *IASSIST Quarterly* 34/35, no. 3/1–2 (2010): 38–40; Brian Kleiner, Claudia Heinzmann, Thomas S. Eberle, and Manfred Max Bergman, "Qualitative Data Archiving in Switzerland," *IASSIST Quarterly* 34/35, no. 3/1–2 (2010): 77–79; Arja Kuula, "Methodological and Ethical Dilemmas of Archiving Qualitative Data," *IASSIST Quarterly* 34/35, no. 3/1–2 (2010): 12–17; Natasha S. Mauthner and Odette Parry, "Qualitative Data Preservation and Sharing in the Social Sciences: On Whose Philosophical Terms?" *Australian Journal of Social Issues (Australian Council of Social Service)* 44, no. 3 (Spring 2009): 291–307; Irena Medjedović and Andreas Witzel, "Sharing and Archiving Qualitative and Qualitative Longitudinal Research

Data in Germany," *IASSIST Quarterly* 34/35, no. 3/1–2 (2010): 42–46; Bren Neale and Libby Bishop, "Qualitative and Qualitative Longitudinal Resources in Europe: Mapping the Field and Exploring Strategies for Development," *IASSIST Quarterly* 34/35, no. 3/1–2 (2010): 6–11; Dirk Schubotz, Martin Melaugh, and Peter McLoughlin, "Archiving Qualitative Data in the Context of a Society Coming out of Conflict: Some Lessons from Northern Ireland," *Forum Qualitative Sozialforschung / Forum: Qualitative Social Research* 12, no. 3 (September 20, 2011), http://www.qualitative-research.net/index.php/fqs/article/view/1751; Andrea Smioski, "Establishing a Qualitative Data Archive in Austria," *IASSIST Quarterly* 34/35, no. 3/1–2 (2010): 30–35; Andrea Smioski, "Archiving Qualitative Data: Infrastructure, Acquisition, Documentation, Distribution. Experiences from WISDOM, the Austrian Data Archive," *Forum Qualitative Sozialforschung / Forum: Qualitative Social Research* 12, no. 3 (September 16, 2011), http://www.qualitative-research.net/index.php/fqs/article/view/1734; Janez Stebe, Jože Hudales, and Boris Kragelj, "Archiving and Re-Using Qualitative and Qualitative Longitudinal Data in Slovenia," *IASSIST Quarterly* 34/35, no. 3/1–2 (2010): 50–59; Larissa Titarenko and Olga Tereschenko, "Qualitative and Qualitative Longitudinal Research and Resources in Belarus," *IASSIST Quarterly* 34/35, no. 3/1–2 (2010): 60–63; Miguel S. Valles, "Archival and Biographical Research Sensitivity: A European Perspective from Spain," *Forum Qualitative Sozialforschung / Forum: Qualitative Social Research* 12, no. 3 (September 16, 2011), http://www.qualitative-research.net/index.php/fqs/article/view/1744.

9. Karsten Boye Rasmussen, "Barking up the Right Tree," *IASSIST Quarterly* 34/35, no. 3/1–2 (2010): 5.
10. Louise Corti, "Re-Using Archived Qualitative Data—Where, How, Why?" *Archival Science* 7, no. 1 (2007): 38.
11. Ibid.
12. Uwe Flick, ed., *The SAGE Handbook of Qualitative Data Analysis* (Los Angeles, CA: SAGE, 2014).
13. Norman K. Denzin and Yvonna S. Lincoln, eds., *The SAGE Handbook of Qualitative Research*, 3rd ed (Thousand Oaks, CA: Sage Publications, 2005), 3–4.
14. Louise Corti, Veerle Van den Eynden, Libby Bishop, and Matthew Wollard, *Managing and Sharing Research Data: A Guide to Good Practice*, 2014, Table 2.1, 17–18.
15. The terminology of codes/coding in qualitative research is distinct from quantitative research. Saldaña (2013) defines a "code" as "a short word or phrase that symbolically assigns a summative, salient, essence-capturing, and/or evocative attribute for a portion of language based or visual data" (p. 3). Johnny Saldaña, *The Coding Manual for Qualitative Researchers*. 2nd ed. (Los Angeles, CA: SAGE Publications, 2013).
16. Corti, "Re-Using Archived Qualitative Data—Where, How, Why?"; Louise Corti, "Recent Developments in Archiving Social Research," *International Journal of Social Research Methodology* 15, no. 4 (2012): 281–90; Corti et al., *Managing and Sharing Research Data*.
17. Larry Hoyle, Louise Corti, Arofan Gregory, Agustina Martinez, Joachim Wackerow, Eirik Alvar, Noemi Betancourt Cabrera, et al., "A Qualitative Data Model for DDI" (Data Documentation Initiative (DDI), ca. 2013), http://www.ddialliance.org/system/files/AQualitativeDataModelForDDI.pdf.
18. Corti, "Re-Using Archived Qualitative Data—Where, How, Why?"; Louise Corti, Andreas Witzel, and Libby Bishop, "On the Potentials and Problems of Secondary Analysis. An Introduction to the FQS Special Issue on Secondary Analysis of Qualitative Data," *Forum Qualitative Sozialforschung / Forum: Qualitative Social Research* 6, no. 1 (2005), http://www.qualitative-research.net/index.php/fqs/article/view/498.
19. Explicit mention of Geographic Information System (GIS) support, an increasingly popular form of data support provided by social sciences librarians, is absent in this chapter. Gauging from some of the GIS literature, while GIS traditionally has been used more frequently to analyze quantitative data, GIS visualization and analysis of qualitative data are on the rise. For the sake of simplicity, this chapter does not explicitly discuss GIS data support. See Ryan Burns

and André Skupin, "Towards Qualitative Geovisual Analytics: A Case Study Involving Places, People, and Mediated Experience," *Cartographica* 48, no. 3 (Fall 2013): 157–76; Jin-Kyu Jung and Sarah Elwood, "Extending the Qualitative Capabilities of GIS: Computer-Aided Qualitative GIS," *Transactions in GIS* 14, no. 1 (February 2010): 63–87; Agnieszka Leszczynski, "Quantitative Limits to Qualitative Engagements: GIS, Its Critics, and the Philosophical Divide," *Professional Geographer* 61, no. 3 (August 2009): 350–65.

20. Youngok Choi and Edie Rasmussen, "What Qualifications and Skills Are Important for Digital Librarian Positions in Academic Libraries? A Job Advertisement Analysis," *Journal of Academic Librarianship* 35, no. 5 (September 2009): 457–67; Jeffrey M. Stanton, Youngseek Kim, Megan Oakleaf, R. David Lankes, Paul Gandel, Derrick Cogburn, and Elizabeth D. Liddy, "Education for eScience Professionals: Job Analysis, Curriculum Guidance, and Program Considerations," *Journal of Education for Library & Information Science* 52, no. 2 (Spring 2011): 79–94; Jingfeng Xia and Minglu Wang, "Competencies and Responsibilities of Social Science Data Librarians: An Analysis of Job Descriptions," *College & Research Libraries* 75, no. 3 (May 2014): 362–88.
21. "About IASSIST | IASSIST Home," accessed July 20, 2015, http://iassistdata.org/about/index.html.
22. International Association for Social Science Information Services & Technology, "Job Postings," *International Association for Social Science Information Services & Technology*, 2015, http://iassistdata.org/resources/jobs/all.
23. Xia and Wang, "Competencies and Responsibilities of Social Science Data Librarians: An Analysis of Job Descriptions," 366.
24. Ibid. 384.
25. "Carnegie Classifications | Basic Classification," accessed August 15, 2015, http://carnegieclassifications.iu.edu/descriptions/basic.php.
26. Xia and Wang, "Competencies and Responsibilities of Social Science Data Librarians: An Analysis of Job Descriptions," 383.
27. The data were collapsed because, when running the chi-square tests on the original separate data categories, the assumptions of the chi-square test were violated; per McHugh, "The value of the cell *expecteds* [expected outcomes as generated during the chi-square test] should be 5 or more in at least 80% of the cells, and no cell should have an expected of less than one" (p. 144). Mary L. McHugh, "The Chi-Square Test of Independence," *Biochemia Medica* 23, no. 2 (2013): 143–49.
28. Kate Dougherty, "Getting to the Core of Geology LibGuides," *Science & Technology Libraries* 32, no. 2 (April 2013): 145–59; Kate Dougherty, "The Direction of Geography LibGuides," *Journal of Map & Geography Libraries* 9, no. 3 (September 2013): 259–75; Nestor L. Osorio, "Electrical Engineering Reference Resources: A Survey from LibGuides," *Collection Building* 34, no. 1 (January 2015): 6–12; Tony Stankus and Martha A. Parker, "The Anatomy of Nursing LibGuides," *Science & Technology Libraries* 31, no. 2 (June 2012): 242–55.
29. "LibGuides Community Site," accessed August 2, 2015, http://libguides.com/community.php.
30. Mandy Swygart-Hobaugh, "NVivo Qualitative Data Analysis Software," accessed August 2, 2015, http://research.library.gsu.edu/nvivo.
31. Mandy Swygart-Hobaugh, "Sociology—Graduate Research: Finding Data (Primary Research)," accessed August 2, 2015, http://research.library.gsu.edu/gradsoc/finddata.
32. Mandy Swygart-Hobaugh, "Data Management: Identifying Repositories for Data Sharing," accessed August 2, 2015, http://research.library.gsu.edu/datamgmt/datasharing.
33. "The Brady Bunch."

CHAPTER 12

Data in the Sciences

Karen Stanley Grigg

THIS CHAPTER PRESENTS an introduction to scientific data and its relevance to librarians and libraries. The characteristics of science data in general, and in relation to a number of scientific disciplines, are identified. The disciplines discussed have been chosen because they demonstrate notable aspects of data management, either because of the type of data used or because of the requirements external agencies place on researchers. Federal funding agencies' requirements for data management and sharing are discussed, along with initiatives to promote sharing of data, and notable large datasets and repositories are identified. Though the chapter mainly focuses on United States (U.S.) funding agencies, it also lists some international archives. Broad discussion of data management in the sciences, and how libraries and librarians can embed themselves in the data lifecycle, are presented, along with specific examples of how libraries have become involved with research data services.

Science Data Management—Early Adopters

In the United States, federal funding agencies were among the first to issue data management and open access policies for their grant recipients. In 2005, the United States National Institute of Health (NIH) created a public access policy that encouraged researchers to provide open access to its funded research. In 2007, a new NIH Public Access Policy bill was signed by President George W. Bush that required the NIH to provide open access to all the research it funded. Investigators would now be required to submit their final manuscripts to PubMedCentral, the NIH's open access repository. In 2011, the United States National Science Foundation (NSF) required that all proposals submitted to the NSF must include a data management plan of two pages or less. In contrast, other agencies have implemented their data management and sharing policies more recently. For example, the Office of Digital Humanities released its data requirements in 2014, and the Institute of Museum and Library Services implemented its data management plan requirements in 2015.

Scientific research and researchers have unique characteristics and needs that have pushed data management in the sciences to the forefront. One such characteristic of scientific research is that the size of the data presents specific challenges for storage and curation. Another unique aspect of scientific research is that some disciplines, such as medicine, have special privacy and security concerns. Scientific datasets can be extremely large, often taking up terabytes, even petabytes, of storage space. In 2011, *Science* magazine polled its peer reviewers about the size of the datasets used and found that "about 20% of the respondents regularly use or analyze datasets exceeding 100 gigabytes, and 7% use datasets exceeding 1 terabyte. About half of those polled store their data only in their laboratories—not an ideal long-term solution. Many bemoaned the lack of common metadata and archives as a main impediment to using and storing data."[1] Additionally, 80 percent said that their institution did not have sufficient funding for data curation.[2] While more recent data was not available, datasets are unlikely to have become any smaller.

Genomics and astronomy generate some of the largest datasets, often reaching one or more petabytes (PB). The Sloan Digital Sky Survey, for example, produces about five PB a day, and the proposed Large Synoptic Survey Telescope (LSST) will record 30 trillion bytes of image data daily from the top of a mountain in Chile, a data volume equal to two daily Sloan Digital Sky Surveys.[3] Not only can storage be a limiting factor, but due to their size, these datasets can be difficult to move to remote locations, download, or process. Scientific data are expensive and complex to analyze and manipulate, as the data require high performance computer servers and storage solutions that strain the budgets of individual institutions. These servers must manage and transfer petabytes and terabytes of data in distributed computing environments, generate simulations, and provide the ability to share and transfer large sets of data to remote or local sites.

Scientific data are often decentralized, generated in a laboratory by many researchers. This dispersion often leads to data being spread across multiple storage devices and without a standardized method of naming conventions or metadata. Additionally, many of the people in the laboratory producing the data are graduate students and postdoctoral researchers, who may take their data with them when they leave or leave the institution without a schema to allow those who come after them to interpret data results. Those researchers who direct the workflow are not necessarily those who produce and manipulate the research data. Because of this decentralization, it is crucially important that the researchers create detailed plans for data preservation, curation, storage, and metadata conventions in their initial data management plan. Creating standardized conventions for file naming and formats is important for long-term curation of research data. It is useful for entire disciplines to discuss standards, rather than leaving the decisions to be carried out institution by institution, in order to enable useful sharing of data between researchers.

The willingness to openly share scientific data varies by discipline. MacMillan states, "Data sharing among the sciences does not have an all-inclusive, uniform or over-arching data culture, a function of both values and of sheer quantities and types of data produced."[4]

Tenopir et al. surveyed a total of 1,329 scientists in a variety of disciplines regarding their data sharing practices and perceptions. Survey data revealed that those in basic sciences, such as atmospheric science, environmental science and ecology, and biology are cultures that most favor data sharing, while health sciences, computer science, and engineering are disciplines less likely to share data.[5] Disciplines in which data are costly to obtain and store, such as astronomy or meteorology, tend to have a culture that favors and encourages the open sharing of data.[6] Confidential data are a significant concern with medical research in the United States and in other countries, and highly competitive disciplines that are financially lucrative are likely to be more reluctant to share data.[7] While science data share some commonalities, large size and production in laboratory environments among them, individual scientific disciplines have varying characteristics and attitudes towards sharing data. This chapter focuses on some of the major scientific disciplines that have unique datasets, funding agency requirements, or challenges with analyzing, storing, and sharing data. As science librarians should become familiar with the major datasets and repositories in their subject areas, this chapter lists some of the major data repositories for each discipline.

Genomics/Biomedical Sciences

Genomics datasets require a massive amount of storage space and are expensive to sequence and store. An early genomic project that garnered much attention is the Human Genome Project, which mapped the "human genome" and was declared complete in 2003. The field of Bioinformatics has emerged in order to deal with the complexity of organizing and analyzing genomic data.

Though the cost of DNA sequencing is high, it has decreased sharply due to the increase over time in computing power. In 2009, the average raw genome cost $154,714 to sequence. In 2014, the cost had dropped to $4,905.[8] As cloud storage solutions become increasingly common, the cost of sequencing raw genomic data will continue to decrease, though cloud solutions must guarantee data security for wide scale adoption to be possible. Some non-commercial cloud data solutions include Bionimbus Protected Data Cloud (PDC), an open source cloud-computing platform developed at the University of Chicago, and NCI Cancer Genomics Cloud Pilots, an NIH trusted partner. Commercial cloud computing solutions include the Amazon Web Services Cloud and the newly released Google Genomics Cloud Platform.

Biomedical human research presents many barriers to creating a culture of data sharing. Due to privacy concerns, researchers are often reluctant or unable to make their data publicly available. A study on gene sequence data articles published between 2006 and 2009 showed that cancer researchers who use human subjects tended to not share their datasets, and only a fourth of the studies had stored their raw data in repositories. Data sharing was more prevalent when studies were funded by NIH, and thus were covered by the NIH Data Sharing Policy.[9] A more recent survey of biomedical researchers in the U.S. Southwest confirmed that about 88% of respondents agreed with the NIH Resource Sharing Plan, and over half would be likely to participate in a virtual biorepository of human cancer biospecimens.[10]

Genomics and Biological Sciences Datasets/Repositories

- 1000 Genomes (http://www.ncbi.nlm.nih.gov/geo/): Launched in 2008, this international project is a catalog of human genetic variation. Scientists have sequenced genomes of over a thousand participants in a variety of ethnic groups.
- Entrez Databases (http://www.ncbi.nlm.nih.gov/genbank/): Entrez is a web portal that consists of a number of health sciences databases at the National Center for Biotechnology Information (NCBI) web site. Entrez provides a federated search engine that allows users to search across all databases.
- National Center for Biotechnology Information (NCBI)'s Gene Expression Omnibus (NCBI GEO) (http://www.ncbi.nlm.nih.gov/geo/): One of the NCBI databases and an international public repository for functional genomic datasets.
- GenBank (http://www.ncbi.nlm.nih.gov/genbank/): GenBank, another NCBI database, is an annotated collection of all publicly available DNA sequences.
- The cBio Cancer Genomics Portal (http://cbioportal.org): This portal is an open access repository that provides access to large-scale cancer genomics datasets.
- Dryad Digital Repository (http://www.datadryad.org/): Dryad is a scientific data repository that makes the data corresponding to scientific journal articles available and re-usable. Authors, journals, and publishers can facilitate data archiving at the time of article publication and receive a permanent Digital Object Identifier (DOI), which can be included in the published article.

Astronomy

Astronomical research, like genomics, produces large amounts of data and can create great challenges for processing and archiving. Telescopes are becoming larger and more sophisticated than ever before. In a 2012 interview, Alberto Conti explained:

> Over the past 25 to 30 years, we have been able to build telescopes that are 30 times larger than what we used to be able to build, and at the same time our detectors are 3,000 times more powerful in terms of pixels. The explosion in sensitivity you see in these detectors is a product of Moore's Law—they can collect up to a hundred times more data than was possible even just a few years ago. This exponential increase means that the collective data of astronomy doubles every year or so, and that can be very tough to capture and analyze.[11]

Astronomy has long fostered a culture that is receptive and proactive in terms of data sharing, and, indeed, there are a number of large open access datasets. Norris discusses the culture of sharing in astronomical research: "Because the advance of astronomy frequently depends on the comparison and merging of disparate data, it is important that astronomers have access to all available data on the objects or phenomena that they are studying. Astronomical data have therefore always enjoyed a tradition of open access, best exemplified by the astronomical data centres, which provide access to data for all astronomers at no charge."[12]

a. Managing and archiving these large databases is often difficult due to understaffing, which makes the creation of metadata challenging. Other issues include a lack of standardization of formats, inadequate nomenclature, and the fact that many of the classic, seminal articles in astronomy have not been converted to electronic formats.[13] As so much astronomy discovery depends on the collaborations of astronomers internationally, common data standards and formats have been necessary in order to process and make sense of data from a variety of observatories and laboratories. Community standards have been developed to handle large-scale astronomy projects. For example, the Flexible Image Transport System (FITS), published in 1981, is the standard format for the interchange of astronomical images and arrays.

Astronomy Datasets/Repositories

- The Sloan Digital Sky Survey (http://www.sdss.org): This project has detailed three-dimensional maps of the Universe, containing images of one third of the sky. It also contains spectra for over three million astronomical objects.

- Earth Observing System Data and Information System (EOSDIS) (https://earthdata.nasa.gov/about-eosdis): Processes, archives, and distributes data from a large number of Earth observing satellites and represents a crucial capability for studying the Earth system from space and improving prediction of Earth system change. EOSDIS consists of a set of processing facilities and data centers distributed across the United States that serve hundreds of thousands of users around the world.
- NASA Space Science Data Coordinated Archive (http://nssdc.gsfc.nasa.gov/): NASA's archive for space science mission data,
- NED: NASA/IPAC Extragalactic Database (https://ned.ipac.caltech.edu/): This site collects and distributes astronomical data worldwide, for millions of objects outside the Milky Way galaxy and connects the public to observatories around the world and makes use of data collected from powerful telescopes.

Chemistry

Chemistry research data management practices have lagged behind other disciplines for a variety of reasons. Often, the research work of chemists takes place at the lab group level, and is guided by academics who must focus on managing the project rather than interacting directly with the data. This lack of hands-on contact with the laboratory's data can result in differing opinions among chemists on standards for data management. Chemists often store data in formats that are subject to technological obsolescence, and labs rarely create metadata for research. As graduate students and junior researchers leave for other institutions, data and knowledge become lost.[14]

While researchers in fields such as astronomy and physics are organizing and storing their data on a cross-institutional basis, partially due to the expense of equipment, chemistry is still largely campus-based, and faculty often believe their field is slow to innovate.[15]

Given that the culture of chemistry is more campus-based and less collaborative, chemists are less likely to value sharing their data than researchers in disciplines such as astronomy and geology. In a 2011–2013 study of their research support needs, 67% of interviewed chemists surveyed responded that they had never utilized an online repository, though many did state that they would be more likely to do so if mandated by their institution.[16] While chemists tend to not openly share their data, they do frequently make their data available to colleagues when requested.[17]

Chemistry Datasets/Repositories

- Cambridge Structural Database (http://www.ccdc.cam.ac.uk/about_ccdc/): The Cambridge Crystallographic Data Center (CCDC) compiles this database, which is an international repository of organic and metal-organic crystal structures obtained via experimental data.

- Chemical Synthesis Database (ChemSynthesis) (http://www.chemsynthesis.com/): ChemSynthesis is an open access chemical database. It contains physical properties of over 40,000 compounds and over 45,000 synthesis references.
- ChemXSeer (http://chemxseer.ist.psu.edu/): Hosted and administered by Pennsylvania State University, ChemxSeer is an integrated digital library and database that hosts published articles and experimental data obtained from chemical kinetics.
- PubChem (http://pubchem.ncbi.nlm.nih.gov/): From the U.S. National Center for Biotechnology Information of the National Institutes of Health (NIH). This database provides chemical information on the biological properties and activities of small molecules. It is organized as three linked databases within NCBI's Entrez Information Retrieval system.

U.S. Federal Agency Requirements on Data Management and Data Sharing†

As previously discussed, given that scientific researchers have varying approaches to sharing data, and that scientific data can be large and complex, the importance of data sharing to further development and expansion of research ensures that data sharing matters to federal agencies. Scientific federal agencies were the first to impose requirements for data management and sharing. The three federal agencies with the largest research and development budgets are the National Institute of Health, The National Science Foundation, and the Department of Defense.[18] This section discusses the requirements from these three agencies, as well as from other important federal granting agencies that support scientific research.

The first federal funding agency to develop and implement a data sharing policy was the National Institute of Health in 2008. In this public access policy, scientists funded by NIH grants are required to submit their final peer-reviewed journal manuscripts to PubMed Central immediately upon acceptance for publication. Increasingly, journals are now automatically submitting these publications to PMC on behalf of authors. However, authors can upload manuscripts themselves via the NIH Manuscript Submission (NIHMS) system, which submits articles to PubMedCentral.

Additionally, researchers who submit an application seeking $500,000 or more in NIH funding for a single year must include their plan for data sharing, or, if data sharing is not possible, their reasons for not sharing. NIH states that "data

† U.S. policies and agencies have been mainly discussed, as the author is most familiar with them. The situation in other countries will vary.

intended for broader use should be free of identifiers that would permit linkages to individual research participants and variables that could lead to deductive disclosure of the identity of individual subjects."[19]

In January 2015, the NIH-instituted Genomic Data Sharing (GDS) Policy became effective, and it applies to all NIH-funded research that generates large-scale genomic data. All researchers applying for NIH grants where large-scale genomic data will be generated must create a Genomic Data Sharing plan in their proposal and outline in the budget section of their application the resources they will need to prepare the data for submission to the appropriate repositories. If the sharing of human data is not possible, applicants should provide a justification as to why the data cannot be shared.

Following on the heels of NIH, in 2011 the National Science Foundation (NSF) began requiring that researchers submit a two-page data management plan as part of each funding proposal. This data management plan must include information about the types of data to be gathered, the metadata standards to be used, the policies and provision for reuse, and plans for long-term archiving. Although the NSF has guidelines for archiving, saving, or providing of samples, collections, or research data, it does not mandate how these practices should be done.

The Department of Defense (DoD) has released a draft of its proposed public access plan, which requires that all proposals for research funding include a data management plan, as well as the deposit of metadata for all created datasets to the Defense Technical Information Center (DTIC.) Other federal funding agencies with data management mandates or guidelines include the Environmental Protection Agency, the Department of Energy, National Aeronautic and Space Agency, and the National Oceanic and Atmospheric Administration.

In March 2012, the Obama-Biden administration rolled out the Big Data Research and Development Initiative from the Office of Science and Technology Policy (OSTP), which will invest $200 million to store and provide access to large collections of digital data. This effort involves Defense Advanced Research Projects Agency (DARPA), the NIH, and the NSF. Some of the initiatives include a partnership between the NIH and Amazon Web services to host the 1,000 Genomes Project data on Amazon Web Services, grants for "EarthCube" (a collaborative partnership between the U.S. National Science Foundation's Geosciences Directorate (GEO) and the Division of Advanced Cyberinfrastructure (ACI) and DARPA's XDATA, which develops computational techniques for analyzing large volumes of defense data.

Science Librarian Support for Data Management

Given the increasing emphasis of data management practices in the sciences, the Association of Research Libraries (ARL) began to discuss the roles that libraries might take as partners in research in the mid-2000s. In 2006, ARL hosted a workshop funded by the National Science Foundation to discuss and explore the roles academic research libraries could serve in order to partner with organizations in the science and engineering research lifecycle. A subsequent report (*To Stand the Test of Time: Long Term Stewardship of Digital Data Sets in Science and Engineering*) presented recommendations for data stewardship.[20]

Furthermore, a survey of science librarians at ARL member institutions in 2012 asked respondents about participation in data management and data repositories. The survey showed that 8% of respondents' institutions accepted and stored data, and 11% indicated that the institution was working on implementing a repository. Thirty-two percent indicated assistance with data management was available, and 24% responded that librarians offered data management plan consultations. Forty-four percent of respondents indicated that their job duties included working with institutional/data repositories or data management, with 17% indicating that these duties were forthcoming.[21]

Librarians knew that data services were a newly emerging role and opportunity but were grappling with the scope of what could and should be done. The gradual emergence of federal agency requirements provided a framework of current and future services libraries could provide. As science funding agencies, such as the NLM and NIH, are increasingly mandating data management plans and data sharing, science librarians have a unique opportunity to participate in library efforts to develop and define data management and support services at academic research institutions.

Research Data Management Lifecycle

It is helpful for librarians, in planning support services, to consider the research data management lifecycle. This basic model[†] shows the research lifecycle as an iterative process with many points of opportunity for libraries to provide services and guidance to researchers. Most scientists begin by formulating and refining a research question while consulting previous studies via journal articles and data analysis. Librarians have long been involved in this stage of the research project, assisting researchers with locating appropriate background information, scholarly journal articles, and datasets, which is the data search/reuse stage of the research data management lifecycle. Assisting users with literature reviews and finding information has been the specialty of the liaison, and liaisons should become familiar and knowledgeable about locating data in their subject areas. The library may have a data services librarian who specializes in locating data in a variety of

† This model has been formulated in various ways. In brief, the idea is that a data management plan needs to take into account initial research, data collection, documentation, analysis, storage and archiving, discovery, and reuse (which starts the cycle over again). See a version of the lifecycle at http://guides.library.ucsc.edu/datamanagement/.

disciplines, but the liaison is often the first point of contact and should have some background knowledge. Liaisons often focus on serving faculty individually but may also embed themselves in a laboratory at the beginning of a research project.

When the research question has been formulated, and the initial data has been gathered, researchers are often required by the funding agency to create a data management plan. Even when such a plan is not required, librarians should emphasize the importance of going through the exercise. Many libraries are offering assistance with data management plans by offering information on data management tools, locating standards for different agencies, and even providing assistance in the writing of these plans.

During the data storage phase, as well as the archival phase, libraries can provide services such as advising on best practices in organizing, naming, and storing research data. Science librarians should take leadership in advising researchers on current standards for metadata and file naming in relevant subject areas, such as the Darwin Core and Integrated Taxonomic Information System (IT IS) for Natural History, the Standard for the Exchange of Earthquake Data (SEED) for Earth Sciences, and the Geospatial Interoperability Framework (GIF) for Geographic and Geospatial Data. Librarians already possess skills in organization and description of materials, and development and assistance with metadata are an opportunity to offer a valuable service to researchers and stay relevant in the university setting.

Institutional and Other Repositories

Given the role libraries already serve in hosting and offering research materials to the university, they are well positioned to offer services for storing, hosting, and archiving scientific research data. Many libraries are already offering institutional repositories to host manuscripts, so hosting, storing, and sharing researcher data are natural extensions. However, libraries with limited budgets and staff are frequently unable to take on this major commitment, and certainly should not try to if a long-term commitment is not possible. When libraries cannot store data internally, librarians should advise and guide researchers to the appropriate repositories for storing their data, and liaisons should become familiar with repositories in their subject areas.

Dedicated Professional Staff

Some libraries have dedicated data services librarians who work with all the colleges and departments who produce data. These librarians work closely with Information Technology staff, faculty, and other relevant library staff to provide a central source for data management and support initiatives. Other libraries do not have a centralized research and data support librarian, and, hence, have distributed data support work among liaisons, technical services, and library IT staff. Though libraries without dedicated research and data support librarians and with a small staff may have to scale down the services that can be provided to institutional researchers, it is important for the library to define the needs of the researchers, to define the capabilities of library staff, and to begin to make strategic decisions as to what the library can offer. Administrators considering library-wide initiatives should assess the feasibility of having dedicated positions for data support.

Subject Guides

Many academic libraries have created subject guides specifically on data management to assist campus researchers in all areas of data, from discovering existing datasets, to working with data management plans and tools, to finding subject-specific repositories. Researchers, however, may not discover these guides unless they are heavily marketed and easy to locate from library web sites. Science librarians should make sure that these subject guides are presented to their affiliated departments.

Assessment

Before undertaking wide-scale data management services, it is important to assess the needs and practices of researchers across campus. Assessment tools (such as survey instruments, focus groups, and interviews) can be used to determine how faculty in different departments are approaching creating data management plans and processing and storing research data, and to identify their attitudes and practices when it comes to sharing data. Researchers in departments can indicate which services both in the library and also throughout campus would be valuable.

Partnering across the Organization

Librarians involved with data services and management should also identify other campus entities that are already providing data management assistance and reach out to these offices and offer to partner.[†] Many times, research faculty are not aware of all the services available to them on campus, and the library can serve a valuable role in marketing and communicating on behalf of these entities. A few examples demonstrate how university libraries are participating in providing data management services and resources to researchers. These efforts are not specifi-

† For more information and examples on collaborative support for research data management initiatives, see the chapter in this volume by Hofelich Mohr, Johnston, and Lindsay called "The Data Management Village."

cally limited to science data, but science librarians can use these models as starting points in their own efforts to provide data support.

Purdue University took an early leadership role in offering data services to its researchers, focusing initially on science and engineering research. Through an initiative that evaluated interest in collaborating with researchers, the results led to the creation of a full-time data research scientist position.[22] Purdue built a data curation profiles toolkit that provides a snapshot of the researcher's data at any given time. Additionally, in 2011, the university launched the Purdue University Research Repository (PURR), which provides a collaborative, virtual research environment and working space enabling researchers to create a data management plan, upload research data, and publish datasets.

In 2009, Georgia Tech decided to assess data management practices on campus in advance of the upcoming NSF requirement for data management plans. At that time, 40% of researchers surveyed believed that creating data management plans was unnecessary, and 47% indicated that they did not know much about data management. Seventy-three percent were interested in data storage and preservation assistance, and 40% were interested in information about developing data management plans.[23] As a result, Georgia Tech now offers assistance with data management plans, allows data to be included in SMARTech (Georgia Tech's institutional repository that is comprised of many different communities and collections), and offers a "Data Management Planning" course to help satisfy Georgia Tech's "Responsible Conduct of Research Compliance Policy."

The Johns Hopkins Libraries, in response to big data challenges, developed and implemented Data Management Services in 2010, which provides data management planning support, data consulting, and archival services across disciplines. Researchers can use the JDH Data Archive to store their data if no other repositories are available. The consultants work with researchers to determine their data management needs (how they are planning to manage, store, and share their data) and advise on metadata standards.

The University of Virginia Library's Research Data Services provides extensive and robust data management services to campus researchers. One of the original contributing institutions in the development of the DMPTool, which provides templates for major funding agencies' required formats for DMPs. In addition, librarians offer data management workshops to researchers and are available to help with data management plans for all University of Virginia researchers. The StatLab provides consulting and workshops for researchers on using statistical methods and software.

Health Science librarians are keenly poised to assist researchers with NIH compliance issues. Duke Medical Center Library started monitoring the NIH Public Access policy in 2006 and created a web-based guide to inform researchers on how to comply. Librarians reached out to key research offices around campus and were given the ability to take the lead on addressing researcher compliance.

NIH has created the Public Access Compliance Monitor (PACM), an online system that lists citations found in PubMed citing grants that should fall under the NIH Public Access Policy. Librarians can download reports of non-compliant PIs; researchers who are out of compliance are individually contacted by the library about their compliance issues, given instructions on how to comply, and given contact information so that they can work with librarians to get assistance on uploading manuscripts and other required functions. All library staff receive training in order to handle basic compliance issues, and a core team is available for more complex problems.

Science librarians who want to add data support to their job descriptions should begin by assessing the needs of their departments and researchers. Meeting department heads and head researchers, talking with graduate students, and finding out what services and dedicated staff already exist in each department is important in order to ascertain what service gaps may exist. Important types of information to gather include types and formats of data generated, storage and backup practices, methods used to organize data, whether data management plan help is needed, sharing habits, and identification of units across campus that assist researchers in their departments. Social science data librarians wanting to expand their services to include science data can partner with science librarians, who can provide subject expertise, knowledge of research practices, and connections to key contact people, even if these science librarians lack expertise in data management and support.

Due to the increasing complexity and expense of working with scientific research data, along with the push towards making publicly funded research available to all, scientists are straining to keep abreast of agency policies, data management plan creation, compliance, metadata standards, and all the other aspects of research data management that compete with their other duties in the laboratory and the classroom. Librarians have the organizational and, often, the technical skills to be valuable partners with our researchers to assist with their data service needs. Even smaller libraries with scant budgetary resources can develop expertise in helping researchers write data management plans, develop helpful guides, and connect their researchers to the appropriate data repositories. Finally, as data are becoming increasingly important as resources for scholarly research, science librarians should become familiar and keep current with the major datasets and repositories in their subject areas.

---

1. Science Staff, "Challenges and Opportunities," *Science* 331, no. 6018 (2011): 692–93, doi:10.1126/science.331.6018.692,693.
2. Ibid.
3. Randal Bryant, Randy H Katz, and Edward D Lazowska, *Big-Data Computing: Creating Revolutionary Breakthroughs in Commerce, Science and Society*, December 22, 2008, http://cra.org/ccc/wp-content/uploads/sites/2/2015/05/Big_Data.pdf, 2.

4. Don MacMillan, "Data Sharing and Discovery: What Librarians Need to Know," *Journal of Academic Librarianship* 40, no. 5 (September 2014): 541–49, 542.
5. Carol Tenopir, Suzie Allard, Kimberly Douglass, Arsev Umur Aydinoglu, Lei Wu, Eleanor Read, Maribeth Manoff, and Mike Frame, "Data Sharing by Scientists: Practices and Perceptions.," *PLoS ONE* 6, no. 6 (June 2011): 1–21.
6. Abigail Goben, Dorothea Salo, and Claire Stewart, "Federal Research," *College & Research Libraries News* 74, no. 8 (September 2013): 421–25.
7. Carol Tenopir et al., "Data Sharing by Scientists: Practices and Perceptions."
8. National Human Genome Research Institute, "DNA Sequencing Costs: Data from the NHGRI Genome Sequencing Program (GSP)," *DNA Sequencing Costs: Data from the NHGRI Genome Sequencing Program (GSP)*, October 31, 2014, http://www.genome.gov/sequencingcosts/.
9. Heather A Piwowar, "Who Shares? Who Doesn't? Factors Associated with Openly Archiving Raw Research Data," *PloS One* 6, no. 7 (2011): 1–13.
10. Mai H. Oushy, Rebecca Palacios, Alan E. C. Holden, Amelie G. Ramirez, Kipling J. Gallion, and Mary A. O'Connell, "To Share or Not to Share? A Survey of Biomedical Researchers in the U.S. Southwest, an Ethnically Diverse Region," ed. Xu-jie Zhou, *PLOS ONE* 10, no. 9 (September 17, 2015): e0138239, doi:10.1371/journal.pone.0138239.
11. Ross Anderson, "How Big Data are Changing Astronomy (Again).," *The Atlantic*, April 19, 2012, accessed March 20, 2015.
12. Ray P Norris, "Can Astronomy Manage Its Data?," *arXiv Preprint Astro-ph/0501089*, 2005. 2–3.
13. Ibid, 3.
14. Matthew P Long and Roger C Schonfeld, "Supporting the Changing Research Practices of Chemists," *New York: Ithaka S+ R,* 2013, http://www.sr.ithaka.org/publications/supporting-the-changing-research-practices-of-chemists/ 11–12.
15. Ibid, 7.
16. Ibid, 35.
17. Ibid, 12.
18. U.S. Office of Science and Technology Policy, "The 2014 Budget: A World-Leading Commitment to Science and Research: Science, Technology, Innovation, and STEM Education in the 2014 Budget," 2008, https://www.whitehouse.gov/sites/default/files/microsites/ostp/2014_R&D-budget_overview.pdf.
19. "NIH Guide: FINAL NIH STATEMENT ON SHARING RESEARCH DATA," February 26, 2003, http://grants.nih.gov/grants/guide/notice-files/NOT-OD-03-032.html.
20. Amy Friedlander and Prudence Adler, "To Stand the Test of Time: Long-Term Stewardship of Digital Data Sets in Science and Engineering. A Report to the National Science Foundation from the ARL Workshop on New Collaborative Relationships–The Role of Academic Libraries in the Digital Data Universe," *Association of Research Libraries*, 2006, http://www.arl.org/publications-resources/1075-to-stand-the-test-of-time-long-term-stewardship-of-digital-data-sets-in-science-and-engineering#.VpZvkfkrLRY.
21. Karen Antell, Jody Bales Foote, Jaymie Turner, and Brian Shults, "Dealing with Data: Science Librarians' Participation in Data Management at Association of Research Libraries Institutions," *College & Research Libraries* 75, no. 4 (July 2014): 557–74.
22. Catherine Soehner, Catherine Steeves, and Jennifer Ward, "E-Science and Data Support Services: A Study of ARL Member Institutions.," *Association of Research Libraries*, 2010. http://www.arl.org/storage/documents/publications/escience-report-2010.pdf.
23. Susan Wells Parham, Jon Bodnar, and Sara Fuchs, "Supporting Tomorrow's Research," *College & Research Libraries News* 73, no. 1 (January 2012): 10–13.

PART III

Data Preservation and Access

CHAPTER 13

Scholarly Communication and Data

Hailey Mooney

Introduction

The Internet and digital data are strong forces shaping the modern world of scholarly communication, the context within which academic librarians operate. Scholarly communication entails the ways by which scholarly and research information are created, disseminated, evaluated, and preserved.[1] Recognition of the broader forces at play in research and scholarship is imperative to keep ourselves from obsolescence and to simply function as effective librarians. The operation of the scholarly communication system is the "bedrock" of academic information literacy and forms the "sociocultural frame of reference" for understanding library research skills.[2] The purpose of this chapter is to provide foundational knowledge for the data librarian by developing an understanding of the place of data within the current paradigm of networked digital scholarly communication. This includes defining the nature of data and data publications, examining the open science movement and its effects on data sharing, and delving into the challenges inherent to the wider integration of data into the scholarly communication system and the academic library.

The Nature of Scientific Knowledge and Data

The sociology of science provides a basis from which to understand the fundamental underpinnings of the norms and values that govern the institution of science and the production of scientific knowledge. In basic information literacy instruction, librarians teach the difference between popular and scholarly information. We identify scholarly information based on a set of criteria such as a peer-reviewed publication venue and the presence of citations. These identifiers are normative practices in the production of scientific knowledge, a particular type of knowledge which requires certification based on conformance to the methods and values of the scientific community; what Robert Merton calls the scientific ethos.

According to Merton,[3] the ethos of science is based upon four institutional imperatives: universalism, communism, disinterestedness, and organized skepticism. Universalism requires that claims be objectively and impersonally supported, rather than based on the particularities of the author. Communism is the common ownership of goods. Within the institution of science, this means that scientific findings are meant to be widely communicated and shared. Disinterestedness implies lack of personal interest created by conformity to the institution of science that monitors the activity of individual scientists, as through the process of peer-review, in order to verify results. And finally, organized skepticism is the practice of suspending personal belief systems in favor of empiricism and logic. These imperatives of science as an institution support the implementation of the scientific method, which is based upon continual input of observations, or data, in order to build the body of scientific knowledge.[4]

Data, therefore, form the basis of information and knowledge[5] and the use and provision of data can be integrated into Merton's theory of the scientific ethos. For the objective claims of universalism, data provide evidence. The sharing of scientific findings, found in the imperative of communism, conceivably includes the sharing of data that form the basis of those findings. Disinterestedness and the need to validate results are strengthened by the ability to scrutinize and replicate results from data. Favoring empiricism, as necessitated by the norm of organized skepticism, rests on the scientific method and the use of data. Yet despite the intrinsic value of data to the creation of scientific knowledge, the exchange of scientific findings generally do not occur at the level of data, but through the sharing of information—explanations and interpretations of data through the vehicle of the written word in standard forms of scholarly communication such as the journal article, the conference paper, or the book.

There are two important and problematic issues with the nature of data that explain why the written publication has been prioritized over the provision of data within the scholarly record. The first is that data, by themselves, have no meaning to the outside reader. Data require context, documentation, and explanation. The second problem is that data take multiple forms and datasets lack standard structure.

Whereas the sociological frame provides a useful viewpoint to understand the institution of science, an anthropological perspective illuminates the process of data creation within the individual research projects that create the overall body of scientific knowledge. A number of studies have examined the particular practices by which data are created within various scientific projects; here in this section we look at two. Carlson and Anderson[6] selected four projects for study ranging across hard, soft, pure, and applied disciplines: an astronomy data grid, a social survey project, a digital curation project for a collection of museum artifacts, and a collection of anthropological studies of foreign cultures. They found that in all cases, data are characterized by their problematic heterogeneity and the need for careful formatting. Project materials only become usable data through unique processes that allow for materials to be "transportable" as a discrete object and "intelligible" to outsiders. For example, in the social survey project, words are converted to numbers, variables are coded, and files are restructured in order to create usable and intelligible data. The processes of conversion, formalization, and provision of documentation for the data are rarely self-explanatory or self-contained and therefore required "complementary external information" in order for the data to be understood.[7] This is particularly difficult for anthropology projects where private field data has traditionally not been made available for outside use beyond analysis and summary in books or articles.

Ribes and Jackson, in their study of ecological water stream sample data, likewise find data to be a sticky entity, a "commodity fiction," in that data are not easily made into an undifferentiated and universal form.[8] Traveling with the ecologists in field, they find that the creation of data is mutually constructed into the everyday work of scientists and that careful rituals are observed in order to ensure comparability of measurements in the creation of the stream data. Despite the presence of an online database, the stream dataset is "not singular; rather it is...distributed across databases, field sheets, and a physical archive of samples."[9] The project data are constituted of multiple parts; their production require coordination and documentation (for example, one scientist bemoans the possibility of walking into the cold storage room and finding labels have fallen off the samples: "I think the extra label tape we put on the lids will hold up."[10]). Within a single project, and indeed between different projects, data take multiple forms, are made up of multiple parts, and require documentation.

The proliferation of forms that data can take engenders debate on what exactly data are, resulting in a multiplicity of definitions. Data take as many forms as there are disciplines and methodologies. There are as many definitions of data as there are people doing research.[11] Despite this variation, there are a couple of key commonalities across definitions that provide us with a basis to understand data:

1. *Data are evidence.* Data have an evidentiary function and requires analysis and interpretation in order to derive meaning.[12]
2. *Data can take multiple forms.* Many definitions of data provide examples of data forms and formats. However, no list can be complete; note how some definitions will include a listing of research methodologies by which data can be produced in addition to specific types. Forms can include both file types and variant aggregations of data.[13]

In addition to taking multiple format types, data may be aggregated at varying levels and characterized as a *dataset* or a *data collection*. Sets or collections of data may include multiple files of data (potentially of different types) along with accompanying documentation. The dataset is generally a smaller collection of data records, such as a single social science dataset created from a social survey.[14] A data collection refers to an aggregation of data and/or datasets, and so it is larger in scope. For example, the Data Citation Index defines the dataset as "a single or coherent set of data or a data file" which may be part of a data study (generally a description of associated datasets), and at the top level of aggregation makes up the overall data collection of a data repository.[15] The National Science Board[16] identifies three levels of data collections based on functional categories. *Research data collections* include data from one or several focused research projects, serve a small specific group, and are unlikely to persist beyond the life of the research project. *Resource* or *community data collections* are the result of community-level standards and research areas and may be directly funded by stakeholder agencies, but often do not have a clear commitment to long-term maintenance. *Reference data collections* are created for the benefit of large general scientific communities, employ or set standards for data creation, and have large budgets, which often include the capacity for long-term access and preservation.[17]

Therefore, more common than the single file of data is the conception of data as compound objects that can take myriad forms, resulting in a "fuzzy conception" of data.[18] This is in part, a philosophical dilemma to define a relative concept. However, there are very real and practical implications for the integration of data into the scholarly communication system. If we cannot structure, define, and extract meaning from data, then how can we expect to systematically collect, organize, and disseminate data? In order for data to fit into a system that is largely based on dealing with discrete information commodities (e.g., the journal article, book) it must conform to a publication based paradigm. If the compound object of the dataset can be wrapped up into a distinct object, then it may appear logical to conceive of data as a publication—however, it has been proposed that conceiving of data as publication is a problematic metaphor.[19] By attempting to make data fit an old paradigm, we may limit the ability of the scholarly communication system to evolve and adapt to new models of scholarship.[20] The shift to digital technologies is an opportunity to redefine communication models, and by attempting to make data fit into the existing molds we inhibit the creative potential to share data in multiple modalities and fully embrace new forms of scholarship. Even within the realm of information sharing (as opposed to data sharing) forward-thinking scholars are experimenting with emerging formats (e.g., interactive books, blogging) that do not have a clear place within the existing formal modes of scholarly communication.[21]

Despite the rhetorical and practical issues around the fuzzy conception of data, datasets, and data collections, pragmatism dictates that fitting data into the mold of publication is the path forward for integration into the scholarly communication system as it currently stands. Publication, after all, serves an important purpose within the social system of science by legitimizing, creating a priority claim for the author, and allowing for dissemination, access, and preservation.[22] Data publication allows for data to be recognized as "first-class objects" within the scholarly record at-large through the implementation of management and curation.[23] At the micro-level, data publications provide recognition to data creators by affording the ability to bestow citations: the currency of scholarly and scientific achievement. Furthermore, *data publication* stands as a formalization of other methods of *data sharing*. For example, sharing data directly with collaborators or other vetted scholars (as through email) does not afford data with the same level of access, curation, and preservation given to an item housed within the collection of a research library.

Open Data and the Forces Behind Data Sharing and Publication

The open access movement is predicated on the value of science as a public good and leverages Internet technology to provide free and unrestricted access to scholarly literature.[24] The jump from open access for literature to open access to data is not a particularly big one given that the knowledge transferred by the scholarly literature is built from the creation and analysis of data.[25] Although certain types of data have been long published and shared, and calls for increased data sharing date back decades,[26] the recent open access movement has shifted the attention on data sharing into high gear. The reasoning behind open data rests upon two levels of social ideologies: within the scientific community as an ethical imperative, and within government as an economic and political issue.

Advances in science can benefit society. Science is conceived of as a public institution wherein it is the duty of scientists to share their findings. For example, although the United States is a capitalist economy with ongoing tension between private and public goods, knowledge is widely considered to be a public good that would otherwise be under-produced if not supported by government funding.[27] U.S. government agencies fund significant amounts of research through the provision of grants, with the federal government spending $31.0 billion on basic research in FY 2012, 50.8% of which was awarded to universities and colleges.[28] The U.S. government is itself a major data producer, with 13 major statistical agencies and over 100 total agencies that also produce statistical information as part of their mission.[29] However, the issue of transparency and access to data produced directly by government agencies is distinct from access to data funded by government grants but produced by extramural researchers within academia and non-government research institutes. Both may be referred to as *open data*, but the more distinct terms of *open government data* and *open science data* serve to clarify the difference. There are shared ideological tenets, such as right of access to work resulting from public funds, accountability, and the value of knowledge sharing, but open government data (although used in scholarly research) is not a direct component of the scholarly communication system.[†]

In the United States, the legislative debate over open access (as seen in bill proposals such as the Federal Research Public Access Act, Fair Copyright in Research Works Act, and the Fair Access to Science and Technology Research Act) has focused largely on traditional publications.[30] However, as recounted by the Congressional Research Service, federal debate over the right of public access to government funded research data dates back to 1980.[31] The Supreme Court ruled in *Forsham v. Harris* that a grantee's research data were not subject to a Freedom of Information Act (FOIA) request because the files were not federal agency records. In 1999, the issue was raised again with the revision of OMB Circular A-110, the regulatory document which stipulates requirements for grants. Senator Richard Shelby shepherded the inclusion of the Data Access Act of 1999 (a provision within the omnibus P.L. 105-277, also known as the Shelby Amendment) which provided for the revision Circular A-110 "to require Federal awarding agencies to ensure that all data produced under an award will be made available to the public through the procedures established under the Freedom of Information Act." The America Competes Reauthorization Act of 2010 (P.L. 111-358) stipulated that the Director of the Office of Science and Technology Policy (OSTP) coordinate agency policies related to the dissemination and stewardship of scholarly publications and digital data produced by government funded research. This mandate eventually resulted in the February 22, 2013 OSTP memo, *Increasing Access to the Results of Federally Funded Research*, which requires federal agencies with annual research and development expenditures of at least $100 million to develop plans for public access to publications and data.[32] The gap between the 1999 Shelby Amendment and the 2010 America Competes Reauthorization reflect a period of building momentum within the open access movement and the parallel attention paid to the merits of open data.

Many government research grant funders have complied with policy mandates to support the concept of public access to data by requiring data management plans. Current data management plan policies generally require discussion of whether or not data sharing is feasible and how it will be accomplished, but they are vague as to how data sharing should be accomplished and do not specifically require formal publication of data through deposit in a recommended archive or other means.[33] For example, the National Science Foundation (NSF) requires that data management plans discuss policies for sharing and access, reuse, archiving, and preservation, and also that investigators are expected to share their primary data with other researchers; however, there is no specific requirement that data

† For an introduction to open government data, see the *Open Data Barometer Global Report*, 2nd ed. (World Wide Web Foundation, 2015), http://barometer.opendataresearch.org/.

be deposited in a public database.[34] Likewise, the National Institutes of Health data sharing policy guidance offers multiple methods for data sharing. Archiving data with a repository is a possibility, but so is handling data requests individually under the auspices of the primary investigator.[35] Although the NSF and other data management plans do not actually require data publication, they are widely seen as an important step in the direction of increased data sharing.

The recent focus on increasing access to government-funded scientific research data as a matter of public good is also reflected in international policy initiatives. The Organisation for Economic Co-operation and Development endorsed a set of recommended principles and guidelines for the provision of access to publicly funded research data, noting that "the power of computers and the Internet has created new fields of application for not only the results of research, but the *sources* of research; the base material of *research data*."[36] UNESCO supports open access for wide and equitable dissemination of research and recommends that open access policies developed by governments, institutions, and funding agencies consider including data as a relevant research output for policy inclusion.[37] As part of their open access strategy to increase the impact of funded research, the European Commission explicitly includes research data in addition to publications as reflected in their *Recommendation on access to and preservation of scientific information*, which states that "Open access to scientific research data enhances data quality, reduces the need for duplication of research, speeds up scientific progress and helps to combat scientific fraud."[38] The Research Councils UK abide by a common set of principles on data wherein "publicly funded research data are a public good, produced in the public interest, which should be made openly available with as few restrictions as possible."[39]

A common thread throughout U.S. and international governmental policy discussions is the public's right to transparency and accountability. Data can form the basis of legislative decision-making. In 1997, a controversial air quality regulatory standard proposed by the U.S. Environmental Protection Agency was based in part on scientific research conducted by Harvard and funded by the National Institutes of Health. Questioning the validity of the research, legislators and industry groups requested access to the underlying data and were told that it was unavailable.[40] This prompted Senator Shelby's work towards the OMB Circular A-110 revision. Shelby advocated for data access arguing that "public confidence in the accuracy and reliability of information being used to drive public policy ultimately is in the best interest of scientific research. Increasing access to such data promotes the transparency and accountability that is essential to building public trust in government actions and decision-making."[41] Interest in the availability of scientific data in environmental decision-making in particular continues to this day.[42] The National Academies promote the principles of data integrity, sharing, and access, making the point that that "sharing research data enhances the data's integrity by allowing other researchers to scrutinize and verify them."[43] Legislative concern over open data is based on ensuring scientific integrity through verification and reproducibility of results in order to provide for scientific accountability and public trust in science.[44]

Another component of policy-maker and taxpayer right to access government funded research is the trend toward demanding increased "return on scientific capital."[45] Data sharing has the potential to maximize funding impact by reducing redundancy and enabling reuse for new scientific findings, providing for a higher return on investment.[46] Scientific innovation can be translated into economic benefits. When information and data are made available, knowledge can be leveraged to create new products and services.[47] This economic argument is not limited to politicians, but is ensconced within the philosophy of the scholarly open access movement, wherein public funding ought to equal public access.

Scholars recognize their role in advancing public knowledge. Scientists share the beliefs that transparency within the research process produces better science and that data sharing extends research dollars by allowing for innovative reuse. Sharing information and data is positioned as an ethical obligation to the scientific community and the public.[48] Data sharing and publication is viewed as a beneficial for multiple reasons, such as:

- *Providing access for reuse.* Maximizes the contribution of research subjects. Reduces overall research costs. Increases research impact through secondary analysis studies that ask new questions of the data or develop new analysis methodologies, or by initiating collaborations with the primary investigator.
- *Allows for replication and validation.* Reproducible science reduces risk of errors or outright fraud. Improves research practices by encouraging transparency. Enhances public trust in science.
- *Ensuring preservation.* Prevents data loss and redundant research efforts. Protects valuable resources.

Internal pressure within the scholarly community is exerted through editorials and essays promoting these data sharing benefits.[49]

The ethic of data sharing is written into the scholarly ecosystem via the adoption of policies by professional associations and scholarly journals. For example, the American Psychological Association code of ethics and the American Sociological Association ethical standards require researchers to make their data available.[50] A growing number of journals include policies for data sharing and publishing (such as the British Ecological Society journals, *The American Naturalist*, *Nature*, *Public Library Of Science (PLOS)*, American Geophysical Union journals, etc.) that serve to encourage the practice.[51] Declarations from scholarly groups in support of open data further contribute to the movement. The Panton Principles, developed by the Open Knowledge Foundation, provide guidance on licensing data publications within the public domain based on the premise that "for science to effectively function, and for society to reap the full benefits from scientific endeavours, it is crucial that science data be made open."[52] Taking a wider view, the Denton Declaration asserts the value of promoting "collaboration, transparency, and accountability across organizational and disciplinary boundaries" in best practices for data management in support of open access to data.[53]

The scholarly communication system is shifting under the weight of the open access movement. Open data places a unique strain as a non-traditional format, which substantiates the need for system-wide change and adaptation in regards not to just the economics of scholarly publications, but to the very nature of communication formats and technologies and the social ecosystem of communication.[54] Political, economic, and social concerns over access to data are evidenced by advances in policy. These are the forces pushing the scholarly communication system toward integrating data.

Data Sharing Realities

Despite the existence of strong rhetoric in favor of data sharing and publication, the status quo in most fields is low rates of data sharing and publication.[55] A disconnect exists between data sharing ideals and reality. Even when authors publish in journals with data sharing policies, most authors do not actually make their data available.[56] In a study of a group of scientists' data practices and perceptions, Tenopir et al.[57] found that 67% of respondents agree that lack of access to data is an impediment to scientific progress, yet just 36% agreed that others can easily access their data and only 6% make all of their data available for use by others. When it does happen, informal data sharing is more likely to occur than formal publication.[58] The ideal of openness and transparency in research is widely held by researchers, but normative practice does not include regular incorporation of data into formal scholarly communication outputs.

Publishing data has not been a universal feature of scholarly communication practice in the same way as publishing journal articles, books, and conference papers. Until recently, communication technologies lacked the ability to easily facilitate data storage and transfer. Widespread integration of data sharing as a standard feature of the scholarly communication process will take time as change is needed to overcome a variety of challenges. Whereas some academic communities have been early adopters and can easily see value from the open exchange of data (take for example, the adoption of the Bermuda Principle supporting the sharing of human genome sequence data[59]), others may have valid reasons for not expanding their published communications to include data. A key finding of the Research Information Network's report on data sharing is the extent to which behaviors vary by discipline; research cultures, standardization of common data types, and the concordant availability of data archives are major factors in determining the viability of open data within particular research domains.[60]

Reasons for lack of data sharing and publication range across social and technical issues. Reluctance to share and publish data includes the following considerations:[61]

- *Data sharing norms.* Many research cultures rely primarily on informal data sharing, which allows for control over who can gain access and creates collaborative opportunities for further research. In some cases, applications for data reuse may not be apparent to data creators. Published data brings a loss of control and fear that data may be misused or misinterpreted. Academic competitiveness is a concern: when rewards and recognition accrue only to traditional publications, there are no perceived benefits to sharing data.
- *Inadequate support for data management.* Preparing data for sharing and publication takes a considerable investment of time and effort. Limited knowledge or actual lack of metadata standards and other best practices for data documentation inhibit the ability of researchers to prepare data for sharing and publication.
- *Inadequate infrastructure and publication mechanisms.* Lack of publication options. Data repositories do not exist for all data types in all fields. Descriptive metadata standards may not exist to adequately make data visible.
- *Legal and ethical concerns.* Data may be of a sensitive nature and unable to be shared due to privacy and confidentiality concerns. Institutional policies governing ownership of data may not be clear.

Getting There: Data Publication Practices

Some of the data sharing obstacles are easier to solve than others. Embargoes and timelines for data publication can be set so that researchers are able to fully exploit the fruits of their labor before data are released. Sensitive data can be released through archives that handle restricted data access protocols, such as vetting research projects and enforcing data protection plans. However, these are details underlying the larger paradigm shift necessary to create a social norm of data publication within academic cultures and supplementing scholarly communication infrastructures to accommodate data.

As previously discussed, data publication is a fuzzy concept, complicating the ability to arrive at a straightforward approach to implementation. Publishing data, rather than informally sharing it, provides legitimizing factors that allow for the recognition of data contributions as first-class scholarly objects. As Kratz and Strasser explain, for data to be considered published it must be made publicly available, it must be adequately documented to support reproduction and reuse, and it must be citable.[62] These objectives are obtained through a publication process that includes deposition (as with a repository), description, and assignation of a persistent identifier. Additionally, data publications may be subject to validation (as through peer review), although the feasibility and methodology for data validation, as well as its necessity for publication remain a matter of open debate.[63] There are several models of data publication currently in use. Data may be published via deposit into a digital repository, or with journals as supplementary material to an article, or as a data paper.[64] These publication options are discussed further in the remainder of this section.

A *digital repository* provides an infrastructure for storage, management, retrieval, and curation of digital materials.[65] There is wide variation in the availability of digital repositories for data. Data may be included as one of several content types, as within an *institutional repository*. A *data repository* implies dedication to housing data as the primary content type. The scope of a data repository can be institutional, disciplinary, or multidisciplinary. The term *data archive* comes from the social sciences and refers to organizations dedicated to the long-term preservation and curation of data in order to make them available for secondary analysis; archives may be disciplinary or national in scope.[66]

Among the various options for publishing, the data archive is the most long-standing option for data publication and best fulfills the criteria for formal data publication. In addition, disciplinary data archives afford the ability to specialize in a particular type of data and can serve as a community hub by acting as a bastion for development of standards (for data formatting, metadata, and documentation) and best practices in research methodologies, data management, and sharing cultures. For example, the Inter-university Consortium for Political and Social Research was founded in 1962, curates and preserves datasets, actively supports the Data Documentation Initiative for social survey metadata standards, engages in community outreach for data management best practices, and hosts the Summer Program in Quantitative Methods of Social Research. A more recent data archiving model in the earth sciences is the Data Observation Network for Earth (DataONE), which is a unifying coordinator for a distributed network of data centers. DataONE provides a common search interface to link data archives, provides guidance on data citation and best practices for data management, and offers resources and educational opportunities to support increased community engagement in data sharing and publication activities.[67]

Whereas data archives often specialize in a disciplinary area, institutional repositories gather research outputs from across the entire range of research produced by their home universities. Institutional repositories have been built primarily to accommodate traditional publication formats, although some universities are beginning to include data collections within the institutional repository or create standalone data repositories. Heterogeneity of data types and formats presents a challenge to the ability of the institutional repository to successfully accommodate collection and curation of research data. However, when a disciplinary data archive is not available for a particular data type, the multidisciplinary nature of institutional repositories allows them to provide a home for data publication. Private data repository services, such as Figshare, also seek to fulfill the need for multidisciplinary data publication, in addition to providing a low-barrier method for researchers to make data easily available. The issue of adequately curating heterogeneous data remains problematic for multidisciplinary repositories. For example, ensuring that sufficient documentation is provided to describe the data is difficult to accomplish without subject area and research methodology expertise.[68]

Rather than attempting to independently handle all possible data outputs, institutional repositories may find that building partnerships with data archives provides a better option for supporting disciplinary data cultures and taking advantage of specialized data curation knowledge and practices.[69] For example, a librarian at a college or university may be able to work with faculty to identify data to add to the library collection, but may lack the resources or expertise to recover and convert old software formats, review and clean the data, or guarantee preservation for all file types. A data archive may be able to provide tools and expert advice to assist the institutional repository staff, or add the dataset directly to their collection.[70] Additionally, Akers and Green provide a case study of a library leveraging a membership with a disciplinary data repository to provide financial assistance toward publication fees, integrating data publication with the university press, and offering local assistance and promotion.[71]

Data publishing with journals, as supplementary material or as a *data paper*, can be problematic for achieving publication of data as first-class scholarly objects. Providing data as supplementary material to a journal article does not achieve the desired effect of a standalone data publication. Furthermore, supplementary data are usually provided only for replication purposes and do not offer a complete and fully documented dataset for original reuse in a secondary analysis study. While a data paper typically provides in-depth description of a dataset (without engaging in analysis), it reinforces the standard of the journal article as the desired publication mechanism, keeping data as a second-class citizen. Data papers are essentially "data publication by proxy" because they provide a straightforward bibliographic reference and allow authors to accrue credit, but they normally do not provide access to the actual dataset being described.[72]

Although publishing data along with articles was initially a relatively popular option with the move to electronic publishing and the corresponding removal of space limitations, there have long been issues with standardization for supplementary materials.[73] Journal publishing platforms are by and large not equipped to handle the specialized and heterogeneous needs for data curation. Recent developments provide evidence that journal publishers are moving away from directly hosting data as supplementary materials.[74] Some journal publishers have contracted with digital repositories to handle the display and storage of supplemental materials, such as with the partnership between Taylor & Francis journals and Figshare.[75] Another example is the Dryad data repository, which has over 80 integrated journals and focuses on publishing data underlying peer-reviewed articles in science and medicine. In the absence of formal partnerships, journal data sharing policies may guide authors towards trusted archives for common disciplinary data types. For example, the Geoscience Data Journal provides a list of almost 20 approved repositories covering the range of expected data types.[†] PLOS journals specify that authors are required to utilize field-specific standards and data repositories where they exist. That these policies provide a multiplicity of options for data repositories reflects the steps ahead in establishing data publication norms. The advantage to working with a third-party repository is that supplementary data can be given a separate unique identifier, tracked for reuse, and directly cited.

Additionally, although it is a positive step forward that many journal publishers have turned their attention to the creation of links between articles and supporting data (as per Elsevier[76]), links may stop short of full citation. This is especially true in the case of self-citation, wherein a journal article details the analysis of the author's own data as opposed to a secondary analysis study. An argument against self-citation is that it can disproportionately inflate citation counts.[77] However, for self-citation of other published material the standard practice for an entry is the reference list. Without self-citation, data are still treated as supplementary material to the article, rather than as a discrete publication, in that the data are not listed in the article's bibliography but rather linked directly in-text, via a side-bar, or mentioned in a note. Establishing links between journal articles and datasets is an important component of integration. Those links should serve to recognize data as a publication through inclusion of a complete data citation.

The key reason to treat data as a publication is to allow for it to find a place within existing scholarly communication structures and the paradigmatic norms of the scientific ethos. Importantly, publication allows for citation. Citation is a chief characteristic of scholarly writing. It is the mechanism that establishes priority claims and enables reward. Data citation supports the parallel treatment of literature and data as equal scholarly outputs. This includes the ability to create metrics around data reuse, which has the potential to incentivize data publication by measuring usage and impact for researchers, their institutions, and funding bodies.[78]

Although there have been mechanisms for data publication and citation for decades, only recently has there been widespread acknowledgement within the publishing, library, archival, and data communities of its importance.[79] This is evidenced by the recent adoption of the 2014 Joint Declaration of Data Citation

---

† This list of approved repositories does include multidisciplinary options that accept all data types, such as Figshare and Zenodo.

Principles, which has been endorsed by over 90 scholarly organizations.[80] The importance of data citation is also acknowledged in legislative policy discussions[81] and government open data directives.[82] Still, there is significant change to be made in scientific culture as long-standing status-quo communication practices largely ignore formal data citation.[83] Even where data are formally published, the largely informal data sharing cultures are reinforced through informal citation practices—namely the passing in-text mention or a brief statement in an author's note or acknowledgements note.[84]

Advances in data publishing and data citation go hand-in-hand. Scientists indicate that they would be more likely to publish data if they were assured citation.[85] Implementation of data citation requires that data publication venues build systems that provide adequate metadata, unique identification, and persistence guarantees.[86] Tools such as the DataCite program to provide data repositories with Digital Object Identifiers and establish metadata standards for datasets are helping to create the infrastructure necessary to support citation.[87] The Data Citation Index (DCI) essentially provides the application of bibliographic citation indexing and metrics to data, supporting the integration of data into the scholarly record. The DCI enables data discovery, data citation, and examination of current data publication and citation practices.[88] By indexing data from repositories, it recognizes the primacy of the data repository as the preferred method of data publication (rather than supplementary materials and data papers). Although the DCI may be somewhat premature given the current state of citation practices, the database was developed in part to serve as a driver for change.[89] Although research data publication and citation infrastructure and practices are still in early stages, there are sufficient tools and models to continue moving forward.

Steps for Libraries

The place of data within the scholarly record is in flux. We are in a period of rapid development that will likely continue for some time before infrastructures, policies, scientific norms, and cultural practices are settled. Next steps in supporting the full integration of data into the scholarly communication system include sustained and increased attention to constructing infrastructures (both technical and human), including positioning libraries to build data collections.

Policies in support of data sharing and publication require clear and accessible routes to data publication. However, robust and established data publication options are not available across all domains. The current system is in the unfortunate position of embodying the chicken/egg conundrum: people are not going to publish data until sufficient mechanisms for data publication are in place.[90] Existing policies tend towards vagueness in acknowledgment of the present reality that not all fields have established norms for the publication of data. For example, the

NSF offers this guidance in response to the question, "Am I required to deposit my data in a public database?":

> What constitutes reasonable data management and access will be determined by the community of interest through the process of peer review and program management. In many cases, these standards already exist, but are likely to evolve as new technologies and resources become available.[91]

The *PLOS* journal policy on data sharing is similarly open-ended, requiring that "authors comply with field-specific standards for preparation and recording of data and select repositories appropriate to their field" and encourages authors to "select repositories that meet accepted criteria as trustworthy digital repositories."[92] Although these are laudable policies, the difficulty of navigating the data publication landscape make compliance a struggle when even the policy-makers cannot specify how to best accomplish data publication. In some cases, data librarians may be better informed regarding the range of data sharing and publication options than faculty researchers, putting librarians in a valuable advisory role.

The nascent data publication systems require investment, both inside and outside of libraries. In order to support data management and open data policy directives, there must be investment in both the technical and human infrastructures required to facilitate data sharing and publication. The focus on cyberinfrastructure development in the United States by the NSF includes the vision to create a national digital data framework that would support development of community standards for data management and build architectures for data collections across many different stakeholders, including recognition of the role of digital libraries within colleges and universities to house data produced by their faculty.[93] This has manifested in the NSF's data management plan requirement for grant proposals and funding for programs through the Sustainable Digital Data Preservation and Access Network Partners program (better known as DataNet).[94] For example, the Data Conservancy at the Sheridan Libraries at Johns Hopkins University is a DataNet funded program that provides data management and curation services. Vision, however, has not yet caught up to reality. There is a perception that data management and curation is an unfunded mandate as many researchers still lack institutional support.[95]

Viable economic models for setting up and maintaining data publishing infrastructures are yet to be fully developed. The U.S. federal mandate from the OSTP for government agencies to provide public access to publications and data did not come with any additional funding to accomplish this measure.[96] Research libraries also have competing demands on the allocation of their resources, although many see involvement in research data as a growth area and endorse the NSF value proposition for the role of digital libraries in creating a digital data framework.

Setting up and maintaining data publishing infrastructures is a challenge that requires participation from stakeholders across public and private sectors. Cooperative efforts like the Research Data Alliance are working toward solutions to create and enhance technical and social infrastructures in support of data sharing. Areas of concentration include development of guidance around data citation, persistent identifiers, shared metadata frameworks, common organizational policies and practice, data standards, and shared best practices for data access and preservation.[97] Academic libraries can both extend the reach of their impact and gain support in building new programs by participating in relevant interest groups and associations (e.g., International Association for Social Science Information Services & Technology), as well as partnering with data archives.

Libraries can support data publication through expanding the scope of their services to engage with our community members not just as readers, but as authors and producers of data and information.[98] Publishing data is the final step at the end of the data management process for researchers. Efforts towards data management education, integrating data management into research ethics instruction (e.g., Responsible Conduct of Research programs), and embedding with research teams are all in the service of facilitating the progression of behavioral norms in scholarly communication to include data sharing and publication.

Data librarians can work to build collections of faculty data and reposition existing collections to support data intensive research. Libraries may find that they already hold significant collections of data as part of their legacy collections. For example, humanists consider the library their laboratory and our collections as their data. Digitizing special collections and serving them in formats amenable to computational analysis is one way for libraries to actively engage in data publication.[99] With regard to collecting faculty data, institutional repository infrastructures can be adapted or supplemented to include data.

Librarians should be aware that repository models that work for publications may not always work for data given the unique and varied nature of data publications.[100] In addition, flexible definitions of data can confound attempts at defining the scope of data collections.[101] Offering data publication services, as through an institutional repository, is likely to be a high-touch proposition which may require the development of additional infrastructure, processes, procedure, and expertise. Reports of pilot projects indicate that collection of faculty data involves a curation process which requires a significant time investment and challenges existing digital collection workflows.[102]

Library administrators and librarians should take heed from lessons learned in the development of scholarly communication and article-based institutional repository programs, as they speak to issues that will be faced in developing data collections and data management services. To point, the open access movement for literature was not immediately translated into wholesale use of institutional repositories; under-resourcing and a lack of supportive policies have been an impediment to success.[103] Libraries seeking to develop data collections should ensure an ongoing commitment to fund resources both human and technical as data librarians cannot succeed in isolation. This includes both the back-of-house repository support as well as outward facing interactions with faculty researchers. Subject area liaison librarians are important partners in vocalizing the centrality of library resources and services to all aspects of scholarship across the research lifecycle and integrating data into the library's overall collection building.[104]

Library-based data repositories should seek to track the development of standards for data publication. Starting points in the development of standards for data repositories are evident within the digital preservation community, where assessment measures for trusted digital repositories (i.e., Data Seal of Approval, Trusted Repositories Audit & Certification, and DRAMBORA) are now available.[105] These benchmarks provide the opportunity to elucidate best practices and certify the ability to provide long-term preservation and access to quality data. The implementation guidelines for repositories around metadata and identifiers stemming from the Joint Declaration on Data Citation Principles[106] demonstrate how ongoing discussion and initiatives from the scholarly community are also contributing to the development of best practices. Although disciplinary data archives are best suited to aid the creation of community-based standards within a particular niche area, library repositories will likely fill a need given the large diffusion of data types and practices and can apply broad-based standards to promote data publication and citation.

Conclusion

Data librarianship is a field that requires its members to keep on the forefront of current policies and practices. There are multiple stakeholders within the system of scholarly communication (e.g., authors, publishers, research funders), with libraries serving as an important part of the overall infrastructure, allowing librarians the opportunity to actively contribute to shape developments in scholarly communication concerning the role of data. The open data movement is pushing researchers toward data publication as they attempt to comply with policy mandates. The library can position itself as an integral part of the institutional ecosystem as universities work to develop programs and policies to meet researcher needs for grant funder and publishing requirements. An understanding of the complexities of the scholarly communication system, including scientific knowledge and data sharing practices, the nature of research data and data publication, and funder and journal policy requirements, will aid the academic data librarian as they navigate local institutional environments and endeavor to support their research communities. These are the broader forces that impact our day-to-day work.

1. Joan M. Reitz, *Online Dictionary for Library and Information Science* (Westport, CT: Libraries Unlimited, 2004), http://www.abc-clio.com/ODLIS/odlis_A.aspx.
2. Kim Duckett and Scott Warren, “Exploring the Intersections of Information Literacy and Scholarly Communication: Two Frames of Reference for Undergraduate Instruction,” in *Common Ground at the Nexus of Information Literacy and Scholarly Communication*, ed. Stephanie Davis-Kahl and Merinda Kaye Hensley (Chicago: Association of College and Research Libraries, 2013), 41.
3. Robert K. Merton, “The Normative Structure of Science,” in *The Sociology of Science: Theoretical and Empirical Investigations* (Chicago: University of Chicago Press, 1973), 267–78.
4. Randall Frost, “Scientific Method,” in *The Gale Encyclopedia of Science*, ed. K. Lee Lerner and Brenda Wilmoth Lerner, 5th ed., vol. 7 (Farmington Hills, MI: Gale, 2014), 3862–65.
5. Jennifer Rowley, “The Wisdom Hierarchy: Representations of the DIKW Hierarchy,” *Journal of Information Science* 33, no. 2 (2007): 163–80, doi:10.1177/0165551506070706.
6. Samuelle Carlson and Ben Anderson, “What Are Data? The Many Kinds of Data and Their Implications for Data Re-Use,” *Journal of Computer-Mediated Communication* 12, no. 2 (2007): 635–51, doi:10.1111/j.1083-6101.2007.00342.x.
7. Ibid., 647.
8. David Ribes and Steven J. Jackson, “Data Bite Man: The Work of Sustaining a Long-Term Study,” in *“Raw Data” Is an Oxymoron*, ed. Lisa Gitelman (Cambridge, MA: MIT Press, 2013), 147, http://ieeexplore.ieee.org/servlet/opac?bknumber=6451327.
9. Ibid., 164.
10. Ibid., 162.
11. Chaim Zins, “Conceptual Approaches for Defining Data, Information, and Knowledge,” *Journal of the American Society for Information Science and Technology* 58, no. 4 (2007): 479–93, doi:10.1002/asi.20508.
12. R. L. Ackoff, “From Data to Wisdom,” *Journal of Applied Systems Analysis* 16, no. 1 (1989): 3; Laura Wynholds, “Linking to Scientific Data: Identity Problems of Unruly and Poorly Bounded Digital Objects,” *International Journal of Digital Curation* 6, no. 1 (2011): 218, doi:10.2218/ijdc.v6i1.183; National Academy of Sciences (U.S.), National Academy of Engineering, and Institute of Medicine (U.S.), *Ensuring the Integrity, Accessibility, and Stewardship of Research Data in the Digital Age* (Washington, D.C: National Academies Press, 2009), 22; Office of Management and Budget, “Circular A-110 Revised 11/19/93 As Further Amended 9/30/99,” *The White House*, September 30, 1999, http://www.whitehouse.gov/omb/circulars_a110/.
13. National Academy of Sciences (U.S.), National Academy of Engineering, and Institute of Medicine (U.S.), *Ensuring the Integrity, Accessibility, and Stewardship of Research Data in the Digital Age*, 22; Consultative Committee for Space Data Systems, “Reference Model for an Open Archival Information System (OAIS)” (National Aeronautics and Space Administration, June 2012), http://public.ccsds.org/publications/archive/650x0m2.pdf; National Science Board (U.S.);National Science Foundation (U.S.), *Long-Lived Digital Data Collections Enabling Research and Education in the 21st Century* (Washington, D.C. : National Science Foundation, 2005), 13, www.nsf.gov/pubs/2005/nsb0540/nsb0540.pdf.
14. Inter-university Consortium for Political and Social Research, “Glossary of Social Science Terms,” *Inter-University Consortium for Political and Social Research*, accessed January 21, 2015, http://www.icpsr.umich.edu/icpsrweb/ICPSR/support/glossary; Reitz, *Online Dictionary for Library and Information Science.*
15. Thomson Reuters, “Repository Evaluation, Selection, and Coverage Policies for the Data Citation Index within the Thomson Reuters Web of Science,” *Web of Science*, accessed January 21, 2015, http://wokinfo.com//products_tools/multidisciplinary/dci/selection_essay/.
16. *Long-Lived Digital Data Collections Enabling Research and Education in the 21st Century.*
17. Ibid., Appendix D.

18. Wynholds, "Linking to Scientific Data," 218.
19. M. A. Parsons and P. A. Fox, "Is Data Publication the Right Metaphor?," *Data Science Journal* 12 (2013): WDS32–46, doi:10.2481/dsj.WDS-042.
20. Christine L. Borgman, *Big Data, Little Data, No Data: Scholarship in the Networked World* (Cambridge, MA: MIT Press, 2015).
21. Kathleen Fitzpatrick, *Planned Obsolescence: Publishing, Technology, and the Future of the Academy* (New York: New York University Press, 2011).
22. Christine L Borgman, *Scholarship in the Digital Age: Information, Infrastructure, and the Internet* (Cambridge, MA: MIT Press, 2007).
23. Clifford Lynch, "Jim Gray's Fourth Paradigm and the Construction of the Scientific Record," in *The Fourth Paradigm: Data-Intensive Scientific Discovery*, ed. Tony Hey, Stewart Tansley, and Kristin Tolle (Microsoft Research, 2009), http://research.microsoft.com/en-us/collaboration/fourthparadigm/contents.aspx.
24. "Budapest Open Access Initiative," February 14, 2002, http://www.budapestopenaccessinitiative.org/read.
25. J. Klump, R. Bertelmann, J. Brase, M. Diepenbroek, H. Grobe, H. Höck, M. Lautenschlager, U. Schindler, I. Sens, and J. Wächter, "Data Publication in the Open Access Initiative," *Data Science Journal* 5 (2006): 79–83, doi:10.2481/dsj.5.79.
26. Stephen E. Fienberg, Margaret E. Martin, and Miron L. Straf, eds., *Sharing Research Data* (Washington, D.C: National Academy Press, 1985).
27. Paula E. Stephan, "Robert K. Merton's Perspective on Priority and the Provision of the Public Good Knowledge," *Scientometrics* 60, no. 1 (2004): 81–87, doi:10.1023/B:-SCIE.0000027311.17226.70.
28. Michael Yamaner, "Federal Funding for Basic Research at Universities and Colleges Essentially Unchanged in FY 2012," InfoBrief (Arlington, VA: National Science Foundation, National Center for Science and Engineering Statistics, September 2014), http://www.nsf.gov/statistics/infbrief/nsf14318/.
29. "FedStats," accessed January 27, 2015, http://fedstats.sites.usa.gov/.
30. Bart Ragon, "The Political Economy of Federally Sponsored Data," *Journal of eScience Librarianship* 2, no. 2 (2013), doi:10.7191/jeslib.2013.1050.
31. Eric A. Fischer, "Public Access to Data from Federally Funded Research: Provisions in OMB Circular A-110," Congressional Research Service, (2013), HTTP://congressional.proquest.com.proxy2.cl.msu.edu/congressional/docview/t21.d22.crs-2013-rsi-0116?accountid=12598.
32. John Holdren, "Increasing Access to the Results of Federally Funded Scientific Research" (Office of Science and Technology Policy, February 22, 2013), http://www.whitehouse.gov/sites/default/files/microsites/ostp/ostp_public_access_memo_2013.pdf.
33. Dianne Dietrich, Trisha Adamus, Alison Miner, and Gail Steinhart, "De-Mystifying the Data Management Requirements of Research Funders," *Issues in Science and Technology Librarianship* 70, no. 1 (2012), doi:10.5062/F44M92G2.
34. National Science Foundation, "Grant Proposal Guide" (National Science Foundation, January 2013), http://www.nsf.gov/pubs/policydocs/pappguide/nsf13001/gpg_2.jsp.
35. National Institutes of Health, Office of Extramural Research, "NIH Data Sharing Policy and Implementation Guidance," March 5, 2003, http://grants.nih.gov/grants/policy/data_sharing/data_sharing_guidance.htm.
36. Organisation for Economic Co-operation and Development, *OECD Principles and Guidelines for Access to Research Data from Public Funding* (Paris: OECD Publishing, 2007), 9, http://www.oecd-ilibrary.org/content/book/9789264034020-en-fr.
37. Alma Swan, "Policy Guidelines for the Development and Promotion of Open Access" (United Nataions Educational, Scientific and Cultural Organization, 2012), http://unesdoc.unesco.org/images/0021/002158/215863e.pdf.

38. European Commission, "Commission Recommendation of 17.7.2012 on Access to and Preservation of Scientific Information" (European Commission, July 2012), 3, https://ec.europa.eu/digital-agenda/node/66216.
39. Research Councils UK, "RCUK Common Principles on Data Policy," accessed January 28, 2015, http://www.rcuk.ac.uk/research/datapolicy/.
40. Fischer, "Public Access to Data from Federally Funded Research: Provisions in OMB Circular A-110"; Richard Shelby, "Accountability and Transparency: Public Access to Federally Funded Research Data," *Harvard Journal on Legislation* 37 (2000): 369–89.
41. Shelby, "Accountability and Transparency," 379.
42. Government Accountability Office, "Climate Change Research: Agencies Have Data-Sharing Policies but Could Do More To Enhance the Availability of Data from Federally Funded Research," 2007, http://www.gao.gov/products/GAO-07-1172; David Goldston, "Big Data: Data Wrangling," *Nature News* 455, no. 7209 (September 3, 2008): 15–15, doi:10.1038/455015a.
43. National Academy of Sciences (U.S.), National Academy of Engineering, and Institute of Medicine (U.S.), *Ensuring the Integrity, Accessibility, and Stewardship of Research Data in the Digital Age* (Washington, D.C: National Academies Press, 2009), 63.
44. Subcommittee on Research; Committee on Science, Space, and Technology. House, *Scientific Integrity and Transparency*, 2013, http://www.gpo.gov/fdsys/pkg/CHRG-113hhrg79929/pdf/CHRG-113hhrg79929.pdf.
45. Hans E. Roosendall and Peter A. Th. M. Geurts, "Forces and Functions in Scientific Communication: An Analysis of Their Interplay" (CRISP '97, Cooperative Research Information Systems in Physics, Oldenburg, Germany, 1997), http://www.physik.uni-oldenburg.de/conferences/crisp97/roosendaal.html.
46. J. Klump et al., "Data Publication in the Open Access Initiative," *Data Science Journal* 5 (2006): 79–83, doi:10.2481/dsj.5.79; Heinz Pampel and Sünje Dallmeier-Tiessen, "Open Research Data: From Vision to Practice," in *Opening Science*, ed. Sönke Bartling and Sascha Friesike (Springer International Publishing, 2014), 213–24, http://link.springer.com/chapter/10.1007/978-3-319-00026-8_14.
47. National Academy of Sciences (U.S.), National Academy of Engineering, and Institute of Medicine (U.S.), *Ensuring the Integrity, Accessibility, and Stewardship of Research Data in the Digital Age*; Subcommittee on Research; Committee on Science, Space, and Technology. House, *Scientific Integrity and Transparency*.
48. Beth A. Fischer and Michael J. Zigmond, "The Essential Nature of Sharing in Science," *Science and Engineering Ethics* 16, no. 4 (November 2010): 783–99, doi:10.1007/s11948-010-9239-x; Patricia A. Soranno, Kendra S. Cheruvelil, Kevin C. Elliott, and Georgina M. Montgomery, "It's Good to Share: Why Environmental Scientists' Ethics Are out of Date," *BioScience* 65, no. 1 (2014): 69–73, doi:10.1093/biosci/biu169; John Willinsky and Juan Pablo Alperin, "The Academic Ethics of Open Access to Research and Scholarship," *Ethics and Education* 6, no. 3 (2011): 217–23, doi:10.1080/17449642.2011.632716.
49. see for example Daniel S. Caetano and Anita Aisenberg, "Forgotten Treasures: The Fate of Data in Animal Behaviour Studies," *Animal Behaviour* 98 (2014): 1–5, doi:10.1016/j.anbehav.2014.09.025; Fischer and Zigmond, "The Essential Nature of Sharing in Science"; Russell A. Poldrack and Krzysztof J. Gorgolewski, "Making Big Data Open: Data Sharing in Neuroimaging," *Nature Neuroscience* 17, no. 11 (November 2014): 1510–17, doi:10.1038/nn.3818.
50. Barbara Schneider, "Building a Scientific Community: The Need for Replication," *The Teachers College Record* 106, no. 7 (2004): 1471–83; Joan E. Sieber, "Will the New Code Help Researchers to Be More Ethical?," *Professional Psychology: Research and Practice* 25, no. 4 (1994): 369, doi:10.1037/0735-7028.25.4.369.
51. Katherine W. McCain, "Mandating Sharing Journal Policies in the Natural Sciences," *Science Communication* 16, no. 4 (June 1, 1995): 403–31, doi:10.1177/1075547095016004003; Fiona Murphy, "Data and Scholarly Publishing: The Transforming Landscape," *Learned Publishing* 27, no. 5 (2014): 3–7, doi:10.1087/20140502; Hazel Norman, "Mandating Data Archiving: Experi-

ences from the Frontline," *Learned Publishing* 27, no. 5 (2014): 35–38, doi:10.1087/20140507; Michael C. Whitlock, Mark A. McPeek, Mark D. Rausher, Loren Rieseberg, and Allen J. Moore, "Data Archiving," *The American Naturalist* 175, no. 2 (2010): 145–46, doi:10.1086/650340.

52. Peter Murray-Rust, Cameron Neylon, Rufus Pollock, and John Wilbanks, "Panton Principles: Principles for Open Data in Science," February 19, 2010, http://pantonprinciples.org/.
53. Spencer D. C. Keralis, "Denton Declaration: An Open Data Manifesto," May 22, 2012, http://openaccess.unt.edu/denton-declaration.
54. Force11, "Force11 White Paper: Improving the Future of Research Communication and E-Scholarship," ed. Phil E. Bourne, Tim Clark, Robert Dale, Anita de Waard, Ivan Herman, Eduard Hovy, and David Shotton, October 28, 2011, https://www.force11.org/white_paper.
55. Patrick Andreoli-Versbach and Frank Mueller-Langer, "Open Access to Data: An Ideal Professed but Not Practised," *Research Policy* 43, no. 9 (November 2014): 1621–33, doi:10.1016/j.respol.2014.04.008; Bryn Nelson, "Data Sharing: Empty Archives," *Nature News* 461, no. 7261 (September 9, 2009): 160–63, doi:10.1038/461160a; Maggie Puniewska, "Scientists Have a Sharing Problem," *The Atlantic*, December 15, 2014, http://www.theatlantic.com/health/archive/2014/12/scientists-have-a-sharing-problem/383061/.
56. Alawi A. Alsheikh-Ali et al., "Public Availability of Published Research Data in High-Impact Journals," *PLoS ONE* 6, no. 9 (September 7, 2011): e24357, doi:10.1371/journal.pone.0024357; Caroline J. Savage and Andrew J. Vickers, "Empirical Study of Data Sharing by Authors Publishing in PLoS Journals," *PLoS ONE* 4, no. 9 (September 18, 2009): e7078, doi:10.1371/journal.pone.0007078; J.M. Wicherts, D. Borsboom, J. Kats, and D. Molenaar, "The Poor Availability of Psychological Research Data for Reanalysis.," *American Psychologist* 61, no. 7 (2006): 726, doi:10.1037/0003-066X.61.7.726.
57. Carol Tenopir, Suzie Allard, Kimberly Douglass, Arsev Umur Aydinoglu, Lei Wu, Eleanor Read, Maribeth Manoff, and Mike Frame, "Data Sharing by Scientists: Practices and Perceptions," *PLoS ONE* 6, no. 6 (2011): e21101, doi:10.1371/journal.pone.0021101.
58. Christine L. Borgman, *Big Data, Little Data, No Data: Scholarship in the Networked World* (Cambridge, MA: MIT Press, 2015); Amy M. Pienta, George C. Alter, and Jared A. Lyle, "The Enduring Value of Social Science Research: The Use and Reuse of Primary Research Data," November 22, 2010, http://hdl.handle.net/2027.42/78307; Jillian C. Wallis, Elizabeth Rolando, and Christine L. Borgman, "If We Share Data, Will Anyone Use Them? Data Sharing and Reuse in the Long Tail of Science and Technology," *PLoS ONE* 8, no. 7 (2013): e67332, doi:10.1371/journal.pone.0067332.
59. Eliot Marshall, "Bermuda Rules: Community Spirit, With Teeth," *Science* 291, no. 5507 (February 16, 2001): 1192–1192, doi:10.1126/science.291.5507.1192.
60. Aaron Griffiths, "The Publication of Research Data: Researcher Attitudes and Behaviour," *International Journal of Digital Curation* 4, no. 1 (2009), doi:10.2218/ijdc.v4i1.77; Research Information Network, "To Share or Not to Share: Publication and Quality Assurance of Research Data Outputs," June 2008, http://www.rin.ac.uk/system/files/attachments/To-share-data-outputs-report.pdf.
61. Djoko Sigit Sayogo and Theresa A. Pardo, "Exploring the Determinants of Scientific Data Sharing: Understanding the Motivation to Publish Research Data," *Government Information Quarterly* 30 (2013): S19–31, doi:10.1016/j.giq.2012.06.011; Suenje Dallmeier-Tiessen, Robert Darby, Kathrin Gitmans, Simon Lambert, Brian Matthews, Salvatore Mele, Jari Suhonen, and Michael Wilson, "Enabling Sharing and Reuse of Scientific Data," *New Review of Information Networking* 19, no. 1 (2014): 16–43, doi:10.1080/13614576.2014.883936; Research Information Network, "To Share or Not to Share: Publication and Quality Assurance of Research Data Outputs"; Poldrack and Gorgolewski, "Making Big Data Open"; Benedikt Fecher, Sascha Friesike, and Marcel Hebing, "What Drives Academic Data Sharing?," SSRN Scholarly Paper (Rochester, NY: Social Science Research Network, May 1, 2014), http://papers.ssrn.com/abstract=2439645.
62. John Kratz and Carly Strasser, "Data Publication Consensus and Controversies," *F1000Research*, October 16, 2014, doi:10.12688/f1000research.3979.3.

63. Ibid.; Mark A. Parsons, Ruth Duerr, and Jean-Bernard Minster, "Data Citation and Peer Review," *Eos, Transactions American Geophysical Union* 91, no. 34 (2010): 297–98, doi:10.1029/2010EO340001.
64. Don MacMillan, "Data Sharing and Discovery: What Librarians Need to Know," *Journal of Academic Librarianship* 40, no. 5 (2014): 541–49, doi:10.1016/j.acalib.2014.06.011.
65. Najla Semple, "Digital Repositories," DCC Briefing Papers: Introduction to Curation (Edinburgh: Digital Curation Centre, 2006), http://www.dcc.ac.uk/resources/briefing-papers/introduction-curation/digital-repositories.
66. Louise Corti, "Data Archive," in *The SAGE Encyclopedia of Qualitative Research Methods*, by Lisa Given (Thousand Oaks, CA: SAGE Publications, 2008), http://dx.doi.org/10.4135/9781412963909.
67. Suzie Allard, "DataONE: Facilitating eScience through Collaboration," *Journal of eScience Librarianship* 1, no. 1 (February 2012), doi:10.7191/jeslib.2012.1004.
68. Kratz and Strasser, "Data Publication Consensus and Controversies"; Gail Steinhart, "Partnerships between Institutional Repositories, Domain Repositories and Publishers," *Bulletin of the American Society for Information Science and Technology* 39, no. 6 (2013): 19–22, doi:10.1002/bult.2013.1720390608.
69. Ann G. Green and Myron P. Gutmann, "Building Partnerships among Social Science Researchers, Institution-based Repositories and Domain Specific Data Archives," *OCLC Systems & Services: International Digital Library Perspectives* 23, no. 1 (2007): 35–53, doi:10.1108/10650750710720757.
70. Lyle, Alter, and Green, "Partnering to Curate and Archive Social Science Data."
71. Katherine G. Akers and Jennifer A. Green, "Towards a Symbiotic Relationship Between Academic Libraries and Disciplinary Data Repositories: A Dryad and University of Michigan Case Study," *International Journal of Digital Curation* 9, no. 1 (2014), doi:10.2218/ijdc.v9i1.306.
72. Kratz and Strasser, "Data Publication Consensus and Controversies."
73. Todd Carpenter, "Standards Column—Journal Article Supplementary Materials: A Pandora's Box of Issues Needing Best Practices," *Against the Grain* 21, no. 6 (November 1, 2013), http://docs.lib.purdue.edu/atg/vol21/iss6/6.
74. Kratz and Strasser, "Data Publication Consensus and Controversies"; MacMillan, "Data Sharing and Discovery."
75. Taylor & Francis, "Taylor & Francis and Figshare: Making Research More Discoverable," January 2014, http://newsroom.taylorandfrancisgroup.com/news/press-release/taylor-francis-and-figshare-making-research-more-discoverable#.VNFEKy558mE.
76. Elsevier, "Database Linking Tool," accessed February 4, 2015, http://www.elsevier.com/about/content-innovation/database-linking.
77. Rodrigo Costas et al., "The Value of Research Data: Metrics for Datasets from a Cultural and Technical Point of View" (Knowledge Exchange, April 2013), http://www.knowledge-exchange.info/datametrics.
78. Ibid.
79. Micah Altman and Mercè Crosas, "The Evolution of Data Citation: From Principles to Implementation," *IASSIST Quarterly* 37, no. 1–4 (March 2013): 62–70, http://www.iassistdata.org/downloads/iqvol371_4_altman.pdf.
80. Data Citation Synthesis Group, "Joint Declaration of Data Citation Principles," *Force11*, 2014, http://www.force11.org/datacitation.
81. Subcommittee on Research; Committee on Science, Space, and Technology. House, *Scientific Integrity and Transparency*.
82. Holdren, "Increasing Access to the Results of Federally Funded Scientific Research."
83. Joan E. Sieber and Bruce E. Trumbo, "(Not) Giving Credit Where Credit Is Due: Citation of Data Sets," *Science and Engineering Ethics* 1, no. 1 (1995): 11–20, doi:10.1007/BF02628694.
84. Hailey Mooney and Mark Newton, "The Anatomy of a Data Citation: Discovery, Reuse, and Credit," *Journal of Librarianship and Scholarly Communication* 1, no. 1 (2012), doi:10.7710/2162-3309.1035.

85. Tenopir et al., "Data Sharing by Scientists."
86. Joan Starr, Eleni Castro, Merce Crosas, Michel Dumontier, Robert R. Downs, Ruth Duerr, Laurel L. Haak, Melissa Haendel, and Ivan Herman, "Achieving Human and Machine Accessibility of Cited Data in Scholarly Publications," *PeerJ PrePrints*, 2015, https://peerj.com/preprints/697/.
87. Joan Starr and Angela Gastl, "isCitedBy: A Metadata Scheme for DataCite," *D-Lib Magazine* 17, no. 1/2 (2011), doi:10.1045/january2011-starr.
88. Megan M. Force and Nigel J. Robinson, "Encouraging Data Citation and Discovery with the Data Citation Index," *Journal of Computer-Aided Molecular Design* 28, no. 10 (October 1, 2014): 1043–48, doi:10.1007/s10822-014-9768-5; Nicolas Robinson-García, Evaristo Jiménez-Contreras, and Daniel Torres-Salinas, "Analyzing Data Citation Practices Using the Data Citation Index," *Journal of the Association for Information Science and Technology*, 2015, doi:10.1002/asi.23529.
89. Force and Robinson, "Encouraging Data Citation and Discovery with the Data Citation Index."
90. Nelson, "Data Sharing."
91. National Science Foundation, Office of Budget, Finance and Award Management, "Data Management & Sharing Frequently Asked Questions."
92. PLOS, "PLOS Editorial and Publishing Policies," accessed February 5, 2015, http://www.ploscompbiol.org/static/policies#sharing.
93. National Science Foundation, Cyberinfrastructure Council, "Cyberinfrastructure Vision for 21st Century Discovery," March 2007, http://www.nsf.gov/pubs/2007/nsf0728/.
94. Dharma Akmon, "NSF DataNet Partners Update," *Bulletin of the Association for Information Science and Technology* 40, no. 6 (September 2014): 22–25. http://www.asis.org/Bulletin/Aug-14/AugSep14_Akmon.html.
95. Science Staff, "Challenges and Opportunities," *Science* 331, no. 6018 (February 11, 2011): 692–93, doi:10.1126/science.331.6018.692.
96. Francine Berman and Vint Cerf, "Who Will Pay for Public Access to Research Data?," *Science* 341, no. 6146 (August 9, 2013): 616–17, doi:10.1126/science.1241625.
97. Fran Berman, Ross Wilkinson, and John Wood, "Building Global Infrastructure for Data Sharing and Exchange Through the Research Data Alliance," *D-Lib Magazine* 20, no. 1/2 (January 2014), doi:10.1045/january2014-berman.
98. Kara J. Malenfant, "Leading Change in the System of Scholarly Communication: A Case Study of Engaging Liaison Librarians for Outreach to Faculty," *College & Research Libraries* 71, no. 1 (2010): 63–76, doi:10.5860/crl.71.1.63; Todd Bruns, Steve Brantley, and Kirstin Duffin, "Scholarly Communication Coaching: Liaison Librarians' Shifting Roles," in *The 21st Century Library: Partnerships and New Roles*, ed. Brad Eden (Lanham, Maryland: Littlefield and Rowman/Scarecrow Publishing, 2015), http://works.bepress.com/steve_brantley/22.
99. Thomas G. Padilla and Devin Higgins, "Library Collections as Humanities Data: The Facet Effect," *Public Services Quarterly* 10, no. 4 (2014): 324–35, doi:10.1080/15228959.2014.963780.
100. Dorothea Salo, "Retooling Libraries for the Data Challenge," *Ariadne*, no. 64 (July 2010), http://www.ariadne.ac.uk/issue64/salo/.
101. Hans Jørn Nielsen and Birger Hjørland, "Curating Research Data: The Potential Roles of Libraries and Information Professionals," *Journal of Documentation* 70, no. 2 (2014): 221–40, doi:10.1108/JD-03-2013-0034; Borgman, *Big Data, Little Data, No Data*.
102. David Minor, Matt Critchlow, Arwen Hutt, Declan Fleming, Mary Linn Bergstrom, and Don Sutton, "Research Data Curation Pilots: Lessons Learned," *International Journal of Digital Curation* 9, no. 1 (June 17, 2014): 220–30, doi:10.2218/ijdc.v9i1.313; Tyler O. Walters, "Data Curation Program Development in US Universities: The Georgia Institute of Technology Example," *International Journal of Digital Curation* 4, no. 3 (2009): 83–92; Lisa R. Johnston, "A Workflow Model for Curating Research Data in the University of Minnesota Libraries: Report from the 2013 Data Curation Pilot" (University of Minnesota Digital Conservancy, January 19, 2014), http://hdl.handle.net/11299/162338; Mark P Newton, C. C. Miller, and Marianne Stowell Bracke, "Librarian Roles in Institutional Repository Data Set Collecting: Outcomes of a

Research Library Task Force," *Collection Management* 36, no. 1 (2010), doi:10.1080/01462679.2011.530546.
103. Dorothea Salo, "Innkeeper at the Roach Motel," *Library Trends* 57, no. 2 (2008): 98–123, doi:10.1353/lib.0.0031; Dorothea Salo, "How to Scuttle a Scholarly Communication Initiative," *Journal of Librarianship and Scholarly Communication* 1, no. 4 (2013), doi:10.7710/2162-3309.1075.
104. Bruns, Brantley, and Duffin, "Scholarly Communication Coaching."
105. Inter-university Consortium for Political and Social Research, "Trusted Digital Repositories," accessed February 5, 2015, http://www.icpsr.umich.edu/icpsrweb/content/datamanagement/preservation/trust.html.
106. Starr et al., "Achieving Human and Machine Accessibility of Cited Data in Scholarly Publications."

CHAPTER 14

Data Sharing Policies in Social Sciences Academic Journals:

Evolving Expectations of Data Sharing as a Form of Scholarly Communication

Joel Herndon, Ph.D. and Robert O'Reilly, Ph.D.

DISCUSSIONS ABOUT DATA sharing and data availability are widespread in the public and private sectors and within academia. For academic researchers, these discussions often focus on how data sharing and transparency can increase the rigor and credibility of scholarship. In response to these discussions, many academics have argued that academic journals should adopt sharing/replication policies to address these concerns. In this chapter, we analyze whether academic journals in the social sciences have been adopting such policies over time and whether such adoption varies by field.[†] Our conclusion is that while journals are indeed adopting such policies, they are doing so in an incomplete and varied manner. Moreover, the adoption of such policies and the debates that surround them are matters with which libraries should engage themselves, as doing so has the potential to strengthen connections between libraries and researchers with regard to data services and support.

Background and Context

It is now quite common to see stories and commentary about growth in the availability of digital data and about the various implications of that growth. In 2012,

† Data and syntax that produce the tables in this chapter are available at http://dx.doi.org/10.15139/S3/12157.

the *New York Times* announced that we have entered "The Age of Big Data," one in which the amount of digital information being accumulated is growing at a non-linear rate.[1] A few years earlier, *The Economist* magazine made similar points in its cover story on what it called the "Data Deluge": the rapidly-increasing quantities of data that are being created, the implications of those data for both the public and private sectors, and the challenges involved in storing, managing, and making effective use of those data.[2]

While there are many facets to the "Data Deluge," one of the more salient issues in academia is the concept of "open data": the idea, and even expectation, that data gathered and assembled for research purposes should be readily-accessible to the public, especially when such undertakings receive support from the public sector. In the United States, the "Shelby Amendment" to the Omnibus Appropriations Act for FY1999 required the Office of Management and Budget to ensure that all data gathered via grants from federal agencies would be available through the Freedom of Information Act.[3] Since 2003, the National Institutes of Health has required grant applications with costs greater than $500,000 in any single year to include data sharing plans as part of those applications.[4] Since 2011, the various directorates within the National Science Foundation have required all grant applications to include data management plans that spell out what data will be generated and how those data will be managed and shared both during and after the duration of any grant.[5] In a similar vein, the Office of Science and Technology Policy announced in 2013 that agencies with research and development budgets greater than $100,000,000 are required to develop plans for greater public sharing of funded research, including data collected from or for that research.[6]

Nor is this trend confined to the United States. In the United Kingdom, governments have been increasing the availability of government-gathered data.[7] There are now numerous "open data sites"[8] operated by national statistical offices. At an international level, the OECD Committee for Scientific and Technical Policy issued a communiqué in 2004 encouraging increased public access to research data, and the OECD followed that statement up by publishing a set of "principles and guides for access to research data from public funding."[9] The European Union has similarly endorsed principles of open access to research data to encourage greater use and re-use of such resources.[10]

These trends have not gone unnoticed by academics, nor have they gone unnoticed by academic libraries. Gary King has written extensively about the opportunities and challenges presented by the growth of potentially-available data, noting that the social sciences "appear to be in the midst of a massive collision between unprecedented increases in data production and availability about individuals and the privacy rights of human beings worldwide, most of whom are also effectively research subjects."[11] Academic libraries, meanwhile, have discussed and debated how to respond to such developments, with many of them now offering or contemplating offering research data management as a new service, such as by assisting grant applicants in crafting language for inclusion in data management plans.[12]

However, it should also be noted that calls and demands for greater access to data and related discussions of the potential impacts and benefits of such access are not anything new. Long before the media was awash with references to "big data" and long before libraries were deliberating over how to address funder mandates for data sharing plans, academics in the social sciences were deliberating over whether scholars should be more open and sharing with data used in their research. Likewise, academics have engaged in related debates for several decades over whether academic journals should have policies that require scholars to make data available as part of, or even as a condition for, publication.

Data Sharing, Transparency, and Replication

The Benefits of Reuse

Why do various academics value and encourage data sharing as a behavior in which researchers should engage? Likewise, why do they advocate for policies that require authors to make data available? In a nutshell, many of the offered reasons are variations on a theme stated by the OECD: "the value of data lies in their use," as greater availability of research data provides various positive externalities in the form of benefits that accrue to parties other than those who did the original data collection.[13] Shared data provide opportunities for reuse outside of the context in which they were collected and allows other researchers opportunities to combine data collections to address novel questions that would be otherwise be difficult to empirically evaluate. For example, data initially collected to study ethnic conflict could later be repurposed to test for the effects of property rights on economic growth.[14] Greater reuse of research data also reduces unnecessary duplication of effort, as scholars do not need to expend time collecting data that others have already gathered if they can access those data. Gleditsch and Metelits and others argue that sharing research data offers benefits in the form of greater visibility and more citations to those scholars who do so.[15] Jeremy Freese, meanwhile, notes that the common practice of selectively sharing data amongst colleagues and within informal networks creates asymmetries of access that disadvantage graduate students and other less-established researchers. Greater sharing of data thus provides for more egalitarian levels of data access.[16]

The Benefits of Transparency and Replication

The main reasons for and benefits from greater sharing of research data emphasized by its advocates, however, relate to matters of transparency in research practices and replication of research findings. In a nutshell, data sharing promotes transparency in research and makes it easier for others to evaluate and assess empirical scholarship. When data used in a given work are readily available, other scholars can see how the data were assembled and used, the choices and assumptions that went into their usage, and how the analyses were conducted. Ideally, shared data allow the research community to determine and assess the entire sequence of steps from the collection of the raw/original data to the empirical findings of the analysis. In being able to do so, researchers can uncover any flaws or weaknesses in the analysis, thus improving the likelihood that errors are both identified and shared with the larger academic community while simultaneously offering new opportunities to extend and expand promising research. By sharing data and conducting research in a more transparent manner, academics make their work more accessible and their findings more credible—their work is easier to evaluate and engage with, and their findings have additional legitimacy precisely because it is easier to determine how those findings were produced.[17]

Greater sharing of data also enhances the scientific rigor of research. For research to be "scientific," it must, in principle, be *replicable*. Other scholars should be able to take the data used in a publication and reproduce the results using the methods described by the authors. If the social sciences are to be truly scientific in terms of applying the scientific method to the explanation of social phenomena, empirical research in the social sciences must likewise be reproducible by others. King argues that replication of existing findings is "the most common and scientifically productive method of building on existing research"[18] while Anderson et al. note that, "in theory, economic research is scientific research—that is, economic theory suggests empirically falsifiable hypotheses and investigators seek to confront those hypotheses with data."[19] Similarly, they argue that "empirical economics, by actively discouraging replication, does not incorporate the self-correcting mechanism of the scientific method."[20] Data sharing, then, is a means of promoting replication and thus making research more scientific. As Lupia and Elman put it, "a claim's perceived legitimacy is grounded in the fact that the results are the product of publicly described processes that in turn are based on a stable and shared set of beliefs about how knowledge is produced. Such open access to the origins of others' claims is the hallmark of scientific ways of knowing."[21] Or, as Ben Bernanke (yes, **that** Ben Bernanke) notes, "Replicability is essential if empirical findings are to be credible and usable as a starting point for other researchers."[22]

We should note here that these discussions and debates are not merely theoretical. Instead, they have been inspired in part by recurring questions about the extent to which empirical research in the social sciences can be replicated and about the research practices of academics in various fields. Within political science, for instance, the Data Access and Research Transparency initiative (DA-RT)† grew in part out of a "growing concern that scholars could not replicate a significant number of empirical claims that were being made in the discipline's top journals."[23] Dafoe similarly notes that "it is not uncommon for the key results of scientific research to be non-reproducible or to arise from errors."[24] Eubank undertook an attempt to replicate twenty-four empirical papers submitted to the *Quarterly Journal of Political Science* and found that "13 (54 percent) had results in the paper that differed from those generated by the author's own code."[25] Numerous attempts to replicate articles in various top-ranked economics journals have resulted in similar conclusions: the empirical findings in such works are often—even usually—difficult to successfully reproduce.[26] Within the field of psychology, debates about replication have been motivated by cases of outright fabrication of data.[27] More generally, some academics have suggested that most empirical findings in academic research are effectively false.[28] Not just an esoteric debate amongst academics, this matter has even received attention from the mass media.[29]

The increased usage of data harvested from social media has further raised questions about replication, given how highly asymmetrical access to such data can be.[30] A particularly vivid instance of how replication can uncover non-trivial issues with research involves the case of an article by Harvard economists Carmen Reinhart and Kenneth Rogoff on the relationship between public-sector debt and economic growth. The article attracted considerable attention because its findings suggested that public-sector debt has a marked, negative effect on economic growth when debt levels rise above 90% of GDP. A replication of their study by graduate students at the University of Massachusetts, however, concluded that their findings were a function of decisions on how to aggregate observations within and across countries and of spreadsheet errors in the underlying data. The macroeconomic policy implications of their original findings were such that this specific case generated a great deal of commentary amongst academics and the media about replication and transparency in general, and about the usage of Microsoft Excel in particular and its suitability (or lack thereof) for producing robust, replicable analyses.[31]

Implications for Scholarly Communication—The Role of Journal Policies

Given the potential benefits of greater sharing of research data, the question then becomes one of how such sharing can be encouraged. Toward this end, many advocates of data sharing argue that one effective way to promote greater data availability is for academic journals to adopt policies that expect or require authors

† See Elman and Lupia, "The (DA-RT) Data Access and Research Transparency Joint Statement" for additional information about this initiative and its origins.

of submitted manuscripts to provide data used to produce the results in those manuscripts as part of the publication process. As Stodden, Guo, and Ma put it, "the journal publication process is a key lever shaping the nature of scholarly communication and promoting the integrity of the scholarly record."[32] Consequently, the presence of journal policies that require data sharing as a condition of publication provide a strong incentive for authors who wish to publish to make their data publicly available. Anderson, et al, succinctly summarize the role that journals can play here:

> As a form of collective action, journals can assure that published research is sufficiently documented—including data and program archives—and that published articles' results are replicable. Absent such a journal structure, both economic models of rational choice—and the evidence—suggests that most authors will not voluntarily choose to incur the costs of creating archival files and documentation.[33]

Journal policies, then, are a "key lever" that can be used to pry open data resources that might otherwise remain closed, and to enhance the methodological soundness of quantitative research by encouraging academics to be more thorough in their work.[34]

Data Sharing—What Is It?

Such discussions of data sharing and its benefits and how journals might encourage it in turn raise the questions of what data sharing actually entails and what forms data-sharing policies should take. Early statements on this topic from researchers such as Robert Hauser and Gary King mainly focus on providing the data themselves and are not otherwise that detailed in specifying what policies should require. King's proposed "replication standard," for instance, stated that "sufficient information exists with which to understand, evaluate, and build upon a prior work if a third party could replicate the results without any additional information from the author."[35]

With time, however, proposals for data sharing and transparency have become much more detailed. Certainly, the data themselves and/or detailed lists of data sources used are important, as is detailed documentation of those data that explains units of measure, response categories, and methods used for data collection. But if the points of data sharing are to permit replication and to provide greater transparency in terms of how the data produced a given collection of empirical findings, then the data and documentation alone are not enough. Researchers must also provide the code that implemented the analyses that produced those results so that others can see how data were weighted, how observations were filtered, what specific variables were used, and what specific estimators and options were employed. Ideally, the code used for the analyses should provide enough information for an independent observer to understand the data sources used in the study and the steps used to process those resources for the final analysis. A researcher may even need to provide or identify the software used, as different programs or versions of a program may produce different results.[36] As empirical analyses increase in complexity, space limitations in articles often preclude providing the level of detail necessary to allow for replication and to meet standards of transparency. This makes it all the more important that policies for data sharing and replication include requirements to provide code in addition to the data themselves.[37] Indeed, the code may still be useful even if the data themselves cannot be provided due to their proprietary or sensitive nature.[38]

Such considerations about the importance of providing both data and code have in turn worked their way into specific proposals for policies that journals should adopt. The data-sharing policy suggested by Gleditsch et al. is an illustrative example:

> Authors of quantitative empirical articles must make their data available for replication purposes. A statement of how that is done should appear in the first footnote of the article. Required material would include all data, specialized computer programs, program recodes, and an explanatory file describing what is included and how to reproduce the published results.[39]

Freese's proposed policy is of a similar nature:

> Authors of accepted articles of empirical quantitative research are expected to use online archives to deposit maximum possible information pertinent to the verification of presented results at the time of publication. Ideally, data, code and other materials would be provided that would allow others to duplicate the analysis procedures that lead from original data to presented results without the need for any additional information about what was done from authors.[40]

Hoffler and Kneib, commenting on the aftermath of efforts to replicate Reinhart and Rogoff's work on debt and economic growth, make a similar point:

> In the narrow sense, replicability means that the raw data for an analysis can be accessed, that the transformation from the raw data to the final data set is well documented, and that software code is available for producing the final data set and the empirical results. Basically, this comes down to a question

> of data and code availability, but nonetheless it is a necessary prerequisite for replication.[41]

Finally, there is the "Data Access and Research Transparency Joint Statement," proposed by a group of political scientists and data archivists as a standard for data-sharing policies used by political science journals. This statement includes the following language, as part of the requirements journals should have for authors of submitted manuscripts:

> Require authors to delineate clearly the analytic procedures upon which their published claims rely, and where possible to provide access to all relevant analytic materials. If such materials are not published with the article, they must be shared to the greatest extent possible through a trusted digital repository.[42]

In other words, there is a common (if not unanimous) view among academics that if replication of empirical findings and transparency in research practices are to be more than abstract notions, then journals should require more than just provision of the data (or a listing of the data sources) used in a given work. Authors must also provide a detailed explanation of how the data were assembled and analyzed so as to clearly show how a given data resource or collection of data resources were used to produce a given set of empirical findings. The need is for transparency in terms of data access, data production, and data analysis.[43]

Measuring Journals' Data-Sharing Policies

Given the growing specificity of proposed standards for data sharing, transparency, and replication, how have social sciences journals responded? Have journals been adopting such policies? If so, what is the content of those policies? Is there any variation over time, or across academic fields?

These are questions that have not been systematically addressed in an empirical manner. The Association of Learned and Professional Society Publishers, for instance, produced a report in 2008 on scholarly publishing practices, based on a survey of publishers of academic journals. The survey included a question about availability of datasets associated with journal articles, and presented the results in summary form: 46.63% of publishers had such a policy. However, the report did not make the underlying data from the survey available for others to examine.[44] Therefore, the report does not necessarily offer much insight into our questions.

There has been some field-specific work on social sciences journals' data and replication policies. Gleditsch and Metelits look at the policies of a collection of

27 journals in Political Science and International Relations and found that 18% of them had a stated replication policy.[45] Gherghina and Katsanidou examine 120 journals in Political Science that publish studies which make intensive use of data and found that 16% (19/120) of those journals had a policy about data availability, with the likelihood of a journal having such a possibility being a function of characteristics such as the age of the journal and its ISI Impact Factor.[46] In a study of data-sharing behavior of individual economists, Andreoli-Versbach and Mueller-Langer discuss the data sharing policies of 147 Economics journals and Business journals and identified 20% (30/147) of them with a data-availability policy.[47] However, none of these works is a comparative analysis that looks for differences across a comparable set of journals in different fields within the social sciences. Nor does any one of them look at changes over time to see whether more journals are adopting such policies.

To fill this gap, we conduct a comparative analysis in which we look at the policies of journals in different fields at different points in time and in which we do the following: (1) identify major academic journals in several disciplines in the social sciences; (2) determine whether they have policies about sharing data associated with articles published in them; and (3) evaluate the nature of those policies in terms of what they expect or require authors to do. Our starting point here is the aforementioned Gleditsch and Metelits study, which is one of the earliest empirical examinations of journals' data-sharing policies. In that study, the authors identify the top 15 journals in both International Relations and Political Science based on the number of citations reported for journals in the *Journal of Citation Reports*. We expand upon that approach by looking at a wider range of fields in the social sciences that make extensive use of quantitative data: Business/Finance, Economics, International Relations, Political Science, and Sociology. In addition, we identify the top 20 journals in each field, but based on each journal's 2003-vintage ISI Impact Factor score rather than the raw number of citations. This initial cut gives us 92 unique journal titles, as some journals are duplicated across two fields. In instances when a title is duplicated, we then assign it to one field and select the next-highest-ranked title in the other field until we are left with 100 unique titles overall that are evenly distributed across our 5 fields (i.e. 20 journals/field). We then code the data-sharing policies of each of these journals at two points in time, 2003 and 2015, so that we have a panel dataset of journals that will allow us to compare variation in journal policies both across fields and over time.†

In other words, we analyze the policies of top-ranked journals from 2003 to see how or whether the policies of that group of journals have changed over time. Since the publication of Gleditsch and Metlits' study, academics in the social sciences have continued to discuss and debate data sharing and transparency, to

† The final list of journals is available on the companion website (https://databrarianship.wordpress.com/). The list indicates which journals were duplicated across fields and to which field a duplicated journal was assigned.

propose that journals adopt data-sharing policies, and to flesh out what those policies should expect of authors. Our approach allows us to see to what extent these discussions have subsequently affected the behavior of journals that Gleditsch and Metelits examined, as well as allowing us to see whether such discussions have influenced the policies of journals in other fields that were likewise top-ranked at the time of their study.

To code journal policies, we develop a 10-point ordinal index for these policies, which we have used in earlier presentations on this topic.[48] This policy consists of the following 5 elements:[†]

1. whether the journal has a stated policy about data availability/replication
2. the terms/language of policy, such as whether authors are "encouraged" to make data available or whether they are "expected" or "required" to make data available
3. the materials that authors have to provide as part of the policy, such as whether they have to provide data only or whether they also have to provide code/syntax to reproduce the analyses in the submission
4. the time-frame for providing data/replication materials, such as whether they have to be available upon request from other researchers post-publication versus whether they have to be provided prior to publication
5. the location at which the data must be available, such as whether authors are required to make the data available via a journal's website or Dataverse

To collect data for journal policies from 2003 and construct index values, we consult issues of journals available via either print or microfilm. When print issues are not readily available, we rely on any digitized front or back matter available for issues from 2003 accessible in J-STOR. When print issues or issues in J-STOR referred to any URLs for a given journal, we also check any 2003-vintage copies of those sites that are accessible via the Internet Archive. For data on policies from 2015, we consult websites for individual journals and look specifically for submission instructions, any instructions for "Supplemental Materials," editorial policies, and guidelines from publishers.

Journal Policies—Findings

Our results, presented in Table 14.1 below, indicate that a considerably greater fraction of our journals of interest has data-sharing policies now relative to 2003. In 2003, 10% (10/100 journals) had policies, while 39% (39/100) have such policies in 2015. While many of the journals that were top-ranked in 2003 adopted

† The index components in their entirety are available on the companion website (https://databrarianship.wordpress.com/).

policies between 2003 and 2015, most of them have not. In addition, the results also clearly indicate that the adoption of such policies has varied greatly across fields within the social sciences. Most of our Economics journals (13/20, or 65%) have adopted policies since 2003. For our remaining fields, however, half or fewer of the journals now have policies: 50% (10/20) for Business/Finance, 35% (7/20) for Political Science, 30% (6/20) for International Relations, and 15% (3/20) for Sociology. Even with all the ensuing discussion since 2003 about data sharing and replication, most of the journals that were top-ranked in 2003 did not subsequently adopt data-sharing policies.

Table 14.1. Summary Statistics by Academic Field and Year for 2003 Top-Ranked Journals in 2003 and in 2015

Field	Year	Number of Journals with Policies	Mean Policy Index Value	Maximum Policy Index Value	Minimum Policy Index Value
Business/ Finance	2003	3	0.70	7.0	0
	2015	10	2.33	7.0	0
Economics	2003	1	0.15	3.0	0
	2015	13	4.45	9.0	0
International Relations	2003	4	1.00	6.5	0
	2015	6	2.23	9.0	0
Political Science	2003	1	0.20	4.0	0
	2015	7	2.30	10.0	0
Sociology	2003	0	0.00	0.0	0
	2015	3	0.90	8.0	0
Total	**2003**	**9**	**0.41**	**7.0**	**0**
	2015	**39**	**2.44**	**10.0**	**0**

As for the values for our 0–10 policy index score, we see similar patterns over time and across fields. Overall, the mean value for our index increased from 0.41 in 2003 to 2.44 in 2015. The mean value for the index has increased across all fields, with Economics again being the field with the largest mean value in 2015 (4.45), followed by Business (2.33), Political Science (2.30), International Relations (2.23), and Sociology (0.90). The minimum and maximum values also suggest considerable variability across journals within fields. While Sociology has not adopted journal policies to the same degree as have our other fields, for instance, the 2015 policy for *Sociological Methods & Research*, which has a value of 8, is amongst the most exacting policies in our list.

Table 14.2. Summary Statistics by Academic Field and Year for 2003 Top-Ranked Journals v. Current Top-Ranked Journals

Field	Year	Number of Journals with Policies	Mean Policy Index Value	Maximum Policy Index Value	Minimum Policy Index Value
Business/ Finance	2003	3	0.70	7.0	0
	2015	12	2.67	8.0	0
Economics	2003	1	0.15	3.0	0
	2015	17	5.63	9.0	0
International Relations	2003	4	1.00	6.5	0
	2015	8	2.40	9.0	0
Political Science	2003	1	0.20	4.0	0
	2015	11	3.83	10.0	0
Sociology	2003	0	0.00	0.0	0
	2015	7	1.52	8.0	0
Total	**2003**	**9**	**0.41**	**7.0**	**0**
	2015	**55**	**3.21**	**10.0**	**0**

As an alternate approach to looking at our questions of interest, we also compare top-ranked journals from 2003 to current top-ranked journals. Our basic methodology is the same as above, except that we are now also looking at the policies of top journals based on their most recent (2014) JCR impact rankings. Instead of using a panel dataset to compare past and present policies for journals that were top-ranked in 2003, we are comparing the policies of journals that were top-ranked in 2003 to the policies of journals that are currently top-ranked.[†] The results from this analysis, shown in Table 14.2, are quite similar in terms of variation over time and across fields. For journals that are currently top-ranked, a majority of them now have data-sharing policies. Economics and Business/Finance are once again the fields with the most journals with policies, followed by Political Science, International Relations, and Sociology. Economics and Political Science, meanwhile, are the fields with the highest mean policy index values, followed by Business/Finance, International Relations, and Sociology. In comparison to journals that were top-ranked in 2003, then, a small majority of journals that are currently top-ranked do have data-availability policies.

Journal Policies—Discussion

As both of our sets of results make clear, there is still considerable variation in data-availability policies, even as more journals have adopted such policies over time. Some examples taken from different journals in different fields provide illustrative examples of how policies vary. The *Review of Financial Studies*, for instance, does not have any formal policy on data availability. Instead, it "encourages our authors to post on the RFS Oxford University Press web page any material that they think will help others productively use their published research" and lists datasets as one example of such supplemental materials.[49]

Public Opinion Quarterly has an explicit data policy, but it is relatively limited in terms of what authors are expected to do:

> To permit competent professionals to confirm the results and analyses, authors are expected to retain raw data for a minimum of 5 years after publication of the research. Other information related to the research (e.g., instructions, treatment manuals, software, details of procedures) should be kept for the same period. This information is necessary if others are to attempt replication. Authors are expected to comply promptly and in a spirit of cooperation with such requests.[50]

---

† The list of journals by field are available on https://databrarianship.wordpress.com/.

Authors for *Public Opinion Quarterly* are expected to retain and provide data, but only for a specific period of time. There are no additional requirements to deposit the data at a designated archive or that the data be available prior to publication, nor is there any explicit requirement to provide code explaining how the original data were transformed into whatever dataset was analyzed.

The *American Journal of Political Science*, meanwhile, has a very exacting policy. In a very lengthy statement on its new policies, the *AJPS* notes that authors have to deposit data in the journal's Dataverse site, have to provide code or instructions for how the analysis dataset was produced from the source data, and have to provide these materials prior to publication. Moreover, the *AJPS* makes final publication conditional upon the successful replication of the analysis in any submission; until the results can be successfully reproduced, there will be no publication of the manuscript.[51] While the data policies for *Comparative Political Studies*[52] and the *Journal of Conflict Resolution*[53] are not as strict as that of the *AJPS*, they do similarly go beyond stating that provision of data are "required" to explicitly state that even articles that have otherwise cleared the review process will not be published in the absence of replication files.

The *AJPS* language about replication of results being part of the review process is, it should be noted, not exclusive to that journal. While they are not in our list of journals under study, the *Quarterly Journal of Political Science*[54] and *Political Science Research and Methods*[55] have similar policies of conducting in-house reviews of submissions for replication purposes. While it is likewise outside of the scope of our study, we should also note that *Science* employs a similar approach.[56] This is a striking development, as it is an approach that very much goes beyond what proponents of data-sharing policies for journals have generally advocated.

Another noteworthy development involves whether journals designate specific locations for where data might reside. In earlier debates about data-sharing policies, various participants often did not get into the specifics of where replication data and materials should be deposited, and some even expressed skepticism about the notion of placing replication materials in the likes of data archives such as the ICPSR.[57] More recent proposals for replication policies, however, are more explicit about this matter and less inclined to endorse private communications or individual websites as appropriate means to share data. The recent DA-RT statement mentioned earlier, for instance, explicitly calls for the requirement that authors deposit replication materials in a "trusted digital repository."[58] Similarly, various scholars of inter-state and intra-state conflict argue that researchers are not trained archivists and that individual websites do not constitute data archives. Consequently, researchers should instead deposit data at "an organization that has professional staff and resources dedicated to that effort," with the likes of the ICPSR or the Dataverse Network given as examples.[59] While our focus is journals in the social sciences, we also note in passing that both *Nature* and *Science* likewise recommend that authors deposit data at bona fide archives such as Dryad.[60] This particular thread of the discussions about data sharing is also reflected in the policies of journals such as the *World Bank Economic*

Review, the *Journal of Money, Credit, and Banking*, the *American Journal of Political Science*, and *Sociological Methods & Research*, which now expect authors to make data available via journal websites and/or journal Dataverses.

Continued Barriers and Obstacles to Sharing

Our results indicate that a growing number of academic journals in different fields within the social sciences have been adopting data-sharing/replication policies since 2003. Our results also indicate that such adoption is not uniform across disciplines, and that many journals still do not have such policies. While our methods and list of journals differ from those of Gherghina and Katsanidou's study of political science journals and those of Andreoli-Verbach and Mueller-Langer's study of economics journals, our findings are nonetheless similar in that they likewise show that data-sharing/replication policies are not yet a standard practice for journals in the social sciences. Despite decades-long deliberations about this matter, it is still only partially the norm for academic journals to require authors to submit data and code as part of the publication process. Moreover, even when journals have policies, they do not always produce the desired results. McCullough and McCullough, et al. undertook various attempts to replicate findings in articles published in economics journals with replication policies and had only limited success in doing so, in part because the policies of the journals they looked at were not necessarily actively monitored and enforced at the time of writing.[61] Likewise, Eubank's assessment of the in-house replication policy of the *Quarterly Journal of Political Science* noted that there were issues replicating findings in 13 out of 24 submissions under review from 2012-2014.[62] More generally, data sharing is still not a common practice amongst academics, as evinced by Andreoli-Versbach and Mueller-Langer's study of data-sharing behavior amongst economists, which concluded that roughly 80% of their sample of scholars did not share data and code from their research.[63] Wicherts et al. similarly found that psychologists were not in the habit of sharing research data used in publications, even when requested to do so.[64] Why is this still the case, even when the potential benefits from data sharing seem so compelling?

We should note here that there are legitimate reasons why research data may not be readily sharable. Proponents of data sharing readily concede that data resources that are proprietary often cannot be shared. Likewise, the potential for disclosure risk is a sound and defensible reason to not share data that contain sensitive information about potentially-identifiable individuals.† Furthermore, we

† Questions about protecting the identity of individuals have been particularly salient in debates among political scientists over how or whether to apply DA-RT to qualitative research. See the many commentaries at http://dialogueond-art.org/ for an overview of this particular debate.

should note that the debates about data sharing and replication policies are precisely that—debates. That these discussions have been ongoing for decades in and of itself suggests that there is not unanimity on this matter. While their focus is not replication specifically, Herrera and Kapur note that repeated reuse of pre-existing data can result in datasets having legitimacy in the eyes of researchers regardless of their quality in terms of measurement accuracy and the like.[65] Herrnson makes a related point that data-availability policies may have the effect of dissuading researchers from collecting their own data, thereby stunting the development of valuable skills that can result from such efforts.[66] Various participants in and observers of debates on data sharing and replication policies have also raised concerns about the de facto outcomes of such policies, such as focusing on minutiae and minor errors that then get undue levels of attention and have the potential to damage reputations because of relatively small mistakes and good-faith errors.[67] This in turn leads to questions such as how much replication is "enough" for a finding to be deemed robust and credible, how serious an error or discrepancy in an attempted replication has to be for the results to be called into question, and how to ensure that the replications themselves are conducted in a transparent and sound manner.[68] Even proponents of data sharing and transparency recognize that there may be practical difficulties in implementing replication policies. As Carsey notes, there are nuts-and-bolts considerations such as when replication materials should be submitted, how to address concerns about keeping replication materials secure during the review process, and whether providing replication materials may effectively identify submitters of manuscripts.[69]

We should also note here that the incentive structures that researchers often face are not necessarily conducive to encouraging data sharing or replication. Preparing data and code and documentation so that others can readily attempt to replicate one's work is a time-consuming process that becomes especially difficult as time passes and recollections fade. The rewards for such work may not be readily forthcoming. Data sharing is not necessarily something that will result in favorable tenure decisions or other such professional benefits. Indeed, from the perspective of individual researchers, sharing data may instead result in costs such as being "scooped," losing the ability to maximize the benefits of one's work, having one's results be undermined via the replication efforts of others, and losing one's competitive advantages in the context of a tight academic job market.[70] Moreover, replication work itself is not necessarily rewarded or even encouraged in the first place. While Ishiyama is very much in favor of data sharing and replication and transparency, he is also of the view that replication studies should not necessarily be published in major journals, where the focus should be more on "original" research. But, as Ishiyama acknowledges, such a position raises the questions of where replication studies should be published and why scholars should undertake efforts to replicate findings if such efforts are unlikely to be published in major journals.[71] And as Andreoli-Versbach and Mueller-Langer point out, the lack of reward for undertaking replication studies further reduces the incentives of individual researchers to make the effort necessary to ensure that their work can be replicated: why undertake such efforts when the likelihood of having one's work undergo replication is minor due to the lack of incentive for others to do so?[72]

The incentives being what they are, it is thus not surprising that Hamermesh drily notes that "Economists treat replication the way teenagers treat chastity—as an ideal to be professed but not to be practiced."[73] And while such sentiments may cause the heart of many a librarian to skip a beat or two, it should likewise not be a surprise for Gleditsch and Metelits to note that for many academics, "documentation, for instance, is often thought of as a waste of time."[74] In the abstract, greater sharing of research data and transparency in their use can constitute a genuine public good for academics, and journal policies that encourage such behavior thus offer many potential collective benefits to the social sciences. However, the philosophical and practical questions about such policies and the incentive structures that weigh against such behavior still constitute considerable barriers to data sharing and the adoption of replication policies.

Implications for Data Sharing and Data Management

Our findings here suggest that the ongoing efforts of proponents of data-sharing policies for academic journals in the social sciences have not been entirely in vain. Our reviews of the policies of top-ranked journals to see how many have adopted policies over time shows that many of them have, and that the policies they are adopting are increasingly demanding. However, our results also show that such adoption has not been uniform across the social sciences. In our collection of journals, many more of them have such policies now than then. But many still do not. This suggests that there are continued issues for replication of empirical findings and transparency in research practices. If one agrees that replication is a crucial part of the scientific method and that transparency is key if academic research is to be credible, then one may still be concerned about the scientific rigor and credibility of much empirical research in the social sciences. Due to reasons such as practical considerations and problematic incentive structures, the level of data sharing is one that is still not socially-optimal within the social sciences.

Having said that, we want to emphasize that our findings show that the number of journals in different fields with data policies is on the increase, and that those policies are increasingly rigorous. And, there is some evidence in the social sciences (and in the sciences) that such policies have a positive effect on data sharing. Andreoli-Versbach and Mueller-Langer are, in general, downbeat about the willingness of economists to share research data. But they also find that economists who publish in journals with replication policies are more likely to make data available, as the sunk costs of prepping data to meet those policies are such that the additional marginal costs of making data available more generally are minor.[75] Dafoe compares data availability for articles published in the *American Political Science Review* to those published in the *American Journal of Political Science* and concludes that the more exacting replication policy of the latter journal, while not perfect, "seems to have substantially increased the actual availability of replication files" when compared to the less exacting policy of the former.[76] In the sciences, both Piwowar and Piwowar and Chapman find that replication policies have a positive effect on availability of data associated with journal articles.[77] As previously noted, there is a tension between the social benefits for academic disciplines from data sharing and the potential costs for individual researchers in meeting such expectations. These findings, however, suggest that the adoption of data-sharing policies by academic journals provides an institutional means for resolving that tension in favor of greater data availability. This suggests that as initiatives such as DA-RT gain traction in fields such as political science, we should witness an even greater level of data sharing over time. At a minimum, we have a hypothesis which we will be able to test in the future.

Implications for Libraries

Our findings and reviews are also relevant for considerations of how librarians and libraries might interact with researchers with regard to data management and data sharing. While academic discussions have focused on issues of replication and incentives for sharing, libraries and librarians have focused on the rise of e-science and e-research and how libraries can and should respond to the rise of data-driven, networked research.[78] Environmental scans of the current data management landscape in research libraries reveal a fairly diverse set of institutional responses to campus needs for research data support, ranging from more traditional library services in the area of identifying data to highly engaged consulting services providing data management and sharing support for research teams.[79] In general, libraries supporting Ph.D. programs and research intensive programs tend to demonstrate a deeper set of services around data management plan support, data curation, and training. Additionally, some libraries have actively explored expanding librarian roles in working on research teams and providing data and information literacy training to teams charged with managing and sharing research.[80]

Despite increased emphasis on research data at many university libraries, however, there is something of a gap between faculty and librarian perspectives of the availability and form of research services.[81] The language used by academics in discussions about data sharing is often strikingly different than that used by librarians. For libraries providing research data management services, the focus is often on funder mandates and statements from entities such as the Office of Science and Technology Policy and how libraries should respond to such developments, for example, by assisting researchers with writing data management plans for grants or by developing institutional repositories as a means to store and preserve and disseminate data produced by grants. For academics, however, the focus is more often on replication and methodological considerations such as scientific rigor and transparency and credibility of findings. The 2014 symposium on data access and research transparency published in *PS: Political Science & Politics*, for instance, mentions funder mandates for data management plans in passing.[82] The main focus is instead on how data sharing promotes research transparency and how such transparency might be further encouraged. As for where research data might reside, we have also noted that the tendency amongst academics and journal policies is to recommend usage of established archives such as the ICPSR or the Dataverse Network (or, in the sciences, the likes of Dryad or GenBank).

While data management plans for grant applications are certainly important for various fields and in certain contexts, they are not what academics tend to focus on when they talk about data management and data sharing. Instead, academics focus much more on matters of replication and transparency. As an example, a proposed open letter from a Director of Graduate Studies in the Political Science department at the University of Missouri says nothing about NSF mandates, but does mention transparency and the need to satisfy journals' replication policies.[83] Indeed, funder mandates are likely not applicable to many, if not most, researchers in the social sciences—whereas assistance in meeting the data availability policy of a journal as a step in the publication process is a service that likely will resonate with many researchers whether they are graduate students or faculty.[84] Likewise, data management support might also be better focused on helping researchers identify appropriate external options for depositing and archiving research data and on helping them with how to best prepare data for submission to such archives, as academics and journals are increasingly recommending pre-existing archives as suitable locations to place research data. Once more, the point here is not so much that libraries' efforts in data management support are misplaced, per se. It is instead that such efforts will be more effective if their scope is adjusted to incorporate the concerns and considerations expressed by academics in their own debates and deliberations about how they should best handle and use data. To the extent that librarians discuss such issues with the same language as do academics, they are more likely to make effective connections with them.

Given how academics are increasingly emphasizing evidence, transparency, and sharing, we suggest that librarians should incorporate such arguments and concerns into their deliberations about data management support and their interactions with researchers about data services, so that their proposed services and conversations address and inform faculty concerns about data as a scholarly object. This shift would largely be a matter of placing more emphasis, services, and instruction on many of the scholarly communication themes and workflows surrounding research data and data driven research. Indeed, much of the early planning for librarian roles in e-science initiatives noted this connection such as Soehner et al., who specifically note that "the libraries may not see these scholarly communication issues as being connected to e-science, when, in fact, the connection is closer than is realized."[85]

Writing in *PS: Political Science & Politics* in 1995, Kenneth J. Meier predicted that "in 2010 A.D. every journal in political science will have some form of replication policy."[86] Suffice it to say that this prediction has not proved to be entirely accurate. The findings of our analysis in this chapter show that top-ranked journals in political science and other fields within the social sciences have indeed been adopting such policies over time, but that such adoption has been incomplete and uneven across the disciplines. However, the apparent effectiveness of data-availability policies in promoting data sharing suggests that the increased adoption of such policies bodes well for the future promotion of data services. The academic literature and commentaries on matters of data sharing also offer suggestions for how librarians can discuss data management with academics in ways that more directly relate to researchers' concerns and interests. Data sharing and data management already are and will likely continue to be central topics in larger discussions of scholarly communications and open access. Such discussions will only benefit from a greater awareness of the debates amongst academics about the benefits of data sharing and the means for best providing it.

---

1. Steve Lohr, "The Age of Big Data." *New York Times*, February 11, 2012, http://www.nytimes.com/2012/02/12/sunday-review/big-datas-impact-in-the-world.html.
2. "The Data Deluge," *The Economist*, Feburary 25, 2010, http://www.economist.com/node/15579717.
3. National Research Council, *Access to Research Data in the 21st Century: An Ongoing Dialogue Among Interest Parties: Report of a Workshop*, (Washington, D.C.: The National Academies Press, 2002), viii.
4. National Institutes of Health, "NIH Data Sharing Policy," last modified April 17, 2007, http://grants1.nih.gov/grants/policy/data_sharing/index.htm.
5. National Science Foundation, "NSF Data Management Plans," accessed April 20, 2015, https://www.nsf.gov/eng/general/dmp.jsp.
6. Office of Science and Technology Policy, "Increasing Access to the Results of Federally Funded Scientific Research," last modified February 22, 2013, https://www.whitehouse.gov/sites/default/files/microsites/ostp/ostp_public_access_memo_2013.pdf.
7. Chris Thorpe and Simon Rogers, "Ordnance Survey Opendata Maps: What Does It Actually Include?" *The Guardian*, April 2, 2010, http://www.theguardian.com/news/datablog/2010/apr/02/ordnance-survey-open-data.
8. Office of Citizen Services and Innovation Technologies, "Open Government," accessed April 20, 2015. https://www.data.gov/open-gov/.
9. Organization for Economic Co-Operation and Development, "Science, Technology and Innovation for the 21st Century. Meeting of the OECD Committee for Scientific and Technological Policy at Ministerial Level, 29–30 January 2004—Final Communique," accessed April 19, 2015. http://www.oecd.org/science/sci-tech/sciencetechnologyandinnovationforthe21stcentury-meetingoftheoecdcommitteeforscientificandtechnologicalpolicyatministeriallevel29-30january2004-finalcommunique.htm; Organization for Economic Co-Operation and Development, "OECD Principles and Guidelines for Access to Research Data from Public Funding," accessed

April 19, 2015. http://www.oecd.org/science/sci-tech/oecdprinciplesandguidelinesforaccesstoresearchdatafrompublicfunding.htm.

10. European Commission, "Guidelines on Open Access to Scientific Publications and Research Data in Horizon 2020," last modified December 11 2013, http://ec.europa.eu/research/participants/data/ref/h2020/grants_manual/hi/oa_pilot/h2020-hi-oa-pilot-guide_en.pdf.
11. Gary King, "Ensuring the Data-Rich Future of the Social Sciences." *Science* 331 (2011): 719, doi: http://dx.doi.org/10.1126/science.1197872.
12. Anne R. Diekema, Andrew Wesolek, and Cheryl D. Walters, "The NSF/NIH Effect: Surveying the Effect of Data Management Requirements on Faculty, Sponsored Programs, and Institutional Repositories," *Journal of Academic Librarianship* 40 (2014): 322–331, http://dx.doi.org/10.1016/j.acalib.2014.04.010; Regina Raboin, Rebecca Reznik-Zellen, and Dorothea Salo, "Forging New Service Paths: Institutional Approaches to Providing Research Data Management Services." *Journal of eScience Librarianship* 1 (2012): 134–147, doi: http://dx.doi.org/10.7191/jeslib.2012.1021.
13. Organization for Economic Co-Operation and Development, "OECD Principles and Guidelines for Access to Research Data From Public Funding," 11.
14. Terra Lawson-Remer, "Property Insecurity," *Brooklyn Journal of International Law* 38 (2012): 145–191. http://www.terralawsonremer.com/wp-content/uploads/2012/12/13_LawsonRemer_145_191-1_Property_Insecurity_Brooklyn_Law.pdf. More generally, see Kenneth J. Meier, "Replication: A View from the Streets," *PS: Political Science & Politics* 28 (1995): 456–459, http://www.jstor.org/stable/420303.
15. Nils Petter Gleditsch, Claire Metelits, and Havard Strand, "Posting Your Data: Will You Be Scooped or Will You Be Famous?" *International Studies Perspectives* 4 (2003): 89–97, doi: http://dx.doi.org/10.1111/1528-3577.04105; see also Amy Pienta, George C. Alter, and Jared A. Lyle, *The Enduring Value of Social Science Research: The Use and Reuse of Primary Research Data* 2010, http://hdl.handle.net/2027.42/78307; Jeremy J. Albright and Jared A. Lyle, "Data Preservation Through Data Archives," *PS: Political Science & Politics* 43 (2010): 17–21, doi: http://dx.doi.org/10.1017/S1049096510990768; and Heather A. Piwowar, Roger S. Day, and Douglas B. Fridsma, "Sharing Detailed Research Data Is Associated with Increased Citation Rate," *PLoS ONE* 2 (2007): e308, doi: http://dx.doi.org/10.1371/journal.pone.0000308.
16. Jeremy Freese, "Replication Standards for Quantitative Social Science: Why Not Sociology?" *Sociological Methods & Research* 36 (2007): 153–172, doi: http://dx.doi.org/10.1177/0049124107306659.
17. Freese, "Replication Standards for Quantitative Social Science;" Arthur Lupia and George Alter, "Data Access and Research Transparency in the Quantitative Tradition;" *PS: Political Science & Politics* 47 (2014): 54–59, http://dx.doi.org/10.1017/S1049096513001728; Arthur Lupia and Colin Elman, "Openness in Political Science;" *PS: Political Science & Politics* 47 (2014): 19–42, doi: http://dx.doi.org/10.1017/S1049096513001716; Marcia McNutt, "Raising The Bar," *Science* 345 (2014): 9, doi: http://dx.doi.org/10.1126/science.1257891; Richard G. Anderson, William H. Greene, B. D. MuCullough, and H. D. Vinod, "The Role of Data & Program Code Archives in the Future of Economic Research," *Federal Reserve Bank of St. Louis Working Paper 2005-014*, (St. Louis, MO. 2005), http:// research.stlouisfed.org/wp/2005/2005-014.pdf; Nils Petter Gleditsch and Claire Metelits, "The Replication Debate," *International Studies Perspectives* 4 (2003): 89–97, doi: http://dx.doi.org/10.1111/1528-3577.04105; James Lee Ray and Brandon Valeriano, "Barriers to Replication in Systematic Empirical Research on World Politics," *International Studies Perspectives* 4 (2003): 79–85, doi: http://dx.doi.org/10.1111/1528-3577.04105; William G. Dewald, Jerry G. Thursby, and Richard G. Anderson, "Replication in Empirical Economics: The Journal of Money, Credit and Banking Project," *American Economic Review* 76 (1986): 587–603, http://www.jstor.org/stable/1806061; King, "Replication, Replication," *PS: Political Science & Politics* 28 (1995): 444–452, http://www.jstor.org/stable/420301; Meier, "Repliation: A View from the Streets."
18. Gary King, "Replication, Replication," 445.

19. Richard G. Anderson, William H. Greene, B.D. MuCullough, and H.D. Vinod, "The Role of Data & Program Code Archives in the Future of Economic Research," 2.
20. Ibid, 3.
21. Lupia and Elman, "Openness in Political Science: Data Access and Research Transparency." *PS: Political Science & Politics* 47 (2014): 20.
22. Ben Bernanke, "Editorial Statement," *American Economic Review* 94 (2004): 404, http://www.jstor.org/stable/3592790.
23. Luipa and Elman, "Openness in Political Science," 19.
24. Allen Dafoe, "The Imperative to Share Complete Replication Files," *Lux et Data* (blog), September 2013, http://isps.yale.edu/news/blog/2013/09/the-imperative-to-share-complete-replication-files.
25. Nicholas Eubank, "A Decade of Replications: Lessons from the Quarterly Journal of Political Science," *The Political Methodologist* (blog), December 9, 2014, http://thepoliticalmethodologist.com/2014/12/09/a-decade-of-replications-lessons-from-the-quarterly-journal-of-political-science/.
26. Dewald, Thursby, and Anderson, "Replication in Empirical Economics;" Anderson, Greene, McCullough, and Vinod, "The Role of Data & Program Code Archives;" B.D. McCullough, "Got Replicability: The Journal of Money, Credit, and Banking Archive," *Econ Journal Watch* 4 (2007): 326–337, http://econjwatch.org/file_download/170/2007-09-mccullough-econ_practice.pdf; B.D. McCullough, Kerry Anne McGeary, and Teresa D. Harrison, "Do Economics Journal Archives Promote Replicable Research? *Canadian Journal of Economics / Revue canadienne d'Economique* 41 (2008): 1406–1420, http://www.jstor.org/stable/25478330; B.D. McCullough and H.D. Vinod, "Verifying the Solution from a Nonlinear Solver," *American Economic Review* 93 (2003): 873–892. doi: http://dx.doi.org/10.1257/000282803322157133.
27. David Funder, "Does 'Failure to Replicate' Mean Failed Science?" *LiveScience*, May 15, 2013, http://www.livescience.com/32041-revisiting-science-studies.html; Henry L. Roediger, III, "Psychology's Woes and a Partial Cure: The Value of Replication," *Observer* 25 (2012), http://www.psychologicalscience.org/index.php/publications/observer/2012/february-12/psychologys-woes-and-a-partial-cure-the-value-of-replication.html; Ed Yong, "Replication Studies: Bad Copy," *Nature* 485 (2012): 298–300, http://www.nature.com/news/replication-studies-bad-copy-1.10634.
28. John Ioannidis, "Why Most Published Research Findings Are False," *PLoS Medicine* 2 (2005): e124, doi: http://dx.doi.org/10.1371/journal.pmed.0020124.
29. George Johnson, "New Truths That Only One Can See," *New York Times*. January 20, 2014. http://www.nytimes.com/2014/01/21/science/new-truths-that-only-one-can-see.html; "Trouble in the Lab," *The Economist*, October 19th, 2013, http://www.economist.com/news/briefing/21588057-scientists-think-science-self-correcting-alarming-degree-it-not-trouble.
30. Bernardo A. Huberman, "Sociology of Science: Big Data Deserve A Bigger Audience," *Nature* 482 (2012): 308, doi: http://dx.doi.org/10.1038/482308d; Nathaniel Beck, "Research Replication in Social Science," *OUPblog* (blog), August 24 2014, http://blog.oup.com/2014/08/research-replication-nathaniel-beck/; Nathaniel Beck, "Replication Redux and Facebook Data," *OUPblog* (blog), January 19, 2015, http://blog.oup.com/2015/01/replication-redux-facebook-data/; John Markoff, "Troves of Personal Data, Forbidden to Researchers," *New York Times* May 21, 2012, http://www.nytimes.com/2012/05/22/science/big-data-troves-stay-forbidden-to-social-scientists.html.
31. Jan Hoffler and Thomas Kneib, "Economics Needs Replication," *The Institute Blog* (blog) April 23, 2013. http://ineteconomics.org/blog/inet/economics-needs-replication; James Kwak, "The Importance of Excel," *The Baseline Scenario* (blog) February 9, 2013, http://baselinescenario.com/2013/02/09/the-importance-of-excel/; James Kwak, "More Bad Excel," *The Baseline Scenario* (blog). April 18, 2013, http://baselinescenario.com/2013/04/18/more-bad-excel; Paul Krugman, "The Excel Depression," *New York Times* April 18, 2013, http://www.nytimes.com/2013/04/19/opinion/krugman-the-excel-depression.html.

32. Victoria Stodden, Peixuan Guo, and Zhaokun Ma, "Toward Reproducible Computational Research: An Empirical Analysis of Data and Code Policy Adoption by Journals," *PlosONE* 8 (2013): e67111, doi: http://dx.doi.org/10.1371/journal.pone.0067111.
33. Anderson, Greene, McCullough, and Vinod, "The Role of Data & Program Code Archives in the Future of Economic Research," 13.
34. Daniel S. Hamermesh, "Viewpoint: Replication in Economics." *Canadian Journal of Economics / Revue canadienne d'Economique* 40 (2007): 715–733, doi: http://dx.doi.org/10.1111/j.1365-2966.2007.00428.x.
35. King, "Replication, Replication," 444; Robert M. Hauser, "Sharing Data: It's Time for ASA Journals to Follow the Folkways of a Scientific Sociology," *American Sociological Review* 52 (1987): vi–viii, http://www.jstor.org/stable/2095829.
36. Nils Petter Gleditsch, Patrick James, James Lee Ray, and Bruce Russett, "Editors' Joint Statement: Minimum Replication Standards for International Relations Journals," *International Studies Perspectives* 4 (2003): 105, doi: http://dx.doi.org/10.1111/1528-3577.04105; Anderson, Greene, McCullough, and Vinod, "The Role of Data & Program Code Archives;" Freese, "Replication Standards for Quantitative Social Science;" Lupia and Alter, "Data Access and Research Transparency in the Quantitative Tradition." For discussion of the effects of software choices on replication specifically, see Anderson, Greene, McCullough, and Vinod, pp. 16–17.
37. Anderson, Greene, McCullough, and Vinod, "The Role of Data & Program Code Archives;" Freese, "Replication Standards for Quantitative Social Science."
38. Freese, "Replication Standards for Quantitative Social Science."
39. Gleditsch, James, Ray, and Russett, "Editors' Joint Statement," 105.
40. Freese, "Replication Standards for Quantitative Social Science," 167.
41. Hoffler and Kneib, "Economics Needs Replication."
42. Colin Elman and Arthur Lupia, "The (DA-RT) Data Access and Research Transparency Joint Statement," accessed April 1, 2015, http://www.dartstatement.org/.
43. Lupia and Elman, "Openness in Political Science."
44. John Cox and Laura Cox, *Scholarly Publishing Practice: Academic Journal Publishers' Policies and Practices in Online Publishing* (Brighton: Association of Learned and Professional Society Publishers, 2008),74–75, 112.
45. Gleditsch and Metelits, "The Replication Debate."
46. Serigu Gherghina and Alexia Katsanidou, "Data Availability in Political Science Journals." *European Political Science* 12 (2013): 333–347, doi: http://dx.doi.org/10.1057/eps.2013.8.
47. Patrik Andreoli-Versbach and Frank Mueller-Langer, "Open Access to Data: An Ideal Professed but not Practiced," *Research Policy* 43 (2014) 1621–1633, doi: http://dx.doi.org/10.1016/j.respol.2014.04.008.
48. Joel Herndon and Robert O'Reilly, "Data Sharing Across the Disciplines: An Empirical Study," presented at the Annual Meeting of the International Association for Social Science Information Services and Technology, Tampere, Finland, May 2009, http://www.iassistdata.org/downloads/2009/c4_herndon_oreilly.pdf; Robert O'Reilly, "Data Sharing Across the Disciplines, Revisited: Academic Journals and Replication Policies," presented at the Annual Meeting of the International Association for Social Science Information Services and Technology, Washington, D.C., June 2012, http://www.iassistdata.org/downloads/2012/2012_a3_oreilly.pdf.
49. "Paper Addenda," *Review of Financial Studies*, accessed April 6, 2015, http://rfssfs.org/paper-addenda/.
50. "Note to Contributors, *Public Opinion Quarterly*, accessed April 20, 2015, http://www.oxfordjournals.org/our_journals/poq/for_authors/general.html.
51. William G. Jacoby, "The AJPS Replication Policy: Innovations and Revisions," *AJPS Editor Blog* (blog), March 26, 2015, http://ajps.org/2015/03/26/the-ajps-replication-policy-innovations-and-revisions/.
52. "Submission Instructions," *Comparative Political Studies*, accessed April 14, 2015, http://www.sagepub.com/journals/Journal200828/manuscriptSubmission#tabview=manuscriptSubmission.

53. "Submission Guidelines," *Journal of Conflict Resolution*, accessed April 14, 2015, http://www.sagepub.com/journals/Journal200764/manuscriptSubmission.
54. "Author Instructions," *Quarterly Journal of Political Science*, accessed December 19, 2014, http://www.nowpublishers.com/Journal/AuthorInstructions/QJPS.
55. "Editorial Statement," *Political Science Research Methods*, accessed December 19, 2014, http://journals.cambridge.org/images/fileUpload/documents/RAM_ifc.pdf.
56. McNutt, "Raising the Bar."
57. Ray and Valeriano, "Barriers to Replication."
58. Elman and Lupia, "The (DA-RT) Data Access and Research Transparency Joint Statement."
59. Christian Davenport and Will H. Moore, "Conflict Consortium Standards & Best Practices for Observational Data," last updated April 7, 2015, http://conflictconsortium.weebly.com/uploads/1/8/3/5/18359923/cc-datastandardspractices7apr2015.pdf; Idean Salehyan and Henrik Urdal, "Data Challenges in Conflict Research," *Political Violence @ a Glance* (blog), February 6, 2015, http://politicalviolenceataglance.org/2015/02/06/data-challenges-in-conflict-research/.
60. "Availability of Data, Materials, and Methods, *Nature* accessed December 19, 2014, http://www.nature.com/authors/policies/availability.html; "Data and Materials Availability," *Science*, accessed February 17, 2015, http://www.sciencemag.org/site/feature/contribinfo/prep/gen_info.xhtml#dataavail.
61. McCullough, "Got Replicability?"; McCullough, McGeary, and Harrison, "Do Economics Journals Promote Replicable Research?"
62. Nicholas Eubank, "A Decade of Replications: Lessons from the *Quarterly Journal of Political Science*."
63. Andreoli-Versbach and Mueller-Langer, "Open Access to Data."
64. Jelte M. Wicherts, Denny Borsboom, Judith Kats, and Dylan Molenaar, "The Poor Availability of Psychological Research Data for Reanalysis," *American Psychologist* 61 (2006): 726–728, doi: http://dx.doi.org/10.1037/0003-066X.61.7.726.
65. Yoshiko M. Herrera and Devesh Kapur, "Improving Data Quality: Actors, Incentives, and Capabilities," *Political Analysis* 15 (2007): 365–386, http://www.jstor.org/stable/25791902.
66. Paul Herrnson, "Replication, Verification, Secondary Analysis and Data Collection in Political Science." *PS: Political Science & Politics* 28 (1995): 452–455, http://www.jstor.org/stable/420302.
67. James L. Gibson, "Cautious Reflections on a Data-Archiving Policy," *PS: Political Science & Politics* 28 (1995): 473–476, http://www.jstor.org/stable/420310; Nicole Janz, "'Replication Bullying:' Who Replicates the Replicators?" *Political Science Replication* (blog), May 25, 2014, https://politicalsciencereplication.wordpress.com/2014/05/25/replication-bullying-who-replicates-the-replicators/.
68. Thomas Carsey, "Making DA-RT A Reality," *PS: Political Science & Politics* 47 (2014): 72–77, doi: http://dx.doi.org/10.1017/S1049096513001753; Janz, "'Replication Bullying;'" John Ishiyama, "Replication, Research Transparency, and Journal Publications: Individualism, Community Models, and the Future of Replication Studies," *PS: Political Science & Politics* 47 (2014): 78–83, doi: http://dx.doi.org/10.1017/S1049096513001765.
69. Carsey, "Making DA-RT A Reality."
70. Andreoli-Versbach and Mueller-Langer, "Open Access to Data;" Anderson, Greene, McCullough, and Vinod, "The Role of Data & Program Code Archives;" Hernnson, "Replication, Verification, Secondary Analysis;" Piwowar, Day, and Fridsa, "Sharing Detailed Research Data."
71. Ishiyama, "Replication, Research Transparency, and Journal Publications."
72. Andreoli-Versbach and Mueller-Langer, "Open Access to Data."
73. Daniel Hamermesh, "Viewpoint: Replication in Economics."
74. Gleditsch and Metelits, "The Replication Debate."
75. Andreoli-Versbach and Mueller-Langer, "Open Access to Data."
76. Allen Dafoe, "Science Deserves Better: The Imperative to Share Complete Replication Files," *PS: Political Science & Politics* 47 (2014): 61, doi: http://dx.doi.org/10.1017/S104909651300173X.

77. Heather A. Piwowar, "Who Shares? Who Doesn't? Factors Associated with Openly Archving Raw Research Data," *PLoS ONE* 6 (2011): e18657, doi: http://dx.doi.org/10.1371/journal.pone.0018657; Heather A. Piwowar and Wendy W. Chapman, "A Review of Journal Policies for Sharing Research Data," In *Open Scholarship: Authority, Community, and Sustainability in the Age of Web 2.0—Proceedings of the 12th International Conference on Electronic Publishing (ELPUB)* June 25–27 2008, Toronto Canada, http://www.researchremix.org/wordpress/wp-content/uploads/2009/09/ELPUB_2008_Piwowar.pdf.
78. Amy Friedlander and Prudence Adler, "To Stand the Test of Time: Long-Term Stewardship of Digital Data Sets in Science and Engineering," *A Report to the National Science Foundation From the ARL Workshop on New Collaborative Relationships: The Role of Academic Libraries in the Digital Data Universe* (Washington, D.C.: Association of Research Libraries, 2006), http://www.arl.org/storage/documents/publications/digital-data-report-2006.pdf; Anna Gold, "Cyberinfrastructure, Data, and Libraries, Part 1: A Cyberinfrastructure Primer for Librarians," *D-Lib Magazine* 13 (2007), http://www.dlib.org/dlib/september07/gold/09gold-pt1.html; Anna Gold, "Cyberinfrastructure, Data, and Libraries, Part 2: Libraries and the Data Challenge," *D-Lib Magazine* 13 (2007), http://www.dlib.org/dlib/september07/gold/09gold-pt2.html; Catherine Soehner, Catherine Steeves, and Jennifer Ward, *E-Science and Data Support Services: A Study of ARL Member Institutions* (Washington, D.C.: Association of Research Libraries, 2010), http://www.arl.org/storage/documents/publications/escience-report-2010.pdf; Amanda L. Whitmire, "Thoughts on 'eResearch:' A Scientist's Perspective," *Journal of eScience Librarianship* 2(2013): 68–72, doi: http://dx.doi.org/10.7191/jeslib.2013.1045.
79. Carol Tenopir, Ben Birch, and Suzie Allard, *Academic Libraries and Research Data Services: Current Practices and Plans for the Future* (Washington, D.C.: Association of Research Libraries, 2012) http://www.ala.org/acrl/sites/ala.org.acrl/files/content/publications/whitepapers/Tenopir_Birch_Allard.pdf; David Fearon, Betsy Gunia, Barbara E. Pralle, Sherry Lake, and Andrew L. Sallans, *ARL Spec Kit 334: Research Data Management Services.* (Washington, D.C.: Association of Research Libraries, 2013) http://publications.arl.org/Research-Data-Management-Services-SPEC-Kit-334/.
80. Jacob Carlson, Michael Fosmire, CC Miller, and Megan Sapp Nelson, "Determining Data Information Literacy Needs: A Study of Students and Research Faculty," *Portal: Libraries and the Academy* 11 (2011): 629–57, doi: http://dx.doi.org/10.1353/pla.2011.0022; Jennifer Muilenburg, Mahria Lebow, and Joanne Rich, "Lessons Learned From a Research Data Management Pilot Course at an Academic Library," *Journal of eScience Librarianship* 3 (2014): 67–73, doi: http://dx.doi.org/10.7191/jeslib.2014.1058; Mary Piorun, Donna Kafel, Tracey Leger-Hornby, Siamak Najafi, Elaine Martin, Paul Colombo, and Nancy LaPelle, "Teaching Research Data Management: An Undergraduate/Graduate Curriculum," *Journal of eScience Librarianship* 1 (2012): 46–50, doi: http://dx.doi.org/10.7191/jeslib.2012.1003; Donna Kafel, Andrew Creamer, and Elaine Martin, "Building the New England Collaborative Data Management Curriclulum," *Journal of eScience Librarianship* 3 (2014): 60–66, doi: http://dx.doi.org/10.7191/jeslib.2014.1066.
81. Anne R. Diekema, Andrew Wesolek, and Cheryl D. Walters, "The NSF/NIH Effect: Surveying the Effect of Data Management Requirements on Faculty, Sponsored Programs, and Institutional Repositories," *Journal of Academic Librarianship* 40 (2014): 322–331.
82. See Dafoe, "Science Deserves Better," and Carsey, "Making DA-RT A Reality."
83. Amanda Murdie, "An Open Letter From the New DGS," *Duck of Minerva* (blog) July 2, 2014, http://duckofminerva.com/2014/07/an-open-letter-from-the-new-dgs.html.
84. Katherine G. Akers, "Going Beyond Data Management Planning: Comprehensive Research Data Services," *College & Research Libraries News* 75 (2014): 435–436, http://crln.acrl.org/content/75/8/435.full.
85. Soehner, Steeves, and Ward, "E-Science and Data Support Services."
86. Meier, "Replication: A View from the Streets," 458.

CHAPTER 15

Selection and Appraisal of Digital Research Datasets

Christopher Eaker

> *"Data is the currency of science .... To be able to exchange data, communicate it, mine it, reuse it, and review it is essential to scientific productivity, collaboration, and to discovery itself."*[1]
>
> ~ Anna Gold

ACADEMIC RESEARCH INSTITUTIONS are adding a new type of resource to their collections in today's data-intensive research environment. Historically, libraries have collected physical materials. More recently, libraries have purchased datasets for secondary use. And now, libraries are accepting digital research datasets for archiving. This move has become important as both public and private grant funding agencies are requiring that data from funded research be made publicly accessible and preserved. Emphasizing this, Paul Uhlir calls on academia to consider datasets as valuable assets that should be preserved rather than as disposable by-products of research.[2] Digital research datasets are different from the traditional items libraries historically have collected, and, therefore, have additional characteristics to consider when deciding whether to archive them.[3] How does an institution decide which datasets to accept into its collection? This chapter introduces selection and appraisal criteria and policies to help institutions answer that question.

The need for selection and appraisal policies lies upon the assumption that since scientific research is producing ever-increasing volumes of data, it is impossible to preserve it all.[4] Even if it were possible to preserve every dataset, some datasets do not need to be preserved.[5] For example, data generated by climate models are often discarded since they can be easily recreated by re-running the model. Furthermore, accuracy improves from one generation of a model to the next, so the data generated by an earlier generation is less precise than data obtained from a more current version. On the other hand, climate data gathered during a one-time event, such as a hurricane, cannot be reproduced and is, therefore, more valuable. For this reason, institutions need policies and criteria governing which datasets will be preserved and how to appraise them against those criteria.

Selection and appraisal policies are commonplace in academic libraries for traditional materials and even other digital collections, such as photographs or audio/video materials, but few have complementary policies for datasets. This chapter will introduce and explain the range of selection criteria institutions may consider when developing selection policies, such as scientific or historical value, scarcity, relevance to institutional mission, and others. Lastly, it will discuss life cycle management of datasets, including the periodic refreshing of files and determining when to deaccession, or remove, datasets from the collection. Readers will find an overview of the issues surrounding selection and appraisal of digital research datasets and will be equipped with the knowledge and resources to develop such policies in their institutions.

Definitions

Data, as defined in the introduction, are electronic files of information that have been collected systematically and structured to serve as input for research. For purposes of this chapter, the term *dataset* is defined as one or more files containing multiple data observations. *Metadata* are additional information accompanying a dataset that provides contextual information. Metadata takes the form of descriptive information about the project and its data and is necessary for discovery and crucial for reuse. A *selection policy* is a policy containing specific criteria outlining which types of materials will be accepted into an institution's collection. Selection policies may specify preferences for materials of certain subject matters over others. It may also include criteria pertaining to author/creator; for example, materials created by authors affiliated with a specific institution could be given higher priority. An *appraisal policy* is a policy that outlines a set of processes and procedures to determine if a specific resource meets the selection criteria and will be archived. Appraisal procedures may include tools such as checklists or decision trees, which are discussed in more detail later. The selection policy is the "What?" while the appraisal policy is the "How?"

A Brief History of Collection Development

Collection development of library resources, however rudimentary, has happened since libraries existed. Early libraries served mostly as places of preservation, not dissemination, of information. Today's libraries, however, exist not to keep information in a vault, but to share it with their user communities. These user communities, specifically their interests and characteristics, determine which resources libraries acquire. The term *selection* was originally applied to the process by which librarians determined which items to purchase for the library's collection. Later, in the 1960s, the term *collection development* emerged and implied more than simply selecting items to acquire, but also studying user communities and designing a collection to meet their needs. Even later, in the 1980s, the term *collection management* was introduced, which implied a life-cycle approach to managing a library's collection. Tasks ranged from studying the user community, selecting items to meet their needs, and periodically evaluating the items in the collection to determine whether they should continue to be supported or removed from the collection, a process known as *weeding*.[6] Appraisal and selection of digital materials is closely related to collection management in that files must be managed throughout their lifecycles, from ingest to disposition. It also contains aspects of collection development, as the choice of which datasets to obtain is, in part, related to how they will serve the user communities for which they are intended.

Developing Selection and Appraisal Policies

Development of selection and appraisal policies involves both practical and conceptual questions. Institutions may decide that digital datasets are covered under the traditional collection development policies already in place. However, digital datasets often have different requirements that need to be considered, such as intellectual property issues and the need for greater metadata about the projects that created the data, the data creators, and the data themselves. It is for this reason that Harvey says traditional selection and appraisal criteria cannot be applied to digital materials without some level of modification.[7] Thus, institutions may want to create separate policies regarding datasets because of the additional needs and different characteristics they have when compared to traditional materials. This determination must be based on what is best for the institution's operations.

The different intellectual property issues surrounding datasets often arise because the result of a research project may be a patentable product or procedure or a copyrightable work. The data generated in these projects support those copyrights and patents and are considered intellectual property. Intellectual property issues are discussed later in *Monetary Value*.

Additionally, datasets must have a high degree of metadata to make them useful for reuse. The data creators must provide information about the purpose of the project; the data collection, processing, and analysis techniques; the meaning of variable names; and the spatial and temporal coverages of the data. This information is crucial for data to be meaningful to researchers not originally involved in the research. Metadata are discussed in more detail later in *Level of Documentation*.

Selection Policy Criteria

Selection policies include criteria related to a dataset's content, authorship, value, and potential reuse to determine whether or not a dataset should be obtained for an institution's collection. Ideally, the institution evaluating the dataset for archiving should make this determination in coordination with the original data producer, who has the most intimate knowledge of the data. In their report "How to Appraise and Select Research Data for Curation," Whyte and Wilson[8] provide several criteria to consider when evaluating a potential dataset. Their criteria include relevance to institutional mission, value (scientific, monetary, and historical), scarcity, level of documentation, and readiness for redistribution. These criteria are also identified in Harvey's chapter "Appraisal and Selection" in the Digital Curation Centre's *Digital Curation Manual*, but Harvey goes further and adds vulnerability as an important criterion.[9] Institutions must evaluate each of these criteria and assess how each will be applied to archiving datasets at their institution.

Relevance to Institutional Mission

Relevance to institutional mission should be considered the primary primary criteria for judging which datasets are to be preserved. If a dataset does not serve an institution's mission, then its archiving should be considered a lower priority. For example, if an institution focuses heavily on marine sciences, then archiving a dataset about the effects of climate change on deepwater fish species would be a higher priority than archiving a dataset about deciduous trees in Kansas. Additionally, datasets produced by the institution's own researchers are relevant to the institution and may be considered a higher priority than those produced by researchers at another institution. Last, the institution's goals in archiving datasets is one more element of institutional relevance. In other words, if an institution's goal in archiving datasets is to support education of its students, then datasets that support educational opportunities are considered higher priorities than those that do not.

Institutional relevance also applies to data centers. Data centers archive datasets based on their mission, which is often dictated by their funders. For example, the Inter-University Consortium for Political and Social Research primarily archives datasets useful to social science and political science researchers.[10] Likewise, the Oak Ridge National Laboratory Distributed Active Archive Center focuses primarily on archiving datasets related to NASA's Terrestrial Ecology Program.[11] These data centers' selection policies are discussed in more detail later.

Value

Once it is determined that a dataset supports the needs of an institution's constituents, a further determination must be made based on a dataset's value. Value can be defined in one or more ways, including *scientific*, *historical*, and *monetary*.

Scientific Value. One primary purpose of archiving a dataset is to foster reuse in scientific research. Reuse of datasets serves two purposes: 1) supporting the replicability of the initial study and 2) supporting the creation of new knowledge beyond the data creator's original intent. Reproducibility of research allows for greater transparency and accountability, thereby increasing research integrity.[12] However, reusing research data can be challenging. For example, locating suitable data to answer a potential user's specific research question may be difficult, and even if a potential dataset is located, it may lack enough documentation to be useful.[13] Even so, Paul Uhlir indicates that the value of a dataset increases as it is reused for new research.[14] In other words, as more research is conducted with a dataset and new findings are discovered, its inherent value increases. In determining if a dataset should be archived, institutions must decide its potential and readiness to serve future, even unintended needs. This concept, called *analytic potential*, is determined by two main components: a dataset's fit for serving research outside the original field and its readiness for preservation.[15]

A dataset's potential to serve researchers in communities other than the originally intended community must be evaluated at the point of archiving. Which potential user communities may be able to reuse this data? Which potential research questions might this dataset be able to answer? The answers to these questions may be difficult to anticipate, but should be evaluated by the institution and the original data creator. Furthermore, to support future reuse, datasets must be fit for this purpose, which means the dataset is verified as high quality and is accompanied by adequate descriptive metadata. Quality assurance builds trust for the dataset and encourages its reuse in new research.[16]

Historical Value. Similarly to acquiring physical resources with scientific value, datasets having historical value may be considered a high priority for preservation.[17] Datasets with historical value may include those from research projects that were significant in scope or were especially groundbreaking. The Data Center is an example of how archiving historical data is central to an institution's mission. The

Data Center collects and maintains data related to southeastern Louisiana. After Hurricane Katrina in 2005, The Data Center began a special collection of data related to the storm's damages and the region's subsequent recovery.[18] Archiving of these datasets is part of preserving the record of a historical event, and thus their preservation might be considered a higher priority.

Monetary Value. Some datasets have monetary or commercial value and may support intellectual property, such as copyrights or patents. These datasets might be considered a high priority for preservation. Indeed, many institutions have policies governing the length of time a dataset must be preserved if it supports intellectual property. These datasets should be preserved for at least the life of the patent or copyright they support. However, in situations where data support intellectual property with monetary value, it may not be feasible to make them publicly available. Thus, the goal in these cases is simply preservation of the datasets rather than sharing.

Scarcity and Irreplaceability

Datasets that record a one-time occurrence are more valuable since the collection is unique and cannot be reproduced.[19] One example of irreplaceable data is data collected during the Deepwater Horizon oil spill in the Gulf of Mexico in 2010. These data were collected during an event that occurred once (we hope!) and can never be collected again. A dataset's scarcity also affects its historical value, thereby adding to the priority in the archiving decision. More commonplace situations where the scarcity principle governs are in the daily recording of weather conditions. Today's weather will not be repeated. In these cases, the institution should preserve the datasets and be careful to maintain accessibility.

Level of Documentation

As mentioned earlier, clearly described datasets are better suited to serving future research, both in the original discipline and in other disciplines.[20] The question must be asked: Will another researcher to be able to make sense of the dataset to reuse it for his or her research? If the answer is no, the institution should determine if it should supplement the metadata on its own. This may be possible in limited cases when the dataset meets other important criteria for acceptance. For example, if the dataset is valuable and cannot be replicated easily or at all, then the library may decide to accept the dataset and create the necessary metadata on its own. For example, when processing a submitted dataset for archiving, Oak Ridge National Laboratory Distributed Active Archive Center creates a document detailing the dataset. The level of documentation provided by the data creator varies, and when that is found lacking, DAAC staff will read publications that used the data to extract information important to reusing the dataset, such as procedures and variable used, which they will describe in the documentation. However, staffing levels and time constraints may prevent the institution from augmenting the metadata. Datasets initially provided with a high level of metadata should be considered higher priority than those without it.

Readiness for Redistribution

Datasets that contain sensitive information, such as medical information or locations of sensitive species, must be given extra attention to determine if this information has been properly and thoroughly removed.[21] Datasets that have been properly prepared for sharing may be given higher priority than those that have not. However, even if a dataset has been properly anonymized, it should not be made publicly available if the human participants in the research were not informed of this possibility when they agreed to participate in the research. This dataset must be embargoed unless other agreements or situations supersede the informed consent.

Vulnerability

Harvey adds vulnerability to the list of criteria to assess when making the determination of whether to archive a dataset.[22] Vulnerability is determined based on special requirements to read or access the data or the condition and age of the media on which they reside. For example, if the dataset requires special hardware or software to be accessed, it is considered vulnerable. The institution must determine if the additional cost to provide special access to the dataset outweighs the financial benefits of providing that access. Similarly, if the data are on aging media (over 15 years old) or on obsolete media, such as a 5.25-inch floppy disk, they are considered vulnerable. In situations where the data reside on vulnerable media, the institution may decide it is important to transfer the data from that media onto more stable media in order to provide continuing access.

Economic Viability

One final criterion for determining whether or not a dataset should be archived is the costs associated with preparation, archiving, and maintaining those data. Maintaining data accessibility over the long term is not free. Thus, institutions should estimate all associated costs and weigh them against the potential value of maintaining the dataset for future reuse. Costs should be estimated for items such as the storage space for hosting the data, the storage space for providing geographically dispersed backup copies, labor costs for periodic reappraisal and refreshing, and costs to serve up the data when requested.[23] The UK Data Service has produced a useful tool for estimating costs associating with managing and archiving research. It outlines eighteen activities with questions to consider and suggestions about how those activities add cost.[24]

Appraisal Policies

The selection policy must be accompanied by an appraisal policy that identifies procedures to follow each time a dataset is considered for preservation. These procedures reduce redundant activities, eliminate subjectivity, and improve the efficiency of the appraisal process. Appraisal policies should also include life-cycle management tasks, such as periodic refreshing, reappraisal, and deaccessioning. Those processes, as well as two helpful appraisal tools, are discussed below.

Checklists

Checklists help determine whether or not a dataset should be preserved by providing a clear outline of selection criteria. Checklists also reduce oversight by providing a list of all tasks that must be completed before an archival determination is made. The checklist should include all important items, and the institution's personnel must go through the list systematically to verify each item. Once the checklist has been completed, a determination can then be made whether or not to preserve the dataset based on the information the checklist provides. Does the dataset meet enough of the criteria on the checklist to warrant preservation? If so, it can be preserved. If not, the dataset can be rejected or sent back to the data producer for more information, if necessary.

Decision Trees

Decision trees are another helpful way of determining whether or not to preserve a dataset. Decision trees provide a graphical representation of a logical progression of thought. Questions are presented with possible answers. Each answer then leads to another possible question and set of answers. Once a path of questions and answers is exhausted, the end result is an answer of "YES, this item should be preserved," "NO, this item should not be preserved," or "MAYBE, this item may be preserved, but more information is needed." Decision trees take the guesswork out of appraisal and provide an objective answer rather than relying on sometimes subjective criteria. An example of a decision tree developed by the Digital Preservation Coalition is shown in Figure 15.1.

Figure 15.1. Example of an Appraisal Decision Tree

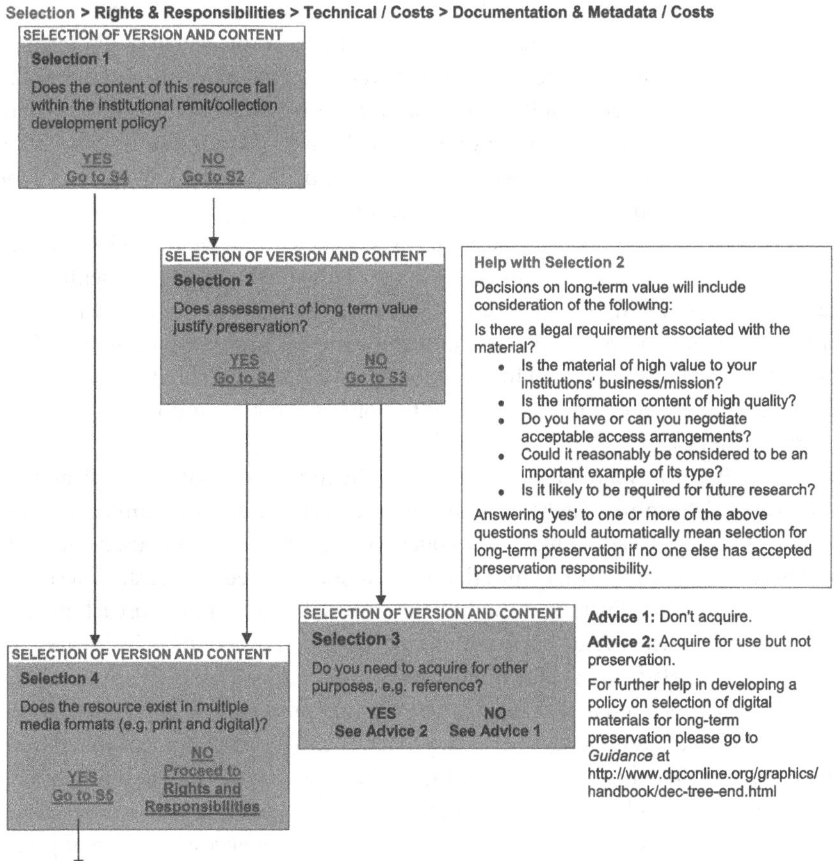

(Used with permission from Neil Beagrie, Maggie Jones, and Digital Preservation Coalition. *Preservation Management of Digital Materials: The Handbook*, 2008, http://www.dpconline.org/pages/handbook/)

Periodic Refreshing, Reappraisal, & Deaccessioning

Periodic reappraisal of preserved files serves two purposes: 1) to determine if the datasets are still accessible; and 2) to determine if continuing preservation is warranted. Long-term accessibility of digital files can be a challenge if steps are not taken to periodically check the files for file format obsolescence. If the file format is in danger of becoming obsolete, it should be refreshed to a newer format as necessary. However, in cases where file formats are periodically refreshed, it is important to remember that some special formatting may be lost in the process. In these cases, it must be determined whether or not saving the content is the most important goal, to the detriment of the formatting. File format obsolescence happens when the file formats in which the data were created are no longer supported by modern computer software and hardware. In these cases where file formats may become obsolete over time, institutions must migrate these data to newer file formats to maintain accessibility. To avoid format obsolescence, ideally the data should be initially archived in a preservation-friendly file format, such as .TXT for documents with textual information and Comma Separated Values (.CSV) for documents with tabular numerical information.

Likewise, files should be periodically checked for data degradation, also known as bit rot. Over time, physical storage media degrade, thus preventing access to the files stored on them. This degradation is a breakdown of the electrical, optical, or magnetic properties of the storage media, thus causing them to lose their ability to hold the digital information. To avoid this potentiality, institutions must continually check the integrity of the physical media and upgrade to new media as necessary.

In addition to maintaining accessibility, institutions should periodically reappraise to determine whether to continue preserving a dataset. Similar to a collections librarian weeding his or her collection based on changing usage patterns and user needs, libraries may find that they no longer need to maintain access to a particular dataset. Further, it might be discovered that there is a breach of confidentiality or a legal issue surrounding its continued archiving. This process of removing datasets from a collection is known as deaccessioning. There should be a process by which a dataset's need for continuing preservation is assessed. If it is determined that it is no longer necessary to maintain, it can be deaccessioned from the collection. Even in those situations, institutions may consider simply hiding the dataset from public view instead of permanently deleting it from the server, as a situation may arise when the dataset needs to be re-accessioned. In any case of deaccessioning, the archive should provide a note at the dataset's usual location explaining why it was deaccessioned and who to contact for more information or access.

Examples of Selection and Appraisal Policies

To demonstrate the types of selection and appraisal policies that currently exist and how they utilize the criteria previously explained, the following are descriptions of policies at data centers and academic institutions. While these examples are primarily from data repositories or data centers, they are meant to provide an example of the types of policies an academic institution might implement.

*Oak Ridge National Laboratory Distributed Active Archive Center (*http://daac.ornl.gov/*)*

The Oak Ridge National Laboratory Distributed Active Archive Center (DAAC) is a NASA-funded data archive that archives datasets about the interactions between the biological, geological, and chemical components of the Earth's environment from NASA's Terrestrial Ecology programs and projects.[25] Datasets in good condition when they are submitted to the DAAC, meaning they do not require much effort to prepare them for archiving, are given a higher priority than those that require extensive work or for which the data producers are less responsive to the DAAC's requests for information.

In addition to terrestrial ecology data, the DAAC will archive datasets associated with manuscripts. Many publishers now require data associated with their publications to be archived in a publicly accessible place. The DAAC provides a place for datasets related to its mission to be publicly accessible and, once archived, provides a Digital Object Identifier to the publisher for inclusion in the article. Last, the DAAC will also archive datasets recommended to it by its User Working Group, which is made up of researchers and scientists from other data centers and from universities across the United States. These datasets are given the lowest priority for archiving.

*Inter-university Consortium for Political and Social Research (*http://www.icpsr.umich.edu/*)*

The Inter-university Consortium for Political and Social Research (ICPSR) is a data archive that seeks to preserve and provide access to social science research data. In particular, datasets that show "demonstrated importance" to the research community are given high priority.[26] Emphasis areas may change over time, but currently include datasets that are interdisciplinary, complex, and focused on cultural diversity. These datasets are checked against the selection criteria, which include availability of data, confidentiality concerns, data quality, data documentation, and data format. Datasets that meet its selection criteria are curated and made available to the research community.

*The Odum Institute (*http://www.odum.unc.edu/*)*

The Odum Institute hosts a data archive based at the University of North Carolina at Chapel Hill. Similarly to ICPSR, the Odum Institute hosts significant social science datasets and provides access to them via the Dataverse network of repositories. The archive solicits datasets and then determines if they meet their selection criteria by using an appraisal checklist.[27] The Odum Institute's criteria include institutional mission and different aspects of the dataset's value, namely its scientific value, historical value, and monetary value. In addition to value, the archive looks at the level of documentation and whether it is complete and readable.

Based on the results of the appraisal checklist and the dataset's current level of documentation and preparation, the dataset undergoes varying levels of processing. Minimal processing is conducted on datasets that come to the archive with a high level of documentation already completed and in the preferred data format (SPSS or Stata). Datasets that have a lower level of documentation may undergo a high level of processing called "routing processing." Datasets considered especially important or valuable or are part of multi-site or multi-year studies may undergo a high level of processing called "intensive processing."[28] In these cases, the archive has determined the extra processing required to prepare the dataset for ingest is warranted due to its high value.

University of Minnesota Libraries (https://www.lib.umn.edu/)

The University of Minnesota (UM) Libraries' data repository requires that at least one of the dataset's producers be a researcher at that university.[29] It also requires data depositors to make sure their datasets are prepared properly before submitting them to the repo7sitory. Proper preparation includes providing files in a preservation-friendly file format, providing an adequate level of metadata, and ensuring any sensitive information has been removed. Datasets are expected to be open access once deposited, and all go through a curatorial review process before submission to ensure compliance with the selection criteria.

Conclusion

After an extensive search for samples of selection and appraisal policies and requests for written policies from colleagues at academic libraries, it became clear that it is far more common for data centers to have publicly accessible, written policies than it is for academic libraries. Academic libraries have only recently begun archiving datasets as a part of their collection, and many still do not have data repositories in place. Those having data repositories may be processing ingest of datasets on a case-by-case basis without written policies. Even so, it is important to be proactive rather than reactive. Having a policy in place before researchers require services would help eliminate confusion and uncertainty. An additional benefit of establishing selection criteria and appraisal procedures is that academic institutions, namely academic libraries, will have a clearer understanding of the types of datasets they want in their collections. This clarity will help when determining how to promote their repository services by identifying where to focus outreach efforts. Especially now that almost all federal granting agencies and many private granting agencies require the results of research they fund to be publicly accessible, data archiving services are becoming increasingly important and valuable services. Having well-described, trusted datasets in its institutional repository will improve not only an institution's reputation, but also the reputations of its researchers.[30]

---

1. Anna K. Gold, "Cyberinfrastructure, Data, and Libraries, Part 1: A Cyberinfrastructure Primer for Librarians," *D-Lib Magazine* 13, no. 9/10 (2007), doi: 10.1045/september20september-gold-pt1.
2. Paul F. Uhlir, "Information Gulags, Intellectual Straightjackets, and Memory Holes: Three Principles to Guide the Preservation of Scientific Data," *Data Science Journal* 9 (2010):ES1-ES5, doi: 10.2481/dsj.Essay-001-Uhlir.
3. Ross Harvey, "Appraisal and Selection," *DCC Digital Curation Manual*, January 2007, http://www.dcc.ac.uk/resources/curation-reference-manual.
4. Angus Whyte and Andrew Wilson. "How to Appraise and Select Research Data for Curation," *DCC How-to-Guides* (Edinburgh: Digital Curation Centre, 2010), http://www.dcc.ac.uk/resources/how-guides/appraise-select-data.
5. Ross Harvey, "Appraisal and Selection."
6. Peggy Johnson, *Fundamentals of Collection Development and Management* (Chicago: ALA Editions, 2014).
7. Ross Harvey, "Appraisal and Selection."
8. Angus Whyte and Andrew Wilson. "How to Appraise and Select Research Data for Curation."
9. Ross Harvey, "Appraisal and Selection."
10. Inter-university Consortium for Political and Social Research, "ICPSR Collection Development Policy," accessed April 27, 2015, http://www.icpsr.umich.edu/icpsrweb/content/datamanagement/policies/colldev.html.
11. Les Hook, personal communication regarding ORNL DAAC selection policies, 2014.
12. Louise Corti, Veerle Van den Eynden, Libby Bishop, and Matthew Woollard, *Managing and Sharing Research Data: A Guide to Good Practice* (London: Sage Publications Ltd. 2014).
13. Ibid.
14. Paul F. Uhlir, "Information Gulags, Intellectual Straightjackets, and Memory Holes."
15. Carole L. Palmer, Nicholas M Weber, and Melissa H Cragin, "The Analytic Potential of Scientific Data: Understanding Re-Use Value," *Proceedings of the American Society for Information Science and Technology* 48, no. 1 (2011):1–10, doi: 10.1002/meet.2011.14504801174.
16. Ibid.
17. Angus Whyte and Andrew Wilson. "How to Appraise and Select Research Data for Curation."
18. The Data Center, "Katrina-Related Data," 2015, http://www.datacenterresearch.org/data-resources/katrina/.
19. Ibid.
20. Ibid.
21. Ibid.
22. Ross Harvey, "Appraisal and Selection."
23. Angus Whyte and Andrew Wilson. "How to Appraise and Select Research Data for Curation."
24. UK Data Service, "Data Management Costing Tool," 2013, September 2015, http://www.data-archive.ac.uk/create-manage/planning-for-sharing/costing.
25. Les Hook, personal communication regarding ORNL DAAC selection policies, 2014.
26. Inter-university Consortium for Political and Social Research, "ICPSR Collection Development Policy," accessed April 27, 2015, http://www.icpsr.umich.edu/icpsrweb/content/datamanagement/policies/colldev.html.

27. The Odum Institute, "Appraisal, Content Selection, Acquisition and Processing Policies," accessed April 27, 2015, http://www.odum.unc.edu/odum/contentSubpage.jsp?nodeid=627.
28. Ibid.
29. University of Minnesota Libraries, "Data Repository for U of M: About the Data Repository." 2014, https://conservancy.umn.edu/pages/drum/.
30. University of California Santa Barbara, "Data Curation and Management," accessed April 27, 2015, http://www.library.ucsb.edu/scholarly-communication/data-curation-management.

CHAPTER 16

Local Data Success Story:

The University of Calgary Library's Ten Years with the City of Calgary

Susan McKee

AS WITH MOST academic libraries in Canada, the University of Calgary Library has a specialized unit that collects, manages, and delivers geospatial and statistical data to students and researchers, as well as providing data software and related services. The Maps, Academic Data, Geographic Information Centre (MADGIC) was created in 1999; MADGIC combined the library's existing Map and Airphoto Collection unit with the library's Academic Data Centre. Like other libraries with cartographic collections, MADGIC's geospatial data services developed as an extension of the map and air photo services. Geospatial and academic (statistical) data differ in theme, structure, and user groups but were natural partners in the merged unit.

At that time, MADGIC had access to Statistics Canada data and geography files, a small collection of national and provincial-level geospatial data, and data software. However, there was a lack of local data in the collection, in particular for the City of Calgary, which like many municipalities creates a large amount of geospatial and other data files.[1] Up to the mid-2000s, campus students and researchers could only obtain Calgary geospatial files by purchase from the city, but there was a growing demand for this level of data on campus. Researchers and students who wished to carry out city-related projects were frustrated with the lack of availability of local data in MADGIC's collection. After several years of requests and negotiation by MADGIC staff, in 2004 we signed a three-year academic license with the City of Calgary for a few geospatial data files. Ten years later, Spatial and Numeric Data Services (SANDS, formerly MADGIC) renewed our agreement with the city for the third time. The situation has changed substantially, as SANDS now manages a large collection of local geospatial data and provides specialized data reference services for campus users. This chapter will discuss the acquisition of City of Calgary data files for the library's collection, other local data developments, SANDS reference services, and the challenges involved with managing this collection. Finally, it provides suggestions for other libraries interested in acquiring local data.

Data Collections in the Early 2000s

By the early 2000s, data and GIS units in Canadian academic libraries were well established. Data collections were growing, GIS and other data software was available, and libraries were providing various levels of data services, from basic data delivery to advanced mapping.[2] At that time most data files were licensed for academic use only; this meant that data were restricted to an institution's students and researchers. Some national and provincial datasets, such as the DMTI SMART program[3] and the National Topographic Data Base,[4] were acquired through library consortiums, an efficient and cost-effective method of collection development. However, though there was now national and provincial level data available, most Canadian libraries did not have local municipal data in their collections. One early success story came from the University of Ottawa and Carleton University, where an agreement was reached in 1998 for local data from the Regional Municipality of Ottawa-Carleton and the National Capital Commission.[5]

There has always been strong interest in this level of data on university campuses. Local data provide a greater level of detail and accuracy than national or provincial level datasets, and students and researchers are interested in local projects. Also, with local data, instructors can include fieldwork as an element of class assignments. Unfortunately, prior to the 2000's, there was reluctance on the part of many municipalities to engage in data provision to academic institutions. Municipalities often operated under a business model that did not allow for academic licensing. Also there were concerns about data liability and fear of data leakage to commercial users. To overcome these concerns, data librarians across Canada worked on the important task of trust and relationship building with local data providers.[6]

Data at the University of Calgary

In the early 2000s demand for City of Calgary geospatial data was high on campus, in particular from the Planning, Architecture, Geography, Geomatics Engineering, and Urban Studies programs. MADGIC received frequent requests for local data, as many as several a week, which we passed on to the city. Also, city staff regularly fielded requests for data directly from students and researchers from the University of Calgary and other city educational institutions. University of Calgary researchers and city departments had a history of working together on municipal projects, where local data were provided in exchange for research results. However, data-sharing policies at the city were not consistent over the years, and payment and licenses were sometimes required.[7]

MADGIC had a pre-existing relationship with the city's cartographic unit. From the 1970s to the 1990s, the Map and Airphoto unit had received donations of historic Calgary maps and photos for the collection. We also regularly purchased city maps and air photos and had built up a substantial collection of these materials. This collection was available to the public as well as students for viewing and sign out. Our local map and air photo collection was heavily used, and the air photos remain very popular.

In response to the demand for local data, MADGIC approached the city's GIS unit in 2002 with a proposal for an academic data license agreement. Unfortunately, at that time we did not have contacts in that department; they were not aware of us or our data collection and likely did not perceive us as GIS experts. The city didn't recognize our growing data collection and skills, but we felt we were ready to take on this agreement. By 2002 we had proven experience not only with cartographic materials and data but also with data licensing. MADGIC had already successfully negotiated the GEODE license with AltaLIS, distributor for Alberta government GIS data.[8] This ongoing agreement provided access to provincial geospatial datasets for a consortium of academic libraries in Alberta.

Some of the arguments that MADGIC used in discussions with city representatives in 2002 included: we were experienced with data licensing and management; data was needed to train students and advance academic research; with the data, researchers could undertake studies on important city issues; and we could assume the role of data intermediary and thus take that burden off city staff. Unfortunately we could not claim to have great data management practices; at that time our data was stored on CD-ROMs rather than a secure repository. The city was reluctant. Their concerns were similar to those experienced in the early days of national and provincial data licensing, characterized by fears of liability for incorrect data and data management and security issues. The city had always sold their data to businesses and individuals, so the concept of academic licensing was unknown.

MADGIC was persistent and after a series of meetings the city finally agreed to our proposal. In 2004 we signed a three-year educational license. We believe one of the factors involved was the amount of time city staff spent fielding requests from campus data users. By giving us some data, they assumed the requests might slow down or stop. We were provided with a set of data files for academic use, fortunately at no charge. The city signed similar agreements with two other local educational institutions, SAIT (Southern Alberta Institute of Technology) and Mount Royal College (now University). In hindsight, MADGIC could have tried a collective approach with the other local academic libraries; however at that time we were unaware of their interest. A collective or consortium type approach to negotiating, similar to the University of Ottawa's experience mentioned above, probably would have given more strength to our position.

The data package we received was small, consisting of twenty-eight DAS (Digital Aerial Survey)[9] files, DEMs (digital elevation models), and cadastral files covering the downtown and communities in the northwest, and a few city-wide base files (roads, water, boundaries). The city wanted MADGIC to hold only about 10% of the detailed DAS set that covered the entire city. There was no reason given for this decision, but we assumed they were reluctant to provide a large amount of data because it was a new and untested venture. At that time all data was in CAD file format. This was popular with architecture students who used AutoCAD software, but other campus users preferred shapefiles for use with ArcGIS software.

All users were required to pick up the files at the MADGIC desk and sign a data release agreement. The terms of the agreement included using the data for educational purposes only, maintaining data security, and returning the data when no longer needed. Students and researchers were pleased to have access to some local data, but MADGIC continued to get requests for data covering other themes and areas of the city. At that time the city did not wish to discuss the agreement further or expand the data package, despite our requests. In 2007 MADGIC's agreement with the city was renewed for another three years, and we received a refresh of the original data package.

A few years later, there were several positive changes that affected our data agreement and collection. By 2009 there was a more open attitude to data provision at the city and a climate of closer relationships with the academic research community. Also the city was continuing to receive numerous data requests directly from students and researchers. By this time they were more confident that MADGIC was managing the data within the terms of our license. We were good data stewards, getting data release agreements signed, and there had not been any data leakage. With this more open climate and confidence, they were willing to meet with us once again to discuss the agreement.

With some persuasion, we were able to change the original three-year data package refresh model to a system of data by request. MADGIC would act as intermediary for campus data requests. If we did not have the data files we could simply ask, and in most cases they were supplied. Also, for the first time, a city staff member was appointed as our contact for data requests. The new files we received were informally added to our data license. From that year, our city data collection grew rapidly, although we were still not allowed to have the entire DAS set. At about the same time, MADGIC finally got access to a secure file server for better data management.

A significant local data development was the launch of the city's Public Data Catalogue in 2010. At this time, the open data movement, where government departments make data freely available, was starting to spread across Canada.[10]

Along with the federal and provincial levels, many municipalities across Canada participated in this initiative. Delivery platforms, data files, and goals and motivations vary greatly among municipalities.[11] Calgary's original pilot project was restructured in 2013 and renamed the Open Data Catalogue, making data easier to download with fewer restrictions.[12] Open data access is a policy challenge for the City of Calgary; they are committed to providing open data but at the same time want to generate revenue through data licensing.[13] A few of the open data files are identical to the licensed city files in our collection; others are similar but with less detail and fewer attributes. There are a number of open files that we do not have, such as the city's Civic Census in shapefile format.

SANDS (formerly MADGIC) joined the local Community Data Program in 2013.[14] An initiative of the Canadian Council on Social Development, this is a national network of more than twenty municipal consortia that purchase mainly socio-economic data files at the smallest geographies possible. Through this City of Calgary-led program, SANDS has access to federal Census and National Housing Survey files at the community level and other custom products from Statistics Canada, Environics Analytics, and other sources. Custom community-level Census products are among the most heavily used data files on campus.

In 2014 SANDS celebrated our ten-year anniversary with the City of Calgary and again renewed our data license agreement. We now have a large collection of city-wide shapefiles, DEMs, orthophotos, cad format utility and cadastral files, and the entire DAS set. Even though we now have the complete DAS set, there is still a restriction in that we can only provide nine files at a time. Our city data files are in constant use by campus students and researchers for class assignments and projects.

About SANDS and Data Services

Spatial and Numeric Data Services is a small library unit with four staff members—two librarians and two support staff. Data and GIS are specialized areas that require years of experience and training to master, and staff skill levels vary widely. Ideally, in a combined data and GIS unit, all staff would be knowledgeable in both areas, but in reality staff tend to specialize in one area or the other. Training can take place through formal courses and tutorials or by informally watching or shadowing other experienced staff. Also we have two other library staff members that help out at the desk at busy periods. We provided some initial training for them, but most learning takes place through hands-on experience at the reference desk. When unable to answer a question, staff call for backup or refer the question for later follow up.

We maintain a large collection of spatial and numeric data from a variety of sources, as well as cartographic materials. Collecting the data involves downloading new files as they become available, processing the files, and loading them to our file server and reference desk hard drives. We also maintain web guides for information and data access.[15] The data files on our file server are available to campus users remotely, with the exception of city data. The City of Calgary does not allow SANDS to provide remote access to their data, so users must visit the SANDS desk in person. All users of city data must sign a hard copy data release agreement for licensed files. No other data providers require this.

Data files in general are not easy to find, so many users come to our desk for assistance with finding and downloading data. SANDS staff perform a mediated service: users tell us about their projects and what types of data they are interested in; we advise on what is available and assist with downloading. Also, we are often asked to assist with opening and manipulating data files in our data and GIS software. This specialized reference service involves an in-depth knowledge of the data collection—including sources, themes, and file types—and also software skills. Software assistance is a growth area for us; for many users, there is no other place on campus to get technical assistance. Producing basic maps using ArcGIS software and data is another service that we provide for users. We offer these reference and technical assistance services to all students, undergraduate and graduate, and researchers.

Our growing data collection has led to increased workload, and our service levels have become more sophisticated as we learn more about data and software. Also, SANDS increasingly acts as data intermediary with the city for student and researcher data needs; we relay requests for data we do not have in our collection and download and distribute files as they are sent to us. We work closely with our city contact for data requests. This is an informal and successful arrangement that evolved over the years of our agreement; it is an efficient method of data discovery and saves the time of city staff. Users are pleased to have their city data needs fulfilled but are sometimes frustrated with wait times and the need to pick up files in person at the SANDS desk and sign the city's data release agreement.

Challenges

There are some ongoing challenges with our city data collection. First, the city continues to require a signed hard copy data release agreement for all licensed files. This is a procedural relic. Users do not like signing the form and do not always understand the purpose, and it is unlikely that most users remember the terms of the agreement after they have signed it. However, the city still wants to be able to track individual users to ensure compliance with the license terms. We continue to store the hard copy agreements in case the city wants to look at them. This has never happened, although we do get regular requests for statistics on usage.

Second, remote access is a challenge. SANDS has a file server for data management and remote access to data files, but the city does not want their data remotely accessed. Access to licensed city data remains a mediated in-person service where users must come to our desk to get data during SANDS open hours. In addition, as our collection grows, this mediated service becomes more challenging. SANDS staff must retain a detailed knowledge of the data collection, both licensed and open, in order to respond to requests. Staff are not equally knowledgeable of the collection or skilled with data and GIS software, so ongoing training and back-up availability for questions is important.

Finally, the open data has created new user expectations. Users are finding and using the city's open data portal, but generally these files are not sufficient for a project or assignment, and users also need licensed data from the SANDS collection. Open data has likely increased demand for our services, but because of our mediated service the impact remains to be seen. We do not know if there will be more open data available in the future, since the city continues to use their data as a revenue generator.

Suggestions for Libraries

For other library data units contemplating acquiring local data and developing a similar reference service, here are some suggestions and lessons that SANDS learned.

- Develop data expertise: Dedicated GIS and data librarians and staff with a good knowledge of GIS and data files and software are essential. Service levels can range from basic data delivery to advanced software assistance. More advanced reference service, including mediated service, develops with experience, collection size, and campus demand.
- Data management: Having a secure data repository or file server is important, as it provides evidence of proper data management practices and data security.
- Relationship building: Contacts are valuable. Take any opportunity to meet and get to know local data providers. This could be done through attendance at seminars and conferences or informal gatherings such as open houses and GIS events.
- Collective approach: Seek out partners in the community. A group of libraries with similar local data needs can make a stronger case to a data provider than a single institution.
- Data intermediary role: Local data providers spend a lot of time with campus requests. Point out the time-saving benefits of taking this burden off their staff.
- Value of local data: Emphasize to the data provider that local data are valuable not only for training students, but also for research on pressing local issues.
- Start small: Start with a small local data collection and prove your competence, then push for expansion.

- Be persistent: Keep trying if initial efforts to acquire local data are unsuccessful.

Conclusion

Spatial and Numeric Data Services has acquired a large geospatial data collection over the last ten years. Although it happened slowly, we have moved from a climate of reluctance to one of confidence and cooperation with our local data provider. At the same time, SANDS data and GIS reference services have evolved and matured to a more advanced level. Ten years after our first city data agreement was signed, we consider our local data experience a success.

SANDS now manages a robust city geospatial data collection of well over a thousand files; city data represent about 75% of SANDS total geospatial data usage. Use of the city collection has increased along with growth of the collection. Data and GIS files are used extensively for research projects and assignments in Planning, Architecture, Geography, Engineering, and Urban Studies, but we also have growing interest from users in the social and natural sciences. SANDS and the University of Calgary are very fortunate to have this extensive local geospatial data collection and we look forward to many more years with the city. We are very grateful to the City of Calgary for providing their data to the campus.

---

1. City of Calgary, "CITYonline," accessed April 7, 2015, https://cityonline.calgary.ca/Pages/Home.aspx.
2. Colleen Beard, "Reference Service Levels for Spatial Data Delivery and GIS Activity in Libraries: A Local Assessment," *Association of Canadian Map Libraries and Archives Bulletin* no. 118 (2003): 14.
3. Directions Magazine, "DMTI Spatial Celebrates Ten Years of Support to Canadian Academia with SMART Program," accessed July 21, 2015, http://www.directionsmag.com/pressreleases/dmti-spatial-celebrates-ten-years-of-support-to-canadian-academia-with-smar/233158.
4. James Boxall, "Advances and Trends in Geospatial Information Accessibility—Part I," *Journal of Map & Geography Libraries* 1, no, 1 (2004): 22, doi: 10.1300/J23v01n01_02.
5. Heather McAdam-Ferrarotto and Grace Welch, "Inter-Library Cooperation for GIS Services: A Road to Success," *Association of Canadian Map Libraries and Archives Bulletin* no. 111 (2001): 14.
6. Richard Pinnell, Richard Grignon, and Laura Cole, "Forging Municipal Partnerships for Data Acquisition" (presentation for Association of Canadian Map Libraries and Archives Conference, Montreal, Quebec, May 30–June 2, 2001).
7. Nigel Waters, "Imagine Calgary as a GIS-Friendly City," *Geoworld* 19, no. 2 (2006): 18–19.
8. Laurie Schretlen and Leah Vanderjagt, "Fundamentals of Geographic Information Systems and Spatial Data (presentation for Netspeed Conference, Edmonton, Alberta, October 20, 2005), https://www.ualberta.ca/~leahv/Netspeed-GIS.ppt.
9. City of Calgary, "Digital Aerial Survey," accessed April 7, 2015, http://www.calgary.ca/CS/IIS/Pages/Mapping-products/Digital-Aerial-Survey.aspx.
10. Government of Canada, "Open Government Across Canada," accessed April 17, 2015, http://open.canada.ca/en/maps/open-data-canada.

11. Liam James Currie, "The Role of Canadian Municipal Open Data Initiatives: A Multi-City Evaluation" (M.A., Queen's University, Canada, 2013), http://search.proquest.com/docview/1511453884?accountid=9838.
12. City of Calgary, "Open Data Catalogue," accessed April 7, 2015, http://www.calgary.ca/CS/IIS/Pages/Licensing-city-data/Open-Data_Catalogue.aspx.
13. Dale McNamee, "Open Data at the City of Calgary" (presentation for the Office of the Information and Privacy Commissioners' Right to Know Forum, Calgary, Alberta, September 2014), http://www.oipc.ab.ca/Content_Files/Files/Docs/CoC_Open_Data_RTK_2014.pdf.
14. Canadian Council on Social Development, "Community Data Program: CCSD's Flagship Initiative," accessed April 7, 2015, http://communitydata.ca/.
15. "Spatial and Numeric Data Services," accessed April 20, 2015, http://library.ucalgary.ca/sands.

CHAPTER 17

Metadata for Social Science Data:

Collaborative Best Practices

Jane Fry and Amber Leahey

IN CANADA, SOCIAL science data libraries and archives have existed since the mid-1960s, with some academic departments and libraries establishing data reference services.[1] The Social Science Data Archives at Carleton University in 1965 and the Data Library at the University of British Columbia in the 1970s are examples of this early establishment in Canada.[2] As previous chapters have discussed, data resources found in library collections may include licensed or commercial data, institutional data, government data, and research data (i.e., data produced for the purpose of generating original research results). Data types found in libraries can include survey microdata, aggregate data, and databases. Other data resources provided include training workshops and statistical consultations for statistical analysis software packages and GIS software.

In 2012, the Data Liberation Initiative (DLI) division of Statistics Canada conducted a survey of its contacts who help users with their data needs and found that the majority of these specialists help their users find datasets from surveys, including individual-level microdata, aggregate data, and other statistical products.[3] In addition to answering data reference questions, most provide training on the use of DLI data, which primarily consists of social and economic survey microdata and aggregate data. The widespread adoption of these services illustrates the need to make data findable and useable in libraries, and as such, data librarians need to be able to ensure that data, regardless of type, have sufficient metadata to inform the user. Metadata are especially important for data librarians and those who are tasked with finding, selecting, providing access to, and facilitating secondary use of data resources.

From Cataloging to Metadata

Libraries provide cataloging for items in a library's collection to enable the discovery, access, and retrieval of resources. Effective cataloging provides the necessary information about the item, its abstract, its subject, where it is located (physical or digital), and how to access it. Cataloged records often appear in a library database in MARC record format. Since it was introduced in the mid-1960s, MARC has been used as the main format standard for the library catalog, using the Anglo-American Cataloging Rule (AACR) as a content standard for description.[4] MARC, however, only provides a minimal set of descriptive elements, often not sufficient or appropriate for the description of numeric datasets. Data are rarely described or cataloged using MARC in libraries, and early attempts to do so relied heavily on a physical (paper) data codebook in the library's collection to provide additional documentation.[5] The catalyst of change for the description of numeric data files from cataloging to metadata, including survey microdata in libraries, was largely due to the increasing volume of descriptive information required for machine-readable data files and accompanying documentation.[6]

Since raw data are rarely self-explanatory, metadata are required to ensure data are easily findable, understood, and managed appropriately in a library or archive. Without appropriate metadata, it would be very time consuming (if not impossible) to determine the relevance of a raw dataset for secondary use. Examining a raw numeric data file provides a good illustration of the importance of metadata for social science datasets. A numeric data file consists of numbers or alphanumeric codes with no apparent order or logic (see Figure 17.1). The data that appear are representing something much richer than what appears at first glance; when examined line-by- line, the data can represent individual responses to a survey, cases,[†] categories, codes, or variables[‡] that are part of a larger research study.

A study that seeks to understand people's sense of belonging to their community might look at multiple characteristics related to feelings of "belonging," such as closeness to neighbors, or use of local recreational facilities, and these representations may be developed for analytical purposes and coded as "variables" in a dataset. The use of variables and concepts is a common practice in social science research, and documentation should support these important dataset elements. At a basic level, metadata facilitate understanding of the raw dataset, including cases and variables, which is necessary for replication and reuse of the data.

---

† Cases represent individual responses or observations to a particular research test or instrument used for data collection, such as a question asked in a survey questionnaire.

‡ Variables found in a dataset can represent coded or summarized responses to questions in a survey. Variables can also represent complex concepts made up of multiple observations or instruments such as questions asked in a survey.

Figure 17.1. Excerpt from a Dataset


```
1000014646904322221661614133333222112221222212222222222266 902 903996699669966 901996699669
10000235359013211222616141141131142122222222222222222669966 501996699669966996699669
100003595990122112166121321111314411222222222222122221226 904  349966996699669966996699669
100004353590412112166 4 41411161442222112121221122222121226996699669966 284 2129966  249
100005242490131222661 3 3246666666666666666666666666666669966996699669966996699669
100006121290131422661 3 3246666666666666666666666666666669966996699669966996699669
100007242490132322166 5 6144121213112122222222222222112266 282  439966  149966996699669
100008474790122612166 5 72421132342222122222222222222226699669966996699669966  249966996699669
100009353590421112661 3 3246666666666666666666666666666669966996699669966996699669
100010464690132522226 5 7245722103221112222222212222222226699669966 124 122 901996699669669
1000113535904421121661313235225103222222222222222222222166996699669966996699669966
10001213139012232216612121382244932122122222222222222669966  7499669966  249966996699669
100013131390141421661 4 5246666666666666666666666666666669966996699669966996699669
100014464690331522661 4 4146666666666666666666666666666669966996699669966996699669
1000153535903224211661614133533122222222222222222222221669966996699669966996699669
100016484890142322166 8101421142342222222222222222222121299669966996699669966996699669
100017242490141612666 2 2246666666666666666666666666666669966996699669966996699669
100018474790142712166 5 724322312312122222222222212221222266 9019966  3399669966996699669
100019353590342322166 5 61421332322212222222122122222122669966996699669966  21996699669966996699669
100020353590441522661 4 5246666666666666666666666666666669966996699669966996699669
1000212424901424222261212122113234122121222222222212222266 36399669966 6049966 242996699669
100022474790131612666 2 2246666666666666666666666666666669966996699669966996699669
100023464690132112166 8101421231331222222222222222222222266 182996699669966996699669
100024242490112422166 8112311132441222222222112222222222266 363996699669966996699669
100025353590231112661 4 5246666666666666666666666666666669966996699669966996699669
```


Source: Statistics Canada. "Canadian Community Health Survey, 2005, Cycle 2.2 [Public-Use Microdata File]." 2005.

Typically, a codebook (also referred to as a data dictionary) is needed to make sense of the dataset. The codebook features detailed metadata about what the data actually mean or represent, including the position and length of a variable, the provenance of a variable, codes, and summary counts (see Figure 17.2).

Figure 17.2. Excerpt from a Codebook

Variable Name GEOEGPRV **Length** 2 **Position** 7 - 8

Question Name

Concept Province of residence of respondent - (G)

Question

Universe All respondents

Note

Content	Code	Sample	Population
NEWFOUNDLAND AND LABRADOR	10	4,111	448,812
PRINCE EDWARD ISLAND	11	2,031	117,478
NOVA SCOTIA	12	5,066	795,983
NEW BRUNSWICK	13	5,100	638,232
QUEBEC	24	29,165	6,467,615
ONTARIO	35	41,766	10,570,076
MANITOBA	46	7,352	935,340
SASKATCHEWAN	47	7,765	787,765
ALBERTA	48	11,800	2,686,119
BRITISH COLUMBIA	59	15,407	3,601,945
YUKON/NORTHWEST/NUNAVUT TERRITORIES	60	2,658	76,800
Total		132,221	27,126,165

Source: Statistics Canada. "Canadian Community Health Survey, 2005, Cycle 2.2 [Data Dictionary]." 2005.

Standards for the Description of Data

Since the early 2000s, emerging web content standards, including the Dublin Core metadata standard, have been widely used in libraries and digital archives for the description of many kinds of digital objects in repositories. The emergence of metadata standards, including Dublin Core, is largely attributed to the need to provide resource description for a wide variety of information and resources, including born-digital objects and non-traditional formats, which require metadata for discovery and access in online repositories.[7] Metadata, simply put, are information about data, including descriptions of the study, methodology, associated files, and variable information. An example of metadata for data would be the study abstract that usually accompanies a survey dataset to inform a secondary user. Without the abstract, the researcher would have to read through any documentation associated with the survey to ascertain its purpose and any other relevant information. This abstract helps the researcher to determine the usability of a particular survey for their research. In addition, metadata in machine-readable formats, such as extensible markup language (XML), enable computer software and systems to read, search, and use metadata alongside data for statistical analyses.

Dublin Core is used by digital library projects worldwide, especially in archival and repository systems, such as the Open Archives Initiative and DSpace. Dublin Core provides a simple, interoperable, and semantic web-enabled set of elements for the description of digital objects, including digital scientific data.[8] With the advent of research data repositories and archival systems, such as DSpace and the Dryad repository (http://datadryad.org/) for scientific datasets, metadata standards such as Dublin Core play an important role in making repository systems interoperable, and have facilitated improved access to research data worldwide.[9] However, there are other descriptive metadata standards that provide more detailed description for datasets in particular. Dublin Core only provides a set of top-level elements to describe a dataset's study and descriptive elements for discovery purposes, not the internal data elements, such as the variables, required for deep content searching and reuse in statistical analysis software.

The DataCite metadata schema provides a set of descriptive elements based on Dublin Core and aims to improve the ubiquitous discovery and access to datasets online. DataCite has also been instrumental in promoting the need for and ability to systematically cite data in scholarly research publications, supporting the digital object identifier (DOI) standard for persistent identification and access to data. The incorporation of dataset publication into the traditional academic publishing and accreditation process requires effective metadata and data standards, especially as it relates to the ability to properly identify data and replicate research findings. DataCite provides a centralized registry of datasets registered with a DOI and this has been a tremendous contribution to the data community around the promotion and improvement of data citation in scholarly research and publishing.

Both Dublin Core and DataCite attach descriptive metadata to digital objects, but unlike embedded standards, neither standard considers the structure or inherent content of the resource to be part of the core elements for description.[10] Embedded standards, such as the Text Encoding Initiative (TEI), embed markup into the document or dataset itself, providing documentation on individual elements within the object as well as on the object as a whole. The use of embedded markup for datasets is an important aspect to making data findable, comprehensible, and reusable.

Other metadata standards are rooted in disciplinary or domain knowledge, such as the FGDC-CSDGM (digital geospatial metadata) and ISO 19115 (digital geographic metadata standard) for geographic and earth science information, and have varying opportunities for application across academic disciplines and in libraries. One such standard, the Data Documentation Initiative (DDI) standard, comes out of the social sciences and offers a rich set of descriptive and structural metadata elements for describing social science research datasets in libraries and data archives, and includes descriptors such as publisher, data type, data collection information, spatial and temporal parameters, variables, and concepts.

The Data Documentation Initiative (DDI)

DDI was first envisioned in 1995 as a metadata standard that aimed to reproduce a full dataset codebook (see Figure 17.2) to describe and exchange data and metadata in machine-readable form.[11] DDI includes a set of study-level elements, as well as file and variable-level elements, to enable the description and embedded markup of the dataset's content (including variables, categories, cases, etc.). Simply put, DDI provides a set of specialized vocabulary to appropriately describe and capture data throughout the full data lifecycle. In this way, DDI facilitates the markup of datasets by providing a consistent language and set of machine-actionable elements necessary for the effective management and reuse of datasets and the accompanying metadata that is required to understand data. Consistency and granularity of metadata, especially if it is enabled by the use of standards including DDI, vastly improves the ability to search across datasets. As a result, end users of the data can easily discover and select datasets on a particular subject or topic, access variable-level metadata, and exchange and reuse data and metadata elements easily. Beyond discovery and access, rich metadata help to inform appropriate reuse and replication of data for a variety of research purposes.

Throughout its history, DDI was developed to support a diverse user community of researchers, survey managers, data centres, libraries, and archives. Libraries, repositories, and archives utilize the DDI standard for a variety of reasons. Use of DDI in libraries enables the enhanced discovery and searching of data in online retrieval systems, as it has done for many repositories and archives, such as the Inter-university Consortium for Political and Social Research (ICPSR, https://www.icpsr.umich.edu). In Canada, the adoption of DDI by Ontario libraries for the Ontario Data Documentation, Extraction Service and Infrastructure (<odesi>, http://odesi.ca) service has tremendously improved access to data in Ontario universities.

Other purposes and applications of DDI include its use for the standard exchange of data and metadata within an organization, such as for the management of longitudinal data or by large survey data banks. There are some challenges in using DDI, and these challenges include its complexity in terms of the XML structure (see Figure 17.3) and the low level of researcher buy-in, that is, researchers are more concerned with their data and analyses rather than the metadata used for description.[12]

Figure 17.3. A DDI Excerpt in XML


```
<?xml version='1.0' encoding='UTF-8'?>
<codeBook version="1.2.2" ID="cipo-E-2000-01" xml-lang="en" xmlns="http://www.icpsr.umich.edu/DDI"
xmlns:xsi="http://www.w3.org/2001/XMLSchema-instance" xsi:schemaLocation="http://www.icpsr.umich.edu/DDI
http://www.icpsr.umich.edu/DDI/Version1-2-2.xsd">
<docDscr>
<citation>
<titlStmt>
<titl>
Canadian Gallup Poll, January 2000
</titl>
<IDNo>
cipo-E-2000-01
</IDNo>
</titlStmt>
<rspStmt>
<AuthEnty affiliation="&quot;Carleton University. Data Centre&quot; ">
Fry, Jane
</AuthEnty>
<AuthEnty affiliation="&quot;Carleton University. Data Centre&quot; ">
DeSouza, Victoria
</AuthEnty>
<AuthEnty affiliation="&quot;Carleton University. Data Centre&quot; ">
Leahey, Amber
</AuthEnty>
</rspStmt>
```


Source: Canadian Gallup Poll, January 2000, XML File. odesi.ca

Currently, DDI has two supported versions. DDI Codebook, first published in 2000, closely models a physical dataset codebook that includes study-level and variable-level metadata required for understanding and use of survey microdata.[13] DDI Lifecycle was developed in 2009 to reflect the full research data lifecycle, and enables the reuse of many metadata elements for the establishment of workflows, and metadata and data frameworks. Both versions, also known as streams, are currently used by researchers and organizations all around the world, depending on their use case. The DDI Alliance, a self-sustaining membership organization established in 2003, is an active organization in which all members are encouraged to participate in guiding the development of DDI (http://www.ddialliance.org/alliance).

Within Canada, the adoption of DDI is ongoing, with some academic libraries and government data producers, such as Statistics Canada, utilizing the standard. Popular data repository platforms for the description and retrieval of numeric datasets, including Nesstar and Dataverse, incorporate the DDI standard and have established easy-to-use metadata tools and data publishing frameworks. A variety of Canadian research libraries and organizations have adopted these frameworks, including the University of British Columbia Libraries, Simon Fraser University Libraries, University of Alberta Libraries, the DLI, and the Ontario Council of University Libraries (OCUL), to name a few. Metadata support and enhancement is crucial to ensuring that data collections in libraries are well understood, documented, shared, and reused, especially in Canada where there is a growing emphasis on improved data management and stewardship for federally funded research data.[14]

Challenges for Wider DDI Adoption in Libraries

The requirements for standard metadata make their creation inherently complex and, at times, resource-intensive and tedious.[15] Often the process of creating high-quality metadata requires specific skills, tools, and resources that can seem excessive for a comparably small amount of data.[16] In other words, the amount of resources that are required to produce the necessary metadata often do not seem justified. Dietrich explains that creating metadata for multiple related datasets, sometimes working with multiple standards, can be too labor-intensive a process, and that this practise is unsustainable, especially for librarians who are working with researchers to describe and publish datasets.[17] Researchers themselves are often very reluctant to provide detailed metadata for their own data, finding the creation to be burdensome.[18]

Initiatives aimed at reducing costs, such as collaborative markup and metadata reuse, as well as automated, semantic web, and linked data approaches, are driving the future of metadata projects in libraries. While linked data and automated approaches to metadata creation are not well developed in libraries yet, especially for scientific datasets, one common approach that can be adopted is around greater collaboration and metadata reuse, and the use of standards greatly facilitates these efforts.

Collaborative approaches to metadata creation and reuse can involve individual researchers, research groups, administrators, data producers, government bodies, and librarians and other library staff, using a variety of collaborative models including local, cross-disciplinary, cross-institutional, and consortia approaches to describing datasets. For example, within the Ontario Council of University Libraries (OCUL), collaboration around the description of shared licensed numeric data, including government and commercial datasets, has been ongoing since 2008. In that year, <odesi> was developed: a data portal for digital numeric data that allows subscribing institutions (mostly in Ontario) the ability to download over 3500 datasets for the social sciences (see http://odesi.ca/). As well, there is access to the metadata for an additional 13,000-plus datasets that can be used for data discovery. With the development of <odesi>, libraries are able to collaborate and share resources around the creation and management of rich standards-driven metadata for data. Together, all OCUL libraries benefit from this shared metadata collection that has greatly improved discovery and access to datasets for academic use both inside and outside Ontario.

The <odesi> portal provides access to thousands of datasets through a shared search and data retrieval interface, built on the Nesstar platform that uses the DDI Codebook metadata standard. Collaborative markup of data for <odesi> is facilitated through the OCUL MarkIt! student metadata program, which seeks out interested OCUL libraries annually to receive funding to pay for student workers to markup and publish data to the shared repository. This process of data preparation and publishing is done remotely through shared Nesstar tools and OCUL's Scholars Portal digital infrastructure environment.† Across all OCUL data services, there is a model workflow for collaborative data management, ingest, and metadata markup (see Figure 17.4).

Through the OCUL MarkIt! program, resources are pooled and allocated to enable more efficient use of library resources and greater knowledge exchange to build community expertise around metadata in libraries. To date, the program has accomplished the high quality markup of thousands of datasets. Ongoing loading and maintenance costs associated with metadata creation facilitated through the program are less than the cost of one full-time library employee on a per-year basis (roughly Can$30,000 per year), although the start-up costs were much higher. Even given the need for a considerable initial investment, over time the program has proved very economical. Collaborative approaches for maintenance and data loading, such as those described above, present a consortium-based metadata program and data repository infrastructure that improves access to data in libraries.

---

† Scholars Portal (SP) is the digital library project of the Ontario Council of University Libraries, a consortium of academic libraries in Ontario, Canada. It supports digital infrastructure projects that are aimed at supporting the work of OCUL libraries. SP hosts a variety of digital library materials including journal articles, eBooks, digital numeric and geospatial data, researcher data, accessible text, and more. For more information see http://scholarsportal.info.

Figure 17.4. Collaborative Markup Model

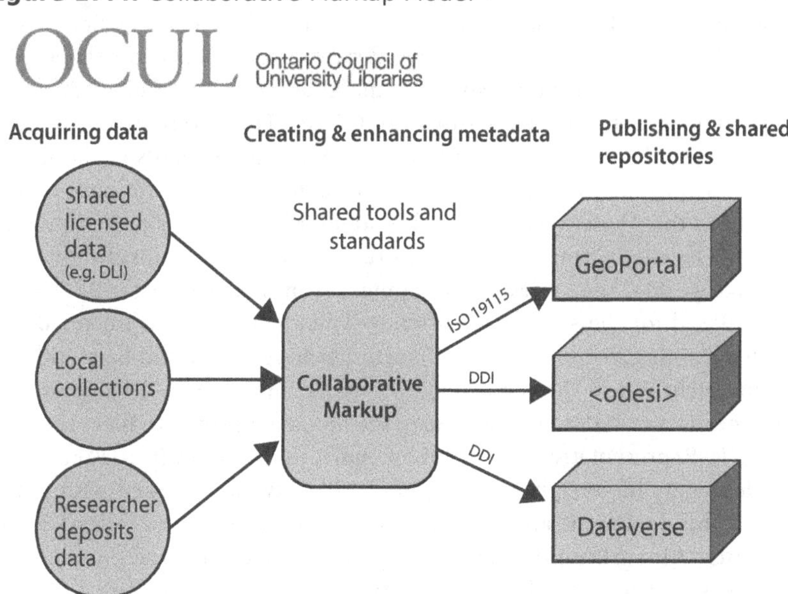

Source: Leahey, Amber. "A collaborative markup model," OCUL 2015.

Establishing Best Practices for Describing Data

Standard metadata are only effective in so far as guidelines and best practices are established and adhered to for the creation and editing of metadata records. Describing social science datasets requires knowledge about data production and its use throughout the research lifecycle, as well as understanding of data structures, such as variables and codes. Creating complete and accurate metadata requires the skills and knowledge of a range of types of data and standards for description. At times, specialized software and tools are needed for the creation and editing of metadata, and time is required to bring everything together for end use.[19]

When collaborating with other libraries, it is important that common practices be in place for consistency and accuracy across metadata markup. This consistency is required from the point of training, initial metadata creation, maintenance, and ongoing quality control of records in a system; thus the need for a Best Practices Document (BPD). Given that metadata are costly to produce, the establishment of best practices is essential to a standard library metadata processing model.[20] Best practices can be established around the utilization of a standard and are necessary in aiding non-experts in interpreting the standard.

For the <odesi> project, the DDI standard was adopted since it was already heavily used for the description of data in the social sciences. At the time of the project's development, few libraries had established best practices for the description of data resources, and there was little knowledge about this particular metadata standard within OCUL. There were two <odesi> developers (Jane Fry, one of the authors, and Michelle Edwards at the University of Guelph), and as we started to input data and metadata into <odesi>, we realized that there were no available standard procedures or best practices to follow. As the intention for the future was for different institutions to be marking-up data, the <odesi> development team realized that a BPD should be composed for the sake of consistency. This document was intended to be used for training purposes in the Ontario libraries that would be marking up data for inclusion in the repository. A further intention in developing these guidelines was to tailor and customize the metadata profile to meet the needs of OCUL. Representatives from three Ontario universities (Carleton University, University of Guelph, and Queen's University) were tasked with putting together this document, and this led to the development of the <odesi> BPD in 2008 (http://tinyurl.com/j5g429e). The guide primarily focuses on microdata, as this was determined to be one of the types of data that our users demanded, and it required the most attention to detail and consistency in terms of the creation of metadata. While this best practices document is only intended for use with <odesi>, it has also been used as a guide for other researchers and organizations using their own Nesstar interface.

Best practices are used for a variety of standard metadata fields, including the dataset or study title, producer statement, universe, keywords, and even the identification number for the survey. Multiple examples for metadata fields are provided in the BPD to make it easy to produce consistent metadata for a variety of types of datasets. For example, basic DDI requires the inclusion of a title. BPD standards for a title require the title to contain the name of the dataset or survey, date (which the data cover), subtitle or cycle name, and geographic coverage (e.g. Labour Force Survey, July 2015 [Canada]).

Since the initial Best Practices Document, additional guides and best practices have been developed for other types of data, including aggregate data and synthetic data. Templates have also been formulated based on these guidelines, using the Nesstar Publisher tool, to improve the consistency and accuracy in markup of datasets across the OCUL metadata community. Queen's University, a member of the core training group, provided the initial templates and they continue to be updated and used by the MarkIt! program participants. The program supervisors quickly realized that the BPD was not as necessary for students to use once they were trained, so a supplementary and shorter "How-to" document was composed and shared. It is currently used as a quick look-up of the procedures used for publishing data.

In the past year, Carleton University developed almost 20 short training videos to be used in concert with the "How-to" guides. Video topics were chosen based on questions that had been raised repeatedly by students. Given the positive feedback, the training videos are now the primary form of training used by the students in the different institutions, and more training videos will be made as needed. To ensure that these videos are easily found and accessed, they are distributed on YouTube (http://tinyurl.com/hjcch8g). These training videos are another excellent example of the collaboration among the institutions to enable metadata creation. This work has been extremely helpful to other communities, both within OCUL and outside the province, around metadata best practices and procedures for marking up data using DDI, especially in Canada.

Creating Metadata Content and Publishing to <odesi>

As others, including J. Ma, note, before any metadata can be created, it is first necessary to ask what kind of metadata currently exist for these materials.[21] Typically data received from commercial vendors or government producers come supplied with documentation, sometimes minimal, and most likely in text or PDF form. Datasets are often accompanied by user guides, codebooks, and other documentation useful for reading and using the data for analytical purposes. Sometimes, important information about the dataset's context may be difficult to find and often requires the cobbling together of e-mails, read-me text files, and so forth.[22] For example, it can be difficult at times to determine the dates pertinent to the dataset's production, distribution, or collection as they should be described in the DDI standard. Given that the information is available, OCUL librarians and MarkIt! student employees are tasked with creating standard metadata mainly from scratch, using whatever information and documents they can find, including online supplementary resources.

The approach taken for publishing data to <odesi> needs to be as complete as possible, with great attention to detail. However, it is always a balancing act trying to consider time and resources and the need for accuracy and quality output. Typically, advanced metadata and data transformation and extraction tools such as Nesstar Publisher, StatTransfer, FME, Sledgehammer, Dataverse, MS Excel, MS Access, among others, are required to expedite the process for data librarians and staff involved in data preparation, markup, and publication.

Specialized data publishing software for metadata ingest, preparation, editing, and publishing enable the creation of standard DDI metadata. Nesstar Publisher provides a desktop application that acts as a metadata editing tool and DDI template for the creation of DDI Codebook metadata. The metadata are attached to the publishing of a dataset, which is typically uploaded and published, using the Nesstar Publisher tool, onto the Scholars Portal's servers. This workflow ensures that the DDI metadata capture both the study-level and dataset-level metadata in one machine-readable XML record, which is stored in a shared XML database at Scholars Portal.

To reduce duplication and improve data publishing turnaround, remote data publishing occurs at multiple sites and facilitates collaborative multi-institutional review and publishing of data to the <odesi> platform. Scholars Portal maintains the main server resources and infrastructure to facilitate remote access and publishing. Publishing coordination is typically managed and communicated amongst group members through a shared wiki and spreadsheet that tracks all markup of individual datasets and documentation slated for inclusion and markup in the system. The shared spreadsheet provides columns for coordinating progress, including the name of the institution responsible, dissemination and completion dates, quality control review, and progress notes, if applicable. It should be noted that effective communication is required for this type of collaboration to occur and, to this end, the group holds regularly scheduled meetings every two months for ongoing data review and project discussion. The group members also utilize e-mail communication in between meetings to discuss best practices and technical problems and solutions as well as training and new project ideas.

Maintenance and Ongoing Quality Control

Scholars Portal hosts and manages a metadata store that is part of the Nesstar and data publishing infrastructure. MarkLogic, a proprietary XML database system, is used to store metadata, and build queries and indexing of the metadata for searching in <odesi>. The search engine is quite effective in searching across all <odesi> collections, including external collections that support the DDI standard, such as the collections at ICPSR and CORA, the Canadian Opinion Research Archive (http://www.queensu.ca/cora/). Adding metadata from these collections expands the resources available to OCUL researchers and illustrates the importance of collaboration and shared standards in libraries. The search platform is also an enhancement from the traditional library catalog systems since it indexes all of the variable-level metadata associated with the datasets (including variable names, labels, values, codes, etc.) to allow for granular data and variable searching, in addition to keyword and series searching. Finally, we recognize that metadata created for the description of datasets are not free from errors. Therefore, the group has a set procedure to follow when errors are found, and this method has proved to be quite effective for managing quality control issues as they arise.

Future Directions and Conclusions

This chapter provides a brief history of cataloging and metadata in libraries, including an overview and history of the DDI and its adoption by academic libraries.

The best practices used for <odesi> were detailed including a description of the highly effective model for metadata collaboration within OCUL. The importance of regular collaboration and communication around best practices, as well as the use of shared standards and practices, all help to ensure data are effectively described and made reusable in libraries. Before this model of collaboration existed, access to datasets and standards-compliant metadata was limited in Ontario universities, especially for those institutions that did not have a dedicated data services unit or department. This limitation hampered researchers looking for data to use in secondary analysis. It should also be mentioned the important role that OCUL played in the establishment of this collaboration, in terms of technology, resources, and knowledge transfer. Without the involvement of OCUL in the initial development of <odesi>, it would never have been the success it is today.

In terms of future directions, Scholars Portal staff plan ongoing regular updating of the infrastructure to maintain the shared repository. As well, they plan ongoing involvement in the development of the DDI metadata standard, including membership and participation in the broader international DDI community through conferences and development meetings. At some point, potential adoption of the DDI Lifecycle version may also come to fruition.

For libraries and OCUL, staying abreast of the latest standards and practices for data and metadata management, including developments around research data management services in libraries and the role of metadata, is essential. An important aspect to all future activities is the role for greater collaboration. OCUL has been pursuing collaboration with external organizations, including government partners and data providers such as the DLI, for some time. Overall, collaborations of this kind facilitate the effective creation of metadata to enhance the discovery and greater access to, and reuse of, datasets within libraries.

---

1. Chuck Humphrey, "Canada's long-tail of data," *Preserving Research Data in Canada* (blog), December 5, 2012, http://preservingresearchdataincanada.net/category/introduction/.
2. IASSIST Blog. "Chronology of data libraries and data centres," http://tinyurl.com/o46gcx7
3. Jane Fry, "What is a Canadian data dude?" presentation at *Annual IASSIST Conference, Toronto, 2014*, http://tinyurl.com/hxtyv8f.
4. Myung-Ja Han, "Metadata with levels of description: New challenges to catalogers and metadata librarians," paper presented at the *World Library and Information Congress: 78th IFLA General Conference and Assembly, Helsinki, 2012*, http://conference.ifla.org/past-wlic/2012/80-han-en.pdf.
5. Ann Green and Chuck Humphrey, "Building the DDI," *IASSIST Quarterly* (Spring 2013): 36–44.
6. Ibid.
7. Carolyn Guinchard, "Dublin Core use in libraries: A survey," *OCLC Systems and Services: International Digital Library Perspectives* 18, no. 1 (2002): 40–50, http://dx.doi.org/10.1108/10650750210418190.
8. Jane Greenberg, Hollie C. White, Sarah Carrier and Ryan Scherle, "A metadata best practice for a scientific data repository," *Journal of Library Metadata* 9, no. 3–4. (2009): 194–12, doi:10.1080/19386380903405090.
9. Ibid. 195.

10. Uwe M. Borghoff et al, *Long-Term preservation of digital documents: Principles and practices*, (Berlin: Springer. 2006), 162.
11. Mary Vardigan, Pascal Heus and Wendy Thomas, "Data Documentation Initiative: Toward a standard for Social Sciences," *International Journal of Digital Curation* 3, no. 1 (2008): 107–13.
12. Ibid; Mary Vardigan, and J. Wackerow, "DDI—A metadata standard for the community," Paper presented at the *North American Data Documentation Initiative Conference (NADDI), Lawrence, Kansas, 2013.*
13. Vardigan, Heus and Thomas, "Data Documentation Initiative."
14. Government of Canada, "Draft Tri-Agency Statement of Principles on Digital Data Management," July 20, 2015, http://www.science.gc.ca/default.asp?lang=En&n=547652FB-1
15. Jian Qin and Kai Li, "How portable are the metadata standards for scientific data? A proposal for a metadata infrastructure," proceedings of the *DCMI International Conference on Dublin Core and Metadata Applications, Lisbon, 2013*, http://jianqin.metadataetc.org/wp-content/uploads/2013/08/DC2013-metadatad-portability.pdf.
16. Dianne Dietrich, "Metadata management in a data staging repository," *Journal of Library Metadata* 10, no. 2–3:79–78, doi:10.1080/19386389.2011.544997; Erin Forward, Amber Leahey, and Leanne Trimble, "Shared geospatial metadata repository for Ontario university libraries: Collaborative approaches," *New Review of Academic Librarianship* (forthcoming).
17. Dietrich, "Metadata management in a data staging repository."
18. Vardigan, Heus and Thomas, "Data Documentation Initiative."
19. Erin Forward, Amber Leahey, and Leanne Trimble, "Shared geospatial metadata repository for Ontario university libraries: Collaborative approaches," *New Review of Academic Librarianship* (forthcoming).
20. Ya-Ning Chen, Shu-Jiun Chen, and Simon C. Lin, "A metadata lifecycle model for digital libraries: Methodology and application for an evidence-based approach to library research," Paper presented at the *World Library and Information Congress: 69th IFLA General Conference and Council, Berlin, 2003.* http://archive.ifla.org/IV/ifla69/papers/141e-Chen_Chen_Lin.pdf
21. Jin Ma, "Managing metadata for digital objects," *Library Collections, Acquisitions, and Technical Services* 30, no. 1–2 (2006): 3–17, doi:10.1080/14649055.2006.10766103.
22. Joyce Chapman and Jeff Essic, "Juggling Points and Polygons: GIS Researchers' Metadata and Search Needs," *Journal of Library Metadata* 11, no. 1 (2011): 1–18.

Suggestion for Further Reading

DDI Alliance Structural Reform Group. "DDI Version 3.0 Conceptual Model." June 10, 2004. http://www.ddialliance.org/system/files/Concept-Model-WD.pdf.

CHAPTER 18

Exploring Disciplinary Metadata and Documentation Practices to Strengthen Data Archiving Services

Elizabeth Rolando, Lisha Li, Ameet Doshi, Alison Valk, and Karen Young

IN RESPONSE TO changes in academic research and evolving funding agency public access requirements, research libraries are increasingly engaging with data curation.[†] The development and expansion of research data services in libraries aligns with broader changes in research libraries such as increased emphasis on open access; investment in preserving unique, local collections; and greater involvement in the research process. This expansion also responds to the growing need for research data archiving services.[1]

† We use the term "data curation" as a catchall for services or efforts geared towards "the active and ongoing management of data through its life cycle of interest and usefulness to scholarship, science, and education," as defined by the Graduate School of Library and Information Science at the University of Illinois at Urbana-Champaign (http://www.lis.illinois.edu/academics/degrees/specializations/data_curation).We use the terms "data archiving" or "archiving data" to signify the process of moving research data into long-term storage for preservation and access. This process includes all actions associated with the transfer and ingest of data into a repository, including metadata creation, format normalization, and the assignment of persistent identifiers. As we use the terms here, data archiving is but one element of data curation.

The last decade has seen a broad push to normalize data archiving practices. Between publisher and funder requirements, social norms, and interest in reusing previously collected data, researchers are under pressure to provide evidence that the data underlying their findings and collected over the course of a project are freely available to others.[2] This is a non-trivial endeavor. Researchers often lack the skills necessary to adequately manage, secure, document, and preserve their datasets;[3] the rewards and incentives to do so are often inadequate given competing demands on their time and attention;[4] and sufficient resources are rarely available to help researchers manage, preserve, and share their data.[5]

For some disciplines and communities of practice, archiving data is a long-standing practice. Resources, standards, and curatorial support are available through organizations such as the Inter-university Consortium for Political and Social Research (ICPSR, http://www.icpsr.umich.edu/), the Dryad Repository (http://datadryad.org/), and Data Observation Network for Earth (DataONE, https://www.dataone.org/). However, data archiving is a new effort for many other research communities, and no comprehensive community resources are available to help them. For this reason, and because archiving data has become a serious compliance issue for researchers and institutions receiving federal funding,[6] many research universities are developing institutional services to support data archiving. In many cases, the library, given its mission to collect, organize, and preserve information in all forms, has been a leader and driving force behind the development of campus research data services.

In this chapter, we will explore the Georgia Tech Library's efforts to develop research data services and data archiving services. As we will explain, a significant challenge for institutional data archiving services is acquiring sufficient documentation and metadata about deposited datasets to ensure those datasets can be used in the future. In order to address this problem, we conducted a study of disciplinary metadata and documentation practices at Georgia Tech. Our work builds upon past research examining metadata for research data and demonstrates how the results of these studies can be applied locally to improve data archiving services through the development of metadata templates.

Metadata in Data Archiving

Metadata, the information necessary to discover, retrieve, or manage an information item (the "data about data"),[7] are of particular concern to libraries. Creating and managing metadata to make resources discoverable, accessible, and usable is a central library activity.[8] In libraries, metadata have customarily included things such as catalogs, repository records, or finding aids, and the metadata are structured by schemas such as Dublin Core, Metadata Object Description Schema (MODS), and Preservation Metadata Implementation Strategies (PREMIS). The information recorded in the structured metadata record is often, but not always, derived from the informational items themselves, such as the title page. Within the library community, metadata are usually grouped as descriptive, structural, or administrative.[9] Heavy emphasis is placed on standardization (metadata records are often created in accordance with an industry standard, such as Dublin Core, so that the content of the record is consistent from one library to the next), structure (the metadata records are typically created to follow specific patterns, so machines or patrons can systematically locate sections of the record), and interoperability (when interoperable, a metadata record can pass through multiple systems and still retain the content and functionality of the record).[10]

This paradigm of metadata is problematic for archiving research data. As detailed below, there are four reasons for the disconnect between traditional library metadata and the metadata and documentation needs of researchers depositing datasets: 1) most metadata and documentation for research data are generated by dataset creators; 2) datasets require significantly more metadata and documentation than traditional library materials to be useful in the future; 3) research practices vary far too widely to be fully accommodated by any one metadata standard; and 4) documentation about research data is not standardized.

Dataset Creators Need to Provide Metadata and Documentation

Because the production of datasets does not follow standard practices and the form of a dataset can differ from one project to the next, datasets often lack the equivalent to a title page, that traditional repository for incorporating official metadata into a book. Accordingly, repository and archive curators have to rely heavily on dataset creators or depositors to provide metadata and documentation about a dataset. While curators and librarians have an important role in normalizing and enhancing submitted metadata, the creator is usually the only one with knowledge of why the dataset was collected, how it was cleaned or transformed, what the variables in the dataset mean, or any of the other countless quirks a dataset may present. Yet most data creators have neither the time, training, nor incentive to create comprehensive metadata to support data archiving,[11] and few researchers actually follow any metadata standard or specification when documenting their datasets.[12]

Datasets Need More Metadata to Ensure Future Reuse

Datasets are rarely self-describing, they are extremely diverse, and they typically do not follow standard forms of production, storage, or sharing. Accordingly, datasets usually require significantly more information and explanation, beyond what can be captured in a catalog or repository record, to be used by someone other than the original creator. To be effective, metadata for datasets should provide all of the information future users—separated from the creator by space, time, institution, or disciplinary norms—would need to know about the data to use the data themselves.[13]

Usability metadata, or the information necessary for someone else to use a dataset, are critical to data archiving and subsequent data reuse. Usability metadata can include a range of informational items, from field sensor manufacturer, to a general description of research questions, to a standard protocol used in a lab for all experiments, to the dataset title included in a structured metadata record. Past work exploring how researchers share or reuse data has revealed numerous examples of information that could be considered usability metadata. For instance, researchers consistently indicate that a description of the research methods employed to create or collect the dataset should be included when archiving or sharing data.[14] This information is necessary so that a future user can assess the quality of the data and the level of professionalism of the data collector.[15] Similarly, data reusers need context about how data were collected in order to use them in their own work.[16] For example, a secondary user may need to know why samples were collected from a particular location in order to understand the limitations of the dataset, and the user would be unlikely to know this information without documentation or communication from the original creator. Similarly, secondary users often want to know what software or scripts were used to clean or refine a dataset, in order to understand the final data product. Particularly challenging, though, is the need to document datasets in detail sufficient for unknown future users, since many researchers have not previously needed to identify and record tacit knowledge about their work.[17]

While usability metadata is not a formal category of metadata, nor is it—as we conceive of it—entirely distinct from descriptive, administrative, and structural metadata,[†] it is a worthwhile distinction to highlight because of its importance to data reuse. Given that metadata categories may be most useful when framed in terms of what the metadata are intended to accomplish,[18] usability is a valuable category of metadata because it is uniquely focused on recording information that details or documents how an end user would use the dataset.

Research Practices Vary Widely

Variances in metadata practices between and among disciplines further complicate the process of describing data for archiving.[19] Terminology differs from one community of practice to the next. For example, methods information is represented in many current metadata schemes for research data; yet, the way the elements are named differs in each schema, reflecting dissimilarities in terminology between disciplines.[20]

---

† For example, capturing the name and institutional affiliation of the dataset creator is important to future use and for discovery metadata.

Initiatives and projects have been established to address some of the drawbacks to a one-size-fits-all approach to metadata and to accommodate disciplinary differences. Some communities have established disciplinary metadata standards, which specify precise pieces of information that should be recorded alongside a dataset. Specifications like the Ecological Metadata Language (EML, https://knb.ecoinformatics.org/#external//emlparser/docs/index.html) or the Data Documentation Initiative (DDI, http://www.ddialliance.org/)‡ are examples of this type of structured metadata schema designed to describe ecological or social science datasets, respectively. These specifications include elements about datasets from a particular discipline, and they record and structure information necessary to locate, evaluate, access, and use datasets. However, there is little evidence that researchers use these metadata standards in their own work.[21]

Conforming to a disciplinary schema requires a great deal of effort,[22] especially as the metadata created and used for one project often differs significantly from that for another. As such documentation is often customized to particular needs or datasets and cannot be easily molded to fit a community standard.[23]

Practices Around Research Data are Not Standardized

One of the biggest challenges to using standardized forms of metadata for datasets is that datasets do not readily lend themselves to standardization. Datasets and their metadata are deeply tied to the local practices and needs of the originating investigator or lab,[24] and many projects do not easily fit within community standards for metadata. For example, the methods in the study may be novel, the work may be interdisciplinary and draw from many fields, or the practical realities of the work done in the lab may be in conflict with the disciplinary standard. For many research projects, looser, more ad-hoc forms of documentation are more useful and easier to capture. Further, understandings of what metadata for research data are differ from one group to another.[25] Rigid insistence on structures and standards for machine readable metadata does not accommodate the needs of researchers with complicated datasets that require metadata and documentation to make their work understandable to other people.[26] Moreover, researchers infrequently use metadata standards in their own work, often because the standards do not necessarily help the researcher or their research process, and because metadata standards are typically designed to address the archiving of a dataset, not active use. In these cases, only the metadata that directly support current projects or immediate tasks will be collected and used, regardless of whether a disciplinary or relevant standard ex-

‡ For more information about DDI, see the chapter in this volume by Fry and Leahey called "Metadata for Social Science Data: Collaborative Best Practices."

ists.[27] This suggests that even when metadata standards for research data are available and researchers have the time, expertise, and resources, they still will not record all of the information necessary to support reuse within a structured metadata record.

Beyond the Metadata Record

Frequently, unstructured or non-standardized forms of documentation are included when archiving datasets; they serve as important and powerful complements to the structured, standardized metadata records common in library and repository systems. Because these supplemental forms of documentation are typically flat text files, not bound to any particular structure or standard, depositors and curators can record a much wider variety of contextual information than could be accommodated by highly-structured metadata records that must conform to community specifications. While the information captured in a structured metadata record is critical for ensuring data discoverability, supplemental documentation is needed to capture contextual information or usability metadata necessary to allow for secondary uses. Further, this type of documentation is often used in the research process by researchers themselves. Examples of these types of documentation include README files, lab notebooks, and codebooks.

The README file has become a common form of supplemental documentation used to describe datasets for archiving and later reuse. Originating from computer programming,[28] README files are widely used by software developers today.[†] Given that README files are typically flat text files, they can contain whatever information a data creator chooses to include. Further, while information professionals tend to prefer simple schemes to document datasets, scientists tend to create documentation in the style of a README file.[29]

While data repositories and data centers create and manage structured metadata alongside a dataset, many also require or strongly promote the inclusion of supplemental documentation with data deposits. For example, Dryad and ICPSR use structured metadata schemas (such as Dublin Core, Darwin Core, and DDI) in their repositories.[30] Both also support and provide guidance on creating codebooks and README files that do not necessarily conform to a particular standard in order to capture additional context about a dataset.[31] Despite the disciplinary focus of these services, supplemental documentation is still considered necessary to fully capture the scope of information required to enable reuse.

---

† See the discussion on Stack Overflow about "How to Write a good README" (http://stackoverflow.com/questions/2304863/how-to-write-a-good-readme) for more information about how README files are used in software development.

Metadata Challenges for Institutional Repositories

Herein lies a pressing problem for institutional data archiving services. Given that library services should accommodate all users, how can an institutional data repository support the collection, preservation, and access to rich metadata about datasets? How does a repository acknowledge and support disciplinary differences in metadata and documentation practices, while ensuring consistency of service and interoperability of metadata? These were some of the questions and challenges we hoped to explore in our study.

Research Data Services at Georgia Tech

The Georgia Tech Library first established its Research Data Services department (RDS) in 2010 and has since worked with the Georgia Tech community to better understand local needs and practices, to refine and expand available services, and to develop the digital infrastructure to curate research data. As services mature and new tools are created, we are attentive to questions around how RDS will scale, be flexible, and provide a foundation of support to any researcher, regardless of specialization or disciplinary affiliation. Yet, we also want to leverage disciplinary or research differences and avoid losing unique features of the reseach products in the process of handling their data.

The library supports data deposit into our institutional repository SMARTech (https://smartech.gatech.edu). A major challenge to this approach is the limited metadata support. Our repository was designed to store publications, white papers, and electronic theses and dissertations; accordingly, we use Dublin Core almost exclusively for descriptive metadata. This is simply too narrow for cataloging and describing datasets. As a workaround, we began asking depositors to include a supplementary file with deposits, either documentation they had already created or a README file they created for archiving, using a template we provided. The template was based on examples from the University of Virginia (https://pages.shanti.virginia.edu/libra/datasets) and the University of Indiana-Bloomington (https://scholarworks.iu.edu/dspace/handle/2022/17126)[32] and included information such as standards or calibrations used, uncertainty, precision, or accuracy of measurements, or description of acronyms used in the dataset.[‡]

The metadata submitted by depositors improved, both in quantity and quality, after we provided the template. Over time, however, depositors noted ways in which the template did not meet their needs. Because the template was one-size-fits-all, depositors were asked for information that was not relevant to their work (or the template was worded in such a way that they perceived it to be irrelevant),

‡ The full template can be seen in Appendix 18.A.

and the template missed information depositors knew to be critical. As we are not constrained by structured standards for these supplemental files, depositors can record whatever unique, specialized, custom information they would like. In turn, we wanted to support this effort as best we could.

To help depositors prepare supplemental documentation, we endeavored to create disciplinary-focused metadata templates. We recognized that even within a discipline the practices and needs would vary, but we sought to determine whether enough commonality existed within a disciplinary research community to allow us to offer specialized services under the umbrella of our general research data services. Through interviews and document analysis, we conducted an exploratory review of local research practices, to better understand how researchers create metadata and documentation. We also sought to investigate the conditions and characteristics that inform the decisions researchers make in regards to metadata for their data. Local exploration was augmented by an examination of existing disciplinary metadata standards for datasets.

Methods

In order to explore the feasibility of creating disciplinary README file templates, we narrowed the scope of our investigation to three unique communities at Georgia Tech—faculty from the School of Economics, the School of Civil and Environmental Engineering, and the School of Interactive Computing. We chose these groups because members of each community had previously expressed interest in archiving data, and each community was distinct enough that we expected to find observable differences in their behaviors and needs. To develop an understanding of the metadata practices and needs of these communities, we employed a variety of methods: loosely structured interviews; in-depth review of interviewees' published literature; and a survey of metadata elements from relevant disciplinary metadata standards. The study populations and methods are described in more detail below.

- The School of Economics is one of the six schools within the Ivan Allen College of Liberal Arts. Research areas covered include environmental economics, technological change, and industrial organization. The school currently has 22 faculty and 85 full-time undergraduate and graduate students.
- The school of Civil and Environmental Engineering (CEE) is one of the eight schools within the College of Engineering, and it includes diverse engineering specializations. Currently consisting of 15 research centers, 26 laboratories, 58 tenure-track faculty members and over 30 research faculty and adjunct professors, CEE is home to expertise in construction engineering, environmental fluid mechanics and water resources, geosystems engineering, mechanics and materials, and transportation systems engineering.

- The School of Interactive Computing was formed in 2007 as one of three schools within the College of Computing. The school currently has about 50 faculty. Research within the school focuses on the intersection of the human experience and computing, falling into nine main areas that include Artificial Intelligence & Machine Learning; Geometry, Graphics and Animation; and Social Computing.

Interviews

We conducted eight interviews in total for this study. Each interview was with a different faculty member: three faculty from Civil and Environmental Engineering; two faculty from Economics; and three faculty from Interactive Computing. Potential participants were identified by subject librarians, personal contacts, or records from the Office of Sponsored Programs that indicated a researcher had applied for a National Science Foundation grant since January 18, 2011, the date the data management plan requirement went into effect. Our sample included both tenured and non-tenured faculty, as well as faculty with high levels of research funding (over $1,000,000) and low levels of research funding (under $50,000). Given that our sample consisted of researchers willing to discuss data documentation and sharing practices, our sample likely skews more heavily toward openness and willingness to share or archive data, so results may not be representative of all faculty in the schools studied. However, because the interview protocol included questions about community expectations or community norms, we feel the results illustrate expectations, practices, or needs that are broadly applicable to the respective disciplines.

Interviews were conducted in person, by one or two of the authors, and on average, they lasted 40–60 minutes. The interviewers recorded the audio of the interview and took extensive notes.[†] In the interview, participants were asked to review the current README file template and note any information that was missing or irrelevant to their work.

Project members listened to the recordings and reviewed their notes to create, for each interview, a list of metadata fields based on the interviewee's responses. For example, if an interviewee stated that he or she needed to know the software used to analyze the data, we noted that "software for data analysis" was a possible metadata element. Lists of metadata elements were compared against one another within a particular discipline (i.e., Civil and Environmental Engineering responses were compared to other Civil and Environmental Engineering responses, Interactive Computing responses were compared to other Interactive Computing responses, and so on). We created a representative metadata model for each school by combining duplicate pieces of information and removing items that were too specialized or specific.

† The full interview protocol is available in Appendix 18.B.

Review of Interviewee's Published Literature

Because published literature is the primary form of scientific communication, articles often contain important descriptive information in the "methods" section or in tables or charts. Publications may be important sources of contextual information or data description to be used in curation.[33] Accordingly, as a supplement to the interview, project personnel read examples of published literature from each interviewee and listed items that could be descriptions of data or metadata. These lists generally produced specific examples of descriptive information (for example, the precise manufacturer and model of a sensor), and so they were an important complement to the interviews, which tended to focus more on general types of metadata and description (for example, the method of data collection). Interviewees were shown the list and asked to validate the items as important or unimportant in enabling data reuse. Items interviewees felt were important were included in the individual lists of metadata elements.

Metadata Survey

In addition to seeking input from researchers, our project team also surveyed existing metadata standards and specifications. Similar to the methodology used by Qin & Li,[34] we identified relevant metadata specifications, then parsed out individual elements or metadata fields. These individual elements were entered into a spreadsheet, where we noted the formal and informal name of the element, the name of the specification that included the element, whether any vocabularies or standards were used to normalize metadata in that element, and the disciplinary coverage of the original specification. In total, we analyzed 18 metadata specifications. The full list can be found in Table 18.1.

Table 18.1. List of Metadata Specifications Examined during Metadata Survey

Metadata Specification	Disciplinary Coverage	Link
ADN (ADEPT/DLESE/NASA)	Earth System Learning Materials	http://www.dlese.org/Metadata/adn-item/
Content Standard for Digital Geospatial Metadata (CSDGM)	Geographic	https://www.fgdc.gov/metadata/geospatial-metadata-standards#csdgm
Data Documentation Initiative (DDI)	Social Sciences	http://www.ddialliance.org/

Table 18.1. List of Metadata Specifications Examined during Metadata Survey

Metadata Specification	Disciplinary Coverage	Link
GenBank BankIt Submission Metadata	Genomics	http://www.ncbi.nlm.nih.gov/WebSub/html/help/genbank-source-table.html#modifier
Qualitative Data Exchange Format (QuDEx)	Qualitative Social Sciences	http://www.data-archive.ac.uk/create-manage/projects/qudex
Ecological Metadata Language (EML)	Ecology	https://knb.ecoinformatics.org/#external//emlparser/docs/index.html
Darwin Core	Biodiversity	http://rs.tdwg.org/dwc/
MIxS	Genomics	http://wiki.gensc.org/index.php?title=MIxS
IEDA Marine Geoscience Data System Metadata Form	Marine Geoscience	http://www.marine-geo.org/submit/guidelines.php#metadataforms
Earthquake Engineering Metadata Model	Earthquake Engineering	http://dx.doi.org/10.1007/s11709-010-0036-z
Directory Interchange Format (DIF)	Earth Sciences	http://gcmd.gsfc.nasa.gov/add/difguide/index.html
Service Entry Resource Format (SERF)	Earth Sciences	http://gcmd.gsfc.nasa.gov/add/serfguide/index.html
IEDA EarthChem Data Submission Guidelines	Geochemistry	http://www.earthchem.org/library/help/guidelines
Digital Library for Earth System Education (DLESE)	Earth Science Education	http://www.dlese.org/Metadata/
General Transit Feed Specification (GTFS)	Public Transportation	https://developers.google.com/transit/gtfs/

Table 18.1. List of Metadata Specifications Examined during Metadata Survey

Metadata Specification	Disciplinary Coverage	Link
NEES metadata requirements	Earthquake Engineering	https://nees.org/resources/4759/supportingdocs
NCAR Contrast README Guidelines	Earth and Atmospheric Sciences	https://www.eol.ucar.edu/content/contrast-data-set-documentation-readme-guidelines
W3C Data on the Web Best Practices	General	http://www.w3.org/TR/dwbp-ucr/

Similar to the interviewee analysis, once we extracted the metadata elements from each specification, we manually grouped related elements and removed elements that were too specific or did not fit within the scope of our three sample populations.[†]

Findings

Disciplinary Documentation Needs

The direct outcome of this project was README file templates targeted toward the three schools in our study population, based on the fields identified in this study. Although we uncovered some differences between the Schools, the needs for supplementary documentation were fairly similar across the groups, as can be seen in Figure 18.1. A full listing of the common elements used in the new README file templates are in Appendix C and the distinct elements from the new templates are in Appendices D, E, and F.[‡] In many cases, the disciplinary differences are evident not in the semantic element, but in the precise word choice or description used in the template. For example, "Data Creator(s)" is included as a distinct element for Civil and Environmental Engineering and a shared element between Economics and Interactive Computing because the description of a data creator in Civil and Environmental Engineering is distinct from the others, while the description was the same between Economics and Interactive Computing. Included in these findings are descriptive metadata fields that would also be included in a structured metadata record.

† The raw data collected for this project are available at http://hdl.handle.net/1853/53323.

‡ Appendices C, D, E, and F are available on the companion website https://databrarianship.wordpress.com/.

Figure 18.1. Comparison of Metadata Needs between Interactive Computing, Economics, and Civil and Environmental Engineering

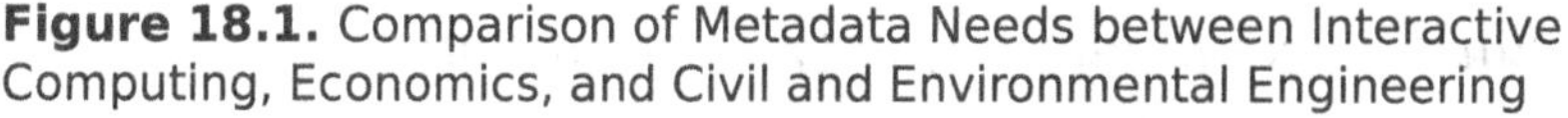

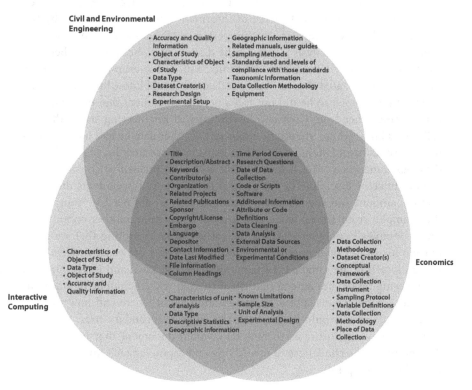

Source: Leahey, Amber. "A collaborative markup model." OCUL 2015.

In addition to the results incorporated into the templates, we also discovered a number of notable themes. Our sample size is quite small, so findings may not be applicable to all researchers in the three colleges. However, despite the small sample, we observed some clear trends and open questions worth highlighting.

Article as Metadata

Every participant felt strongly that archived datasets should be linked to published literature that discusses the research that used the dataset. Many also noted that the article should explain the research design and process of data collection, clean-up, and analysis in enough detail that the publication could stand alone as documentation. However, most noted that while this was the desired practice amongst their research community, articles rarely include such specific information.

Difficult to Document Unspoken Assumptions

Many participants noted that, when reviewing our current template, they struggled to articulate what pieces of information were not captured by the template. Others were unsure whether certain methodologies or decisions in data collection and analysis needed to be documented, because they believed any future data user would know that information. For example, a researcher from Economics stated that any of his colleagues would know how he had randomized his sample, so he did not feel a need to document that process. Similarly, a researcher from Civil and Environmental Engineering stated that his colleagues know where to find the applicable weather data he had incorporated into his traffic simulation, so he felt an explanation of how he acquired those data was unnecessary. Yet, when interviewees were pressed to consider users from a different discipline or the general public, these respondents did agree that the amount and specificity of documentation would need to improve. In the examples from above, when asked about users from another community, the Economics researcher clarified his earlier remarks, noting that someone outside his subset of Economics would need to know the exact process used for randomizing the sample treatment. Similarly, the Civil and Environmental Engineering researcher agreed that when sharing with the public or researchers from a different discipline, documentation about where and how weather data was obtained would be important to support secondary uses. However, respondents were unsure as to how they would document that information. This points to the challenges of identifying and capturing tacit knowledge and unspoken assumptions.

More Investment in Documentation When Researchers Anticipate Sharing Data

Participants who have shared data or anticipated sharing data were more thoughtful about how they document datasets and how that information would be communicated to others. Participants who did not plan to make datasets accessible were less concerned about documenting their work. Perceived future use may drive the level and quality of documentation, as well as completeness of metadata. All interviewees were willing to share some data, although not all had previously done so. For our interviewees, the drive to share stemmed primarily from data sharing requirements, whether from funding agencies or publishers. Less evident in the interviews was a desire to contribute to the knowledge commons as defined by Hess and Ostrom.[35]

Little Use or Knowledge of Any Standards or Community Practices

With some exceptions (an interviewee in genomics and an interviewee who anticipated depositing into the USDA Research Data Archive), participants were unable to identify standards or best practices in their community for creating metadata or documentation. They indicated that their methods for creating documentation were based primarily on past experience. Although participants did not name specific standards or best practices, they did indicate that journal or funding agency requirements are regularly the standard by which they assess how much (or how well) to document their datasets.

Metadata Needs are Very Diverse

The specific pieces of information participants felt were necessary to support future use were incredibly diverse. Although obvious themes were apparent across all interviews (for example, most felt that they needed to define terms used in a dataset), the specifics (for example, precisely what terms would need to be defined) almost never overlapped. A few participants stated that each study is so unique and specific to their research questions that no one standard could ever accommodate their needs. We also found that interviewees felt it was important to acknowledge disciplinary differences, although some reported that they would rather see all possible fields and then pick those that were applicable to their materials. This suggests that a more comprehensive, but flexible, instrument, perhaps with skip logic or other ways of grouping logically similar fields, may be most appropriate to capture the breadth and depth of research being conducted across the disciplines at Georgia Tech.

Discussion

Our investigation into local data documentation practices has confirmed findings from earlier studies. We found that the practices and needs of researchers vary widely (even within a specific discipline),[36] researchers do not employ disciplinary metadata standards in their own work,[37] and published articles contain rich contextual information that can be leveraged to create metadata and documentation about datasets.[38] Our findings further highlight the importance of unstructured forms of documentation for institutional data archiving services. Additionally, our use of these findings to create specialized templates provides other libraries with a model and strategy for capturing usability metadata to support data archiving. Although the specific fields applicable to a particular community may vary between schools or institutions, the methodology described in this chapter could be repurposed and employed elsewhere. Overall, we found the process to be productive and in keeping with the types of support our interviewees wanted when documenting datasets for archiving.

An unexpected outcome of this project was that the interviews with members of the local communities of practice helped to formalize and document community understandings and expectations around metadata and documentation for datasets. This form of engagement not only involves the end users in decisions on how a service is offered, but it is also less prescriptive and more receptive to the fact that researchers' practices and the desires of the library may not always be in alignment. The results of this project, namely the README file templates, can now be used to help establish documentation practices, as the templates are a reflection of community expectations and desired behaviors. This will help future depositors document and share their datasets, but we hope it will also help encourage conversations in the local community about best practices and expectations with respect to documentation and data sharing.

Future Work

Going forward, we plan to investigate how documentation is used when data are reused. Our work has focused on what depositors expect documentation should include, and the next step would be to study what secondary users expect of documentation and how well our templates and metadata meet the needs of secondary users. We are also interested in exploring how to support interdisciplinary research, especially as a means to better understand what unspoken assumptions or tacit knowledge must be documented to make data from one community understandable to another. Future research will also involve exploring different metadata and documentation needs according to data type (i.e., qualitative vs. quantitative) or research method (i.e., experimental vs. simulation).

Given that expectations to share data drive metadata creation, we must still consider the larger scope of issues, including how to encourage data sharing. If researchers consider future users while they work with and document their data, they will ultimately create better documentation, which will help future users, enhance archiving, and assist the immediate research project. We want to explore how the library can promote and foster this type of prosocial behavior, especially when it ultimately benefits the researcher as well.

Conclusions

Research libraries archiving datasets in an institutional repository will face a number of challenges when trying to capture metadata and documentation about datasets to enable future reuse, but there are ways to engage with the local community to alleviate some of the issues. Our project demonstrates that helping researchers create supplemental documentation to record local context and information specific to a particular project is an important way to support data archiving and future data reuse. We have also demonstrated that it is productive to engage the local community of researchers in discussions about documentation and metadata practices, in order to develop disciplinary specific information and advice that can be provided to researchers.

Appendix 18.A. Previous Readme File Template Used for All Data Deposits, Regardless of Discipline

Required information:

1. File names, directory structure (for zipped files), and brief description of each file or file type, including where in the research process each data file lies (e.g. raw/unanalyzed data, processed/analyzed data, rendered/visualized data)
2. Definitions of acronyms, site abbreviations, or other project-specific designations used in the data file names or documentation files, if applicable
3. Description of the parameters/variables (column headings in the data files) and units of measure for each parameter/variable, including special codes, variable classes, GIS coverage attributes, etc. used in the data files themselves, including codes for missing data values, if applicable:
    - column headings for any tabular data
    - the units of measurement used
    - what symbols are used to record missing data
    - any specialized formats or abbreviations used
    - any additional related data collected that was not included in the current data package
4. Uncertainty, precision, and accuracy of measurements, if known
5. Environmental or experimental conditions, if appropriate (e.g., cloud cover, atmospheric influences, etc.)
6. Method(s) for collecting the data, as well as the methods for processing data, if data other than raw data are being contributed
7. Standards or calibrations that were used
8. Specialized software (including version number) used to produce, prepare, render, compress, analyze and/or needed to read the dataset, if applicable

9. Quality assurance and quality control that have been applied, if applicable
10. Known problems that limit the data's use or other caveats (e.g., uncertainty, sampling problems, blanks, QC samples)
11. Date dataset was last modified
12. Relationships with any ancillary datasets outside of this dataset, if applicable

Optional information:

14. Resources, such as books, articles, serials, and/or data files, if any, that served as source of this data collection
15. Methodology for sample treatment and/or analysis, if applicable
16. Example records for each data file (or file type)
17. Files names of other documentation that are being submitted along with the data and that would be helpful to a secondary data user, such as pertinent field notes or other companion files, publications, etc.

Appendix 18.B. Survey Instrument

1. What research data do you create for your work/research?
2. How do you document your data or your work with the data (examples of documentation include lab notebooks, file naming conventions, README files, or change logs)?
3. Who typically creates the documentation?
4. What determines what types of documentation or metadata you collect? Are you following a community protocol, continuing the methods you were taught, or is it determined organically, as you recognize a need?
5. What information would someone need to know about your data in order to use them properly? This could be general concepts, like the methodology of the data collection, or specific pieces of information, like the orientation of the MRI scanner.
6. [Using the list compiled from analyzing the participant's published literature] Which of these elements on this list would someone else need to know?
7. Do you use, or are you aware of, any tools to help with the creation and storage of your documentation and metadata?
8. Have you shared data with people outside your research group?
    a. If yes, what additional information did you provide and/or did they request?

9. Have you ever deposited data into a repository?
    a. If yes, what additional information did you include? Where there pieces of information that were required?
10. Do you use a disciplinary metadata schema to document your data? Are there any standards for collecting metadata or documentation that you use in your work?
11. Does you discipline use any standard file formats or have data standardization guidelines/best practices?
12. Have you ever used data that you yourself did not collect? This could include data collected by graduate students, collaborators, or researchers they have never before worked with.
    a. If yes, what additional information did you need in order to use those data?
13. If you were asked to fill out the metadata template (which was either reviewed ahead of time or are provided at this time), which fields would you fill out? Which fields are confusing? Which fields don't need to be there? Which fields aren't there that you think should be?
14. Do you have any other questions or concerns, or is there something you think we should have asked but didn't?

---

1. P. Bryan Heidorn, "The Emerging Role of Libraries in Data Curation and E-Science," *Journal of Library Administration* 51, no. 7–8 (October 1, 2011): 662–72, doi:10.1080/01930826.2011.601269.
2. V. Van den Eynden and Libby Bishop, "Incentives and Motivations for Sharing Research Data, a Researcher's Perspective" (UK Data Archive, 2014), knowledge-exchange.info/Default. aspx-?ID=733.
3. Research Information Network, "To Share or Not to Share: Publication and Quality Assurance of Research Data Outputs," 2008, http://www.rin.ac.uk/system/files/attachments/To-share-data-outputs-report.pdf.
4. Djoko Sigit Sayogo and Theresa A. Pardo, "Exploring the Determinants of Scientific Data Sharing: Understanding the Motivation to Publish Research Data," *Government Information Quarterly* 30, no. 1 (January 2013): S19–31, doi:10.1016/j.giq.2012.06.011.
5. Lizzy Rolando, Chris Doty, Wendy Hagenmaier, Alison Valk, and Susan Wells Parham, "Institutional Readiness for Data Stewardship: Findings and Recommendations from the Research Data Assessment" (2013), https://smartech.gatech.edu/handle/1853/48188; Christine L. Borgman, "The Conundrum of Sharing Research Data," *Journal of the American Society for Information Science and Technology* 63, no. 6 (June 1, 2012): 1059–78, doi:10.1002/asi.22634.
6. Amanda Whitmire et al., "A Table Summarizing the Federal Public Access Policies Resulting from the US Office of Science and Technology Policy Memorandum of February 2013" (2015), doi:10.6084/m9.figshare.1372041.
7. National Information Standards Organization, "Understanding Metadata" (Bethesda, MD: NISO, 2004), 3.
8. Matthew S. Mayernik, "Metadata Realities for Cyberinfrastructure: Data Authors as Metadata Creators," SSRN Scholarly Paper (Rochester, NY: Social Science Research Network, June 8, 2011), http://papers.ssrn.com/abstract=2042653.

9. Christine L. Borgman, *Big Data, Little Data, No Data: Scholarship in the Networked World* (Cambridge, MA: MIT Press, 2015).
10. National Information Standards Organization, "Understanding Metadata"; Mayernik, "Metadata Realities for Cyberinfrastructure."
11. Jane Greenberg, Hollie C. White, Sarah Carrier, and Ryan Scherle, "A Metadata Best Practice for a Scientific Data Repository," *Journal of Library Metadata* 9 (2009): 194–212, doi:10.1080/19386380903405090; Paul N. Edwards, Matthew S. Mayernik, Archer L. Batcheller, Geoffrey C. Bowker, and Christine L. Borgman, "Science Friction: Data, Metadata, and Collaboration," *Social Studies of Science* 41, no. 5 (October 1, 2011): 667–90, doi:10.1177/0306312711413314.
12. Christine L. Borgman, Jillian C. Wallis, and Noel Enyedy, "Little Science Confronts the Data Deluge: Habitat Ecology, Embedded Sensor Networks, and Digital Libraries," *Int. J. Digit. Libr.* 7, no. 1 (2007): 17–30, doi:10.1007/s00799-007-0022-9; Carol Tenopir, Suzie Allard, Kimberly Douglass, Arsev Umur Aydinoglu, Lei Wu, Eleanor Read, Maribeth Manoff, and Mike Frame, "Data Sharing by Scientists: Practices and Perceptions," *PLoS ONE* 6, no. 6 (2011): e21101, doi:10.1371/journal.pone.0021101; Jillian C. Wallis, Elizabeth Rolando, and Christine L. Borgman, "If We Share Data, Will Anyone Use Them? Data Sharing and Reuse in the Long Tail of Science and Technology," *PLoS ONE* 8, no. 7 (2013): e67332, doi:10.1371/journal.pone.0067332; Mayernik, *Metadata Realities for Cyberinfrastructure.*
13. Edwards et al., "Science Friction."
14. Tiffany C. Chao, "Enhancing Metadata for Research Methods in Data Curation," in *Proceedings of the 77th ASIS&T Annual Meeting*, vol. 51 (Association for Information Science and Technology, Seattle, WA, 2014), https://asis.org/asist2014/proceedings/submissions/posters/249poster.pdf.
15. Ann S. Zimmerman, "New Knowledge from Old Data: The Role of Standards in the Sharing and Reuse of Ecological Data," *Science, Technology & Human Values* (February 5, 2008), doi:10.1177/0162243907306704; Ixchel M. Faniel and Trond E. Jacobsen, "Reusing Scientific Data: How Earthquake Engineering Researchers Assess the Reusability of Colleagues' Data," *Computer Supported Cooperative Work (CSCW)* 19, no. 3–4 (September 2010): 355–75, doi:10.1007/s10606-010-9117-8.
16. Ixchel M. Faniel, David Minor, and Carole L. Palmer, "Putting Research Data into Context: A Scholarly Approach to Curating Data for Reuse" in *Proceedings of the 77th ASIS&T Annual Meeting*, vol. 51 (Association for Information Science and Technology, Seattle, WA, 2014), http://www.slideshare.net/oclcr/putting-research-data-into-context-a-scholarly-approach-to-curating-data-for-reuse.
17. Christine L. Borgman, *Scholarship in the Digital Age: Information, Infrastructure, and the Internet* (Cambridge, MA: MIT Press, 2007).
18. Priscilla Caplan, *Metadata Fundamentals for All Librarians* (Chicago, IL: American Library Association, 2003).
19. Katherine G. Akers and Jennifer Doty, "Disciplinary Differences in Faculty Research Data Management Practices and Perspectives," *International Journal of Digital Curation* 8, no. 2 (2013): 5–26, doi:10.2218/ijdc.v8i2.263; Borgman, "The Conundrum of Sharing Research Data"; Melissa H. Cragin, Carole L. Palmer, Jacob R. Carlson, and Michael Witt, "Data Sharing, Small Science and Institutional Repositories," *Philosophical Transactions of the Royal Society of London A: Mathematical, Physical and Engineering Sciences* 368, no. 1926 (2010): 4023–38, doi:10.1098/rsta.2010.0165; Mayernik, *Metadata Realities for Cyberinfrastructure.*
20. Chao, "Enhancing Metadata for Research Methods in Data Curation."
21. Borgman, Wallis, and Enyedy, "Little Science Confronts the Data Deluge"; Tenopir et al., "Data Sharing by Scientists"; Wallis, Rolando, and Borgman, "If We Share Data, Will Anyone Use Them?"; Mayernik, "Metadata Realities for Cyberinfrastructure."
22. Edwards et al., "Science Friction."
23. Mayernik, "Metadata Realities for Cyberinfrastructure."

24. Yanni Loukissas and Krystelle Denis, "The Life and Death of Metadata," n.d., http://lifeanddeathofdata.org/; Hollie C. White, "Considering Personal Organization: Metadata Practices of Scientists," *Journal of Library Metadata* 10, no. 2–3 (August 31, 2010): 156–72, doi:10.1080/19386389.2010.506396.
25. Mayernik, "Metadata Realities for Cyberinfrastructure."
26. Caplan, *Metadata Fundamentals for All Librarians.*
27. Matthew S. Mayernik, "Research Data and Metadata Curation as Institutional Issues," *Journal of the Association for Information Science and Technology* 66 (2015), doi:10.1002/asi.23425.
28. Kristin Briney, "README.txt," *Data Ab Initio: Managing Research Right, From the Start*, accessed April 10, 2015, http://dataabinitio.com/?p=378.
29. Hollie C. White, "Descriptive Metadata for Scientific Data Repositories: A Comparison of Information Scientist and Scientist Organizing Behaviors," *Journal of Library Metadata* 14, no. 1 (2014): 24–51, doi:10.1080/19386389.2014.891896.
30. Greenberg et al., "A Metadata Best Practice for a Scientific Data Repository"; Inter-university Consortium for Political and Social Research, "Metadata," *ICPSR Data Management & Curation* n.d., http://www.icpsr.umich.edu/icpsrweb/content/datamanagement/lifecycle/metadata.html.
31. Dryad, "Frequently Asked Questions," Dryad, 2015, http://datadryad.org/pages/faq.
32. For example, see Engs, R. and Zhuo-Ping, L (1997). China Research Dataset: Drinking Patterns, Attitudes towards Alcohol, and Health Concerns. [dataset]. Available at http://hdl.handle.net/2022/17232.
33. Tiffany Chao, "Mapping Methods Metadata for Research Data," *International Journal of Digital Curation* 10, no. 1 (2015): 82–94, doi:10.2218/ijdc.v10i1.347; Mayernik, *Metadata Realities for Cyberinfrastructure.*
34. Jian Qin and Kai Li, "How Portable Are the Metadata Standards for Scientific Data? A Proposal for a Metadata Infrastructure," *International Conference on Dublin Core and Metadata Applications*, September 2, 2013, 25–34.
35. Charlotte Hess and Elinor Ostrom, *Understanding Knowledge as a Commons* (Cambridge, MA: MIT Press, 2006).
36. Akers and Doty, "Disciplinary Differences in Faculty Research Data Management Practices and Perspectives"; Borgman, "The Conundrum of Sharing Research Data"; Cragin et al., "Data Sharing, Small Science and Institutional Repositories"; Chao, "Mapping Methods Metadata for Research Data"; Jillian C. Wallis, Christine L. Borgman, Matthew S. Mayernik, and Alberto Pepe, "Moving Archival Practices Upstream: An Exploration of the Life Cycle of Ecological Sensing Data in Collaborative Field Research," *International Journal of Digital Curation* 3, no. 1 (2008): 114–26, doi:10.2218/ijdc.v3i1.46.
37. Christine L. Borgman, Jillian C. Wallis, and Noel Enyedy, "Little Science Confronts the Data Deluge: Habitat Ecology, Embedded Sensor Networks, and Digital Libraries," *Int. J. Digit. Libr.* 7, no. 1 (October 2007): 17–30, doi:10.1007/s00799-007-0022-9; Tenopir et al., "Data Sharing by Scientists"; Wallis, Rolando, and Borgman, "If We Share Data, Will Anyone Use Them?"; Mayernik, "Metadata Realities for Cyberinfrastructure."
38. Chao, "Mapping Methods Metadata for Research Data."; Chao, "Enhancing Metadata for Research Methods in Data Curation."

PART IV

Data: Past, Present, and Future

CHAPTER 19

View from Across the Pond:
A UK Perspective

Robin Rice

WHEN REFLECTING ON the UK perspective, it may be useful to compare the experiences of North American data services with those of the UK in particular, and Europe more generally. The role of the academic library in the provision of data services has changed in recent years in the UK, where unlike North America, national data services and archives have predominated as the European model of data support for decades. The UK Data Archive (UKDA) and other national service providers have contributed to the knowledge and expertise across British institutions that are now struggling to develop local research data services. Those few UK institutions that have hosted data library and equivalent services are in a strong position to roll out new types of research data solutions in their institutions and serve as a role model for others.

UK national funding organisations play a crucial role in creating drivers for cultural change toward both open access publishing and research data management and sharing. Many research institutions have responded to funding council expectations regarding policy, implementation, and support for data management planning through investment in both IT infrastructure and new data librarian and data management coordinator job posts. However, many of these new posts are reactive to the funders' mandates and do not extend the data librarian's role to its more traditional support work of helping staff and student researchers find, access, and analyse secondary sources of research data. This is despite the growing trend of cross-disciplinary computational science and the increasing tendency for disciplines beyond the social sciences to crunch numbers from existing sources of data.

The European Model

Participants in the international community of social science data providers and supporters will have noticed a distinct difference in the shape of academic data services on opposite sides of the Atlantic since their establishment in the 1960s and later. Where small, local academic data libraries proliferated in North America, Europe fostered centralised, government-funded data archives. This probably reflected differences in how higher education was funded in general, with European universities more heavily tied to the public purse and North American universities more often privately funded and competing freely in the marketplace. Thus, as a rule we have European data *archivists* and North American data *librarians* serving social scientists who require access to secondary datasets such as survey and census data. Exceptions to the rule include the large American data archive, Inter-university Consortium for Political and Social Research (ICPSR), based at the University of Michigan, which is not generally funded by the government but by institutional memberships, and the small but growing number of data librarians based in UK universities.

The expertise developed within the centralised European data archives has been extended and consolidated over time through cooperation and communication through the Consortium of European Social Science Data Archives (CESSDA), as well as the International Federation of Data Organisations (IFDO), the International Association for Social Science Information Services & Technology (IASSIST), and other bodies. CESSDA was founded in 1976 as an informal umbrella group. Today it is a permanent legal entity funded by its member states: Austria, Czech Republic, Denmark, Finland, France, Germany, Lithuania, the Netherlands, Norway, Slovenia, Sweden, Switzerland, and the United Kingdom (with the Slovak Republic as an observer). Hosted in Bergen, Norway, the consortium consists of thirteen European countries with designated service providers working to harmonise their holdings and procedures and to support less well-resourced data archives in other European countries. Many of their holdings consist of government-produced surveys and cross-country surveys such as the Eurobarometer series, as well as datasets produced by academic researchers. CESSDA has always worked toward metadata standardisation; it has a search and browsable pan-European data catalogue, and has developed a multi-language social science thesaurus (http://cessda.net/CESSDA-Services/Resources/Data-Catalogue).

In Europe the social sciences have generally opted to build their own infrastructures for data use, focusing on survey and other quantitative datasets with highly structured metadata, particularly metadata using standards such as the Data Documentation Initiative (DDI), once known as the "codebook standard." As is discussed in another chapter,[†] national data archives (including ICPSR in the US) have played a major role in developing DDI, ensuring the standard

† For more information about DDI, see the chapter in this volume by Leahey and Fry called "Metadata for Social Science Data: Collaborative Best Practices."

helps agencies process datasets throughout a curation lifecycle, as well as improve access by providing XML metadata that allow datasets to be fully marked up at the variable level and then browsed, subsetted and even analysed online via web applications.‡ Now that the social sciences are entering the era of Big Data, there may be even more reasons for researchers to work together across disciplines. This is both because of the methodological challenges presented by new forms of computational-based research and the multidisciplinary nature of many contemporary "grand challenges," such as climate change and the results of globalisation.

The advent of Open Data in governments has led to the perceived need for more secure data infrastructures to be built to safeguard against potentially damaging data disclosure about individual human subjects, a problem that the social sciences shares with clinical research. The ability to combine data from different sources offers new methodological promise even as it increases the potential for unethical disclosure. The European Data Protection Directive is privacy legislation which ensures that the need to protect data subjects is a legal, as well as an ethical, obligation for all European states. In the UK, this is policed by Information Commissioner Offices that have the power to mediate disputes about both data protection and freedom of information and can punish (usually through fines) data controllers found to be mis-handling personal data.

An update to the European Data Protection Directive has been agreed on by the European Parliament, Council of Ministers, and European Commission as part of an overhaul of the 20-year-old legislation to take into account newer technologies such as cloud computing and social media, as well as the impact of increasing globalization. The General Data Protection Regulation (GDPR) is due to be finalised by spring 2016, with enforcement to begin in spring, 2018. Research and health organisations were involved in developing the current solutions for ethical, secure data access, especially to medical records, and have been lobbying strenuously for the continuation of the research exemption in some form, which allows some research in the public interest to go ahead without explicit consent.[1] For example, the ability to link administrative records by individual identifiers combined with a system of careful governance for approving access to this sort of linked data has led to innovative new services for providing safe access to medical, welfare, and other important government held records about individuals to approved researchers. Such linkage and access would not be possible if the law determined that all research subjects needed to consent in advance to their data being used for any particular research project.

‡ The system used by the UKDA is Nesstar (www.nesstar.com). Nesstar has various software modules—free and for purchase, developed and owned by the Norwegian Social Science Data Services.

The UK Data Archive

The Social Science Data Bank established at the University of Essex in 1967 was itself an exception to the European model in that it, like ICPSR, was based at a university rather than a government department. With a complement of over 70 staff, the UK Data Archive, as it is known today, has become an internationally regarded centre of expertise in social science data acquisition, curation, and access, as well as a repository of research data management knowledge for both its primary funder, the government-funded Economic and Social Research Council (ESRC), and its grant recipients (researchers in UK institutions). The archive holds several thousand historical and contemporary datasets, including key national and international survey data collections, international databanks, census data, and qualitative data. While government surveys account for the majority of datasets accessed, ESRC has had a longstanding policy that its grant recipients are required to offer all data, including data derived from existing datasets, to the archive for deposit. The archive does not in practice accept all datasets offered, though in the last few years it has set up a self-deposit repository (ReShare) with a broader acceptance policy. More recently, ESRC has updated its data management requirements to allow some of the data creators they fund to deposit data into their institutional repositories instead, given certain circumstances.

Balancing National and Local Support in the UK

In the United Kingdom, the UKDA has always been the standard bearer for quality service provision for social science data. The Essex-based organisation has consistently won bids to be the ESRC's data archive of choice over four decades. In the last decade, as part of a consolidated funding arrangement, it has entered into collaborations with other specialist data providers[†] to offer a broader menu of services, such as international macrodata and population census data, under the umbrella of the UK Data Service (UKDS). UKDA also champions data archiving standards and guidelines for research data management best practices in the UK and Europe.

Like its European counterparts, the UKDA has developed a direct relationship with social science data users in terms of raising awareness, training, registration and data delivery, and omitting institutional liaisons whenever technically

† Currently these include Jisc (formerly Mimas) and the Cathie Marsh Institute for Social Research at the University of Manchester, EDINA at the University of Edinburgh, the School of Geography at the University of Leeds, Geography and Environment at the University of Southampton, and University College London.

feasible. This is in contrast to the ICPSR model of a consortium of universities paying for the services of a social science data archive in the US provided through the role of organizational representatives, and to the Statistics Canada Data Liberation Initiative, which has a programme for training librarians to support data requests.‡ Because the UKDA service is free for all members of UK higher education institutions, no institutional subscriptions are required, nor are there librarians acting in a direct liaison role.§

While perhaps efficient, this arrangement's downside has been the general lack of institutional capacity to support the use of social datasets in secondary analysis, in contrast with the best North American research institutions. For example, as part of a larger investigation into capacity-building needs in England, Wales, Scotland, and Northern Ireland for uptake of quantitative social science research methods funded by the ESRC, a 2008 targeted survey of library and computing professionals at fourteen Scottish universities led to responses from nine institutions about levels and kinds of support for data analysis in the social sciences.[2] The study found that provision of detailed support for an individual's use of quantitative data sources was low, though these results were self-reported and not independently verified. Only one institution provided support in all the areas listed in Table 19.1, the same one that had a data library service (University of Edinburgh).

Table 19.1. Types of Support Provided by Library or Computing Staff (n = 9)

Type of Support Offered	Number Offering Support
Identifying appropriate service/website based on user's query	5
Instruction/assistance in use of search/download interface	5
Downloading/subsetting/reformatting data on behalf of user	4
Troubleshooting problems using data (e.g. in analysis packages)	2
Consultation on methods or research question	2
Assistance with understanding data documentation or codebooks	1

‡ For more information on Statistics Canada and the Data Liberation Initiative, see the chapter in this volume by Hill & Gray called "The Academic Data Librarian Profession in Canada: History and Future Directions."

§ The role of site representative did exist up until the 2000s, when datasets needed to be delivered to a stable postal address on portable media (tapes then CDs and DVDs). Some training in the role was offered, though in the author's experience it was a little understood and peripheral role for many of the librarians and computing officers who found themselves performing it.

Learning from North America

Those few who have had a dedicated data support role in UK universities, such as data librarians and data managers, have often looked to North America for models of support. A couple of years after his appointment to Edinburgh University Data Library in 1983, Peter Burnhill looked at both sides of the Atlantic in his paper for the Librarians and Statisticians Committee of the Library Association and the Royal Statistical Society, "Towards Data Libraries in the UK."[3] A survey statistician himself, he noted the importance of social scientists' own initiative in setting up data libraries and archives to help control access to the burgeoning machine-readable data files (MRDF)† that were the basis of their research. In the UK he pointed to the Department of Government at Essex University and the Department of Politics at Strathclyde University as the "driving force" of the data services that were developed there. He quoted Judith Rowe from the Princeton University Data Library in the US regarding how such services often cropped up outside the controlled library environment: "They usually existed outside the Library and were totally lacking in library procedures for collection, management or bibliographic control."[4] He also called for a union catalogue for data libraries, noting the importance of Sue Dodd's contributions to normalising cataloguing procedures for MRDF.

A decade later, Simon Brackenbury, a History graduate appointed as data librarian at the London School of Economics, was tasked with designing a data library service for the British Library of Political and Economic Science, under the direction of Jean Sykes. After consulting with UK Data Archive staff he identified three sites in the UK which provided deeper data support than that of site representative—the Universities of Edinburgh, Plymouth, and Oxford—and also toured data libraries in the US and Canada‡. His observations and recommendations were written up concisely in his paper, "Ways of Supporting Data Use in the Social Sciences," in which he summarised his visits and covered such varied topics as levels of support, national versus local models of support, staff backgrounds and qualifications, most popular data, storage and media, collection development policies, help for finding data, software, and involvement with taught courses.[5]

---

† This was the common parlance of the time; MRDF meant digital data files that requires software code to render and manipulate them, such as data formatted by SPSS.

‡ The bridge across the Atlantic has been travelled many times, including in 1998 when a data librarian from the University of Wisconsin (the author) took up the vacant post of data librarian at the University of Edinburgh, and in 2014 when another University of Edinburgh data librarian, Stuart Macdonald, completed a 6-month temporary appointment at the Cornell Institute for Social and Economic Research (CISER) for the purpose of professional knowledge exchange. At the same time Laine Ruus, retired data librarian from University of Toronto, filled the vacancy at Edinburgh, extending the knowledge exchange further.

DISC-UK and the Emergence of UK Data Librarians

In 2004 a group of five academic data professionals (data librarians and data managers) based in UK universities formed DISC-UK (Data Information Specialists Committee—United Kingdom) as a "talking shop" to overcome their professional isolation in between international IASSIST conferences,[§] and to compare notes on service provision. Occasional face-to-face meetings were held at the London School of Economics, Oxford University, and the University of Edinburgh, and later Southampton University.

The group engaged in a formal collaboration which was funded nationally as part of a programme of activity to enhance existing institutional repositories across UK higher education institutions. The project, called DISC-UK DataShare (2007-09), involved data librarians, data managers, repository librarians, and technical staff at the four institutions to set up exemplars to show that "institutional repositories can improve impact of sharing data over the internet," among other aims.[6] The project helped to raise the profile of data librarians in the UK, and caught the bleeding edge of libraries entering the realm of research data management support in the UK. A common rhetorical question heard at UK data-related events in those years was, "Should libraries be involved in data support?" The answer was certainly not self-evident at the time. Although this project was arguably ahead of its time, a number of deliverables from the project (http://www.disc-uk.org/deliverables.html), along with a handful of other data-related projects in the same program, laid groundwork for future programs to help institutions create policies and infrastructure for data management. These programs were funded by Jisc[¶] under the rubric of *Managing Research Data* between 2009 and 2013.

After the project, the participants went in separate directions and the DISC-UK "talking shop" came to an end. However, by this time momentum was building for libraries to get involved in data support; the UK Digital Curation Centre—set up in 2004 as a national centre of expertise—was maturing and organising training and events; the original purpose of the group in dealing with professional isolation was gradually becoming a phenomenon of the past.

During this time Jisc commissioned a report to look into the skills needed by and the academic career incentives (or lack of incentives) for data managers, or scientists whose focus was on data curation rather than publication. This led

§ IASSIST, or the International Association for Social Science Information Services and Technology, is an individual membership organisation for social science data librarians and data archivists world-wide.

¶ Jisc, formerly the Joint Information Systems Committee, is itself largely funded by the Higher Education Funding Council for England as well as the equivalent organisations in the other UK countries. Its services and innovation programmes have helped build and strengthen the information infrastructure of UK 'higher and further education' institutions since the 1990s.

to the landmark report, *The Skills, Role and Career Structure of Data Scientists: An Assessment of Current Practice and Future Needs.*[7] The authors had heard of DISC-UK and the DataShare project, and after interviewing a few participants, wrote a section of the report on "the training and supply of data librarians." Suddenly a large proportion of the library community was aware that "although there are some individuals in the UK who are called data librarians, it is thought these currently number around five!"[8] Considering the small number, and that some of the five had other job titles, this was a slight embarrassment, but fortunately the report outlined the need for more and also called for training to be introduced in the library schools.

The Role of Research Funders

For many years, only two or three of the seven Research Councils UK (RCUK) members explicitly supported data sharing by their funded research projects: the Economic and Social Research Council, through its funding of the UK Data Archive and related services; the Natural Environment Research Council, through its network of discipline-specific data centres and long-standing data policy; and the Arts and Humanities Research Council, which funded specialised data archives under the umbrella of the Arts and Humanities Data Service from 1996 until 2008 when it unceremoniously ceased its funding (although funding for the Archaeology Data Service has continued).

However, as a member of the OECD the UK government had to take note of the seminal report *OECD Principles and Guidelines for Access to Research Data from Public Funding,*[9] which set out the principle that publicly funded research should be made publicly available. Moreover, the growing open access (to research publications) movement, combined with data management and sharing mandates by US government funders such as the National Institutes of Health (NIH) and the National Science Foundation (NSF)—and before that, the Australian government—were bound to shake up long-held perceptions of academic norms. Finally, the value for money arguments about research being needlessly repeated due to lack of publication of negative results (known as publication bias) and the moral arguments put forth by scientific opinion leaders such as *Nature* Magazine,[10] along with the positive example set by the private London-based funder, the Wellcome Trust, led to some tentative and then bolder policies emerging from the research councils. In 2011 RCUK issued a set of Common Principles on Research Data Policy.[11]

Since then, the UK-based Digital Curation Centre (DCC), a centre of expertise for the higher education community in digital preservation and data curation, has analysed and tracked both the principles and the (still-changing) individual policies, for stakeholders including academic libraries to make sense of the nuanced differences and similarities (See Figure 19.1).

Figure 19.1. Overview of Funders' Data Policies

● Full Coverage ◐ Partial Coverage ○ No Coverage

	Policy Coverage		Policy Stipulations					Support Provided			
Research Funders	Published outputs	Data	Time limits	Data plan	Access/ sharing	Long-term curation	Monitoring	Guidance	Repository	Data centre	Costs
AHRC	●	●	●	●	●	◐	○	●	○	◐	◐
BBSRC	●	●	●	●	●	●	●	●	●	◐	●
CRUK	●	●	●	●	●	●	●	◐	●	○	○
EPSRC	●	●	●	◐	●	●	●	◐	○	○	●
ESRC	●	●	●	●	●	●	●	●	●	●	◐
MRC	●	●	●	●	●	●	○	◐	●	○	◐
NERC	●	●	●	●	●	●	●	●	●	●	◐
STFC	●	●	●	●	●	●	●	◐	●	◐	◐
Wellcome Trust	●	●	●	●	●	●	●	●	●	◐	●

Reprinted with permission from the Digital Curation Centre. Overview of funders' data policies, accessed October 24, 2015, http://www.dcc.ac.uk/resources/policy-and-legal/overview-funders-data-policies.

At the time that the University of Edinburgh was scoping its Research Data Management Policy, circa 2010, a laissez-faire attitude existed amongst UK university administrations toward the research conduct of its staff. Some researchers invited to the early scoping meetings voiced opinions that the university had no business imposing rules such as data sharing mandates on them. They were already pressured by both teaching-related regulations and paperwork, and the peculiar national obsession of the Research Excellence Framework (REF), a competition and ranking of a selected subset of publications which determines both government funding and individual career rewards in universities. It was one thing for the funders to impose rules on principal investigators regarding funded projects; it was quite another for universities to intervene in research conduct beyond the normal vetting and ethical evaluation of research projects.

For this reason and others, the policy that was eventually passed by the University of Edinburgh in May 2011 (the first such policy in UK universities) was carefully framed to shore up existing policy requirements by funders rather than to impose new mandates. It also laid out the responsibilities of the researchers themselves for the active management of research data during the life of the research project, along with the infrastructural and resourcing obligations of the institution in supporting researchers to manage their data well (such as providing sufficient storage, preservation services, etc.). The wording of the policy made clear that the policy itself was aspirational, and would take several years to fully implement.[12] Many of the UK university research data management (RDM) policies that were developed in the next couple of years copied the tone or words of the Edinburgh policy, which was formulated by the former director of the DCC, Chris Rusbridge, although some of the later ones dared state their requirements more forcefully.

Surprisingly, it was the last research council to formulate a policy that turned out to be the real game-changer. In April 2011, the Engineering and Physical Sciences Research Council (EPSRC) decided to place the requirements for data management and sharing on institutions as a whole, rather than individual grant-holders. They issued expectations of institutions in receipt of their (sometimes quite substantial) research funds, for example that the institution would gather data management plans from every research project—whether EPSRC-funded or not. Yet they did not ask grant-seekers to include a data management plan either as part of their submission, or any time after their proposal was accepted. This was an ingenious way for the council to pass on enforcement of their expectations to institutions. They also mandated that each institution receiving their funds create a "roadmap" of progress toward implementation of the expectations by May 2015; since then they have been conducting various forms of light-touch checks and audits on compliance.

Needless to say, the prospect of losing all future funding from the largest research council in the UK eventually focused minds from the tops of institutions on down. As a rough indicator, in this period (April 2011–May 2015), 34 UK-based data-related jobs appeared in the IASSIST Jobs Repository (http://www.iassistdata.org/resources/jobs/all). Twelve of them were at the UK Data Archive, but the rest were serving individual institutions. For comparison, in the previous three years, only 13 jobs appeared (11 of them at UKDA or its sister service in Manchester).

Europe and Horizon 2020

While many countries' funders still do not require data management plans, these requirements are being piloted in the current round of European Commission funding, known as Horizon 2020. Some projects are automatically added to the data pilot but may choose to withdraw, and others may opt in. Those who do are expected to provide data management plans and deposit their data in a suitable repository for sharing. Although this is a cautious rather than bold step for the funder to take, it should provide a useful experiment for the study of outcomes. In the Commission's own words, "The Pilot will give the Commission a better understanding of what supporting infrastructure is needed and of the impact of limiting factors such as security, privacy or data protection or other reasons for projects opting out of sharing. It will also contribute insights in how best to create incentives for researchers to manage and share their research data."[13]

Academic Libraries Rethinking Research Support

Many of those jobs created at UK institutions were library-based. A few were based in a research office or an IT centre. Academic libraries increasingly have seen these roles as coordinators of research data management support across the institution (hence the commonly seen job title of RDM Coordinator or Service Coordinator). As if to hedge their bets, many of these posts started out as fixed-term, corresponding to the run-up to the EPSRC deadline, or perhaps imagined to become unnecessary once the policy and infrastructure was put in place. It is a bit too early to speculate about the lasting nature of these posts, but recent training events sponsored by the DCC seem to have quite a number of new faces among the delegates, indicating that we may be witnessing a second generation of data professionals already.

Library leaders have been tentatively embracing data support as an important part of a reinvigorated research support role, seen as necessary to redress the balance given in recent years, especially by subject and liaison librarians, toward learning and teaching (such as information literacy skills training). From a North American perspective their approach may seem partial, as in not embracing all areas of data support—such as support for secondary analysis and use of statistical and geospatial data—but rather more narrowly focused on research data management and the strengths they perceive librarians can bring to it, such as metadata, curation, and archival management.

An influential report commissioned by Research Libraries UK (RLUK) in 2012 drew attention to a skills gap among academic librarians, based on a web survey of 169 subject librarians and their managers from 22 RLUK member libraries, in which they were asked about skills that would be important in two to five years and that were important now. The skills that more than a quarter of respondents said would be important in two to five years were:

- Ability to advise on preserving research outputs (49% essential in 2–5 years; 10% now)
- Knowledge to advise on data management and curation, including ingest, discovery, access, dissemination, preservation, and portability (48% essential in 2–5 years; 16% now)
- Knowledge to support researchers in complying with the various mandates of funders, including open access requirements (40% essential in 2–5 years; 16% now)
- Knowledge to advise on potential data manipulation tools used in the discipline/ subject (34% essential in 2–5 years; 7% now)
- Knowledge to advise on data mining (33% essential in 2–5 years; 3% now)
- Knowledge to advocate, and advise on, the use of metadata (29% essential in 2–5 years; 10% now)[14]

While there is some consensus about the direction academic libraries need to go in the UK, it is less clear how they will get there. Library and information schools are attempting to fill those gaps at the Masters level, but it is left to organisations like the Digital Curation Centre (DCC) and institutions themselves to train librarians currently in the workforce. The DCC hosts an annual conference at various locations in Europe and North America, operates a peer review international journal, and provides in-depth support for institutions in the UK (http://www.dcc.ac.uk/resources). Research Data MANTRA (http://datalib.edina.ac.uk/mantra), a free, open, online course hosted by EDINA and the Data Library at the University of Edinburgh provides do-it-yourself training for both researchers and librarians in RDM, and has been adopted and adapted by other institutions for their own training requirements. The Netherlands has a similar resource, in both Dutch and English, for librarians called Essentials 4 Data Support (http://datasupport.researchdata.nl/en/). There is also now a free, cross-Atlantic MOOC (Massive, Open, Online Course) available on the Coursera platform called Research Data Management and Sharing, for researchers and information professionals, delivered by the University of North Carolina-Chapel Hill and the University of Edinburgh, over repeating 5-week enrolment periods. Some European Union-based institutional libraries have taken advantage of an EU-funded travel and training award programme called Erasmus to undertake site visits at institutions such as the Universities of Edinburgh and Glasgow and other places where they perceive RDM services have been rolled out and are somewhat mature.

For university data services to reach maturity in the UK, senior managers need to view staff investment as a response to the changing needs of their academics, rather than a simple reaction to funding council requirements. Data science is the next big trend looming, and it remains to be seen how librarians intend to engage with these new research requirements. Perhaps there is hope in the fact that the Information School at the University of Sheffield now offers a postgraduate data science degree; however, the majority of data science courses in the UK are more computing science based than librarian-focused, so it is unclear what synergies, if any, will develop between the areas of librarianship and data science. It may be observed that academic libraries that have good relations or are integrated with IT services are able to fill these service gaps more quickly than those who are more isolated from university IT and other related academic services. In this sense, it also "takes a village"[†] to produce robust data services in the UK.

† For more about this concept, see the chapter in this volume by Hofelich Mohr, Johnston and Lindsay, "The Data Management Village: Collaboration Among Research Support Providers."

---

1. "Good news for health research from trilogue talks on the Data Protection Regulation," *European Data in Health Research Alliance*, December 15, 2015, http://www.datasaveslives.eu/news-resources/good-news-for-health-research-from-trilogue-talks-on-the-data-protection-regulation/.
2. Susan McVie, Anthony P.M. Coxon, Philip Hawkins, Jackie Palmer and Robin Rice. *ESRC/SFC Scoping Study into Quantitative Methods Capacity Building in Scotland*, Edinburgh: University of Edinburgh, 2008: 30–31, http://www.esrc.ac.uk/_images/Scoping_Study_into_Quantitative_Capacity_Building_in_Scotland_tcm8-2683.pdf.
3. Peter Burnhill, *Towards the Development of Data Libraries in the UK*, Edinburgh: University of Edinburgh, 1985, http://hdl.handle.net/1842/2510.
4. Sue Dodd, *Cataloguing Machine-Readable Data Files: An Interpretive Manual* (Chicago, American Library Association, 1982).
5. Simon Brackenbury, *Ways of Supporting Data Use in the Social Sciences. Report from Visits to UK and US Data Libraries* (London: London School of Economics, 1997) http://www.disc-uk.org/docs/brackenbury.pdf.
6. Robin Rice, "DISC-UK DataShare Project: Building Exemplars for Institutional Data Repositories in the UK," *IASSIST Quarterly*, 31 (2007, Fall/Winter): 21 http://www.iassistdata.org/content/disc-uk-datashare-project-building-exemplars-institutional-data-repositories-uk.
7. Alma Swan and Sheridan Brown, *The Skills, Role and Career Structure of Data Scientists: An Assessment of Current Practice and Future Needs* (London: Joint Information Systems Committee, 2008) http://eprints.soton.ac.uk/266675/.
8. Ibid., 28.
9. Organisation of Economic Co-operation and Development, *OECD Principles and Guidelines for Access to Research Data from Public Funding*, April 2007 http://www.oecd.org/sti/sci-tech/oecdprinciplesandguidelinesforaccesstoresearchdatafrompublicfunding.htm.
10. "Editorial: Data's Shameful Neglect," *Nature* 461, no. 7261 (2009):145. doi:10.1038/461145a.
11. Research Councils UK, *RCUK Common Principles on Data Policy*, April 2011, revised July 2015 http://www.rcuk.ac.uk/research/datapolicy/.
12. University of Edinburgh, *Research Data Management Policy*, May 2011, accessed October 24, 2015, http://www.ed.ac.uk/is/research-data-policy.
13. European Commission, *Commission launches pilot to open up publicly funded research data*, December 2013, http://europa.eu/rapid/press-release_IP-13-1257_en.htm.
14. Mary Auckland, *Re-skilling for Research: An investigation into the role and skills of subject and liaison librarians required to effectively support the evolving information needs of researchers* (Research Libraries UK, January, 2012), 3 http://www.rluk.ac.uk/wp-content/uploads/2014/02/RLUK-Re-skilling.pdf.

CHAPTER 20

The Academic Data Librarian Profession in Canada:

History and Future Directions

Elizabeth Hill and Vincent Gray

FROM THE 1970S onward, Canadians have been active in developing services and establishing structures to support the dissemination of data. In recent years the academic data profession in Canada has largely developed around access to data from the national statistics agency, Statistics Canada, and around the services which have been developed to permit access to these data.[†] This chapter will provide a historical background for these activities and explain how current and emerging trends continue to affect the profession.

Data librarianship in Canadian universities in the 1970s and 1980s was influenced by factors similar to those in other countries. As was happening elsewhere, researchers, particularly in the social sciences, were beginning to collect and analyze machine-readable (MR) data files (MRDF)[‡] and to use already-collected data files as cost-effective resources for secondary analysis. Academic researchers, especially in the social sciences, increasingly looked to Statistics Canada as a source of MRDF for analysis.

The Development of Data Services

Initially, data services were typically located within computing centres as opposed to libraries, and librarians were seldom involved in the delivery of data. Institu-

† Western University (formerly University of Western Ontario) has been a participant in and/or developer of these services both prior and during to the tenure of the authors, who have combined for over 45 years of data experience at Western.

‡ Results of surveys or censuses coded into machine-readable format such as the Social Change in Canada Survey, 1977, conducted by Institute for Behavioral Research at York University.

tions typically chose to establish data services in pre-existing computing centres due to the cost and complexity of computers. The University of British Columbia established a Statistical Centre in 1963–1964.[1] Carleton University's data service, which in 2015 celebrated its 50th anniversary, was the only Canadian record in the publication *Social Science Data Archives in the United States, 1967*. Western University's data service was founded in 1972, in the Social Science Computing Laboratory (SSCL).

An article in a 1982 *Library Trends* special issue on data records that discussions began in the 1960s on how libraries or social science data archives might support data-related inquiries and provide services to support researchers.[2] Initially, discussions occurred within archives as libraries were not seen as logical partners, lacking the technology necessary to support statistical software programs. A second article in the same issue of *Library Trends* reported attempts to influence academic libraries to take responsibility for collections and services pertaining to data.[3]

The 1972 merger of the University of British Columbia's computing centre's data service into the university's library created the first Canadian library-based data service.[4] Generally, however, Canadian university libraries did not see data as part of their service mandate until the mid-1980s. In a 1979 article, Slavko Manojlovich recognized the growing use of computers for data analysis and that machine-readable files from the census were becoming increasingly important to researchers.[5] Canadian census data had been first released in machine-readable format with user summary tapes and public use sample tapes for the 1961 census. Manojlovich contended that the library, being the major depository of information at universities, was the logical home for MRDFs. Using a survey of Canadian government documents librarians, he found that 35 Canadian universities had census data files. Services to assist researchers with the data were found in disparate locations from university to university. Overall he recognized the need to have an information professional mediate access to MR data.

Locating and Providing Access to Data

The model for accessing and acquiring data during these early years was very different from today. If a researcher realized that Statistics Canada had a relevant data file, he or she might purchase it (usually for Can$300 or less), or contact Statistics Canada staff who could, and often would, provide the data for free. Other Canadian providers included the Machine-Readable Archives (subsequently the Government Archives) Division at the National Archives, and specialized centres, such as the Health and Leisure Databank at Waterloo and survey institutes at York, Alberta and Winnipeg, which would produce print catalogues of their holdings.

Researchers usually ordered data independent of any university-wide collections policy or service point; generally, they and their graduate students would be the only users of these files, so files might be duplicated on campus when acquired by different research teams. Data files would arrive on magnetic tapes, which required computer mainframe-based tape drives to read, together with technical staff and the infrastructure to support access and analysis. The Inter-university Consortium for Political and Social Research (ICPSR) marked a contrast to the norm. As a membership-based consortium, data orders were placed through and received by the university's Official Representative.

Print publications, such as *The Machine Readable Archives Catalogue of Holdings* (1981) or word of mouth were the only ways to discover the existence of data collections. An initial Canadian union catalogue, the self-described first annual edition of the Social Science Data Inventory, was produced in 1977 by the Data Clearing House for the Social Sciences. After the release of this catalogue, the Data Clearing House abruptly closed. A subsequent chill around developing national data infrastructure has been attributed in part to this closure.[6] This has been the source of much frustration for Canada's data professionals. Until the broader adoption of e-mail as an information dissemination tool, the creation of the Data Liberation Initiative (DLI), and the proliferation of web-based search tools, the landscape for finding data remained relatively unchanged. Proposals for the creation of a national data archive for Canada came to naught. Had such an agency been founded, the landscape for data discovery, sharing, and access would likely have been different.

Peer-Group Organizations

In the 1980s, data professionals were less likely than now to have campus colleagues who shared their experiences of supporting data. Therefore, they had to find peers from outside their institution to collaborate with or to rely upon for assistance. The International Association for Social Science Information Services and Technology (IASSIST, http://www.iassistdata.org) made up of data producers in government and academia, data librarians, administrators, and researchers, was founded to provide these support mechanisms.

The inaugural meeting which led to the development of the organization was held in Toronto in 1974 concurrent with the 1974 World Sociology Congress.[7] The aim was to use the meeting to "bring issues of common interests to a joint gathering of social science researchers and data service providers."[8] The eighteen members of the first IASSIST Steering Committee represented twelve different countries. Their initial objectives were laid out and their activities were planned in the structure of action groups, including data organization and management, data archive development, data documentation, classification, process-produced data, and data acquisition. The leaders of the IASSIST committees realized that standards were required for citing, formatting, cataloguing and referencing data files. Perhaps the best-known product of these groups was the *Working Manual for Cataloging Machine-Readable Data Files*, prepared by Sue A. Dodd, the U.S. chair of the Classification Action Group.[9]

During the inaugural meetings, Canada was represented by members from the academic community, the Public Archives of Canada, and Statistics Canada. The third IASSIST newsletter included reports of action groups on cataloguing and citation and on standards for data documentation, and a report describing a *Guide to Providing Social Science Data Services* presented at the May 1977 IASSIST conference in Toronto.[10] IASSIST has continued to influence the international profession of data librarians, researchers and producers for four decades with Canadian data librarians making significant national and international contributions to the organization.

The Inter-university Consortium for Political and Social Research (ICPSR), founded in 1962 at the University of Michigan, has long been linked with IASSIST. For example, one of ICPSR's earliest employees became the first president of IASSIST in 1976. ICPSR was created to make datasets available for reuse. The concept of reusing data, rather than the files being proprietary, was a foundational shift that led to the need to have data professionals at campuses who could serve to provide access to these products, technical expertise, and guidance. As described on the ICPSR website:

> The impulse [of ICPSR] to break with proprietary tradition was both strange and much welcomed in the social scientific community. In hindsight, we can think of this data sharing motive as a prerequisite of the "scientific ethic" of verification, replication, and validation. In the early 1960s, though, the concept of giving access to all interested scholars to one's basic (micro) data was so foreign as to be considered "revolutionary" ...likened to a violation of basic economic precepts: data were the scientist's capital, and "they weren't about to share their capital."[11]

ICPSR has been an influential organization in the development of data professionals and data librarians in Canada. Two ICPSR membership consortia, CAPPUL and OCUL/CREPUQ, represent 34 Canadian universities.[12] The twelve-person ICPSR Council includes two Canadian representatives. Canadians have participated in its educational program through courses and webinars in such topics as data curation and management, the ICPSR Summer Program, Official Representative Meetings, and mailing lists. ICPSR has served as a model and exemplar over the years for data service and delivery, and as a participant in and advocate of new projects such as the development of the Data Documentation Initiative.

Impetus for Change within Canada

While Canadian data centres were still few in number and benefiting from organizations such as IASSIST and ICPSR, the academic community faced an unexpected crisis in November, 1984. Canada's Progressive Conservative government announced plans to cancel the quinquennial (1986) census. Less than a month later, the census was reinstated, but under a cost-recovery model unlike anything before in Canada.[13] In 1988, Statistics Canada announced the pricing model for census data. Western had purchased approximately 35 summary files (roughly 65 tables), and the three public use microdata files (PUMFs) from the 1981 Census for approximately Can$5,000. For the 1986 Census, fewer tables would be available, each file would contain one table only, all three PUMFs were not expected, and the cost would be approximately Can$110,000. The same scenario was taking place across Canada, as researchers began to realize the impossibility of affording to work with the Census. Institutions that had previously purchased census data realized that they would be unable to afford holdings comparable to 1981; therefore, a solution was needed to support academic research in Canada.

Laine Ruus had recently established a data library in Canada's largest university, the University of Toronto (UofT). Ruus proposed to the directors of the Canadian Association of Research Libraries/Association des bibliothèques de recherche du Canada (CARL/ABRC) that a consortium of its members be formed to purchase a single copy of all public 1986 Census data. UofT would undertake to copy and disseminate the files to each member of the consortium. Twenty-five[14] CARL institutions agreed to participate, although few were currently providing data services.[15] Without warning, librarians who knew nothing about data would be called upon by their institutions to provide access to and support for data.

"What do I do with this magnetic tape, and with what's on it?" was a question that began to echo throughout CARL/ABRC consortium member institutions. The most frequently designated individual to take on the role of data support was the government documents librarian, well-versed in print materials but frequently unaware of and ambivalent toward machine-readable data and their support. In 1988, at the Washington IASSIST meeting, Canadian attendees developed the idea of forming the Canadian Association of Public Data Users (CAPDU), an association whose objectives, were "to secure and promote efficient access to and use of public data in computer-readable form."[16] This objective meant training the trainers: experienced librarians within data centres undertook to train data neophytes, whether one-on-one or through conferences and meetings. Laine Ruus and Wendy Watkins (Carleton University's data professional) were fundamental in developing these early training programs. Beginning with rather informal gatherings of colleagues from across Canada, they developed into formal meetings held in conjunction with the Association of Learned Societies in Canada or IASSIST.[17]

CAPDU meetings provided the first extensive Canada-specific data training on Canadian files. CAPDU was strictly a volunteer organization: web server space, mailing list management, conference coordination, preservation of records, and other resources were (and remain) at the mercy of those able to provide them. CAPDU's importance in providing training in the early years of the expansion of data services in Canadian libraries cannot be underestimated.

Having established a consortium to acquire data from the 1986 Census, and with the cost-recovery model in place at Statistics Canada, the inevitable next step was to establish additional consortia for surveys such as the General Social Surveys of Canada, the Aboriginal Peoples' Survey, and the Health and Activity Limitation Survey. A second and larger CARL/CREPUQ consortium formed for the 1991 Census, again ramping up training needs. Ultimately, the term "consortium" became a problematic word among the data community in Canada.[18] Whether a file would be included in a consortium, what the cost for the particular consortium might be, and the time and effort involved creating the consortium all contributed to making the availability of data unpredictable and unequal across the country's academic institutions. Something better was needed to provide more equal access to data at a price that might be both predicted and budgeted year over year.

The Data Liberation Initiative

The scope of this paper is insufficient to describe the establishment of the Data Liberation Initiative.[19] After tremendous effort by Ernie Boyko of Statistics Canada and Wendy Watkins of Carleton University, and community buy-in on various levels (government, Statistics Canada, research councils and universities), a five-year pilot project was launched in January 1996. Over 50 Canadian universities joined this project, paying a subscription fee for access to Statistics Canada data including microdata files and aggregated data products.

Immediate and ongoing training was needed to make librarians aware of the range of data provided in the DLI collection, to justify the membership cost, and to provide basic instructions to members who had not participated in the CARL Consortia. Again, institutions were calling upon untrained librarians to act as the local official contact for the DLI and as the hub through which Statistics Canada data would be provided on campus. Individual institutions had to determine the level of service that they might offer. The most basic service was to download data files from Statistics Canada and to provide them directly to users, while at the high end an institution might maintain a statistical support centre and operate a local online data retrieval system. To help new staff learn the tricks of the trade, the DLI's External Advisory Committee (EAC) established an Education Committee to report to the EAC. The Education Committee initiated and has in the years since continued to conduct annual training in each of the four regions of Canada. It established the practice of conducting "boot camps" for new data providers,[20] and developed a first version of what has developed into the *DLI Survival Guide.*[21] On a regular basis the regions have gathered together for national training sessions, with members learning from each other and making useful contacts with colleagues from across the country. These training sessions continue to showcase the *DLI Survival Guide* and highlight the type of data service that might be established at an institution.[22]

For the period from 1996 through 2007, training was generally offered to data librarians at regional and national DLI training sessions and at CAPDU meetings. An institution's DLI fees paid for one representative's travel to a DLI training session, and it became more difficult for data specialists to justify additional travel expenses for separate CAPDU meetings; consequently, CAPDU meetings came to be held in conjunction with DLI training.

The DLI Training Repository

DLI training, delivered by data professionals from DLI-member institutions and by Statistics Canada subject matter experts, is conducted regionally rather than nationally in three out of four years, and topics vary. The Education Committee recognized the need to provide access to the content of all training sessions, and established a training repository (https://cudo.carleton.ca/collection/dli). This repository contains PowerPoint slides, PDFs, and exercises for approximately 500 sessions that have been delivered at DLI training in the period 1997 to 2015. The repository is accessible by anyone interested in learning more about Canadian data or tools and tricks of the trade, and it is well-used: "in 2014, there were 1,676 sessions of the repository which accounted for 7,867 page views."[23]

At many institutions a single professional still provides data support, often devoting only a fraction of his/her time to data. The level of service delivered is impacted by local technical support, skill sets of staff members, and administrative support at the institutional level.[24] For these solo service providers, attending IASSIST, ICPSR or Canadian data meetings provides an essential opportunity to network, to share strategies for providing access to data files, and to consider possibilities for service expansion. Through these various training opportunities, data librarians learn techniques and tricks which they can take back to their local institutions to share with their colleagues and broaden the data culture.

Creation of Online Data Delivery Systems

From the late 1980s into the 2000s, a number of Canadian institutions with technical support teams and experience in data developed tools for delivering data files to users' desktops. In most cases, these systems were developed at institutions where the data service was integrated with computing support. Some systems (e.g., Queen's QWIFS and the Tri-University Groups system) were developed on top of commercial statistical software packages. Others, such as Calgary's LANDRU, UBC's ISLAND, and CREPUQ's Sherlock, were hybrid systems delivering data and statistics. UofT deployed Berkeley's Survey Documentation and Analysis software (SDA). Western's data delivery underwent a number of changes. An early 1980's Cyber computer-based tape delivery system served as the back end of a VAX Fortran-based Network Data Library System (1986). The metadata entered there was transformed into static web pages for the web-based Internet Data Library System (IDLS, 1995). IDLS Version 2 used metadata transferred from IDLS into a searchable database to drive a new web-based system (2001). Finally, elements of IDLS Version 2 and Sherlock were integrated to create the bilingual Equinox Data Delivery System (2009). New data librarians typically received initiation in these various data delivery tools at DLI (or CAPDU) training sessions. Institutions without extensive local technical support could use these tools to access data, since the DLI license agreement allowed them to partner with other institutions to deliver data. It has become the norm to collaborate with peers from other institutions or to piggyback on services developed by other institutions.

For example, the Computing in the Humanities and Social Sciences (CHASS) unit at the University of Toronto obtains data from providers and creates an interface to those data that are offered to other institutions on a subscription basis. Universities across Canada may subscribe to one or more services from CHASS, the most popular being CANSIM (Statistics Canada's time-series database) and the Census Analyzer (a common interface to Canadian geographically-based census aggregated data). Other than CHASS, the system which enjoyed the largest adoption among other institutions were the UWO-based Internet Data Library System and its successor Equinox, which delivered microdata, aggregated data, and geospatial layers to users' desktops. As the DDI standard has spread, the Ontario Council of University Libraries (OCUL) deployed a Nesstar-based DDI-compliant system, <odesi> (http://odesi.ca), launched in 2008 as a common platform to deliver data to all Ontario universities. OCUL also launched a geospatial complement to data delivery, the Scholars Geoportal, in 2012. Coincidental to the retirement of the Equinox Data Delivery System in academic year 2014/2015, <odesi> enjoyed a surge in subscriptions from non-Ontario universities. Even more recently, in 2015, Statistics Canada launched two services, a Nesstar service that disseminates microdata to DLI users, and a Beyond 20/20 Web Data Server delivers aggregated data and geospatial files.

Broadening the Data Community

As more Canadian institutions subscribed to or hosted a user-friendly data delivery service, the number of librarians and library staff who were providing reference service for using data files grew.† Training opportunities for staff could be provided at local institutions as peer training or at regional or national DLI training events. Other specialized training opportunities became available, such as an OCUL-sponsored two-day workshop on using DDI, and a three-day True North Science Boot Camp for Librarians focused on research data management in the sciences (https://truenorth2015.ok.ubc.ca/). In 2007, the University of Alberta Data Library launched the Winter Institute on Statistical Literacy for Librarians (WISLL), a workshop for librarians aimed at training them to a basic understanding of statistical concepts and support.[25] This training series has been an annual event since 2007, attended by librarians from across Canada, including public service librarians as well as data professionals.

Access to Confidential Data

While the Data Liberation Initiative was providing access to microdata and to aggregated data, higher-level researchers continued to need access to non-anonymized data from Statistics Canada to do more robust analysis or to look at variables not included on the public files. To support this research, "in 1998, the Canadian Initiative on Social Statistics … [recommended] the creation of research facilities to give academic researchers improved access to Statistics Canada's microdata files."[26] Support from the Canada Foundation for Innovation (CFI) and the Canadian Institutes of Health Research, as well as local institutional support, has resulted in the establishment of 26 Research Data Centres (RDC) or RDC branches at universities across Canada.[27] The RDC program provides access to non-anonymized files to authorized users within a secure environment. Access to the RDC network is governed by a rigorous project approval process, which includes a police background check of the applicants for access. All analysis of RDC datasets is conducted within a secure data enclave constructed and paid for by the hosting university. An onsite Statistics Canada employee reviews researchers' analysis to ensure no breaches of confidentiality.

In 2012 Statistics Canada launched the subscription-based Real Time Remote Access (RTRA) program as a complement to and partial substitute for establishing a RDC. [28] It offers simpler and faster project approval process, but provides less

† Although there are only 79 DLI institutions, messages to the DLI mailing list today are sent to 323 recipients. As a further example of the broadening of data responsibilities, from discussions with Walter Giesbrecht, and looking at the ads, York University advertisements for reference librarians now generally include a preference for experience with data.

robust access to the data because hands-on access to the data is not provided. Instead, a user sends a SAS syntax file to Statistics Canada, where it is executed. The descriptive statistics created by the analysis are automatically checked for confidentiality and are returned to the user if no breach of confidentiality is found.

The data librarian faces challenges in supporting users who wish to use secure data through either system. RTRA requires the use of SAS, a statistical programming language that is not customarily used by librarians. With either RTRA or the RDC, librarians face barriers in knowing what is contained in the system; while the survey questionnaires are publicly available, no variable-level search tool exists to quickly or easily identify files of interest to researchers.

A concern that has been voiced by data librarians since the launch of the RDC program was a fear that the number of PUMFs produced for the DLI program would be reduced since they are relatively costly to create, and since "real" researchers could use the files in the RDCs. That concern has been magnified by the deployment of RTRA and by budget cuts undergone by Statistics Canada. To some extent this fear has been realized, as a number of files (e.g., Longitudinal Survey of Immigrants to Canada, Community Noise and Health Study, Maternity Experiences Survey) have never been provided to the DLI community as public use files.

Given that Statistics Canada surveys may be released in any, all, or none of these forms, data librarians must be aware of the existence and availability of data and statistics at all levels in order to direct users to the most appropriate resource. The table below is based on the one contained in the current DLI Survival Guide, with the addition of the Real Time Remote Access Service.[29] It shows the Statistics Canada services with which a data librarian should be acquainted.

Table 20.1. Data Librarian Continuum of Access. (Reprinted with permission from DLI Survival Guide)

	Open Statistics ←				→ **Restricted Data**	
Service	Statistics Canada Website	Depository Services Program (DSP)	Data Liberation Initiative	Custom Tabulations	Real Time Remote Access and Remote Job Submission	Research Data Centres

As the number of Statistics Canada's services increase, the need for a common search tool for these services becomes more critical. Librarians need to find the most appropriate information for users and should not omit any service from consideration, whether through neglect, oversight, or lack of familiarity. A common search tool should be made available to end users and the public in reflection of the government's move toward open data, to provide them with self-mediated access to information. They then can approach their libraries knowing what they wish to use and receive instruction in how to use it.

Reflections on Opportunities and Challenges

Canada's academic sector has responded to many challenges around the delivery of data and of training. In this section, we speculate on issues that academic data librarians will likely face in the future. Canada's municipal, provincial and federal governments are increasingly embracing the open data movement and creating their own data catalogues and search engines.[30] While many more data files become available, finding them and determining their comparability will prove to be an issue that confronts us. Additionally, government open data sites are not always maintaining preservation copies of data files: the Government of Canada site indicates that you may "search open data that is relevant to Canadians,"[31] but what is relevant to Canadians may not be the same as what is relevant to Canadian researchers interested in tracking phenomena over time. Data librarians and researchers will need to try to influence government policy to ensure that data are not lost when overwritten by new, "more relevant" versions of the same measures.

Canadian academic funding agencies are moving along similar paths. On February 27, 2015, a new open access policy for research was announced: "all peer-reviewed journal publications funded by one of the three federal granting agencies to be freely available online within 12 months."[32] However, this policy does not require "NSERC or SSHRC grant recipients to make their data openly accessible or archived at this time."[33] It refers users to the SSHRC Research Data Archiving Policy, which encourages users to deposit data within two years of a project's completion,[34] but this recommendation has in the past been largely ignored by researchers, as there is no enforcement or follow-up.

On July 17, 2015, a long-awaited *Tri-Agency Statement on Principles on Digital Data Management* was released in draft form for feedback.[35] The draft declares that "data management planning is necessary at all stages of the research project lifecycle, from design and inception to completion."[36] It proposes responsibilities for researchers, research communities, research institutions, and research funders. Academic institutions and librarians are charged with responsibilities, including providing access to "repositories … that securely preserve, curate, and provide continued access to research data," providing researchers with "guidance to properly manage their data," and to "promote the importance of data management."[37]

As in the past, institutions will rely on collaborative efforts or borrowing from the work of others. The CARL Portage project to develop a community of practice for research data management in Libraries is the leading example, which deployed the Data Management Plan Builder created by the University of Alberta nationally as DMP Assistant (https://portagenetwork.ca/). Providing RDM services entails activities not currently undertaken at many Canadian universities, such as ensuring file integrity and migration from software platforms or storage media. Best practices will need to be established and shared should these support tasks devolve upon data librarians and other public service librarians.

Unless we wish to rely on Google as the default global search engine for Canadian data, an agency will need to develop a comprehensive search engine for data or for data depositories.† This will become even more important as RDM becomes the norm within Canadian universities and research is deposited for long-term access into more and varied repositories.

Canadian data librarians must remain vocal and informed defenders of the Public-Use Microdata Files (PUMF) program at Statistics Canada because PUMFs are the key tool for training users of the future. We need to advocate for the creation of a centre of excellence for the creation of PUMFs within Statistics Canada to improve their quality and documentation, speed their creation, and reduce the cost of creation. DLI contacts echoed this concern at the National DLI Training Day in 2014 by calling on the DLI to initiate a system of quality control for SPSS data set descriptions before distributing them to the user community.

In addition, Canada's academic data librarians were active in the campaign to reinstate the mandatory long form census, which was canceled for the 2011 cycle. On November 5, 2015, the community rejoiced, as the newly elected government reinstated that program in time for the 2016 cycle, and has promised autonomy from ministerial interference for Statistics Canada.

IASSIST was founded in 1974 to address data organization and management, data archive development, data documentation, classification, process-produced data, and data acquisition. As shown in this chapter, Canadian data librarians have been responsive to changes in the data environment in Canada, developing, using and promoting collaborative tools, and developing and delivering training programs to their colleagues. Consequently, today's data librarians have access to many more tools and support for their activities than in the pre-DLI era. However, the issues around which IASSIST was found continue to face the data librarian in Canada and abroad.‡

† An international database similar to OpenDOAR (the Directory of Open Access Repositories, http://www.opendoar.org/) would be ideal.

‡ Maps showing the expansion of Canadian data services are available on the companion web site, http://databrarianship.wordpress.com/ The authors offer our thanks to Christine Homuth and Brent Larue, of the Western Map and Data Centre, for their advice in preparing maps showing the expansion of Canadian data services. Thanks are also due to the DLI staff, particularly Renée Rocan, who located a spreadsheet that allowed us to map the DLI program membership in 2002 and 2015. Finally, we thank the Canadian Association of Research Libraries' Manager of Administration and Programs, Katherine McColgan, for delving through CARL's records to give us a list of the institutions that participated in the two census consortia.

1. Laine Ruus, "The University of British Columbia Data Library: An Overview," *Library Trends* 30, no. 3 (Winter 1982): 397.
2. Barton Clark, "Social Science Data Archives and Libraries: A View to the Future," *Library Trends* 30, no. 3 (Winter 1982): 505.
3. Laine Ruus, "Training of Data Services Professionals: Past, Present and Future," *Library Trends* 30, no. 3 (Winter 1982): 456.
4. Ruus, "The University of British Columbia Data Library," 398.
5. Slavko Manojlovich, "A Library-based Reference Service for Machine-Readable Census Data: The Canadian Experience." *IASSIST Newsletter* 3, no. 3 (1979): 55–64.
6. Chuck Humphrey, Preserving Research Data in Canada: The Long Tale of Data Blog, accessed April 24, 2015, http://preservingresearchdataincanada.net/tag/data-clearing-house-for-the-social-sciences/
7. Margaret O'Neill Adams, "The Origins and Early Years of IASSIST." *IASSIST Quarterly* 30, no. 3 (2006): 5–13. http://www.iassistdata.org/downloads/iqvol303adams.pdf.
8. Ibid., 7.
9. Ibid., 11.
10. "Report of the Joint Canadian-United States Action Groups on Classification," *IASSIST Newsletter* 1, no. 3 (1977): 8–9; "Standards for Data Documentation," *IASSIST Newsletter*, 1, no. 3 (1977): 22; "Organization of Data Archives," *IASSIST Newsletter*, 1, no. 3 (1977): 23.
11. Erik W. Austin, *ICPSR: The Founding and Early Years*, accessed May 21, 2015 http://www.icpsr.umich.edu/icpsrweb/content/membership/history/early-years.html.
12. Queen's and UBC were listed in ICPSR's *Annual Report* for 1964–65; Western in the 1965–66 issue. Thanks to Mary Vardigan at ICPSR for tracking down this information for us.
13. Bill Curry, "Census Debate is Nothing New," *The Globe and Mail*, August 16, 2010, accessed April 26, 2015 http://www.theglobeandmail.com/news/politics/census-debate-is-nothing-new/article1377285/.
14. The figure of twenty-five is drawn from Laine Ruus, "Semi-permeable boundaries among institutions: The Canadian Scene(s)," (presentation at the *International Association for Social Science Information Services & Technology*, Tampere, Finland, 2009), http://www.fsd.uta.fi/iassist2009/presentations/A2_Ruus.ppt.
15. Ernie Boyko and Wendy Watkins, "The Canadian Data Liberation Initiative: An Idea worth Considering?" *International Household Survey Network Working Paper No.006*, November 2011, accessed April 29, 2015 http://www.ihsn.org/home/sites/default/files/resources/IHSN-WP006.pdf; Chuck Humphrey, "Collaborative Training in Statistical and Data Library Services," *Resource Sharing & Information Networks*, 18, no. 1–2 (2005):170, doi: 10.1300/J121v18n01_13.
16. Canadian Association of Public Data Users, *By-Laws*, accessed April 29, 2015 http://equinox.uwo.ca/capdu/CAPDU_by-laws.html.
17. Canadian Association of Public Data Users, *Meetings*, accessed April 29, 2015 http://equinox.uwo.ca/capdu/CAPDU_meetings.html.
18. Ernie Boyko and Wendy Watkins, "Data Liberation in 2004: How Did We Get Here?" (presentation at the *Data Liberation Initiative* Regional Training, Ontario, Canada, 2004), http://hdl.handle.net/1873/232.
19. For a thorough history of the development of the DLI, see Boyko and Watkins, "The Canadian Data Liberation Initiative. An Idea worth Considering?"
20. Boyko and Watkins, "The Canadian Data Liberation Initiative. An Idea worth Considering"?, 6.
21. Data Liberation Initiative Education Committee, *DLI Survival Guide*, last modified December 1, 2015 http://www.statcan.gc.ca/eng/dli/guide/toc/3000279.
22. Vince Gray, "Levels of Service," (presentation at the *Data Liberation Initiative* Regional Training, Ontario, Canada, 2004), https://cudo.carleton.ca/collection/dli/search/levels%20of%20service; Laine Ruus, "User Services in a Data Library," *IASSIST Newsletter* 4, no. 2 (1980), 29–33.

23. E-mail from Statistics Canada (Chantal Ripp) to DLILIST@statcan.gc.ca, May 13, 2015.
24. Vince Gray, "Levels of Data Service: The 2012 Ontario Context," (presentation at the *Data Liberation Initiative* Regional Training, Ontario, Canada, 2004), https://cudo.carleton.ca/dli-training/2766.
25. University of Alberta, "Winter Institute on Statistical Literacy for Librarians (WISLL)," accessed May 18, 2015 https://sites.google.com/site/wisll2014/home.
26. Statistics Canada, "The Research Data Centres (RDC) Program," accessed May 18, 2015 http://www.statcan.gc.ca/eng/rdc/index.
27. Canadian Research Data Centre Network, "Where to Access Data," accessed May 18, 2015 http://www.rdc-cdr.ca/find-a-rdc.
28. Statistics Canada, "The Real Time Remote Access (RTRA) system," accessed May 18, 2015 http://www.statcan.gc.ca/rtra-adtr/rtra-adtr-eng.htm.
29. Data Liberation Initiative Education Committee, "DLI Survival Guide."
30. Statistics Canada, "Open Government Across Canada," accessed May 18, 2015 http://open.canada.ca/en/maps/open-data-canada.
31. Statistics Canada, "Open Data," accessed May 18, 2015 http://open.canada.ca/en/open-data.
32. Government of Canada, "Minister Holder Announces New Open Access Policy for Research," accessed May 20, 2015 http://science.gc.ca/default.asp?lang=En&n=415B5097-1.
33. Government of Canada, "Frequently Asked Questions," *Open Access,* accessed May 20, 2015 http://www.science.gc.ca/default.asp?lang=En&n=A30EBB24-1#wsCD7C9989.
34. Social Sciences and Humanities Research Council, "Research Data Archiving Policy," last modified April 8, 2014 http://www.sshrc-crsh.gc.ca/about-au_sujet/policies-politiques/statements-enonces/edata-donnees_electroniques-eng.aspx.
35. Government of Canada, "Draft Tri-Agency Statement of Principles on Digital Data Management," last modified July 20, 2015 http://www.science.gc.ca/default.asp?lang=En&n=83F7624E-1.
36. Ibid.
37. Ibid.

CHAPTER 21

Data Librarianship: A Day in the Life—Science Edition

Danianne Mizzy and Michele Hayslett

AFTER SURVEYING AND interviewing a cross-section of librarians supporting scientific work, we conclude that there is no one path to data librarianship: some start in the sciences (whether physical or biomedical) and find librarianship later; some start in librarianship and find the sciences later. This agrees with Kellam's observation that "Data librarians ... come from a variety of disciplines and by diverse routes."[1] At least among our sampling, this area of practice has many commonalities with social science data support, but with more of an emphasis on data management and data sharing than on data discoverability and reuse. The growth in the importance of data for all areas of scholarship makes this topic broadly relevant. Advice and insights from current practitioners will offer a useful guide, especially for those considering this area as a profession.

Methodology

The authors followed the approach taken by Kellam of posing informal interview questions about the respondents "experiences becoming and being data librarians."[2] The interview questions were adapted from Kellam's questions but were also based on the authors' professional experience and were fine-tuned with help from a survey expert.

The authors drew upon their professional contacts to compile a list of librarians and informationists who provide data services for scientific, health, and biomedical researchers and invited them to participate. Using snowball sampling, we invited people from the original list to suggest others with whom we should speak.† Thirty respondents completed a brief online survey, and twenty-seven

† Appendix 21.A provides more detail on respondents' locations and affiliations as well as the survey questionnaire.

of them agreed to participate in a personal interview conducted by telephone or Skype.†

Survey Results

Education

Respondents possessed a wide range of educational backgrounds, some with no formal library training, some with no or minimal science training. Most respondents (22/30, or 73%) had a bachelor's degree from a science field; twenty-seven percent (8/30) had degrees in humanities or social science fields or did not specify a field. Twenty-three percent (7/30) had no science-related degrees. Seventeen percent (5/30) had doctoral degrees, all of which were in science fields. All but three had master's degrees in library science or information science. Two had advanced certificates focused in data or data curation; two others had graduate certificates in biomedical or health informatics.

Data-Related Training

When we asked what other data-related training, coursework, and programs of study they had taken, respondents provided 76 answers, describing an enormous variety of programs they employed to gain additional knowledge, including both degree programs and many less formal workshops and courses (See Figure 21.1 for frequency of training by type). Twenty-six percent of the respondents (20/76) indicated use of workshops as a means of gaining data management training, but almost as many, twenty-five percent (19/76), learned the material within degree programs. Four of those who mentioned week-long in-person workshops (counted as part of the shorter workshops category) attended the *Curating and Managing Research Data for Re-Use* workshop usually offered in the summer by the Inter-university Consortium for Political and Social Research (ICPSR). Two people mentioned multi-month workshops without specifying which ones and three mentioned the e-Science Institute co-sponsored by the Association of Research Libraries (ARL) and the Digital Library Federation (DLF). Two more cited a two-week long immersion experience, the DigCCurr Institute, hosted by the School of Information and Library Science at the University of North Carolina.

---

† The data are available at http://dx.doi.org/10.17615/C6RP41.

Figure 21.1. Most Commonly Cited Types of Data-related Training

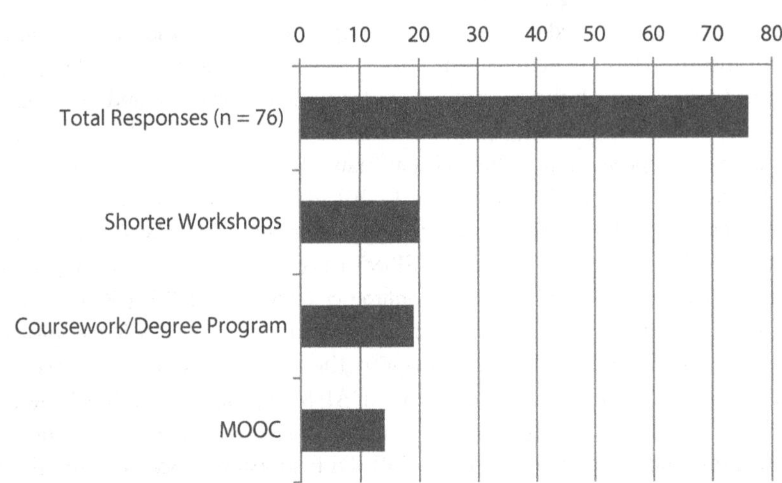

Twenty-five percent (19/76) of responses cited degree programs, and about 8% (6/76) noted certificate programs (although not all were semester- or degree-length certificate programs). One person conducted an independent study, and one took a semester-long online course. The next most frequently cited source of training was MOOCs (Massive Open Online Courses), with 17% (13/76) listing that source. Of those, seven people attended Johns Hopkins' *Data Scientist Toolbox* class via Coursera.‡

While the authors did not ask how long respondents had been practicing, these results seem to suggest a divide between professionals who entered this profession before funding agencies began requiring data management plans, and those who attended graduate school after curricula caught up with developments in the field. The good news for people considering this specialty is that there are plenty of learning opportunities both in and out of graduate school. Likewise, respondents described diverse paths to their current positions so there is no one set of education and experience that qualifies individuals for this profession. The survey also did not explore motivation for choosing one type of program over another, but perhaps some found it easier to complete a MOOC in addition to a full-time job or wanted the formal credential of a certificate program.

‡ For more detail on the programs respondents cited, see Appendix C—Table 1 on the companion website (https://databrarianship.wordpress.com/).

Other Learning Opportunities

For this question, we asked respondents to list specific types of resources they found helpful in their work: conferences/meetings, professional associations, blogs, listservs and other. As with the question about training, coursework, and programs of study, respondents took advantage of an enormous variety of other learning opportunities (each respondent was able to list as many as he or she wished). Conferences were the most popular option, with 57% (17/30) attending the Research Data Access and Preservation (RDAP) Summit, a conference organized by the Association for Information Science and Technology (ASIS&T). Forty-three percent (13/30) attended the International Digital Curation Conference (IDCC) and 23% (7/30) attended the annual conference of the International Association for Social Science Information and Technology (IASSIST). Listservs were the next most popular resource. Forty percent (12/30) of respondents cited the RDAP listserv, and 33% (10/30) the UK-based research-dataman listserv (short for data management). Twenty-three percent (7/30) of respondents participated in the ARL/DLF-sponsored eScience Community blog. Seventeen percent (5/30) cited the data management community on Twitter.†

Tools

Figure 21.2 presents the tools mentioned most frequently. Excel was the most commonly cited tool with 83% (25/30) of respondents mentioning it. Git was the next most frequently cited tool with 57% (17/30) of respondents, followed closely by OpenRefine and R with 50% (15/30) and 43% (13/30) respectively.

Figure 21.2. Most Commonly Cited Useful Tools

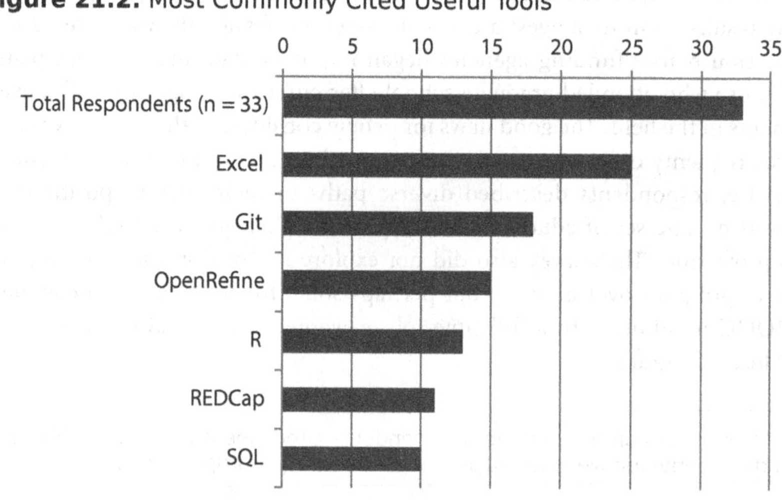

† For a list of these resources, see Appendix C on the companion website (https://databrarianship.wordpress.com/).

Tasks

The survey listed 25 different tasks. The authors gleaned the tasks from job descriptions and data services positions advertised through listservs to which they subscribe and from various library web sites. Respondents were invited to check the ones they performed. Figure 21.3 presents the most commonly selected tasks. As it shows, nearly all respondents assist with writing data management plans, understanding funder requirements, formatting data citations and finding repositories in which to preserve data.

Figure 21.3. Most Commonly Cited Tasks

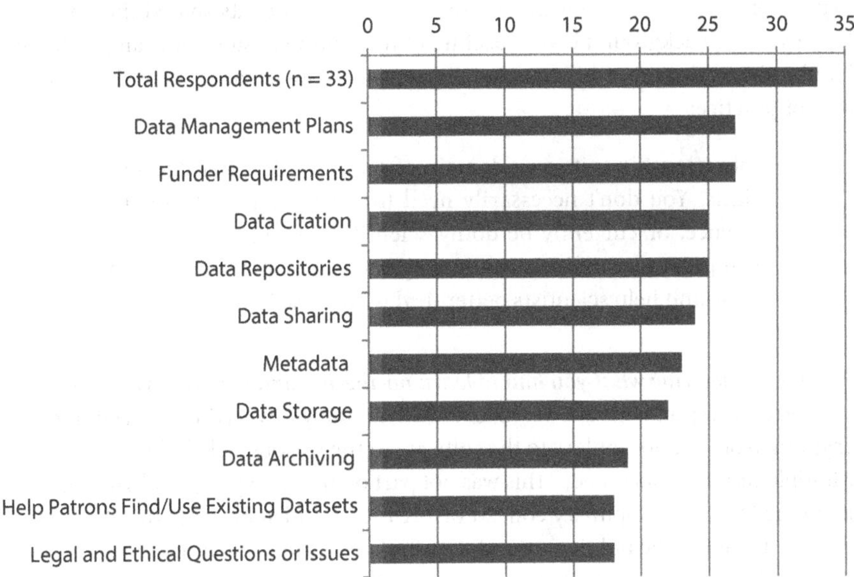

The fact that all 25 tasks listed on the survey had responses speaks to the wide variety of interpretations of what it means to be a data librarian. Each institution has different needs and, while some tasks are common, each position has its own unique mix of job elements. Just as there is no one path to become a data librarian, job seekers in this area will find many different expectations in position announcements. As will be seen in the next section, overall the results of the survey are borne out in the responses from the interviews.

Interview Responses

In addition to a survey, we conducted interviews with several data librarians who support science disciplines. We have organized this portion of the chapter by the interview questions which included several open-ended queries about the training and experiences needed to be a scientific data librarian.†

1. ***How does your educational background relate to the data responsibilities in your current position?***

   The degree of correspondence between formal training and current data responsibilities varied greatly. Some respondents undertook their graduate library work before research data management entered the library science curriculum. Some received statistics, research methods, or data management training as part of their undergraduate or graduate work in non-library- science disciplines. Others sought out data training as an elective, a concentration within their library degree, or a within a certificate program. Many respondents shared the opinion that a science background is very useful but not a prerequisite. For example, Katie Houk offered these words of encouragement for non-scientists considering this area of practice:

   > Librarianship is its own domain of specialized knowledge and skills. You don't necessarily need to have a higher degree in science, or currently be doing scientific research yourself, to bring data or information management best practices to the table and help scientists better deal with these issues.

2. ***Please describe what you had to learn on-the-job and how you went about it.***

   Several respondents answered, only half-jokingly, "Everything!" meaning everything from the vocabulary to the software to the various stakeholders involved. Multiple respondents stated, "This was not part of my MLIS program." They had to learn the local or disciplinary context before they could apply what they had been taught, including the politics around data in their setting. What researchers really do with their data was eye-opening, and the lack of documentation about that data was only one of many ways that actual and ideal practices, as taught in a graduate curriculum, may diverge. Some respondents with scientific training observed that prior experience with research and managing data, while providing an excellent foundation, does not make you a data specialist.

   Many had to discover just what a data librarian does, how reference services for data differ from other kinds of reference interactions, and how scientists use data. Metadata, programming, preservation, and data citation practices were the skills most frequently mentioned as something respondents needed to learn or learn more about on-the-job. Almost all respondents stressed the importance of getting the lay of the land, both within the library and at the institutional level. For

† Respondents reviewed this material and gave consent to include their excerpted answers.

example, those entering a biomedical setting might be interested in Alisa Surkis' early experience:

> I learned about differences in the research process and how data are viewed between basic and clinical researchers. On a clinical research project, beyond the PI (Principal Investigator) everybody is more an employee of the project. In a basic science lab you have a lot of essentially independent or semi-independent researchers who are all doing their own experiments. Post-docs and graduate students cycle through the lab, leaving after a few years. So those create completely different sets of problems.

Whether serving as the first person in this job at an institution, or just joining an established service at a new institution, respondents advised undertaking at least a basic environmental scan. This will help librarians find out who the stakeholders for data management are on campus and what capabilities already exist at the institution. Surkis advises, "Spend time talking to people and gaining awareness of institutional issues before deciding what data management services to offer, rather than basing it on preconceived ideas or what other libraries are doing."

3. ***What is the one thing you wish you had known about being a science data librarian when you started your position?***
   Five major themes emerged for this question, which we will frame as completing the stem sentence, "I wish I had known …"

   a. ***…that the sciences are so diverse***
      Amy Hodge: As soon as we started talking to people about the repository, they began saying things like "I have a thousand files" or "I have 30 TB of data" or "I have protected information" or "I want my deposits to be automatically updated from my GitHub repository." There is always something new or extra that people want and sometimes providing those services is expensive, hard, time consuming or all of the above.

      Heather Coates: You can't really talk about scientific data management practices in any reasonable way. They just don't exist in a consistent way across all scientific research. When we have these high-level conversations about these issues, we tend to gloss over those disciplinary or method specific differences. Don't expect a one solution fits all kind of service.

b. ...that disciplinary attitudes toward data sharing vary so widely

Jenny Muilenburg: The widely variable cultures of data sharing are a particular challenge. Some disciplines have been sharing their data for years. As an example, the GIS community has a culture of sharing their data, sharing certain files so you don't have to recreate them. In other fields that culture doesn't exist yet. You run into different "personalities" in the fields and in labs regarding data sharing and data management. You'll quickly realize that you may have to come up with a customized solution for individual researchers or labs because of their culture.

Dana Bouquin: Everyone wants to use everyone else's data but no one wants to share their data. It's a horrible oxymoron. There is so much cultural push back in medicine to the open data idea. I think it's mostly a literacy issue. Especially in medicine people don't necessarily realize that they can maintain their rights to their data, that they can tightly control what people can do with it if they want and that it's actually a good thing if you share—if you share it you get credit for it and people have to cite you.

c. ...to focus on tools and new processes that people will really use

Sally Gore cautioned about investing a lot of time in developing tools that researchers say they want: "Trying to build something that people will actually use to meet their needs is a hard thing to do. If the resource or the tool isn't something that's easily adopted and integrated into an existing workflow, it's not useful. Or used."

d. ...how researchers view data

Many respondents wished they had a better understanding of how scientists deal with data in the research process. Some expressed that it would have been helpful to have more exposure to some of the underlying science. Others described a time-scale difference, with librarians focusing on the whole data lifecycle and researchers caring about the day-to-day management of data coming in from all the different researchers and projects in their labs.

e. ...the importance of institutional and political awareness

Several indicated the importance of administration and stakeholder support for library involvement in data management as a key factor for success. Some who were new to libraries commented on adjusting to how bureaucratic and political a librarian's position can end up being on a day-to-day basis. Surkis stressed that "at least as important as any subject knowledge is institutional awareness so that you can see where the opportunities are. Making connections and talking to people throughout the institution is probably the most important thing you can do."

4. *What is the most challenging aspect of supporting scientific data services?*

Respondents identified many of the same challenges outlined in the Kellam chapter including "the difficulty of determining which levels of service to offer, in addition to finding the resources with which to support those levels [and] … finding the cutoff point."[3] One respondent expressed it as negotiating the balance between serving the needs of the entire campus versus meeting the complex needs of any one particular group. Infrastructure challenges identified include scalability of services, storage, and sustainable funding models. Lynn Yarmey strongly endorsed "collaborative models for open, distributed, community-based networks" as the way forward. Many respondents echoed Carly Strasser's view of the biggest challenge:

> The biggest challenge facing libraries in this space is a total lack of understanding on the part of researchers about the role of the library. There is a perception that libraries are about books and help desks. I've spoken to tenured professors at major universities who had no idea that their library was involved in anything that had to do with data. Researchers won't show up at the library's doorstep—libraries have to advocate for their role. Librarians should aggressively collaborate with other campus stakeholders, like the vice chancellors of research or the grants offices.

Respondents identified getting buy-in from researchers as a big hurdle. Even getting time to meet with them can be difficult. Surkis' advice is, "Be with or ahead of the curve on what they need to know. Be really careful not to talk to them from a library-centric place using terminology that is not meaningful to them. Try to understand their world, how they think about this stuff and communicate to them where they are." Heather Coates agreed about the challenge and had some additional advice:

> I learned in my first couple years that most of our faculty don't care about data management. It's an activity they have to do but what they care about are their priorities, the things that interest them or are rewarded. I try to find out what those priorities are—funding for a new project, meeting promotion and tenure criteria, etcetera. I tend to start with the incentives and work backwards.

Sarah Oelker identified another big challenge. "The nut we haven't cracked yet is, what structure will encourage them to be thinking about it in small doses routinely rather than in a rush at grant time? Educating graduate students will generate a generation of PIs who are used to thinking about it."

Respondents working with biomedical researchers remarked on some special issues with medical and health data that can best be addressed at the institutional level. Barrie Hayes identified the lack of consistency of data management practices across projects as the biggest challenge, along with the data being sensitive and requiring special handling. Dana Bouquin observed:

> At the institutional level, I'd like to see a shift—even though [biomedical] funders don't necessarily require data management plans, how can we make data curation tasks part of our IRB [Institutional Review Board] process? How can we integrate this into researchers' regular workflows as opposed to trying to just create impetus? How can I facilitate you producing documentation for the institution, not necessarily the federal funder?

5. *If you could give a new science data librarian advice, what would be the first thing you would say?*

We have organized these into ten themes, and have combined answers from both the survey and the interviews in this section.

a. *So what exactly is a data librarian?*

More than one respondent commented that no one knows what a data librarian or databrarian is, so librarians should not focus on trying to build a brand. Instead they should focus on getting services in front of researchers and be prepared with a simple explanation of what a data librarian does. Chris Eaker's answer to this question is, "I do what a traditional librarian normally does for books, but I do it for data. I catalog, organize, describe, preserve and make [data] available for reuse." There is still a lot of confusion about the role of libraries in data management, and researchers do not necessarily see why they should talk to a librarian about data. Even those librarians with domain expertise and relevant degrees may encounter resistance or skepticism from researchers, and it may be that much harder for those who lack these credentials. Sharing specific examples and success stories can help to counter this attitude.

b. *Be patient.*

Many respondents shared that they were surprised at how long it takes to develop connections.

> Chris Eaker: The most surprising thing to me was how slow the process was of getting a data curation program off the ground and starting to accept datasets into our repository. It's going to take a long time and researchers may not always be cooperative about wanting to share and archive their research data. Be

willing to be patient and take things slowly. Try to explain the benefits to them as researchers and to science. Be willing to make concessions, such as making data publicly available two or three years from now.

Amy Hodge: How long the time horizon is for things that go on in libraries. In the business world that I was used to, things get done very quickly, because businesses aren't sure if they are going to be around next quarter. Libraries are planning to be here in one hundred years, so there is a distinctly slower—but more thoughtful—pace to the activities they undertake.

c. *Get out of your office.*

Get in touch with your liaison librarians and research deans. Find champions among researchers who can help promote your services to their colleagues.

Amy Hodge: I sense a tendency for some librarians to sit in their offices and expect that people will come to them. I recommend that you go to seminars and hear about the kind of research that is happening on your campus. Meet in researchers' offices or in their labs so you can get a better feel for the kind of work people are doing. See them in person in their space and in their environment.

d. *Work from the bottom up.*

Carly Strasser: Immerse yourself in the community of researchers you are trying to support. Ask the intro-level grad class professor if you can sit in on his class. You could also casually visit lab groups. Ask them about their work, and introduce yourself and why you're interested in what they do. Talk to graduate students about what they do with their data, and offer to help work through issues they might have. A lot of librarians aren't comfortable inserting themselves in the researcher community at their institution, but it's the only way to really understand what your constituency needs, and shows them you are committed and interested.

e. *...and the top down.*

Regina Raboin: A new science librarian needs to be or learn to become comfortable speaking with your library administration and the administrators at your school, such as the VP for research, provost for research, deans, and department chairs. You must read and learn about the institution's bigger picture, understand its critical mission and how your library's mission

> melds with it. You need to be able to outreach to the offices within research that are charged with moving forward the institution's research interests and mission. Become very familiar with the federal guidelines and agencies and how their policies are going to impact your university.

f. Get your hands dirty.

New practitioners need exposure to working with data, and familiarity with what researchers really do.

> Dana Bouquin: Make sure you have basic numeracy under your belt. With data you can't just talk about how to manage it, catalog it, [and] make sure it is clear and reproducible. You are going to have to talk to people about all the steps of their workflow: the analysis steps, the subsetting, the data clean up, etcetera. Get as much hands-on experience actually cleaning up and manipulating data as you can. Get your hands dirty, get a dirty dataset, and clean it up.

> Sally Gore: If you haven't done so already, do some research yourself. Find a topic of interest to you. Go through the process of collecting data, managing data, building your own dictionary, working through all of the issues and problems that come up. Even if you are already working in a library, do a research project in the library.

g. Find your community then grow it.

Respondents were practically unanimous in stressing the importance of finding a support network of people in similar positions at other universities. There is a very active group of data librarians on Twitter.[†] Yarmey reminds us to think of the data community broadly: "One of the fantastic things about this work is that most data scientists are generous, open and really interested in actual collaboration. Take advantage of that."

Respondents suggested engaging in cross-organization activities as much as possible such as participating on campus task forces or committees, faculty governance (if librarians hold faculty status), and research compliance training. The library data community is currently separate from other data communities, and is also internally divided (e.g., science v. social science and the data discovery v. data management areas). The more we can do to bridge these divides, the better off the data community and the research communities we are trying to support will be.

---

† Use the hashtag #datalibs to begin finding them as well as others listed on Sherry Lake's web page, https://sites.google.com/site/dmsocialnetworks/twitter.

h. Don't overextend yourself.

They also suggest that librarians need to have clear definitions of available services and realistic expectations of the capacity to fulfill obligations such as devoting time to specific research projects versus merely advising on available tools. Over-commitment is an issue especially for librarians with job responsibilities in addition to data management.

i. Don't be intimidated if you don't have a science background—it's very helpful but not a prerequisite for success.

Amy Hodge: I think that if you haven't done scientific research it will be much harder to understand how it works and what the mindset is and how to relate to researchers. The practice of science is often quite different from the idealized theory of it. It's much more about personal interactions as opposed to technical knowledge than I had expected. I didn't realize I was going to spend so much time in one-on-one conversations with faculty and getting to know people. It turns out that the people skills are the most important part of my job.

j. Learn one statistical software package.

Jenny Muilenberg: People in the sciences are using a wide variety of software, and there is no way that a science data librarian could be familiar with every kind that there is. Having said that, it's important that you have at least basic knowledge of one type of software, like R for statistical analysis or ArcGIS for GIS analysis.

6. What training would you advise them to take advantage of?

Respondents were divided on the benefit of taking basic science courses with a lab component. There was general enthusiasm for online and short course curricula for research data management. Some respondents also recommended Software Carpentry (https://software-carpentry.org/) and Data Carpentry (http://datacarpentry.github.io/) workshops, and said the value lay in developing a sense of the capacities of the software, meaning, not to worry about trying to become an expert after one workshop. Science boot camps were lauded for the opportunity to better understand the researcher perspective and were highlighted as especially useful for those without a science background.

Important competencies included appraisal, metadata creation, preservation, project management, communication and negotiation skills, statistical knowledge, data analytics, numeracy, and programming. One respondent observed that there is not as much training available specifically for biomedical librarians while another talked about taking advantage of bioinformatics certification. More biomedical-focused training is expected as an outcome of the recently awarded National Institutes of Health BD2K (Big Data to Knowledge) grants.[4] Multiple respondents stressed the importance of continuing education and we expect this to hold true for the foreseeable future. The data librarian community is a great resource to help you keep up with the ever-changing data landscape.

7. ***Please discuss the balance across your work between data, science, and librarianship.***

This question provoked a wide range of responses. On the practical level, responses partially correlated with the number of staff tasked with data support at their institution. One data librarian exclaimed "You mean the lack thereof?" while a member of a multi-person team talked about the distribution of these areas of responsibility across the team. Several data librarians said they did not do any traditional library work, and informationists had duties typical in their setting but unusual in academic libraries, such as systematic reviews, research evaluations, and support for collaboration and team science.

On the philosophic level, there was great diversity in the ways people view their jobs; some see these aspects as all interwoven with data as just another dimension of being a librarian while some saw them as quite separate.

Here are a few of the different perspectives:

> Katie Houk: Librarianship is its own domain of specialized knowledge and skills. You don't necessarily need to have a higher degree in science, or currently be doing scientific research yourself, to bring data or information management best practices to the table and help scientists better deal with these issues.

> Heather Coates: This is just a different facet of librarianship. Data literacy can be provided using similar structures and services in place for information literacy. The services that I offer are still reference and instruction and research support and consultation. Only the content is different.

> Dana Bouquin: I don't think they are independent at all. Librarianship is about fostering the creation of new knowledge and creating communities. Data science is intensively collaborative, a team science. Getting people to better communicate about their work so they can better execute on their ideas is what librarianship is about. It's a continuum, not a balance.

8. ***Is there anything you would like to add that I haven't asked?***

There were a wide variety of responses to this catch-all question. Many respondents reflected on the challenge of adding data services with no additional or limited staffing. "Adding data to a job that is already chock full is not a strategy for success," "Library administration needs to figure out how to bring sufficient resources to bear and to balance the load," and "There has to be a commitment to data services at the institutional level" were three of the comments. One solution may be building a team. Philippa Broadley spoke about this approach at her university:

> Upskilling our liaison librarians to deal with research data management issues that are arising more and more frequently in their everyday jobs is an exciting opportunity. Our liaison librarians' willingness to embrace this new part of their job is fantastic and makes for a better support service for researchers, especially as they are the "face of the library."

Yarmey encourages a big-tent approach to these challenges:

> Think big in the sense that many people inside and outside of the library community are working on understanding and addressing data challenges. Doing this on your own isn't necessarily sustainable personally, professionally, or programmatically. With those two things in mind, how do we collaborate across communities and get this done together? Find something that you do well and enjoy doing and then contribute it to something bigger.

Observations from the Social Science Perspective

A few respondents touched on ways that data librarianship in the sciences compares to the same specialty in the social sciences. When asked whether they found the week-long workshop on data services hosted by ICPSR to be helpful despite its focus on the social sciences, one interviewee strongly agreed, stating that the principles of data management are pretty much the same for the social sciences versus sciences, and generally applicable regardless of discipline. Margaret Henderson noted:

> Data librarianship is different in the science and social sciences context. It shares a lot of similarities. It's not just [that science is] bigger and [has] more disciplines. The sciences, even broadly, want something different out of data services than the social sciences do. In the social sciences, people explore for

> data because there is a lot of it, but it can be a little difficult to find. They have an idea of the kind of data they want and they have to go out and look for data that matches their question. In the sciences there are few things that everyone uses. Any observational data that is big everybody knows about it and where to get it. Their focus is how you're generating your own data, where to put it. I wasn't prepared for the backend things that scientists wanted, like where to put things and how to comply with …funder mandates.

Henderson and author Michele Hayslett have both observed that scientists are generally more likely to create their own data from observations or measurement ("primary" research data, akin to primary source materials), whereas social scientists are more likely to be able to reuse data created by someone else (i.e., "secondary" data). ICPSR offers perhaps the longest-running training program for new data librarians† and, because ICPSR historically archives social science data, that program focuses on helping researchers obtain secondary data. But if a data librarian focuses only on secondary data, he or she will never connect with a substantial proportion of the researchers at their institution.

Nevertheless, the practices of assigning metadata and managing datasets are virtually identical in the sciences and the social sciences. Outreach to researchers, finding champions and networking on campus and with data colleagues are identical for the two domains. The day-to-day tasks and tools of data librarians are largely the same regardless of the disciplines on which they focus. The advice we would offer colleagues new to the specialty is also largely the same. As a result, data practitioners in the sciences and social sciences are moving closer and closer to one another professionally all the time.

Conclusion

We conceived of this chapter as the scientific counterpart to Kellam's focus on the social sciences. However, this distinction, at least within data librarianship, may be less and less relevant over time. There is a growing acknowledgment of the centrality of data to all disciplines in the digital age, regardless of the diversity of definitions of data. As such, data services provide a way for librarians and their libraries to advance their institution's goals and to prepare the next generation of scholars, be they scientists, social scientists or humanists. The main implication for administrators is the pressing need for additional resources to support this evolving and growing area of practice. Adding data as one more subject liaison area of responsibility is a fine start-up model but is neither scalable nor sustainable. The takeaway

† The summer program as of 2014 was called *Providing Social Science Data Services.*

for LIS students is the broad applicability of this skill set and that having a science background is extremely helpful, but lacking one need not be an impediment to becoming an effective provider of scientific data services. There is a welcoming and supportive community of data librarians to help nurture new practitioners.‡

---

1. Lynda M. Kellam, "Data librarianship: a day in the life," in *Numeric Data Services and Sources for the General Reference Librarian*, ed. Lynda Kellam and Katharin Peter (Oxford: Chandos Publishing, 2011), 151.
2. Ibid., 151.
3. Ibid., 154–5.
4. "BD2K Home Page: Data Science at NIH," last modified August 15, 2015, accessed August 2015, https://datascience.nih.gov/bd2k.

---

‡ Kellam's "Data librarianship: A day in the life" inspired this chapter. Kellam interviewed data librarians supporting the social sciences through statistical and numeric data services. In addition, the authors thank Matthew Leavitt, Erin Moore and Amanda Tickner for their assistance. Finally, we thank the participants for taking the time to share their insights, their passion and their eloquence.

Appendix 21.A. Interview Subjects

Note: Libraries outside of institutions of higher education and outside of the U.S. do not have Carnegie Classifications.

Name	Title	Level	Institution
Daina Bouquin	Data & Metadata Services Librarian	Special Focus Institutions—Medical schools and medical centers	Weill Cornell Medical College of Cornell University
Kristin Briney	Data Services Librarian	Research Universities (high research activity)	University of Wisconsin–Milwaukee
Philippa Broadley	Research Data Librarian	N/A	Queensland University of Technology
Heather Coates	Digital Scholarship & Data Management Librarian	Research Universities (very high research activity)	Indiana University-Purdue University at Indianapolis
Andrew Creamer	Scientific Data Management Librarian	Research Universities (very high research activity)	Brown University
Kiyomi Deards	Assistant Professor	Research Universities (very high research activity)	University of Nebraska-Lincoln
Chris Eaker	Data Curation Librarian	Research Universities (very high research activity)	University of Tennessee
Vessela Ensberg	Data Curation Analyst	Research Universities (very high research activity)	University of California, Los Angeles
Chris Erdmann	Head Librarian	Research Universities (very high research activity)	Harvard University
Jane Frazier	Data Librarian	N/A	Australian National Data Service
Sally Gore	Research Evaluation Analyst, UMass Center for Clinical and Translational Science	Special Focus Institutions—Medical schools and medical centers	Lamar Soutter Library, University of Massachusetts
Barrie Hayes	Bioinformatics and Translational Science Librarian	Research Universities (high research activity)	University of North Carolina at Chapel Hill

Margaret Henderson	Director, Research Data Management	Research Universities (very high research activity)	Virginia Commonwealth University
Amy Hodge	Science Data Librarian	Research Universities (very high research activity)	Stanford University
Katie Houk	Health & Life Sciences Librarian	Research Universities (very high research activity)	San Diego State University
Michelle Hudson	Science and Social Science Data Librarian	Research Universities (very high research activity)	Yale University
Sherry Lake	Data Specialist	Research Universities (very high research activity)	University of Virginia
Jenny Muilenburg	Data Services Curriculum and Communications Librarian	Research Universities (very high research activity)	University of Washington Libraries
Sarah Oelker	Science Librarian	Baccalaureate Colleges—Arts & Sciences	Mount Holyoke College
Regina Raboin	Associate Director for Library Education and Research	Special Focus Institutions—Medical schools and medical centers	University of Massachusetts Medical School
Yasmeen Shorish	Physical & Life Sciences Librarian	Master's Colleges and Universities (larger programs)	James Madison University
Carly Strasser	Program Officer; Formerly Research Data Specialist	N/A	Gordon and Betty Moore Foundation; California Digital Library
Alisa Surkis	Translational Science Librarian	Research Universities (very high research activity)	New York University, Health Sciences Library
Brian Westra	Lorry I. Lokey Science Data Services	Research Universities (very high research activity)	University of Oregon
Amanda Whitmire	Data Management Specialist	Research Universities (very high research activity)	Oregon State University
Stephanie Wright	Data Services Coordinator	Research Universities (very high research activity)	University of Washington Libraries
Lynn Yarmey	Lead Data Curator	N/A	National Center for Atmospheric Research

CHAPTER 22

Teaching Data Librarianship to LIS Students

Michael McCaffrey and Walter Giesbrecht

THIS CHAPTER CONTAINS a discussion of the rationale for designing INF2115, a credit course in Data Librarianship taught by one of the authors (McCaffrey) at the University of Toronto iSchool since 2011. The authors discuss course content and outcomes, teaching methodology and the problems and challenges of teaching data librarianship to a class of library school students with little to no knowledge of the material or discipline. Assignments and other tasks set for the class are described in detail and are tied to certain goals that the instructor felt would be of benefit both for the profession and students' professional development. We conclude by outlining a proposed plan of study leading to a "major" in data librarianship to be offered at schools of library science.

Background

INF2115 was designed, above all, as a course in social science data librarianship. It was the instructor's intent to provide an introduction to the discipline in such a fashion that the beginning data librarian would enter the workforce with a basic but solid foundation in the required skillsets, while training generalists and future "accidental" data librarians (those who become data librarians by circumstance) to deal with questions requiring the use of aggregate data or microdata. In this attempt, the instructor was drawing on his own experience at academic institutions employing the data, map, government (DMG) blended service and collections model. In his experience, DMG reference staff were required to possess data reference skills beyond what would be expected of generalists despite having limited, usually ad hoc, training.

The selection of topics and outcomes was driven in part by the instructor's experience as a government information librarian and department head and was based on his own personal observations, supplemented by discussions with practitioners. The selection of resources and collections to cover was also influenced by geography. While the basic skills taught in the course (identification, retrieval, manipulation, etc.) were transferable and would be of use to the class regardless of their future careers, the fact that it was a course taught in Canada to an audience that would, for the most part, remain in the country after graduation meant that the resources covered had to be mostly Canadian.

When the instructor first developed the idea of teaching INF2115, he performed a quick environmental scan to determine what courses in data librarianship were taught and where they were taught by perusing the websites of peer institutions and of organizations known to train data specialists, such as the International Association for Social Science Information Services and Technology (IASSIST) and the Inter-university Consortium for Social and Political Science Research (ICSPR). For this chapter, a more rigorous and systematic examination was attempted by looking at the course calendars of 59 American Library Association (ALA) accredited schools as well as two institutions under consideration for accreditation. He found that, while there were courses containing "data" or "big data" in the titles or descriptions, they did not meet the needs addressed by INF2115.[1] Government information courses, for instance, often included a discussion of statistical resources, but none addressed microdata in detail. Some courses touched on data librarianship as a part of their coverage of "big data," but in most cases, the connection was tenuous at best. Courses on data management and curation, for instance, were offered at the University of California, Los Angeles by Christine L. Borgman.[2] While the instructor felt that these courses would be invaluable to those managing institutional research data or assisting faculty to comply with National Science Foundation regulations, they did not address the fundamentals of data discovery and reference work. These courses did, however, figure prominently in the plan growing in the instructor's mind for a comprehensive program in data librarianship to be offered as part of a library and information science degree.

Two continuing education programs stood out, but the instructor felt that neither of them was suitable for the audience he had in mind. The University of Alberta had, for a number of years, hosted a Winter Institute on Statistical Literacy for Librarians (WISLL), an impressive program. WISLL, however, was designed as a boot camp for practicing librarians. The three-day workshop appeared to assume a certain amount of prior knowledge. In addition, it was not a credit course, was held during the academic year, and required students to enroll and travel to attend at their own expense.

The instructor also examined ICSPR's Summer Program in Quantitative Methods of Social Research (ICPSR Summer Program, https://www.icpsr.umich.edu/icpsrweb/sumprog/). The vast majority of courses focused on advanced topics such as analysis, survey design, and advanced statistical topics. These courses seemed to be most useful to end users and practicing data librarians wishing to provide a higher level of support to researchers. The instructor felt that they would be useful to his students only after they had acquired the basics through INF2115.

The paucity of attention devoted to data librarianship in library and information science schools is reflected in the relative lack of literature on the topic as well. Library and information science scholars and practitioners rely on three databases: *Library Literature and Information Science*, popularly known as *Library Lit*; *Library and Information Science Abstracts* (LISA); and *Library, Information Science and Technology Abstracts* (LISTA). There is significant overlap between the three databases, but exploring all of them is helpful to see how the notion of data librarianship is covered in the literature. An attempt was made to focus the search on the profession or occupation by searching each database using a form of the term, "data librarian." Apart from a few notable exceptions, virtually all the articles were recent, with most of those addressing the role of librarians in research data management (RDM) and curation.[3] The LIS literature was strangely silent on what was becoming an increasingly important career path choice for library science students, and there was little on the core functions and basic tenets of data librarianship.

The general impression was that data library neophytes had few resources upon which to draw in learning their craft. This appeared to be more the result of a divide between the traditional, library science-centered community and the data librarian community. Individuals already employed as data librarians and those who were about to become data librarians could draw upon a wide variety of pedagogical resources aimed at the career practitioner. Continuing education programs such as WSLL and the ICPSR Summer Institute are, of course, invaluable. Professional associations like IASSIST provide training and educational opportunities at their conferences, and much of the material is available on the conference websites. The Statistics Canada Data Liberation Initiative (DLI) Training Repository is a treasure trove of resources. Attendees of the ICPSR workshop on data librarianship would have had access to the invaluable manual, *Data Basics: An Introductory Text,* authored by Diane Geraci, Chuck Humphrey and Jim Jacobs.[4] Many key articles from, for instance, the *IASSIST Quarterly* do not appear to have been captured in the traditional library literature databases. Data librarianship has not been studied in detail and library science schools are not at present providing the necessary training.

Planning the Course

The instructor decided to make an attempt to bridge that divide and designed INF2115 as a course in data librarianship. It was also, however, designed and structured in response to a number of local factors. The University of Toronto iSchool has a long tradition of excellence in teaching government documents librarianship, with courses having been offered continuously since 1950. The instructor sought to build on this tradition, and by the time INF2115 was launched, his faculty was unique in having three courses in this subject area: Canadian Government Information (INF2136), International Information (INF2137), and United States Government Information (INF2138). He felt that there was an opportunity to build a strong, coordinated program in the management and provision of services in government information and that a course in data librarianship would be a natural complement.

The University of Toronto setting also gave the instructor the opportunity to take advantage of local expertise. At the time, three local institutions employed full-time data librarian specialists who were generous with their time and expertise, advising the instructor on course content and assignments and providing him with a perspective that could only come from seasoned practitioners—something that he felt it was of the utmost importance to introduce to the classroom in a professional school.

Coverage, Goals and Outcomes

INF2115 emphasized the teaching of skills to enable the discovery and delivery of aggregate data (commonly referred to as statistics) and microdata. Specifically, by the end of the course, the students were taught to:

1. Appreciate the significance of the administrative environment in which data are gathered and aggregate data and microdata produced.
2. Locate Canadian statistics and microdata (both current and historical), as well as US, foreign national, and International Governmental Organization (IGO) statistics and microdata, in print and electronic formats.
3. Extract and deliver statistics in a usable file format (.csv or .xlsx).
4. Identify and locate microdata produced by Statistics Canada and US government agencies.
5. Use microdata repositories such as the Ontario Council of University Libraries' <odesi>, the University of Toronto's CHASS data server, ICPSR, and others to identify datasets, to perform basic statistical tasks on these datasets, and to use these repositories to subset, extract, and deliver microdata in a format specified by the end user.
6. Prepare readable microdata files by performing basic SPSS syntax file edits, and using them to create system files in .sav or .por formats.

In compiling the list of course goals and outcomes, the instructor was guided in part by his own experience as a government information specialist and former head of a department offering data services. He relied heavily, however, on discussions and informal interviews with members of the local data librarian community. All were in agreement that it was important to understand the environment in which the microdata most commonly used in academic settings were produced and to be as competent in the discovery and use of aggregated data and analytical products as in the discovery and retrieval of the underlying microdata.[†]

INF2115 met weekly over the course of a twelve-week term. Institutional policies and constraints dictated the format to a large extent, and some of the drawbacks are discussed below. The outline as it was most recently taught is given in Table 22.1.

Table 22.1. INF2115 Class Outline, Winter 2015 Term

Session	Topic
Week 1	Introductory Class: Syllabus Review. Introduction to Statistics and Data
Week 2	Introduction to Statistics and Data (cont.). Statistical Literacy. Administrative Environment
Week 3	Canadian Statistical Programs and Activities
Week 4	Finding Canadian Statistics
Week 5	Foreign and International Statistics
Week 6	Microdata, part I
Week 7	Microdata, part 2
Week 8	Canadian Microdata
Week 9	Foreign and International Microdata, Other Repositories
Week 10	Reference Work
Week 11	GIS and Data Visualization
Week 12	Data Services Administration, Issues and Trends

The main body of the course was divided into two sections: Weeks 1–5 dealt with aggregate data and statistics, and weeks 6–10 dealt with microdata. There was inevitable overlap between the sections; certain topics were visited more than once, but with different emphasis placed each time. Agency policies, for instance, needed to be discussed in terms of the administrative environment, their role in the production of aggregated data, and their impact upon microdata products and release policies.

† Data visualization and data services management, including participation in the Statistics Canada Data Liberation Initiative (DLI), were introduced as topics towards the end of the course. The instructor is of the opinion that this is a less than optimal approach and this will be discussed in detail on page 368 under "Lessons Learned."

Weeks 1 and 2: The Basics

As a certain level of expertise with basic statistical methodology would be necessary in order to understand the material with which the class would work, the first two classes were devoted to a discussion of methods and concepts. The instructor's goal was to enable the students to understand the information needs of their primary clientele. The emphasis was on getting the class to a point where the mathematical aspects of statistics would not scare them and where they would feel comfortable expanding their knowledge as required. Perhaps most importantly, the introductory sessions were designed to enable the class to speak, up to a point, the language of their clientele. Selections from the series of books by Joel Best and John Alan Paulos were assigned to instil confidence, while more substantive readings were drawn from Derek Rowntree's *Statistics without Tears* and *How to Think About Statistics* by John L. Philips.

Weeks 3 and 4: Statistical Literacy (cont.) and Statistics Canada Programs

The instructor felt that the challenges of discovery would best be overcome by a knowledge of the administrative environment in which the data or statistics are collected, produced, or published. Accordingly, weeks 3 and 4 were devoted to the Canadian statistical administrative environment and to the principal tools of discovery. Statistics Canada was, naturally, the primary focus of this part of the course (given that the vast majority of sources used by Canadian data librarians come from there), but the Bank of Canada and the Canadian Mortgage and Housing Corporation were also included. Statistics Canada's history, mandate, the laws governing it, and its organizational structure took up the better part of one class and was followed by a discussion of the principal resources through their website, including CANSIM (a time-series database), the Census of Canada, and the *National Household Survey* (NHS). The NHS, as an ill-conceived (and short-lived) voluntary replacement for the long-form portion of the Census, provided an excellent opportunity for the class both to investigate non-response bias and its effects on data integrity, particularly at the small area level, and to explore the policy and political dimensions of government statistical programs. The instructor was mindful of the needs of historical research and so time was given over to a discussion of the principal tools used to locate print publications, as well as the use of nineteenth-century material, specifically, the *Sessional Papers* of the Parliament of Canada.

Week 5: Foreign and International Statistics

The course then moved to a discussion of United States and other foreign national and international statistics. As with Canadian statistics, the instructor's approach was to focus on the administrative environment and to introduce to the class key products and gateways. Topics covered included the role of the Office of Management and Budget and the value of Statistical Programs of the United States Government as a reference tool, plus the use of fedstats.gov and data.gov as gateways to specific programs. The Census Bureau, Bureau of Labor Statistics, Bureau of Justice Statistics, and the National Center for Education Statistics were highlighted; the amount of attention that could be given was insufficient given the amount of material available but it was necessary to at least introduce the class to the major US sources.

International statistics were also discussed but only in brief, as the material was also covered to some extent in another course (INF2137). The approach taken was to highlight the coordinating role of the United Nations, specifically the UN Statistical Commission and the United Nations Statistics Division (UNSD), and to introduce the resources most likely to be useful to the students in their future work. UNdata and the statistical output of the World Bank, IMF, and the OECD were covered. Here, as with the teaching of US statistical resources, emphasis was placed on determining purview and area of interest as the guiding principles driving the reference process. The instructor had for years been teaching his government information students that, when all is said and done, most work involves answering the question, "Who cares?"—or, put another way, if one knows which agency has responsibility for an issue, one will know where to find information on it. He felt that the principle could be applied to data reference work as well.

Weeks 6 and 7: Microdata Basics

Beginning in week 6 and carrying over into week 7, the course turned to a general discussion of microdata. The students were introduced to basic concepts, such as dependent, independent, control, and weight variables, typical file structures, and the sorts of datasets they were most likely to encounter. The discussion focused on the types of files produced by Statistics Canada: public use microdata files (PUMFs), master files, share files and synthetic files. The students were also introduced to the data repository platforms they would be using in the course, including

- SDA, used by the University of Toronto's Computing in the Humanities and Socials Sciences (CHASS) Centre;
- Nesstar, the platform for <odesi>, a social science digital repository maintained by the Ontario Council of University Libraries (OCUL); and
- Dataverse, also employed by OCUL, which would be used later in the term as the destination for the students' group projects.

The students were taught to use repositories to perform basic tasks, such as subsetting, tabulation, and variable recoding, and to prepare microdata files for downloading and subsequent analysis. The class was required to work with all three, as the instructor knew that they would, in all likelihood, be using one or more of the underlying platforms once they entered the workforce. The class was also taught how to prepare syntax and raw data files for end users. For practical reasons, SPSS was used; this decision is likely to be revisited in future years when the instructor may switch to R or Stata. Codebooks and questionnaires were examined as important reference and discovery tools. The instructor introduced different approaches to finding and selecting appropriate studies and datasets, explaining the circumstances under which one method might be used over another. Student were shown examples of cases where using question and variable databases would yield good results and were also shown examples where searching or browsing study descriptions, to determine descriptions of populations, time frames, and the like would yield even better results.

Weeks 8 and 9: Finding Microdata

Sessions 8 and 9 were devoted to the discovery of social sciences microdata. Two major collections were used: Statistics Canada microdata made available through the Data Liberation Initiative (DLI) program, and the Canadian Opinion Research Archive (CORA) hosted by Queen's University. Session 9 provided an overview of foreign and international microdata, as well as the major non-governmental repositories. Data.gov was the focus here for U.S. data, although the instructor also took the time to highlight a few key surveys including the Census and American Community Survey. A selection of foreign national and international resources and programs received some attention, for instance, CESSDA and the OECD's Program for International Assessment (PISA). The two discovery sessions wrapped up with an examination of selected non-governmental repositories, including the ICPSR, Roper Center, and IPUMS/IPUMS-I collections.

Week 10: Reference Work

By the tenth week, the students were sufficiently well versed in the basics to begin working as data librarians, but they had not yet been exposed to the nuances of assisting data users. The next class was therefore given over to a discussion of reference work. The instructor covered the fundamental nature of the reference interview as it applied to data and statistics. The class looked at the intrusive nature of the process, including the importance of determining eligibility for access (based on license restrictions of individual datasets), intended use, purpose, and level of sophistication of the end user. Various approaches to levels of service were examined in terms of their impact on library staffing and employee skills.

Week 11: Visualization

For week 11 the instructor was able to bring in a guest speaker to discuss data visualization and, briefly, the use of Geographic Information Systems (GIS) and microdata. This was done in part to expose the class to a topic for which there was insufficient time to address adequately and to give the students a break from listening to the instructor.

Week 12: Professional Development and Next Steps

The last class took the form of a wrap-up session together with discussion of associations and continuing professional development. In this class the instructor emphasized takeaways from the course as a checklist of skillsets. It also, however, afforded him the opportunity to let the class know what they had not yet learned and what, perhaps, they should teach themselves.

Delivery

The class met for twelve weeks over the course of one term. The instructor was of the opinion that the class would be better served by his employing the lecture method of instruction and, from time to time, assigning exercises in class in combination with tasks to be performed outside of class. The assigned tasks tended to be technical in nature; for example, the students were required to learn SPSS basics on their own and to explore the discovery, manipulation, and analysis features of the data repositories. The instructor provided tutorials and demonstrated these tasks (by means of slides and screen captures), but the students were left largely on their own. All material prepared for the course was made publicly accessible via the instructor's institutional website. The resources he had developed over the years for his other courses came to be relied upon by alumni and others in the field who needed to update their skills or learn new ones, and he felt it was good policy to continue providing open access. For each class, a "page" was created with links to resources, handouts, and any other material considered in class or made available to the students to consult outside of class time. Slides were prepared in aid of each lecture and a companion set of detailed lecture notes were provided as well.

Wherever possible, humor or anecdotes were employed, as the instructor had found them to be excellent pedagogical tools. For example, the terminology employed to describe different statistical units in the Census of Canada was new to many in the class and required an adjustment in their understanding of certain concepts. To illustrate the difference between families and households in the Census and to demonstrate the different ways in which people living under one roof could be grouped, the instructor distributed cards to a group who stood at the head of the class and held them up on cue. The cards read Mom #1, Mom #2, Brat, Creepy Uncle, Couch Surfer, and Individual.

Table 22.2. Census Units Explained in Class Demonstration

Unit	Summary	Composition
Individual	Each individual in the dwelling	Mom 1, Mom 2, Brat, Creepy Uncle, Couch Surfer
Census Family	Couple/Single parent plus offspring	Mom 1 + Mom 2 + Brat
Economic Family	Everyone related in the dwelling	Mom 1 + Mom 2 + Brat + Creepy Uncle
Household	Everyone in the dwelling	Mom 1 + Mom 2 + Brat + Creepy Uncle + Couch Surfer

The exercise was successful as an icebreaker and as a means to drive home the idea that terms have very specific meanings in social and demographic surveys.

Assignments

Evaluation of student work in INF2115 was achieved by assigning the class a series of highly focused, short tasks designed to give them the opportunity to practice what they would be doing in the field. The instructor set four assignments and mapped them to the course learning outcomes:

Table 22.3. Winter 2015 Session Assignments Mapped to Course Outcomes

Description	Outcomes
Basic statistics and aggregate data identification retrieval (Assignment 1)	1, 2, 3
Microdata subsetting and extraction assignment (Assignment 2)	4, 5, 6
Group Assignment (Assignment 3)	2, 4, 5, 6
Research Guide (Assignment 4)	1, 2, 3, 4, 5, 6

Assignment 1

The first assignment was designed to enable the students to demonstrate a basic understanding of statistical concepts and knowledge of the resources used to locate aggregate data. It was designed as series of questions in a traditional library school "treasure hunt" format. For this assignment, students were required to use a variety of sources to retrieve basic time series or tables of selected values; they also worked with classification schemes and concordances to determine where statistics on goods, activities, and occupations would be found across jurisdictions and over time. Wherever possible the questions were open-ended and designed to force the students to engage with the resources fully, to make judgment calls, and to justify their decisions. Some students complained that the questions were vague, but the instructor's intent here was to avoid a situation where the class was tested only on their ability to mindlessly retrieve values from pre-determined resources and to reflect the reality that reference questions, especially those involving aggregate data and microdata, often are vague.

The assignment drew heavily on the use of CANSIM and the Census/NHS—the two most commonly used Canadian statistical resources—and also data.gov and key IGO resources. One question involved the use of current awareness tools. Students were given an article in a Canadian newspaper and had to work back using the Statistics Canada *Daily* (the weekday publication announcing all of Statistics Canada's data releases) to find the original source and then, using the survey documentation, to outline the release schedule for the survey results quoted in the article. The class also used American Factfinder to pull out some basic numbers from the American Community Survey (ACS). For the Census of Canada/NHS question, they had to retrieve some numbers on the census tract in which they lived and for the ACS question, they were required to retrieve basic statistics for a neighborhood in Evanston, Illinois, and then to list the census/ACS geographies for that address. Bonus marks were given to those who were able to determine that one of the sought values was suppressed below a certain level and would only be found for that address at the census tract level and above.

Assignment 2

The purpose of the second assignment was two-fold: to introduce the class to the processes involved in microdata retrieval and manipulation, and to build their confidence for what was to come. The students were set a small number of simple tasks involving work with predetermined datasets. The tasks included subsetting and extraction for subsequent analysis in SPSS using one of the repository platforms, converting SPSS files for viewing in another format, creation of data and syntax files, and the running of simple tests and processes using both SPSS and the SDA platform. The specific tasks were chosen by the instructor in consultation with the local data library community.† Three types of datasets were selected:

---

† In future years, the instructor may draw upon the series of excellent pre-existing learning modules and exercises from, for instance, the ICPSR and the Data Liberation Initiative, to save class time and to address student concerns.

1. Microdata commonly used in a Canadian academic library setting (the *Statistics Canada General Social Survey* and the *Labour Force Survey*, for example).
2. Microdata not easily found in repositories, forcing the students to work in SPSS completely.
3. One microdata set available only as a *.txt/*.dat file with accompanying syntax file (*.sps), forcing the students to prepare the SPSS file from scratch.

Assignment 3

Assignment 3 enabled students to collaborate on projects that would both test their skills and result in a body of work beneficial to the data library community. Each student group was assigned the creation of a resource or the completion of a study and the preparation of accompanying metadata. Once completed, the group projects were uploaded as studies to the University of Toronto iSchool Government Information Projects Dataverse, which the instructor had created to house and preserve their work.

The projects were drafted in consultation with local data librarians and involved creating finding aids to historical resources, variable data concordances, and retrieving and publishing tables from master files made available via the Statistics Canada Real Time Remote Access (RTRA) system. The instructor's intent was to create resources of enduring value and, where feasible, to create large-scale resources to which subsequent cohorts could add. The instructor's intent is that this become an ongoing project and that the students' work be widely circulated, used, enhanced, and repurposed by others. A selection of student projects appears in Table 22.4.

Table 22.4. Group Projects and Year(s) Assigned
(Open date ranges indicate projects the instructor intends to assign to subsequent cohorts for further development.)

Project	Description
Census Variable Concordance	Expanded and updated a Census of Canada PUMF variable concordance prepared by Walter Giesbrecht. (2013/14)
GSS Variable Concordance	Created a General Social Survey (GSS) PUMF variable concordance. The most recent cohort (2014-2015) built the resource and populated it with the basic background/ demographic variables. In subsequent years students will complete it by adding variables from the cyclical topical modules. (2014/15-)

Table 22.4. Group Projects and Year(s) Assigned
(Open date ranges indicate projects the instructor intends to assign to subsequent cohorts for further development.)

Project	Description
Immigration Statistics Finding Aid	Reviewed the Sessional Papers of the Parliament of Canada to locate reports containing immigration statistics. These reports were authored by immigration agents resident at ports of entry (Halifax, Quebec City, Montreal, etc.) and were included as appendices to the Annual Reports to Parliament of the Departments responsible for immigration. The 2013/14 group mapped out the procedure and created a spreadsheet of reports covering the years 1869-1882. The second group continued to 1894 and added hyperlinks to Internet Archive and other stable digital copies of the Sessional Paper volumes. (2013/14-)
LFS Extraction	Applied for and received permission to query the master files via the Statistics Canada RTRA system for the Labour Force Survey (LFS) to produce a series of tables showing employment by detailed industrial grouping. RTRA access enabled the group to create tables at the 4-digit NAICS level as opposed to the PUMF where the data were provided at the 2-digit level only. (2014/15-)

Assignment 4

The final assignment was designed to bring the course content learned together and to test the students' skills in discovery and extraction. The students were given one of three hypothetical reference queries from members of the faculty at the University of Toronto, and were required to prepare a research guide to relevant data. Students selected three aggregate data resources and three public use microdata files, and were required to subset, extract, and prepare microdata files for use in SPSS. The questions were left purposely vague and the class was instructed that the faculty member requesting the information was unavailable for clarification. Students were thereby forced to interpret (and to make *a priori* assumptions regarding the query) and were required to explain the reasoning that led to their selection of resources. The instructor's intent was to force them to think like reference data specialists and their explanations, as evidence of the extent to which they could field reference queries, factored heavily in the grading.

In the future, the instructor is considering reaching out to faculty members in other departments in an effort to match his students with existing courses and make Assignment 4 the creation of a "real life" library guide for an actual course. While this would involve far more work on the instructor's part, it would benefit the students, both immediately by enabling them to perform tasks they would be assigned in the workplace and in the long run by giving them the opportunity to add to their professional portfolios.

Lessons Learned

The course itself has been a success. Student evaluations were consistently high. In the portion of the course evaluation form focused on core institutional items, the following scores were achieved for the Winter 2015 version of INF2115 (on a scale from 0–5):

Table 22.5. Excerpt from Internal Course Evaluation Summary Report, 2015 (n=14, N=23)

Question	Mean	SD
1. I found the course intellectually stimulating.	4.4	0.6
2. The course provided me with a deeper understanding of the matter	4.8	0.4
3. The instructor created a course atmosphere that was conducive to my learning.	4.9	0.5
4. Course projects, assignments, tests and/or exams improved my understanding of the course material.	4.8	0.4
5. Course projects, assignments, tests and/or exams provided opportunity for me to demonstrate an understanding of the course material.	4.7	0.4
Overall, the quality of my learning in this course was...	4.4	0.5

Students were almost unanimous in their belief that that course prepared them well for working in the field. "This was one of the very few courses in this faculty that made me ready to be a great librarian" was a typical comment. One recurring negative comment was that the students were not in favor of being left to learn SPSS on their own because a hands-on SPSS session was cut when the iSchool moved from a thirteen-week to a twelve-week term. The instructor will explore options for future offerings of the course.

The instructor conducted an assessment of the course content and outcomes based on the findings of a recent article by Jingfeng Xia and Minglu Wang on competencies and responsibilities of data librarians as reflected in job postings and descriptions.[5] He found that, for the most part, he was teaching precisely what employers desired. In a table addressing categories of activities, the two most frequently mentioned requirements ("Data Discovery" and "Data Collection") were addressed in detail in INF2115.[6] Similarly, the four most frequently mentioned types of required experiences were covered in the course.[7]

The skills and competencies discussed by Xia and Wang that the course did *not* address, however, were a concern. Despite positive feedback from students and encouragement from the data library community, the instructor was fully aware of the inadequacy of training data librarians in just one course. Over time, a list of data librarianship competencies and a conceptualization of curriculum required for adequate preparation began to emerge, as the instructor added to his growing list of future INF2115 topics. Three distinct areas stood out: 1) data curation, management, and administration; 2) data visualization and geospatial representation; and 3) advanced reference work. As including or increasing the coverage of any of these would most likely require the deletion of some existing content, the idea of a full-blown data librarianship "major" seemed the best solution. The instructor therefore proposes the following plan of study:†

Program Overview

1. To earn the major, four of the sixteen courses students take to earn their degrees must address the craft of data librarianship.
2. The program is to be in data *librarianship*. Topics such as data science, programming, and data scraping, while useful, should be taken in addition to the four required courses.

Program Requirements

1. INF2115 or an equivalent **foundational course in data librarianship**. At the University of Toronto, INF2115, the existing data librarianship course, is to be the core course fulfilling much the same role as introductory reference courses do in most LIS programs.
2. A course in **government information** focusing on the jurisdiction in which the student will work.
3. A course in **GIS librarianship**.
4. A course in **data management and curation** to include an examination of metadata, the research data lifecycle, the role of librarians in creating RDM plans/services and other topics.

These courses would be required, not only because their content is required for a complete understanding of the broader field of data librarianship, but also because they would make graduating students that much more employable and able to function effectively in the job at an earlier stage. They should, however, be complemented by courses designed to enable prospective data librarians to specialize in and to explore areas of particular interest in greater detail. Most programs offer a sufficient amount of flexibility in course selection.

† This model uses the University of Toronto credit system whereby a "full" course load is four full credits per year and where sixteen half-credit courses are required to complete the two-year MI program at the Faculty of Information.

Recommended Additional Courses

- **Data visualization**: A course in visualization and presentation techniques, beginning with creating simple charts in Excel, moving to visualization techniques available in standard packages (e.g., SPSS, Stata, etc.), and finally to advanced techniques using R or specialized visualization software.
- **Advanced microdata:** A course in advanced data manipulation that addresses other important topics and skills generally acquired only after some time on the job. Such a course might cover bootstrapping, the statistical dimensions of weighting, managing hierarchical files/dealing with longitudinal (panel) studies, and options and techniques for acquiring and working with restricted datasets.
- **Topics in international microdata:** EU initiatives, UN Census 2020, OECD work, World Bank Enterprise Surveys, etc.
- **International government information:** A course in the information practices and policies of International Government Organizations (IGOs). The course would be similar in nature to the required course in government information but would focus exclusively on IGOs.

Establishing a fully-formed, comprehensive, multi-course program in data librarianship is ambitious, but the capacity exists at present. There is already considerable cooperation between institutions who are members of the iSchools Organization. Schools are increasingly offering transferable online credit courses. While the establishment of such a program as the authors propose may indeed be too ambitious for one institution, it is not beyond the capacity of the data library community working closely with LIS faculties.

In sitting down to write this chapter, the authors were aware that they were only beginning a conversation. While there are many factors to be considered in deciding precisely how to teach a single course in data librarianship, the fact that taking only one course provides inadequate preparation should give rise to a larger discussion of what is required to produce professionals capable of working competently with material for which there is both increasing demand and availability. This discussion will be a long and complex one, and the solution to the problem will involve much effort on the part of data professionals and library educators. It is, nevertheless, an important discussion, and the problem is one worth solving.

---

1. American Library Association, "Directory of ALA-Accredited and Candidate Programs in Library and Information Studies," *American Library Association*, accessed April 30, 2015, http://www.ala.org/accreditedprograms/directory.
2. Christine L. Borgman. "Data, Data Practices, and Data Curation, Part I," *The Selected Works of Christine L. Borgman*, accessed April 30, 2015, http://works.bepress.com/borgman/298; Christine L. Borgman. "Data, Data Practices, and Data Curation, Part II" *The Selected Works of Christine L. Borgman*, accessed April 30, 2015, http://works.bepress.com/borgman/299; Christine L.

Borgman. "Syllabus for Data Management and Practice, Part I, Winter 2015," *The Selected Works of Christine L. Borgman,* accessed April 30, 2015, http://works.bepress.com/borgman/358.

3. The notable exceptions included: Carolyn L. Geda, "Training the professional data librarian," *Drexel Library Quarterly* 13, no. 1 (1977): 100–108; James Jacobs, "Providing data services for machine-readable Information in an academic library: Some levels of service," *Public Access Computer Systems Review* 2, no 1 (1991): 144–160; Jingfeng Xia and Minglu Wang, "Competencies and Responsibilities of Social Science Data Librarians: An Analysis of Job Descriptions," *College & Research Libraries* 75, no. 3 (2014): 362–388; For "day in the life" articles, see Elspeth Hyams, "Data librarianship: A Gap in the market," *Library & Information Update* 7, no. 6 (2008): 20–21; Graham Pryor, "Skilling up to do data: Whose role, whose responsibility, whose career?" *International Journal of Digital Curation* 4, no. 2 (2009): 158–170.
4. Chuck Humphrey and Jim Jacobs, "Providing Social Science Data Services: Strategies for Design and Operation," *Inter-university for Political and Social Research,* accessed July 31, 2015 http://www.icpsr.umich.edu/files/sumprog/biblio/2010/Humphrey.pdf.
5. Xia and Wang.
6. Ibid., 384.
7. Ibid., 371.

Author Biographies

Adam Beauchamp is the Research & Instruction Librarian for Social Sciences at Tulane University. He holds an MLIS degree from Louisiana State University, an MA in history from Tulane University, and a BA in history from Niagara University.

Bobray Bordelon joined Princeton University as the Economics and Finance Librarian in 1993, added Head of Data and Statistical Services in 2004, and served as Project Manager/Director of the Cultural Policy and the Arts National Data Archive (CPANDA) from 2006-2015. He just completed a decade of service with the New Jersey State Data Center and is convener elect of the ACRL Numeric & Geospatial Data Services in Academic Libraries Interest Group.

Ryan Clement is the Data Services Librarian at Middlebury Library in Middlebury, VT, where he supports data discovery, use, and visualization for the social sciences and humanities. He completed his MSI at University of Michigan School of Information in 2012 and his MA in Philosophy at Temple University in 2006.

Jen Darragh is the Data Services and Sociology Librarian at Johns Hopkins University. She has been in the data services field for 15 years and has extensive knowledge about social science data resources, reference services, and instruction. Jen is a member-at-large for the International Association for Social Science Information Services and Technology and the founding member of the ACRL Numeric and Geospatial Data Services in Academic Libraries Interest Group.

Harrison Dekker has enjoyed a long career in data as both a librarian and programmer. In 2002 he was hired by the University of California, Berkeley to develop the Library's first data services program and he has been there ever since. He holds an MLIS from San Jose State University and BA in Economics from the University of Colorado.

Ameet Doshi is Director of Service Experience and Program Design at the Georgia Institute of Technology Library in Atlanta, GA. He also serves as the subject librarian for the Schools of Economics and Public Policy at Georgia Tech. He earned his MLS from the University of Tennessee and a Master's in Public Administration from UNC Wilmington.

Christopher Eaker is Data Curation Librarian at the University of Tennessee, Knoxville (UTK), Libraries. He is interested in scientific data curation and integrating sound data stewardship skills into science and engineering curricula. He holds a bachelor's degree in civil engineering from Georgia Institute of Technology and master's degree in information science from UTK.

Jane Fry is the Data Services Librarian at Carleton University (Ottawa, Canada). Research data management, DDI, and helping clients locate and interpret their optimal dataset are her primary responsibilities.

Walter Giesbrecht has been the data librarian at York University in Toronto (and IASSIST member!) since 1998; prior to this he was an organic chemist, atmospheric chemist, seabird biologist, crayfish biologist, medical research technician, and science librarian. He and his co-author, Mike McCaffrey, own an unmatched pair of Daleks.

Vince Gray has been a data librarian at Western University since 1986. He has presented about the various data systems provided by Western at IASSIST and at ICPSR. He is currently a member of Statistics Canada`s External Advisory Committee for the Data Liberation Initiative.

Karen Stanley Grigg is the Science Liaison Librarian at the University of North Carolina at Greensboro Libraries. She received her Master of Science in Library Science at the University of North Carolina at Chapel Hill in 1998, and was the Collection Development Services Librarian at Duke University Medical Center Library before beginning her employment at UNCG Libraries in 2013.

Samantha Guss is a Social Sciences Librarian at the University of Richmond in Richmond, VA. Before moving to Richmond, Samantha was the Data Services & Public Policy Librarian at New York University from 2009-2014. She holds an MSLS from the University of North Carolina at Chapel Hill, an MA in Business & Workplace Education from New York University, and a BA in English from Penn State University.

Michele Hayslett has been a data librarian since 2001, and has worked at UNC at Chapel Hill since December 2008. Prior to that she worked at North Carolina State University Libraries and the State Library of North Carolina. She earned her M.S.L.S. at UNC at Chapel Hill (1999) and her B.A. (with honors) at Earlham College (1990).

Joel Herndon is the Head of Duke Libraries Data and Visualization Services Department, which consults and provides instruction on a wide range of data driven topics including: data management, data visualization, digital mapping, and statistics. He has a PhD in Political Science with a concentration in Comparative Politics.

Elizabeth Hill has been a data librarian at Western University since 1998. She has presented at IASSIST on the Equinox Data Delivery System and on OCUL's Scholars Geoportal. She is currently a member of Statistics Canada`s Education Committee for the Data Liberation Initiative.

Alicia Hofelich Mohr is a Research Data Manager in Research Support Services in the College of Liberal Arts at the University of Minnesota. She received her Ph.D. in Psychology and M.A. in Statistics from the University of Michigan in 2012.

Lisa R. Johnston is an Associate Librarian at the University of Minnesota and is the Research Data Management & Curation Lead and co-director of the University Digital Conservancy. She has a Masters of Library Science and Bachelors of Science in Astrophysics, both from Indiana University.

Lynda Kellam is the Data Services Librarian at the University of North Carolina at Greensboro's University Libraries. She is the co-author with Katharin Peter of *Numeric Data Services and Sources for the General Data Librarian* (2011). She received her MA from the University of Wisconsin, Madison, her MLIS from UNCG, and is currently a doctoral student in History at UNCG.

Paula Lackie has long worked with academic researchers in anticipating and addressing obstacles that arise throughout the research process. Her graduate study was in Political Science, International Relations, and Public Policy but her academic passion remains in the heart of empirical pursuits, the past, present, and future of research data.

Amber Leahey is the Data and Geospatial Librarian at Scholars Portal, a technical infrastructure project of the Ontario Council of University Libraries. Previously, she worked as a Metadata Librarian and has coordinated many metadata projects for data repositories in the social sciences, health sciences, and GIS.

Lisha Li currently works as a science & engineering librarian and patents coordinator at the Georgia Institute of Technology. She has involved in several research data projects and conducted multiple data interviews with research faculty.

Thomas A. Lindsay is the Coordinator for Research Support Services in the College of Liberal Arts at the University of Minnesota. He received an M.A. in History from the University of Minnesota in 2003 and has worked in academic research data services since 1999.

Michael McCaffrey has worked as a government information librarian in academic and think tank settings and run government information, map, and data libraries. He has taught data librarianship and a variety of government information courses at the University of Toronto Faculty of Information.

Susan McKee has worked at the University of Calgary Library for over 17 years, most of that time as Geospatial Librarian with the Spatial and Numeric Data Services unit. She spends most of her time helping students and researchers find and use GIS and statistical data and cartographic materials.

Danianne Mizzy is currently the Head of Kenan Science Information Services at the University of North Carolina at Chapel Hill. Prior appointments include Engineering Librarian at Columbia University and Library Director of The Academy of Natural Sciences of Philadelphia. She received the MLIS from University of Pittsburgh, MFA from Yale School of Drama, and AB from Brown University.

Hailey Mooney is the Social Sciences Librarian for Psychology and Sociology and the University of Michigan. She previously served as the Data Services Coordinator and Social Sciences Librarian at Michigan State University. Hailey has a BA in Sociology from the University of Michigan and an MLIS from Wayne State University.

Christine Murray is the Social Science Librarian at Bates College in Lewiston, Maine. She has an AB in Literature from Harvard University and an MSI in Library and Information Services from the University of Michigan.

Rob O'Reilly is currently a Data Librarian in the Emory Center for Digital Scholarship (ECDS) in the Woodruff Library, where he assists students and faculty with locating data and getting them into usable formats. He has a PhD in Political Science, with a concentration in International Political Economy, from Emory University.

Robin Rice (@sparrowbarley) is Data Librarian at EDINA and Data Library, University of Edinburgh, Scotland, and Service Operations Manager of the University's Research Data Service. She has over twenty years of experience working as a data librarian in both American and British universities, and a Master's degree in Library and Information Studies.

Lizzy Rolando is a Researcher at MailChimp. Prior, she was Research Data Librarian at the Georgia Tech Library.

Nicole Scholtz is a Spatial and Numeric Data Librarian in the Stephen S. Clark Library for Maps, Government Information, and Spatial and Numeric Data Services at the University of Michigan. She received her Master of Science in Information at the University of Michigan in 2007, and has a B.A. in Linguistics with a minor in Physics from Wellesley College.

Joy Suh is the Geospatial Resources Librarian at George Mason University, Fairfax, VA. She received her MLIS at the University of Iowa and her MA in Geography at University of Wisconsin-Milwaukee. Previously she was the Data Files Librarian at Washington State University and the Government Documents and Geography Liaison Librarian at George Mason University.

Mandy Swygart-Hobaugh, M.L.S., Ph.D., is a Sociology, Gerontology, and Data Services Librarian at Georgia State University, where she provides social sciences data reference and instruction, acts as the campus-wide trainer for NVivo qualitative data analysis software, and chairs the Data Management Advisory Team.

Kristi Thompson is the Data Librarian at the University of Windsor and currently heads the systems department. Before coming to the University of Windsor in 2006, she was a Data Services Specialist at Princeton University, and she has also worked as a freelance digital librarian and web developer. She has a BA in Computer Science and Classics and a Masters in Library Science.

Alison Valk is a library liaison to the College of Computing at Georgia Tech and Multimedia Instructional Librarian. She coordinates all the multimedia and software related training through the Georgia Tech library and manages library collection decisions for the College of Computing. She is a member of the Georgia Tech Library's Research Data group, whose purpose it is to support campus research data-related needs.

Cynthia Hudson Vitale is the Digital Data Outreach Librarian in Data & GIS Services at Washington University in St. Louis Libraries. She currently serves as the Visiting Program Officer for SHARE with the Association of Research Libraries.

Karen Young is currently a skilled Metadata Specialist in Scholarly Communication and Digital Curation at Georgia Tech where she assists with the development, implementation, managing and maintenance of digital collections.